perspectives on modern america

PERSPECTIVES on MODERN AMERICA

Making Sense of the Twentieth Century

EDITED BY

Harvard Sitkoff

New York   Oxford
OXFORD UNIVERSITY PRESS
2001

Oxford University Press

Oxford   New York
Athens   Auckland   Bangkok   Bogotá   Buenos Aires   Calcutta
Cape Town   Chennai   Dar es Salaam   Delhi   Florence   Hong Kong   Istanbul
Karachi   Kuala Lumpur   Madrid   Melbourne   Mexico City   Mumbai
Nairobi   Paris   São Paulo   Shanghai   Singapore   Taipei   Tokyo   Toronto   Warsaw

and associated companies in
Berlin   Ibadan

Published by Oxford University Press, Inc.,
198 Madison Avenue, New York, New York 10016
http://www.oup-usa.org

Oxford is a registered trademark of Oxford University Press

Library of Congress Cataloging-in-Publication Data

Perspectives on modern America : making sense of the twentieth century / edited by
Harvard Sitkoff.
    p. cm.
    Includes bibliographical references and index.
    ISBN 0-19-512864-8 (cloth: alk. paper)—ISBN 0-19-512865-6 (pbk. : alk. paper)
    1. United States—Civilization—20th century. 2. United States—Social conditions—20th
century.   I. Sitkoff, Harvard.

E169.1 .M235 2001
973.91—dc21   00-024532

Printing (last digit): 10   9   8   7   6   5   4   3   2   1

Printed in the United States of America
on acid-free paper

contents

contributors

Paul Boyer, Merle Curti Professor of History and Director of the Institute for Research in the Humanities at the University of Wisconsin-Madison, received his Ph.D. from Harvard University in 1966. Boyer has received Guggenheim and Rockefeller Foundation Fellowships, and is an elected member of the Society of American Historians, the American Antiquarian Society, and the American Academy of Arts and Sciences. His most recent books include *When Time Shall Be No More: Prophecy Belief in Modern American Culture* (1992), winner of the Wisconsin Library Association's Banta Award; and *Fallout: A Historian Reflects on America's Half-Century Encounter with Nuclear Weapons* (1998). Professor Boyer is also editor-in-chief of *The Oxford Companion to United States History* (2000), and author of two college-level U.S. history textbooks and many articles and essays, as well as the former editor of the History of American Thought and Culture series for the University of Wisconsin Press.

Kevin Boyle, Associate Professor of History, University of Massachusetts, Amherst, received his Ph.D. from the University of Michigan in 1990. His major books include *The UAW and the Heyday of American Liberalism, 1945–1968* (1995), Choice Outstanding Academic Book of 1996; and *Muddy Boots and Ragged Aprons: Images of Working-Class Detroit, 1900–1930,* coauthored with Victoria Getis (1997). Professor Boyle also edited *Organized Labor and American Politics, 1894–1994: Essays on the Labor-Liberal Alliance* (1998).

Lizabeth Cohen is Professor of History and board member of American Civilization Graduate Program, Harvard University. She received her Ph.D. from the University of California-Berkeley in 1986. Professor Cohen is the author of *Making a New Deal: Industrial Workers in Chicago, 1919–1939* (1990), which was awarded the Bancroft Prize, Superior Achievement of Illinois State Historical Society, and the Philip Taft Labor History Award, and which was also a finalist for Pulitzer Prize in 1991. She has served on the executive board of the Urban History Association and the Immigration History Society, the program committees of the Organization of American Historians and the Berkshire

Conference on the History of Women, and is associate editor of the *Dictionary of American History* (3rd ed., 1999).

Sara M. Evans is Distinguished McKnight University Professor of History, and Adjunct Professor of American Studies, Public Affairs, and Women's Studies at the University of Minnesota. She received her Ph.D. from the University of North Carolina at Chapel Hill in 1976. Professor Evans's major books include *Born for Liberty: A History of American Women* (1989; 2nd ed., 1997); *Wage Justice: Comparable Worth and the Paradox of Technocratic Reform*, coauthored with Barbara J. Nelson (1989), winner of the Policy Studies Organization Award for Best Book of 1989; *Free Spaces: Sources of Democratic Change in America*, coauthored with Harry C. Boyte (1986); and *Personal Politics: The Roots of Women's Liberation in the Civil Rights Movement and the New Left* (1979).

Gary Gerstle is Associate Professor of History at Catholic University of America. He received his Ph.D. from Harvard University in 1982. He is the author of *Working-Class Americanism: The Politics of Labor in a Textile City, 1914–1960* (1989), and co-editor of The Rise and Fall of the New Deal Order, 1930–1980 (1989). Professor Gerstle has just finished co-editing *Immigrants, Civic Culture, and Modes of Political Incorporation* and is writing *The Rise and Fall of an American Nation: A Twentieth-Century History.* He has been selected for the John Simon Guggenheim Memorial Fellowship, Russell Sage Foundation Fellowship, NEH Fellowship for University Teachers, Woodrow Wilson International Center for Scholars Fellowship, Charles Warren Center Fellowship, and National Academy of Education Spencer Fellowship.

Cheryl Greenberg is Associate Professor of History and Director of the American Studies Program at Trinity College. She received her Ph.D. from Columbia University in 1988. A former fellow at the W.E.B. Du Bois Institute for Afro-American Research and at the Charles Warren Center, Harvard University, as well as a Danforth Fellow, Professor Greenberg is the author of the books *"Or Does It Explode?": Black Harlem in the Great Depression* (1991) and *Troubling the Waters: Black-Jewish Relations in the American Century* (forthcoming). She also edited *A Circle of Trust: Remembering the SNCC* (1998). Her "Black and Jewish Responses to Japanese Internment," *Journal of American Ethnic History* (1995), won the Carlton C. Qualey Memorial Article Award of the Immigration History Society.

Jacqueline Jones received her Ph.D. from the University of Wisconsin in 1976, and is now Truman Professor of American Civilization and History at Brandeis University. She is the author of *American Work: Four Centuries of Black and White Labor* (1998); *The Dispossessed: America's Underclass from the Civil War to the Present* (1992), Choice Academic Book of 1992; *Labor of Love, Labor of*

Sorrow: Black Women, Work, and the Family from Slavery to the Present (1985),
winner of the Bancroft Prize, Brown Memorial Publication Prize awarded by
the Association of Black Women Historians, Philip Taft Award in Labor History, Julia Spruill Prize of the Southern Association for Women Historians, and
the Outstanding Book Award from the Gustavus Myers Center; and *Soldiers of
Light and Love: Northern Teachers and Georgia Blacks, 1865–1873* (1980). Professor Jones is an elected member of the Society of American Historians, the
Authors' Guild, and PEN American Center, and is now writing *A Social History of American Workers.*

Jackson Lears is The Board of Governors' Professor of History at Rutgers Uni-
versity. He received his Ph.D. in American Studies from Yale University in 1978.
He is the author of *No Place of Grace: Antimodernism and the Transformation of
American Culture, 1880–1920* (1981), nominated for a National Book Critics
Circle Award; and *Fables of Abundance: A Cultural History of Advertising in
America* (1994), winner of the Los Angeles Times Book Award in History and
the New Jersey Council for the Humanities Book Award. He is co-editor with
Richard W. Fox of *The Culture of Consumption: Critical Essays in American His-
tory* (1983), and *The Power of Culture: Essays in American History* (1993). Professor Lears has been awarded fellowships by the Woodrow Wilson Center,
Rockefeller Foundation, Guggenheim Foundation, Shelby Cullom Davis Center for Historical Studies, Winterthur Foundation, NEH, and the Smithsonian
Institute. He has served on the editorial board of the *American Quarterly, Journal of American History, Wilson Quarterly,* and *Rethinking History,* and is currently writing *Fortune's Fancy: Gambling and Luck in American Culture.*

William E. Leuchtenburg received his Ph.D. from Columbia University in
1951 and is now William Rand Kenan, Jr. Professor of History at the University of North Carolina at Chapel Hill. Leuchtenburg is past president of the
American Historical Association, the Society of American Historians, and
the Organization of American Historians, and a former vice-president of the
American Academy of Arts and Sciences. He is the author of many books, including *Franklin D. Roosevelt and the New Deal, 1932–1940* (1963), winner of
both the Bancroft and Francis Parkman prizes; *In the Shadow of FDR: From
Harry Truman to Bill Clinton* (1983; rev. ed., 1993); *The Supreme Court Reborn:
The Constitutional Revolution in the Age of Roosevelt* (1995); and *The FDR Years:
On Roosevelt and His Legacy* (1995). Professor Leuchtenburg's honorary degrees, editorial positions, visiting professorships, senior fellowships, articles,
introductions to books, works in press, and works in progress are simply too
many to enumerate.

Nancy MacLean, Charles Deering McCormick Professor of Teaching Excel-
lence and Associate Professor of History and of African American Studies at

Northwestern University, received her Ph.D. from the University of Wisconsin-Madison in 1989. Her book *Behind the Mask of Chivalry: The Making of the Second Ku Klux Klan* (1994) was the winner of the Frank L. and Harriet C. Owsley Prize awarded by the Southern Historical Association, the James A. Rawley Prize awarded by the Organization of American Historians, and the Hans Rosenhaupt Memorial Book Award of the Woodrow Wilson National Fellowship Foundation. Professor MacLean's article "The Leo Frank Case Reconsidered: Gender and Sexual Politics in the Making of Reactionary Populism," *Journal of American History* (1991) received the Binkley-Stephenson Prize awarded by the Organization of American Historians.

Lisa McGirr, Assistant Professor of History at Harvard University, received her Ph.D. from Columbia University in 1995. A Fulbright Lecturer in Germany, NEH Dissertation Award finalist, and holder of various fellowships from Columbia University, Professor McGirr is the author of *Suburban Warriors: The Origins of the New American Right* (2001), "Black and White Longshoreman in the IWW: A History of the Philadelphia Marine Transport Workers Local 8," *Labor History* (1995), and "Labor History at the Social Science History Conference, A Report," *International Labor and Working Class History* (1994).

Robert J. McMahon, Professor and Chair of History at the University of Florida, received his Ph.D. from the University of Connecticut in 1977. A former Fulbright Lecturer in New Zealand and in India, Professor MacMahon is the author of such books as *The Limits of Empire: The United States and Southeast Asia since World War II* (1998); *The Cold War on the Periphery: The United States, India, and Pakistan* (1994); *Colonialism and Cold War: The United States and the Struggle for Indonesian Independence, 1945–49* (1981); and the editor of *Major Problems in the Vietnam War* (1990; rev. ed., 1995), and *The Origins of the Cold War* (1991; rev. ed., 1998).

Peggy Pascoe, Associate Professor and Beekman Chair of Northwest and Pacific History at the University of Oregon, received her Ph.D. from Stanford University in 1986. She is the author of *Relations of Rescue: The Search for Female Moral Authority in the American West, 1874–1939* (1990). Professor Pascoe is currently on the editorial board of the *Encyclopedia of the American West, Pacific Historical Review, American Studies,* and *Frontiers: A Journal of Women Studies,* and is now writing *What Comes Naturally: Race, Sex, Marriage, and Law in the U.S., 1870 to the Present.*

Charles Payne, Professor and Chair of African-American Studies, Duke University, received his Ph.D. from Northwestern University in 1976. His major books include *I've Got the Light of Freedom: The Organizing Tradition and the Mississippi Freedom Struggle* (1995), winner of the Mississippi Historical Society McLemore Prize for 1996, the 1996 Outstanding Book Award from the Gustavus Myers Center, the 1995 Lillian Smith Award for Nonfiction on the South from the Southern Regional Council, Choice Outstanding Academic Book of 1995, and cowinner of the 1996 Bruno Brand Award for a Book on Tolerance from the Simon Wiesenthal Center; and *Getting What We Ask For: The Ambiguity of Success and Failure in Urban Education* (1984), Choice Outstanding Academic Book of 1985. Professor Payne is currently coauthoring *Debating the Civil Rights Movement* and co-editing *Time Longer Than Rope: A Century of African American Activism.*

Harvard Sitkoff, Professor of History at the University of New Hampshire, received his Ph.D. from Columbia University in 1975. The Mary Ball Washington Professor of American History at University College in Dublin, and the John Adams Professor of American Civilization at Nijmegen University in the Netherlands, he has been awarded fellowships from the National Endowment for the Humanities, Rutgers Center for Historical Analysis, and Charles Warren Center of Harvard University. His major books include *Postwar America: A Student Companion* (2000); *The Struggle for Black Equality, 1954–1992* (1993); *A New Deal for Blacks: The Emergence of Civil Rights as a National Issue* (1978); and *The Enduring Vision: A History of the American People* (4th ed, 1999). Professor Sitkoff also edited *Fifty Years Later: The New Deal Evaluated* (1985), and is co-editor of *A History of Our Time: Readings on Postwar America* (5th ed., 1999).

INTRODUCTION

HARVARD SITKOFF

M uch as our ancestors had approached the milestone year 1000 with esca-
lating trepidation only to escape the disasters expected in the Apocalypse, so January 1, 2000, despite predictions that the world would end, or
worse, came and went with just slightly more of the minor irritants of modernity than we usually expect. We did learn again just how elastic time is, how
entirely a human construction. Reminded frequently of the errors in the Julian
and Gregorian calendars, of the calculations devised by a sixth-century monk,
Dionysius Exiguus or Dennis the Short, that marked this year as year 2000,
and of such wholly different measurements of time contained in the Chinese,
Hebrew, and Mayan traditional calendars, we recalled what Thomas Mann
wrote in *The Magic Mountain* (1924): "Time has no divisions to mark its passage. . . . Even when a new century begins it is only we mortals who ring
bells and fire off pistols." And so the ending and beginning of the decade, the
century, the millennium, proved mainly to be an opportunity for celebration
and crass commercialism.

We devoured a feast of predictions, special editions on "The Next Hundred Years," and the many books like *Predictions for the Next Millennium,* too
often forgetting to remember that, at the turn of the last century, the commi-
sioner of the U.S. Office of Patents opined that everything that could be invented had been invented. Or that *Popular Science Monthly* had boldly predicted that the next century would be the Trolley Age, and Henry Adams fixed
1950 as the year when the world must go to smash. Or that *Modern Mechanix*
promised the 13-hour work week and a nuclear car in every driveway. Or that
Darryl F. Zanuck, head of Twentieth Century–Fox, scoffed at television in
1946, "People will soon get tired of staring at a plywood box every night," and
the president of IBM asserted there was a world market for only about five
computers.

As the former catcher of the New York Yankees, Yogi Berra, reminds us:
"Its tough to make predictions, especially about the future." Consider that at
the start of the twentieth century Europe dominated Asia and Africa and overshadowed the United States. Few imagined a world war probable, and fewer

1

still considered war anything other than a quick and decisive conflict. The *gulag*, totalitarianism, and the Holocaust were as equally unimaginable as the Internet, Velcro, or recombinant DNA. There is little reason to think our insights into the future—imagining either full-blown disaster or utopia—are any better today. Historians, fortunately, look backward not forward. And the coming of the year 2000 provided the occasion for much reflection about the past, especially, in the United States, for thinking about the twentieth century.

From the intervention of the United States in Cuba and the Philippines at the turn of the century to American smart bombs in the Persian Gulf and Balkan Mountains, the twentieth century has been a grim tapestry reddened with the blood of millions: a century of war, a century shaped by war, a century in which Americans fought a half dozen hot wars and one very long cold war, a century in which the United States opened the Pandora's box of atomic weaponry and brought the world close to a nuclear cataclysm in the Cuban missile crisis of 1962. Humankind is still engaged in what novelist and futurist H. G. Wells a century ago warned was a race between education and catastrophe. The past century, unparalleled in the number of those who have been slaughtered, starved, and spewed from their homelands, has also been a century of liberation, one which saw the demise of fascism, communism, and colonialism. However haltingly and unevenly, millions have escaped the scourges of oppression and poverty. It has been, as well, a century of incredible artistic creativity. And a century of revolutions in science and technology that conquered age-old diseases, sent us into space, and fundamentally changed the way we live. Only time will tell whether the new tools will further divide rich from poor and whether they will be used for beneficial or malevolent purposes.

To make sense of what was most important in the past century, of the enormous changes as well as continuities in the United States, the history department of the University of New Hampshire planned a century's end program as part of its ongoing series of historical conferences sponsored by the Dunfey Fund. My colleagues and I saw this program as an opportune chance to offer serious historical introspection to a broad public on a century of incredible troubles and triumphs. So we asked the very best historians of the twentieth-century United States available to come to UNH in the spring of 1999 to reflect upon their particular areas of expertise in ways that would help us better understand a century in which the population grew from 76 million to 275 million, the percentage of foreign-born Americans went from about fourteen to less than four and then back to fourteen, and the average life span of an American woman leaped from 47.3 years to 79.7. What are we to make of a century in which a federal budget measured in millions of dollars became one of trillions, one which enfranchised the many Americans unable to vote in 1900 and ended with the percentage of eligible voters going to the polls half what it had been a century earlier—despite dramatic bursts of reform—which left politics as much in thrall to special interest donors in 2000 as in 1900? Or one which began with African Americans lynched daily and almost everywhere Jim-Crowed, with women still chattel, with children mainly a source of labor, and concluded with a large majority of Americans—including many minorities, women, and the young—so much richer, healthier, and better educated that they think they are living in a golden age.

The conference highlighted both changes and continuities. Particular attention was given to the emergence of a mass consumer society; the United States as a major power on the international scene; the increasing power flowing to Washington and to the presidency; a rights-based liberalism and regenerative conservatism; persistent systems of inequality and the means employed to resist oppression; the growth and decline of organized labor; enduring ethnic, racial, and religious forces; regional heterogenity and homogenization; and the limitations of the American welfare state—when it had one. Each session provided both an overview and analysis of the central features of the twentieth-century United States, adding depth and sophistication to our historical knowledge. Each proved so challenging and judicious, so authoritative, that we resolved to offer its insights and interpretations to a wider audience. Thus this book of essays, *Perspectives on Modern America: Making Sense of the Twentieth Century*, which widens our historical horizons and enables us to see more clearly than ever a remarkably fascinating and complicated American people and century.

The fourteen chapters illustrate how significantly both the nature of the United States and the writing of its history have changed in a century. They provide perspective on the past, as well as on who now is writing about the past and the new ways the past is read. *Perspectives on Modern America* thus reflects the more diverse historical profession—a recent phenomenon—and the new questions, methodologies, and sensibilities now current in the profession. It challenges the claims of the older narratives rooted in deterministic materialism, idealist ideologies, or efforts to study the past in order to provide lessons for the present; and it highlights the recent significance of social and cultural history, especially in its concern with race and gender relations, with class and poverty, with conflicts rooted in religion and region, with the essential pluralism of the American experience. Thus, while avoiding the procrustean imposition of a single theme, the authors adopt a critical stance toward an onward and upward approach to history or toward explanations grounded in the notion of American exceptionalism. The best of current thinking on the key aspects of modern America, *Perspectives on Modern America* depicts the flaws as well as the genuine advances in the American past.

The fourteen chapters, of course, do not constitute a complete history of the twentieth-century United States. Much, much more could have been included about, for example, this century's amazing explosion of scientific and technological discoveries and innovations that changed how we live, how we fight and heal. (The absence of such an essay may be yet another example of the "two cultures" problem, after C. P. Snow's 1959 book deploring the widening gulf between humanists and scientists, and the scientific illiteracy of the former.) And we need to know as much about CNN as IBM, so an essay could have been included about popular culture, about the global dominance of American style, about teenagers around the world fifty years ago wanting to be like James Dean, and about the ubiquity of advertisements featuring Michael Jordan today. The list could go on and on. But the resulting book would be too expensive to purchase and too heavy to lift.

So these essays are offered as end-of-the-century snapshots of our past—of the people, ideas, events, and developments that most mattered, and that most brought us to where we are now. *Perspectives on Modern America* begins, fittingly, with one of the century's premier historians, William E. Leuchtenburg, describing the halting yet accumulated aggrandizement in power of arguably the century's most influential institution—the American presidency. In an essay of enormous breadth and insight, Leuchtenburg charts both the admirable and the deplorable in both huge transformations and surprising constants.

Lisa McGirr and Cheryl Greenberg then put the century's dominant political persuasions in the United States under the microscope of history. In "Piety and Property," McGirr explores the ideological tensions within American conservatism between libertarianism and religious conservatism as well as the core set of concerns that conservatives across the decades have shared. Emphasizing the various manifestations of conservative mobilization, she focuses on the way conservative concerns, targets, and enemies have been reconfigured, and argues that it is a mixture of preservationism and adaptation that explains the Right's strength and endurance. Greenberg, similarly, explains the reasons for and meaning of the changes in American liberalism, but ends on a note of declension. As do virtually all the subsequent chapters, Leuchtenburg, McGirr, and Greenberg emphasize as the century's pivotal turning points the Progressive era, the Roosevelt years of the Great Depression and Second World War, the bitter battles ravaging American society in the 1960s, and the so-called Reagan revolution.

In "The Republic as Empire," Robert J. McMahon argues that the concept of America-as-empire is fundamental to an understanding of the world role of the United States. He particularly emphasizes this point in the section of his essay on the post-1945 years, when the power and influence of the United States reached their zenith. McMahon's sobering rendition of American foreign policy makes it difficult to avoid thinking that the only thing to learn from history is that no one learns from history.

The next three chapters focus on the protean U.S. economy. They make sense of such facts and trends as: forty years ago one American worker in three belonged to a trade union and today it is one in seven; America.com, exploiting the possibilities of the new technologies, dominates the planet in innovation and creativity; 22 percent of American children currently live in poverty; and while we once contemplated jobs for life, the average length of employment in California for one job is now three years. Kevin Boyle describes the economy's major transformations, especially the changing nature of American work. His essay details the development and maturation of a mass-production industrial economy in the first seventy years of the century, and then its decline and replacement by a postindustrial economy. He concludes that at century's end many Americans continue to be haunted by economic insecurity.

Jacqueline Jones agrees. She sketches the historical forces that have created poverty-stricken populations, particularly patterns of immigration, the regional and technological alterations in the economy, and the emergence of a global economy. She probes the ways we have defined poverty, how public policies have been shaped by perceptions of the poor and by structures of power, and the struggles of the poor to provide for themselves and to participate in the larger decision-making process. At a time when increasing millions of Americans are playing the stock market daily on the Internet, Jones reminds us of an enduring paradox most Americans are reluctant to confront: that the political economy of the United States generates poverty as well as prosperity. At the end of the most prosperous decade, and century, ever, some 40 million Americans still live below the poverty level. From a different angle of vision, Lizabeth Cohen demonstrates that mass consumption has done more than increase the quantity and alter the quality of goods available to American consumers. It has redefined the terms of citizenship, and reshaped American political culture, particularly during the postwar era when widespread commitment to what Cohen calls a "Consumers' Republic" emerged as a new vehicle for delivering the democracy and equality long sought by Americans. Her essay traces the way a mass consumption economy and culture influenced Americans' pursuits of social and political goals as well as their choices about where to live and shop.

Turning next to some of the prominent themes and topics of the newer social history and more diverse historical profession, Sara M. Evans contrasts American women at the dawn of the twenty-first century with those at the beginning of the twentieth century, when women were challenging the confines of an ideology that relegated them to the private realm of domesticity. Over the course of the century, as Evans describes, women in America emerged fully (though still not equally) into all aspects of public life—politics, labor force participation, professions, mass media, and popular culture. As they experienced what she terms a "sea change with unanticipated consequences," they experienced a transformation in the fundamental parameters of their private lives—marriage, family, fertility, and sexuality. Charles Payne then takes up the subject of race in a century of both oppression and liberation, at a time of both a substantial and growing black middle class and evermore concentrated pools of poverty and despair in inner cities. " 'You duh Man!' " recalls the horrors of the white supremacy decades and of ghettoization, as well as the struggle of the common folk to make the United States a better, fuller democracy. Payne reminds us, as well, just how much the past is still present. Indeed, in one way or another, all the authors view race and racism as key determinants of the American paths traveled in the twentieth century.

In "From the Benighted South to the Sunbelt," Nancy MacLean charts the changes that have swept the South and altered the region's place in the nation. MacLean's interpretation focuses on the rise and demise of cotton plantation sharecropping and the relationship of that institution to the civil rights movement and subsequent transformation of the region. Then Peggy Pascoe pinpoints the twentieth-century West as the exemplar, anticipator, and precipitator of much about democracy and citizenship in the twentieth-century United States. Rejecting familiar assumptions about western frontier or regional distinctiveness, she emphasizes the links between regional and national developments in culture, race, gender, power, and state formation. Once again, moreover, race and racism are highlighted, and turn-of-the-century imperialism, progressivism, the New Deal and Second World War, the upheavals of the 1960s, and the resurgent conservatism that Pascoe terms "border patrol politics" are the critical turning points.

Appropriately, in a world that has been wired into networks, in which individuals can act on the global stage without the mediation of governments or corporations, American culture and cultural politics come to the fore in the concluding chapters of *Perspectives on Modern America*. Contrary to the predictions of secularization theorists and many early twentieth-century cultural observers, religion remained strong in twentieth-century America—playing a crucial role in Progressive era reform, the culture wars of the 1920s, the civil rights movement, and the right-wing upsurge of the Reagan era—and is still vigorous at the century's end. Paul Boyer's essay, exploring the changing face of American religion, reflects on the reasons for its remarkable tenacity and vitality. American attitudes and prejudices are also forefront in Gary Gerstle's examination of the two great waves of immigration to the United States in the twentieth century—those who came primarily from Europe in the century's early years and those who have been coming from Asia and Latin America since 1965. Comparing the experiences of these two broad waves of immigration with each other and with the American mythology of freedom that often dominates popular perceptions of the immigrant experience, Gerstle pays particular attention to the immigrants' motivations for coming, their quest for opportunity and security, and their encounters with discrimination. Last but not least, linking ideas and beliefs with broad social developments, Jackson Lears encapsulates the huge subject of twentieth-century American thought and culture into the story of the formation of a managerial ethos. Lears explains how and why it reached its apogee in the accommodation of intellectuals with power during World War II and the early cold war, and then analyzes its subsequent fragmentation and deconstruction.

Taken together then, these chapters constitute neither a celebratory history of the United States in the twentieth century nor one that claims a transcendant mission for Americans or their exemption from the contingencies of history. These chapters reveal both mighty changes and powerful continuities over time. And they make no pretence to being a guide to the future on the basis of the past. History, or more accurately historians, did not predict that in just the 1990s Germany would be united, Czechoslovakia divided, the Soviet Union dissolved, and Yugoslavia dismembered (and that we would watch it all happen on TV). Barely a decade ago, moreover, none of us surfed the Web, and only a chosen few had even heard of genetic surgery. Given the hurtling rapidity of current change, brought on by evermore digitalization, satellite communications, fibre optics, biotechnology, and computerization—with calculations measured in nanoseconds, or billionths of seconds, and the computing power of silicon chips doubling every 18 months (soon less), and millions of investors moving a trillion dollars a day around the world with the click of a mouse, triggering economic upheavals, even the downfall of governments—history is hardly the window through which to gaze or gape at what is still to come.

Yet history remains a compelling story. Neither the most recent of profound transformations nor the most enduring of paradoxes can truly be understood without considering its past. As has often been said, to know who we are and where we are going requires knowing how we got here and where we have been: history for a society is like memory for a person. In that spirit the authors offer *Perspectives on Modern America: Making Sense of the Twentieth Century* to the e-mail generation of the twenty-first century.

1 | THE TWENTIETH-CENTURY PRESIDENCY

William E. Leuchtenburg

Early in September 1901, the first American president of the twentieth century, William McKinley, journeyed to Buffalo, New York, to speak at an exposition. With his Prince Albert coat, high collar, and black string tie, and his solemn demeanor, he cut an impressive figure. One diplomat had alerted a French journalist who was about to see the U.S. chief executive, "His face is as serious and distant as that of a Roman emperor." Born nearly two decades before the Civil War in the administration of John Tyler, he conveyed the impression of having come from the premodern era of the early republic.

Late on the afternoon of September 6, McKinley received hundreds of well-wishers queued up in the Temple of Music at the fair. As he reached out to an unprepossessing young man with a cumbersome handkerchief wrapped around his hand, the visitor—an anarchist—pulled the trigger on a short-barreled revolver concealed in the handkerchief and pumped two bullets into him. One caromed off a button, but the other penetrated the president's stomach. "Don't let them hurt him," McKinley instructed his secretary. The assassin was just "some poor misguided fellow." Grievously wounded, he added, "My wife, be careful how you tell her—oh be careful." Early in the morning eight days later, murmuring the comforting words of the hymn "Nearer My God to Thee," President McKinley died.

It seems odd that anyone would target McKinley—though he was the third American president in a generation to be murdered—not only because he appeared to be unprovocative, even benign, but still more because the presidency in 1901 did not begin to resemble the leviathan it was to become. As a candidate, McKinley had not toured the country to seek out voters but had been content to deliver orations from his front porch in Canton, Ohio. When he entered the decrepit executive mansion in Washington, so dilapidated that it was feared the floors might collapse, his entire staff consisted of one secretary and six clerks. In a country of little more than 47 million people, most of whom lived on farms or in villages, the U.S. Army totaled only 25,000. Save for an hour before bedtime, McKinley ended his workday at four in the afternoon when he went for a drive in horse and carriage or for a stroll, then napped before dinner. He spent most of each evening chatting with his wife and friends, frequently reading the Bible aloud. Content to rely on traditional nostrums such as the protective tariff and the gold standard, he had no conception of anything remotely like the New Deal or the Great Society.

McKinley took office at the climax of a long period of congressional dominance of the executive branch of the government. It was the president's obligation, Abraham Lincoln was told in 1864, "to obey and execute" and to "leave political organization to Congress," and in 1866 Thaddeus Stevens thundered that the president "is the servant of the people as they shall speak through Congress. . . . Andrew Johnson must learn that he is your servant and that as Congress shall order he must obey." Nothing demonstrated the hegemony of the legislative branch so vividly as the episode during Reconstruction when Congress impeached President Johnson and came within a single vote of the two-thirds required to remove him. The question, one member of Congress did not hesitate to say during the proceedings against Johnson, was "whether the presidential office . . . ought, in fact, to exist, as a part of the constitutional government of a free people."

The presidency during this era had neither the power nor the prestige it would accrue in the twentieth century, and chief executives were often treated with contempt. "My God!" James A. Garfield cried. "What is there in this place that a man should ever want to get into it?" When the White House telephone rang, President Cleveland had to answer it himself. Henry Adams later commented that scrutinizing the descent from George Washington to U. S. Grant had caused him to lose faith in the Darwinian creed of progress, and a Massachusetts senator observed that in these years his colleagues "would have received as a personal affront a private message from the White House expressing a desire that they should adopt any course in the discharge of their legislative duties that they did not approve. If they visited the White House, it was to give, not to receive, advice."

In his book *Congressional Government* published in 1885, the young scholar Woodrow Wilson concluded that a president "is plainly bound in duty to render unquestioning obedience to Congress," which was "the dominant, nay, the irresistible, power of the federal system." Wilson said of the president: "His duties call rather for training than for constructive genius. If there can be found in the official systems of the States a lower grade of service in which men may be advantageously drilled for presidential functions, so much the better."

The weakness of the office in this period derived in no small part from the commitment of many of the chief executives themselves to a diminutive role for the national government. In 1887, in vetoing a bill to help drought-stricken farmers, Grover Cleveland declared, "I do not believe that the power and duty of the General Government ought to be extended to the relief of individual suffering," adding that he wanted "the lesson . . . constantly be enforced—though the people support the Government, the Government should not support the people."

Nor did presidents think that they had any obligation to make themselves available to the citizenry. So determined was Cleveland to avoid the press that news gathering, complained one reporter, was carried out "much after the fashion in which highwaymen rob a stage-coach." And when a woman asked Chester Arthur about his drinking habits, he retorted, "Madam, I may be President of the United States, but my private life is nobody's damned business."

Consequently, presidents seemed, both at the time and subsequently, insubstantial figures who failed to stir the popular imagination. In "The Four Lost Men," novelist Thomas Wolfe, recalling his father's ruminations on the postbellum age, later wrote of "the strange, lost, time-far, dead Americans . . . who were more lost to me than . . . the lost faces of the first dynastic kings that built the pyramids." He continued:

> For who was Garfield, martyred man, and who had seen him in the streets of life? Who could believe his footfalls ever sounded on a lonely pavement? Who had heard the casual and familiar tones of Chester Arthur? And where was Harrison? Where was Hayes? Which had the whiskers, which the burnsides: which was which? . . .
>
> Had Garfield, Arthur, Harrison, and Hayes been young? Or had they all been born with flowing whiskers, sideburns, and wing collars, speaking gravely from the cradle of their mother's arms the noble vacant sonorities of farseeing statesmanship? Had they not all been young men? . . . Did they not, as we, cry out at night? . . . Had they not known, as we have known, the wild secret joy and mystery of the everlasting earth, the lilac dark, the savage, silent, all-possessing wilderness? . . . Did they not say: "Oh, there are women in the East—and new lands, morning, and a shining city."

McKinley proved to be, to some degree, a transitional leader. Still in the nineteenth-century mold, he foreshadowed a bit of what lay ahead. As commander in chief of the armed forces in the Spanish-American War, he had kept in touch with the far-flung battle zones through a network of telegraph and cable lines. The first suzerain of the American empire, he appointed commissions to govern the new acquisitions, and, without authorization from Congress, sent U.S. forces into China to suppress the Boxer Rebellion. He would not permit the press to quote him directly, but he did become the first president to appear in a motion picture when the Republicans featured him in a primitive campaign movie. Still, these were only rudimentary beginnings. McKinley, it has been said, appeared to be walking like a bronze statue toward its pedestal.

His death catapulted into the executive mansion the vice president of the

United States, Theodore Roosevelt, an infinitely more dynamic figure. He had been placed on the GOP ticket in 1900 by party bosses in good part to get rid of him in New York state. Roosevelt had some hesitation about accepting such a passive role, saying that he would "a great deal rather be anything, say professor of history, than vice president." Afterward, the industrialist Mark Hanna turned to Colonel Roosevelt's sponsors and said, "Don't you realize that there is only one life between this madman and the White House?" After the convention, Hanna told McKinley, "Now it is up to you to live."

Teddy Roosevelt was no madman, but he infused the presidency with a vigor that went far beyond McKinley's reticence. "After McKinley's grey respectability, Roosevelt seemed a roman candle of exuberance and fun," the historian Lewis Gould has written. "Becoming the president in the first year of a new century also helped Roosevelt convey a symbolic sense of change and vitality." Henry Adams concluded: "Roosevelt, more than any other man living, showed the singular primitive quality that belongs to ultimate matter—the quality that medieval theology ascribed to God—he was pure act." He had gone west, a dude called "Four Eyes" who rode horseback wearing spectacles, an aristocratic New Yorker who would call out to the cowhands in a high-pitched voice, "Hasten forward quickly there,"—and had, despite these handicaps, won the lifelong devotion of the wranglers of the Dakota Badlands. At San Juan Hill, he had dashed around shouting encouragement to his men, while sporting a blue polka-dot handkerchief that made him a conspicuous target in the midst of battle.

Roosevelt expounded and exemplified the doctrine of the "Strenuous Life." "I am father of three boys, and if I thought any one of them would weigh a possible broken bone against the glory of being chosen to play on Harvard's football team, I would disinherit him," he said. As he lived out the doctrine of the Strenuous Life, he changed the country's image of what an American president should be: not McKinley sedately reclining on his front porch, but TR leaping to his feet and waving his arms at some new outrage as he prepared yet another message to Congress.

He became the first twentieth-century chief executive to create a cult of personality—so that Americans came to think it natural to follow in minute detail the exploits, antics, and most vagrant thoughts of their chosen leader. No topic seemed beyond his ken. One writer drew a portrait of him "regaling a group of his friends with judgments on Goya, Flaubert, Dickens, and Jung, and discussions of Louis the Fat or the number of men at arms seasick in the fleet of Medina Sidonia." His big teeth, eyeglasses, and frenetic gestures made him a favorite subject of cartoonists in the daily press, and through nearly two terms the country was captivated by tales of the six children of the youngest president ever to hold the office. Newspaper readers devoured stories about the president romping with his young sons, the "White House Gang," and about his acid-tongued daughter, "Princess Alice." When his name was mentioned at the Republican convention of 1908, as his tenure neared an end, a giant teddy bear was lifted to the platform while delegates chanted: "Four, Four, Four Years More."

Roosevelt viewed the White House as a "bully pulpit." More Victorian than Edwardian, he found it virtually impossible to think of a political question in any but moral terms. The complex issue of business consolidation he reduced to a distinction between "good" and "bad" trusts. Pancho Villa, he declared, was a "murderer and a bigamist," and the suicide of Anna Karenina greatly relieved him, for it was only ethically fitting. Speaker Tom Reed said to him on one occasion: "Theodore, if there is one thing more than another for which I admire you, it is your original discovery of the Ten Commandments." Contemplating his predilection for action and for moralism, John Morley caught Roosevelt neatly as "an interesting combination of St. Vitus and St. Paul."

Roosevelt, who has been called "the first media president,"—he established the first press room in the White House—used his bully pulpit to promote favorite causes, especially the conservation movement, and to denounce those of whom he disapproved. He fastened on investigative journalists the epithet of "muckrakers," one they were to wear as a badge of honor, and castigated big businessmen as "malefactors of great wealth." In 1916, the Kansas editor William Allen White wrote of TR: "He, more than any other man in the country, is responsible for our awakening of civic righteousness. He turned us from the materialism of Hanna into a larger and more spiritual life."

Though he was more cautious and more moderate than he appeared to be, he did not merely preach. As champion of a "Square Deal," he defied Congress by setting aside more than seven million acres of public lands only hours before his authority was about to expire; established the Food and Drug Administration and the Department of Commerce and Labor; and shepherded legislation empowering the Interstate Commerce Commission to regulate railroad rates. By intervening in the crippling anthracite coal strike of 1902, he became the first president to mediate an industrial dispute. He gave opportunities to a new class of administrative experts, and he appointed so many commissions that Congress eventually forbade the practice, a stipulation that TR promptly announced he would ignore. In a message to Congress in 1905, Roosevelt warned, "The fortunes amassed through corporate organization are now so large, and vest such power in those that wield them, as to make it a matter of necessity to give to the sovereign—that is, to the government, which represents the people as a whole—some effective power of supervision over their corporate use." It was imperative, he concluded, "to assert the sovereignty of the national government by affirmative action." "Surely," wrote a progressive editor, "history will be just to Col. Roosevelt. It will call him the first American of enormous popularity and ability to question the modern industrial system." Little wonder that when, shortly after leaving office, he set out on safari, conservatives raised a toast, "Health to the lions!"

He left an even deeper mark abroad, where, he said, his motto was an African expression, "Speak softly and carry a big stick!" The war with Spain had elevated the United States into the first rank of the world powers, thereby greatly enhancing the office of the presidency, and Roosevelt reigned over a far-flung empire. He was, as Thomas Bailey has observed, "the first president to operate in the grand manner on the world stage." An unrepentant imperialist, he formulated the Roosevelt corollary to the Monroe Doctrine, proclaiming the duty of the United States to punish "chronic wrongdoing" in Latin America by exercising "an international police power." He connived to get the right to build the Panama Canal—he later boasted of "taking Panama"—and when he subsequently traveled there, where he was photographed at the levers of a gigantic steam shovel digging the big ditch, he shattered the custom that a president must remain within the continental borders of the United States. To impress foreign powers, he sent the great white fleet of the U.S. Navy around the world. Yet, for all his jingoism, his role in mediating the Russo-Japanese War at a conference in Portsmouth, New Hampshire, won him the first Nobel Peace Prize given to an American.

When his second term ended in 1909, Roosevelt bequeathed a presidency much more capacious than the institution he had inherited. "I have used every ounce of power there was in the office and I have not cared a rap for the criticisms of those who spoke of my 'usurpation of power,'" he bragged to an English friend. In like manner, in his *Autobiography* he wrote:

> My view was that every executive officer . . . was a steward of the people, and not to content himself with the negative merit of keeping his talents undamaged in a napkin. I declined to adopt the view that what was imperatively necessary for the Nation could not be done by the President unless he could find some specific authorization to do it. My belief was that it was not only his right but his duty to do anything that the needs of the Nation demanded unless such action was forbidden by the Constitution or by the laws.

Teddy Roosevelt's hand-picked successor, William Howard Taft, had a much more circumscribed view of the presidency. "The president," he said, "cannot make clouds to rain, he cannot make corn to grow, he cannot make business to be good." In a book written after he left office, *Our Chief Magistrate and His Powers* (1916), Taft insisted, "The President can exercise no power which cannot be fairly and reasonably traced to some specific grant of power or justly implied and included with such express grant or proper and necessary to exercise." He denounced Roosevelt's conception of "an undefined residuum of power" as altogether "unsafe." Taft is remembered today less as chief executive than as a personality—a jolly fat man. A Supreme Court justice once reported that Taft "arose in a streetcar and gave his seat to three women." Less kindly, a senator characterized him as "a large, amiable island surrounded entirely by persons who knew exactly what they wanted."

Yet even Taft expanded the reach of the national government. He strengthened the ICC, created postal savings banks, and put through a constitutional amendment for an income tax. Furthermore, Taft withdrew a huge tract of land from the public domain, though he had no congressional authorization to do so, and his action was upheld by the Supreme Court in *United States* v. *Midwest Oil Co.* (1915) on the grounds that Congress had permitted executive orders of this nature to go unchallenged for a long time. "The President," the Court declared, "is the active agent, not of Congress, but of the Nation. . . . He is the agent of the people of the United States, deriving all his power from them." In short, the Court was saying that the president gained authority not only from statutory grants but from the silences of Congress.

Woodrow Wilson, who defeated not only Taft but also two third-party candidates, the Bull Moose Progressive Theodore Roosevelt and the Socialist Eugene Debs, in 1912, showed that he meant what he had said five years before in his Columbia University lectures, published in 1908 as *Constitutional Government in the United States.* Wilson, drastically altering his earlier views as he witnessed TR's performance, said of the president:

> His is the only national voice in affairs. Let him once win the admiration and confidence of the country, and no other single force can withstand him, no combination of forces will easily overpower him. His position takes the imagination of the country. He is the representative of no constituency, but of the whole people.

In 1913, Wilson amplified this notion. The president, he wrote,

> is expected by the nation to be the leader of his party as well as the chief executive officer of the government, and the country will take no excuses from him. He must play the part and play it successfully, or lose the country's confidence. He must be prime minister, as much concerned with the guidance of legislation as with the just and orderly execution of law; and he is the spokesman of the nation in everything, even the most momentous and most delicate dealings of the government with foreign nations.

The only chief executive with a Ph.D., one of the first presidents of the American Political Science Association, Wilson had an abiding interest in the structure of U.S. government and, strongly influenced by the English theorist Walter Bagehot, a great admiration for the British institution of prime minister. While still an undergraduate at Princeton, he had published an essay entitled "Cabinet Government in the United States."

He also revealed the impact of having been raised in a Presbyterian manse. Perhaps he did not say, "God ordained that I should be the next president of the

United States," but he believed something very much like that. He had a strong sense of being the Lord's chosen instrument. After World War I, he would stun world-weary European diplomats by stating: "Why has Jesus Christ so far not succeeded in inducing the world to follow His teachings . . . ? It is because he taught the ideal without devising any practical means of attaining it. That is why I am proposing a practical scheme to carry out His aims."

Not a few of Wilson's contemporaries found his attitude presumptuous and his personality forbidding. A Maryland politician told a bartender: "He gives me the creeps. The time I met him, he said something to me, and I didn't know whether God or him was talking." A journalist, noting that Wilson reflected "the cold analysis of the cloister," observed: "In my study . . . Wilson stands out, clear cut and rigid, in the sharp definite lines of a steel engraving; when I turn to Roosevelt he is revealed in strong human tints, the warm flesh tones of a Rembrandt or a Franz Hals." Responding to rumors connecting Wilson with a divorcee, Teddy Roosevelt remarked: "It wouldn't work. You can't cast a man as Romeo who looks and acts so much like an apothecary's clerk."

Many others, though, responded enthusiastically, even reverently, to Wilson's appeal—righteous, ascetic, intellectual—because he had an unusual instinct for how to arouse in his followers the conviction that they were joining him in a crusade to redeem the American spirit. An exceptional phrasemaker, Wilson, as early as 1884, had confided to his future wife that he aimed for "a style full of life, of colour and vivacity, of soul and energy, of inexhaustible power—of a thousand qualities of beauty and grace and strength that would make it immortal." He concluded his inaugural address by sermonizing:

This is not a day of triumph; it is a day of dedication. Here muster, not the forces of party, but the forces of humanity. Men's hearts wait upon us; men's lives hang in the balance; men's hopes call upon us to say what we will do. Who shall live up to the great trust? Who dares fail to try? I summon all honest men, all patriotic, all forward-looking men, to my side. God helping me, I will not fail them, if they will but counsel and sustain me!

Wilson had hardly taken office in 1913 when he called Congress into special session to enact a series of reforms, and he insisted that it go on meeting until it finished its business. The Sixty-third Congress sat for over a year and a half—the longest session in history. Wilson led that Congress by his use of imaginative tactics: the personal message, legislative conferences, the party caucus, appeals to the country, adroit use of patronage, and relentless pressure by mail, telephone, and in person. He also carried out much more openly the practice that Teddy Roosevelt had begun gingerly of submitting drafts of legislation he expected Congress to enact. The New York Times commented: "President Cleveland said he had a Congress on his hands, but this Congress has a President on its back, driving it pitilessly. . . . Never were Congressmen driven so, not even in the days of the 'big stick.'"

On April 8, 1913, on behalf of tariff legislation, Wilson became the first president since John Adams to appear before Congress. Jefferson had abandoned the practice on the grounds that it too closely resembled the king's speech from the throne. It was bold of Wilson to break such a precedent, especially for the leader of a party that cherished Jeffersonian principles. (One Democratic senator expressed regret at "this cheap and tawdry imitation of English royalty.") Wilson declared:

> I am very glad indeed to have this opportunity to address the two Houses directly and to verify for myself the impression that the President of the United States is a person, not a mere department of the Government hailing Congress from some isolated island of jealous power, sending messages, not speaking naturally and with his own voice—that he is a human being trying to cooperate with other human beings in a common service.

A champion of the "New Freedom," which aimed to use the power of the national government not to create a planned economy but to liberate market forces and give the small businessman a better chance, Wilson got that long Congress to enact three important measures: the Federal Reserve Act, setting up a new banking system; the Clayton antitrust law; and a tariff revision that a London editor called "the heaviest blow that has been aimed at the Protective system since the British legislation of Sir Robert Peel." The tariff act also had one feature of infinite potential for expanding national authority: a federal income tax. So effective was Wilson as a party leader that on the final vote on the bill creating the Federal Reserve system, every Democratic senator fell into line. In the nineteenth century, the Democrats had been the party of states' rights and hostility to national authority. One critic had asked, "Are they but an organized no?" But in 1914 an editor wrote, "The old cry that the Republican party is the only one fit to govern the country . . . will not be heard this year, or, if heard, will provoke only a smile."

Later in his first term, Wilson won approval of a number of measures that were closer to Teddy Roosevelt's "New Nationalism," including a child labor law, the Federal Workmen's Compensation Act, and a statute of questionable authority imposing an eight-hour day on the railroads. Walter Lippmann, who in 1914 had been such a bitter critic of the New Freedom in *Drift and Mastery*, contended in 1916 that Wilson led the only party that was "national in scope, liberal in purpose, and effective in action. . . . He has fashioned the old party into something like a national liberal organization." That same year, Wilson broke another convention when he actively campaigned for his own reelection.

Unexpectedly, and often against his desire, Wilson also staked out a large position in foreign affairs. A reluctant imperialist, he was also a man fired by missionary zeal. (The dissimilarity of Wilson and Teddy Roosevelt has reminded one historian of Nietzsche's contrast of the priest and the warrior.) He sent the marines into Haiti; authorized military occupation of the Dominican Republic; and, to fend off covetous Germany, bought the Danish West Indies, renamed the U.S. Virgin Islands. Unlike those who thought he should be the agent of American investors, Wilson had a high-minded attitude toward Mexico, where he sought to encourage democratic movements. But he wound up shedding blood at the port of Veracruz and dispatching General Black Jack Pershing on a punitive expedition in futile pursuit of Pancho Villa. It would not be the last time in this century that a well-meaning, but paternalistic, American president found his plans go awry in an unfamiliar political culture.

Increasingly, even more than the Caribbean, the First World War, which broke out in Europe during his second year in office, preoccupied him. For well over two years, Wilson strove to keep America neutral, no matter what the provocation. In the very week in 1915 that the country reeled in shock and outrage at the sinking of the *Lusitania* with the loss of more than a thousand lives, he said solemnly, "There is such a thing as a man being too proud to fight. There is such a thing as a nation being so right that it does not need to convince others by force that it is right." He won reelection in 1916 on the slogan "He Kept Us Out of War," and in January 1917 he called for "peace without victory." (Anatole France responded that "peace without victory is bread without yeast . . . love without quarrels, a camel without humps, night without moon, roof without smoke, town without brothel.") Yet he also sent a series of notes to Berlin warning that it would be held to "strict accountability" if it engaged in unrestricted submarine warfare, a course that made war inevitable. When Congress refused to allow merchant vessels to defend themselves against U-boat attacks, Wilson early in 1917 ordered them armed on his own authority.

In April 1917, Wilson asked Congress for a declaration of war against Germany, and he closely supervised the conduct of that war, including the final negotiations for Germany's surrender. Afterward, he sailed to France to take an active part in drafting the Versailles treaty, and he was indefatigable in promoting a League of Nations. In October 1919, during a fatiguing campaign on behalf of American membership in the League, he suffered a disabling stroke, and for the remainder of his presidency Edith Bolling Wilson, whom he had married in 1915, dominated the White House—to such an extent that she has been called, with considerable exaggeration, "the first woman president."

No concatenation of events has done more to expand the powers of the presidency than twentieth-century war, as the country quickly learned in 1917–18. When the United States entered the conflict, John Whiteclay Chambers has pointed out, "power flowed to the commander-in-chief." Congress delegated to Wilson an enormous panoply of authority: to requisition food and fuel, to take over factories and mines, to fix the price of coal, and to run the

railroads and telephone and telegraph systems. Wilson exploited his prerogatives to establish a War Industries Board and a War Labor Board and to set up
a national propaganda agency. The economic mobilization he headed was so
government driven that it was characterized as "war socialism." The War Finance Corporation would have a legatee in the Reconstruction Finance Corporation of President Hoover and the War Industries Board a successor in the
National Recovery Administration of the New Deal. In addition, under authority of the Espionage and Sedition acts, the national government prosecuted dissenters, and after the war Wilson's attorney general launched a series
of raids on radicals and dissenters. During the war years, too, advocates of
women's suffrage converted Wilson to their cause, and in 1920 the Nineteenth
"Susan B. Anthony" Amendment was ratified. Henceforth, presidential hope-
fuls would have to appeal to an electorate composed of women as well as men.
By the time this former professor left the White House, the combination of
Teddy Roosevelt and Woodrow Wilson had made the presidency a vastly more
significant institution than it had been at the turn of the century.

Under Wilson's three Republican successors, the presidency went into decline. None had an imposing political presence. One critic maintained that
Warren Harding's speeches "leave the impression of an army of pompous
phrases moving over the landscape in search of an idea; sometimes these me-
andering words would actually capture a straggling thought and bear it tri-
umphantly, a prisoner in their midst, until it died of servitude and overwork."
An observer described Calvin Coolidge's appearance as "splendidly null,"
while the sculptor Gutzon Borglum said of Herbert Hoover, "If you put a rose
in his hand, it would wilt."

Moreover, each of the men deliberately sought to diminish government involvement and to restrict the influence of the White House. In the 1920 campaign, Harding declared, "America's present need is not heroics, but healing;
not nostrums, but normalcy; . . . not agitation, but adjustment; not surgery,
but serenity; . . . not experiment, but equipoise." Elihu Root once said of
Coolidge that he "did not have an international hair in his head," and in domestic policy Coolidge's most often quoted statement is "the chief business
of the American people is business." H. L. Mencken wrote of Coolidge, "His
ideal day is one on which nothing whatever happens." That sounds like, and
is, characteristic Menckenian excess, but Coolidge did, in fact, often sleep
eleven hours. Hoover, considerably more active, was not the "do-nothing
president" of Democratic caricatures, but he spent much of his presidency
seeking to prevent the country from going down what he feared was the road
to regimentation.

Yet, as was true of Taft, all three contributed in some fashion to the development of the executive branch. It was under Harding that Congress first set
up the Budget Bureau, and under Coolidge that it put through the Railway
Labor Act. After adoption of the Budget and Accounting Act, not only Harding,

but also each of his successors, had to submit an executive budget and accompanying message every year. Far from being "Silent Cal," Coolidge averaged more press conferences per month than FDR, while protesting that "one of the most appalling trials which confront a president is the perpetual clamor for public utterances." In 1926, at the height of the Coolidge presidency, Senator James A. Reed even warned, "The most dangerous trend today is the custom of creating an atmosphere of omnipotence about the Chief Executive, whatever his party." Hoover, altogether on his own authority and in the Teddy Roosevelt style, created numbers of presidential commissions, notably the President's Research Committee on Social Trends; sponsored an Agricultural Marketing Act, which set up the Federal Farm Board; and launched the Hoover Dam project. By Hoover's time, the executive branch numbered well over half a million employees. Each of the three also undertook initiatives in foreign policy, especially in the banana republics.

These three put together, though, do not begin to match the impact on the office of Franklin Delano Roosevelt. He was in the White House far longer than anyone else before or since. He broke the taboo against a third term, and served part of a fourth term too. One of his advisers later wrote of him: "No monarch . . . unless it may have been Elizabeth or her magnificent Tudor father, or maybe Alexander or Augustus Caesar, can have given quite that sense of serene presiding, of gathering up into himself, of really representing, a whole people." At a critical juncture in World War II, the British prime minister came to America to meet with the U.S. president. At a White House banquet, Winston Churchill raised his glass in a gracious toast to the president of the United States. It then became FDR's turn to respond. He dutifully proposed a toast of his own—not to Churchill but to the king—for Roosevelt never forgot that he was not only, like Churchill, the chief elected officer of his nation, but also the head of state, and, in that capacity, his counterpart was not the prime minister but the monarch. As former HEW Secretary Joseph A. Califano, Jr. has said:

> The foundations of the presidency for the final decades of the twentieth century were set more in the terms of Franklin D. Roosevelt than in the terms of George Washington or any of his intervening successors. . . . The combination of domestic crisis and global war focused ever-increasing power in the White House during his unprecedented four-term presidency. The presidency would never be the same again.

Roosevelt assumed a variety of roles. He became chief legislator to an extent that not even Wilson, and certainly not Lincoln, could have imagined. In 1933, in his First Hundred Days, he sent fifteen proposals up to the Hill and Congress approved all fifteen, and in the Second Hundred Days of 1935, he approached the same rate of success with measures such as the Social Security Act as he headed the country in the direction of a "welfare state." He also, as party leader, fostered "the FDR coalition" of lower income groups that has been the dominant element in the Democratic party for over sixty years. During the 1938 "purge," he even sought, though with small success, to liberalize the party by getting rid of conservative Democrats in Congress, especially the Senate. In addition, Roosevelt used his appointing power to name the first woman cabinet member, Secretary of Labor Frances Perkins, and chose enough African Americans to important posts to excite talk of a "black cabinet." In both areas, he received constant prodding from Eleanor Roosevelt, the most influential First Lady of the century. Furthermore, under the Reorganization Act of 1939, Roosevelt, though Congress denied him the full range of authority he sought, created the structure of the modern Executive Office of the President. The political scientist Clinton Rossiter called that action an "epoch-making event in the history of American institutions," which converted "the Presidency into an instrument of twentieth-century government."

Franklin Roosevelt became, too, the champion of executive and legislative authority against the incursions of the judiciary. In his first term, the Supreme Court had struck down a number of his recovery measures, and, in *Humphrey's Executor* v. *United States* (1935), had curbed a president's power to remove members of independent regulatory agencies. Though in his struggle with the Court Roosevelt met defeat on the particular solution he urged—packing the Court—he brought about so decisive a shift in attitude (what has been called "the Constitutional Revolution of 1937") that no significant legislation regulating corporations has been struck down since.

A master of the media, Roosevelt initiated regularly scheduled press conferences at which there were free and easy exchanges, as well as radio addresses, called "fireside chats" because of his manner of appearing to palaver informally with the people as he spoke into the microphone. They led millions of his countrymen to believe that the president was both their guardian and their friend. Before Franklin Roosevelt, Americans rarely thought to write to the White House because it seemed too distant from their everyday lives. Taft had averaged only about two hundred letters a week. But after Roosevelt delivered his electrifying inaugural address in 1933, he got nearly half a million letters. Though one man had been able to cope with all the letters Hoover received, it took a corps of fifty to handle FDR's mail. Above all, FDR cherished Cousin Teddy's "bully pulpit." Even before he took office, he said: "The presidency is not merely an administrative office. That is the least of it. It is preeminently a place of moral leadership. All of our great presidents were leaders of thought at times when certain historic ideas in the life of the nation had to be clarified."

The FDR years also saw an enormous expansion of presidential preeminence overseas. In 1936, in *United States* v. *Curtiss-Wright Export Corp.,* the Supreme Court gave the most sweeping validation ever of the president's powers abroad—in an opinion by Justice George Sutherland who, though an acerbic critic of what he regarded as FDR's abuse of authority in domestic policy, stated that a chief executive had "plenary" power in the conduct of foreign affairs. In *United States* v. *Belmont* in 1937, the Court, in another opinion by Justice Sutherland, ruled that Roosevelt, in recognizing the Soviet Union, had the authority to negotiate agreements without consulting the U.S. Senate, despite the treaty-making role assigned by the Constitution to the Senate, for the president was "the sole organ" of international relations.

As in 1917, war in Europe opened vast opportunities for a president. In 1940, Roosevelt, acting without legislative sanction and, critics charged, in violation of both U.S. statutes and international law, traded fifty navy destroyers to Great Britain. The following year, Congress, in the Lend-Lease Act, gave him virtually unfettered power to disburse billions to belligerent nations engaged in a global war, and, months before Pearl Harbor, Roosevelt seized an aviation plant in California with no justification other than that he had imposed an "unlimited national emergency." He went still farther when, wholly on his own authority and with the country at peace, he ordered the U.S. Navy to escort Atlantic convoys and, if German submarines raised a threat, to open fire.

After the United States entered the war in December 1941, Roosevelt guided the nation to victory over the Axis in the greatest military struggle in history; created, for good or evil, the Pentagon; and sponsored the development of the atomic bomb. He also fostered the creation of new institutions, most notably the United Nations. Furthermore, in mobilizing an economic juggernaut in support of the armed forces, he advanced new claims for presidential power. In September 1942, after peremptorily demanding that Congress repeal certain features of a price control statute, he announced, "In the event that Congress should fail to act, and act adequately, I shall accept the responsibility, and I will act." In essence, he was asserting the right of a chief executive to abrogate a law passed by both houses of Congress. Additionally, Roosevelt took advantage of the occasion of war to articulate an economic bill of rights and to introduce innovations including a withholding tax and the GI Bill of Rights. Unhappily, he also used his executive power to approve the internment of Japanese Americans.

In 1945, at the end of the Roosevelt era, the British scholar Herbert Nicholas summed up what all of this meant:

> When Franklin Roosevelt died on April 12 he concluded a longer period of continuous office than any President of the United States or any British Prime Minister since the Reform Bill. During these twelve crowded years, by political speech and ceremonial proclamation, by executive action and legislative direction, in his three roles of party leader, chief executive and titular head of state, he exercised a cumulative influence on the American public mind

which for duration and intensity can hardly be paralleled in the history of modern democracies.

During the age of Roosevelt and its aftermath, FDR came to seem to many the very model of what a president should be, but he also left a residue of uneasiness. When before he took office he was asked how much authority he expected if he became president, he snapped, "Plenty." He once said that he would like to turn sixteen lions loose on Congress. But, someone objected, the lions might make a mistake. "Not," Roosevelt retorted, "if they stayed there long enough." To speed aid to the Allies in World War II, he bent the law and indeed told outright lies. Only death cut short his tenure; he never relinquished power voluntarily. Not long after he died, Congress responded by adopting the Twenty-second Amendment limiting presidents henceforth to two terms, a stipulation that the states, in what was called a posthumous act of revenge against FDR, ratified in 1951.

So large was the shadow Roosevelt cast on his immediate successor that not even historians have fully appreciated the impact of Harry Truman on the presidency. Truman's Fair Deal expanded the liberal agenda to include both federal aid to education and health insurance. When in the 1960s these programs came to fruition, President Johnson made a sentimental journey to Independence, Missouri, to sign the Medicare bill into law in Truman's presence. Larger still was Truman's contribution to civil rights. He named a president's committee on civil rights and supported a number of its recommendations in a message to Congress; increased the pace of desegregation of the armed forces; and issued an executive order banning racial discrimination in federal employment. In 1948, he drew upon the capacity of a president to make Congress do what it does not at all want to do by summoning the Republican Eightieth Congress back into special session, and he drove the point home by saucily choosing as the time for reconvening a date with no significance other than it was the day Missouri farmers traditionally planted turnips. By cleverly exposing the unwillingness of conservative Republican lawmakers to approve their party's 1948 platform planks, he helped make possible his surprise victory in November.

Even a short list conveys how extensive was Truman's impact on foreign affairs: the conclusion of World War II with the dropping of atomic bombs on Hiroshima and Nagasaki; the birth of the United Nations in San Francisco; the occupation of Germany and Japan; the Truman Doctrine and the concept of containment; the speedy recognition of Israel; the Marshall Plan; the Berlin airlift; the North Atlantic treaty alliance and the creation of NATO; the Point Four program of aid to the Third World; the Korean War, a conflict he dared enter without asking for congressional sanction. The first president of the cold war, the head of the world's superpower, he held in his hands the awesome authority to launch a nuclear strike that would incinerate millions of people.

President Truman also left an important institutional legacy for the executive branch. In the Truman years, Congress unified the armed forces under a newly created Department of Defense; gave the Joint Chiefs of Staff legal status; established the Central Intelligence Agency (CIA); set up the Atomic Energy Commission; authorized the Council of Economic Advisers; and, over Truman's veto, enacted the Taft-Hartley law, which augmented presidential authority in labor disputes. Truman named Herbert Hoover to head a Commission on Reorganization of the Executive Branch, and issued a "loyalty order" affecting many thousands of federal employees. He even asserted that a president has inherent constitutional authority to seize and operate privately owned steel mills in wartime, but, in *Youngstown Sheet & Tube Co. v. Sawyer* (1952), the Supreme Court rejected this claim, thereby establishing limits to executive prerogatives in keeping with the principle of separation of powers.

Truman made the strongest assertion of civilian authority over the military in American history by dismissing General Douglas MacArthur, though he well understood how unpopular that action would be. Senator Joseph McCarthy of Wisconsin, calling Truman a "son of a bitch," traced the firing to a White House coterie addicted to "bourbon and benzedrine," and, from California to Cape Cod, communities mourning the deed lowered flags to half-mast. Shortly before his announcement was to be made, according to one account, a young White House aide suggested that Truman could protect himself by saying that he was acting with the unanimous approval of his advisers. "Son, not tonight," Truman replied. "Tonight I am taking this decision on my own responsibility as President of the United States and I want nobody to think I am sharing it. Tonight it is my decision and mine alone."

Harry Truman left office with ratings lower even than Nixon's would be when he departed, but in later years the country was swept by nostalgia for him that *Time Magazine* called "Trumania," less because of his many accomplishments than because of his character, a consideration in assessing presidents to which commentators have generally paid insufficient attention. He once wrote: "I wonder how far Moses would have gone if he'd taken a poll of Egypt? What would Jesus Christ have preached if he'd taken a poll in Israel? . . . It isn't polls or public opinion of the moment that counts. It is right and wrong." He was not one to mince words. Nixon, he said, was "a shifty-eyed goddamn liar." When a woman, taking umbrage at his use of the word "manure," asked his wife, "Bess, couldn't you get the President to say fertilizer?," the First Lady responded, "Heavens, no. It took me twenty-five years to get him to say manure." "Trumania," observed John Lukacs, "was the national appreciation for a man of the older American type: outspoken, courageous, loyal to his friends, solidly rooted in his mid-American past, and *real*—a self-crafted piece of solid wood, not a molded plastic piece."

The standing among historians of Truman's successor, Dwight Eisenhower, has been steadily rising, but not because he greatly affected the institution of the presidency. Eisenhower had a Whiggish attitude toward governance which one contemporary capsulized as "What shall we refrain from doing today?" Much of his two terms is a story of what he did *not* do: he did not expand the war in Korea, did not go to war in Southeast Asia or in Hungary, did not support the British-Israeli venture in Suez, did not actively back the Supreme Court's desegregation decision, did not directly confront Joe McCarthy. Yet he also undertook a number of actions, including authorizing the CIA to intervene in Iran and Guatemala, building an enormous arsenal of nuclear bombs, sending U.S. airborne troops to back up the U.S. courts in Little Rock, initiating the interstate highway system, and launching construction of the St. Lawrence seaway. On St. Patrick's Day, 1954, Eisenhower asserted that "hanging ought to be the fate of any President who failed to act instantly to protect the American people against a sudden attack in this atomic age." In addition, he left an institutional legacy in the Department of Health, Education, and Welfare (HEW) and the National Aeronautics and Space Administration (NASA). His most important bequest, though, may well be not an institution but a warning, delivered in his farewell address, to "guard against the acquisition of unwarranted influence . . . by the military-industrial complex."

Still, the striking aspect of the presidency of Dwight Eisenhower, in so many ways an admirable man, is how little he changed or sought to change, thereby permitting the Democrats to regain power in 1960 on John F. Kennedy's pledge to get America "moving again." Patrick Anderson has written:

> The misfortune of Eisenhower's presidency is that a man of such immense popularity and good will did not accomplish more. All the domestic problems which confronted the nation in the 1960s—the unrest of the Negro, the decay of the cities, the mediocrity of the schools, the permanence of poverty—were bubbling beneath the surface in the 1950s, but the President never seemed quite sure that they existed or, if they did, that they were problems with which he should concern himself.

Scholars hold Kennedy's presidency in considerably lower esteem than does the American public, in part for the melancholy reason that he was granted so little time. To be sure, there were major confrontations in the Kennedy years—with Khrushchev over Berlin and the Cuban missiles, with segregationist governors in Alabama and Mississippi, with steel barons. Moreover, he did head the nation in new directions on civil rights and on economic policy, especially in his final year, and he committed the United States to outrace the Soviet Union to the moon. The first president to make skillful use of the new medium of television, he inspired the nation with his inaugural address and his insouciant press conferences. But save for the Peace Corps, he did not alter the executive establishment significantly, though he did give impetus to the feminist movement by establishing the President's Commission on the Status of Women. His adviser and admirer Richard Neustadt concluded sadly, "He will be just a flicker, forever clouded by the record of his successors. I don't think history will have much space for John Kennedy."

The assassination of John Fitzgerald Kennedy in November 1963, however, revealed how deeply rooted are the feelings of the American people toward their president. In the days following the murder, 26 percent of people surveyed reported rapid heart beats, 48 percent insomnia, 68 percent nervous tension. That may seem a one-time phenomenon brought on by the murder of a leader so attractive, so young. But it should be remembered that when Warren Harding died, Californians strew flowers on the tracks of the funeral train; 40,000 mourners in Omaha stood in the rain at 2 a.m. to pay tribute; and a weeping crowd of 300,000 impeded the train's progress in Chicago.

In contrast to Kennedy, Lyndon Johnson rolled up an exceptional number of accomplishments in domestic affairs: Medicare, Medicaid, clean air and clean rivers legislation, the Highway Safety Act, sizable appropriations for education, a highway beautification act (Lady Bird Johnson's favorite project), federal aid to the arts, Wilderness and Endangered Species statutes, the Immigration Act of 1965, a "War on Poverty" that produced enduring programs such as Head Start, and, above all, the Civil Rights acts of 1964, 1965, and 1968. Johnson established two new cabinet-level agencies: the Department of Housing and Urban Affairs (HUD) and the Department of Transportation. In an address at Ann Arbor in the spring of 1964, he announced that he wanted to improve the quality of American life in order to achieve a "Great Society." To Lyndon Johnson that meant, as Tom Wicker said, "a promised land in which there will be no poverty, no illiteracy, no unemployment, no prejudices, no slums, no polluted streams, no delinquency, and few Republicans." In 1965, James MacGregor Burns wrote: "The Presidency today is at the peak of its prestige. Journalists describe it as the toughest job on earth, the presiding office of the free world, the linchpin of Western alliance, America's greatest contribution to the art of self-government."

Johnson, though, also created alarm about a too-powerful and a deceitful presidency, especially by his escalation of the Vietnam War and the prolonged agony it entailed. In the 1964 campaign, he stated, "We are not going to send American boys nine or ten thousand miles away from home to do what Asian boys ought to be doing for themselves." But in the very next year he ordered American combat units into Vietnam, and by the middle of 1968 U.S. forces had mounted to more than half a million, with over 100,000 American casualties. Johnson further widened "the credibility gap" when he denounced critics of his feckless policy as "nervous Nellies."

Lyndon Johnson aroused dismay, too, by his egomaniacal self-conception. According to an apocryphal story, when Chancellor Erhard of Germany said to him, "I understand, Mr. President, you were born in a log cabin," Johnson replied, "No, Mr. Chancellor. You have me confused with Lincoln. I was born in a manger." On one occasion at Andrews Field, when a young officer cautioned him that he was heading toward a helicopter that was not his, Johnson replied, "Son, all of them are mine." Distrust of LBJ's policies and character reached such a level that on March 31, 1968, he announced, "I shall not seek and I will not accept the nomination of my party for a second term as your president."

Anxiety about the gargantuan presidency heightened under Richard Nixon, though, like Johnson, he could boast of a number of achievements, both at home and abroad. He left lasting legacies in the creation of the Environmental Protection Agency (EPA), the Office of Management and Budget (OMB), and the Occupational Safety and Health Administration (OSHA), as well as in the substantial expansion of the Equal Employment Opportunity Commission (EEOC), born in the Johnson administration. A longtime foe of economic controls, he froze wages, prices, and rents for ninety days in 1971, and, a man who had made his reputation warning of the Red menace, he made a historic visit to the People's Republic of China the following year.

Nixon got little credit for these accomplishments, however, in part because they were offset by other aspects of his conduct as president. Though he secured a cease-fire accord in Vietnam in 1973, it came only after he had willfully carried out secret bombing of Cambodia, ordered an invasion of Laos, and approved saturation bombing of North Vietnam. In addition, he impounded an unprecedented proportion of congressional appropriations—as much as one-fifth of the total—for projects such as low-cost housing, even in instances where Congress had overridden his veto of the legislation. In pursuit of a "southern strategy" to lure the followers of George Wallace, he sponsored antibusing legislation.

None of these developments, though, provoked so much rancor as "Watergate," a term connoting not only the break-in and bugging of Democratic National Committee headquarters at the Watergate complex in Washington and the subsequent cover-up, but also a number of other "dirty tricks." These violations resulted in the indictment, conviction, and sentencing of twenty of Nixon's appointees, including his chief White House aides, his counsel, and a former cabinet member, Attorney General John Mitchell, the nation's chief law enforcement official. As one revelation followed the next, Nixon lost support even among conservatives in his own party. After the Supreme Court, in *United States v. Nixon* (1974), though acknowledging executive privilege, required him to surrender subpoenaed tapes of White House conversations, and after the House Judiciary Committee, including a number of its Republican members, voted to recommend impeachment, Nixon had no choice but to become the first president in American history to resign.

The events in the eleven years between 1963 and 1974 created widespread apprehension about the future of the presidency. One source of concern was instability. The first chief executive in this period of little more than a decade had

been murdered; the second had not dared run for reelection; the third had re-
signed in disgrace and could not be succeeded by his corrupt vice president,
who also had been compelled to step down. As a result, the United States commemorated its bicentennial of independence in 1976 with a president and a vice
president, Gerald Ford and Nelson Rockefeller, neither of whom had been
elected by the American people. A year earlier, in his State of the Union message, Ford had acknowledged, "The state of the union is not good." The other
reason for distress was abuse of power in the White House. Scholars such as
Arthur Schlesinger, Jr., who for a generation had been celebrating a forceful
chief executive on the FDR model, now warned of "the imperial presidency."
Thomas Cronin questioned textbook celebrations of strong presidents; Richard
Pious asked, "Is Presidential Power 'Poison'?"; and Nelson Polsby came out
"Against Presidential Greatness." In 1973, Congress adopted the War Powers
Resolution to restrict the president's authority to commit armed forces abroad,
and in 1978, it approved the Special Prosecutor Act creating an official, later
called an independent counsel, who could investigate high-ranking members
of the executive branch, including even the president of the United States.

In the quarter of a century since 1974, beginning in the tenures of Gerald
Ford and Jimmy Carter, the imperial presidency has been in disfavor, and expectations of the executive office have been downsized. Ford conducted himself with such modesty that, in an uncharacteristic pun, he said, "I am a Ford,
not a Lincoln." On inauguration day 1977, Carter eschewed a government
limousine and, hand in hand with his wife, Rosalynn, strolled all the way
down Pennsylvania Avenue from the Capitol to the White House like an ordinary citizen. In a televised address to the nation, he wore a simple cardigan.
He got rid of the presidential yacht, and he gave orders to halt the playing of
"Hail to the Chief," a tradition that dated from James K. Polk. In contrast to
the statist emphases of his party from FDR to Johnson, he pushed for the
deregulation of major industries. "Government," Carter declared, "cannot
eliminate poverty or provide a bountiful economy or reduce inflation or save
our cities or cure illiteracy or provide energy."

These tendencies became even more marked under the next presidents.
Ronald Reagan, who asserted in his inaugural address, "Government is not the
solution to our problem; government is the problem," hung portraits of
William Howard Taft and Calvin Coolidge in the cabinet room. To Secretary of
State Alexander Haig, Reagan was a "cipher." Haig remarked, "To me, the
White House was as mysterious as a ghost ship; you heard the creak of the rig-
ging and the groan of the timbers and sometimes even glimpsed the crew on
deck. But which of the crew had the helm?" With the president often disen-
gaged, some regarded Nancy Reagan as "the de facto chief of staff." George
Bush advocated not expansion of the state but reliance on voluntary efforts by
a myriad of individuals—"a thousand points of light"—to create "a kinder,
gentler America." Bill Clinton abandoned the welfare system initiated in 1935

and announced that the era of big government was over. One writer entitled a recent article on Clinton, "Honey, I Shrunk the Presidency."

Especially during the Ford-Carter years, observers who had been warning about excessive power in the White House began to fret about the ineffectiveness of the country's chosen leaders. As Schlesinger noted:

> Pundits confidently predicted an age of one-term Presidents. The impression arose . . . of a beleaguered and pathetic fellow sitting forlornly in the Oval Office, assailed by unprecedentedly intractable problems, paralyzed by the constitutional separation of powers, hemmed in by congressional and bureaucratic constraints, pushed one way and another by exigent interest groups, seduced, betrayed, and abandoned by the mass media.

In 1980, Gerald Ford declared, "We have not an imperial presidency but an imperiled presidency."

Yet even in this period, the American presidency continued to loom large. Ford exercised his prerogative to grant an unconditional pardon to Richard Nixon, and he vetoed more bills in fifteen months than Hoover had in four years. (One of Gerald Ford's assistants perceived him as "the kind of guy who would take his shirt off his back and give it to a poor kid he saw on the street and then walk in and veto the day care program.") Carter set aside an enormous area of Alaska for posterity; created a superfund to clean up toxic wastes; sought (but failed) to secure ratification of the Equal Rights Amendment; got Israel and Egypt together at Camp David; against all odds put through a Panama Canal treaty; established an office of human rights in the State Department; and left behind him both a Department of Education and a Department of Energy.

That pattern persisted even under chief executives who professed to be foes of "big" government. Reagan broke the air traffic controllers' strike; named enough right-wing judges to the federal courts to shape the contours of jurisprudence well into the twenty-first century; and sent troops to Grenada and Lebanon. While cutting back on food stamps and school lunches, he engaged in an extraordinarily costly arms buildup, including billions on a "Star Wars" project military experts warned would not work. The government payroll actually grew at a faster rate under Reagan than under Carter. Moreover, some historians view the Iran-Contra affair, in which he circumvented the law by furnishing arms both to Iran and to Nicaraguan guerrillas, as a more serious transgression than Watergate. Bush ordered an invasion of Panama and massed the power of the United States and its allies in the Gulf War. And Clinton, who sent U.S. forces to Somalia, Haiti, and the former Yugoslavia, and won approval for the North American Free Trade Agreement (NAFTA), turned away from big government only after failing to put through a colossal health care plan.

The nation also discovered that, however much suspicion it harbored toward 1600 Pennsylvania Avenue, it counted on the president to inspirit the country. In that regard, it found wanting both Ford, portrayed as a bumbler, and Carter, derided as the village scold. Jimmy Carter got into trouble, it has been pointed out, because he "told the American people what they did not want to hear—that they would have to renounce their profligate lifestyles." It was also said that when Carter delivered a fireside chat, even the fire fell fast asleep. Ronald Reagan, though frequently misinformed and inattentive, came as a welcome relief. In his inaugural address, he declared, "It is time for us to realize that we're too great a nation to limit ourselves to small dreams. We're not, as some would have us believe, doomed to an inevitable decline." Too often, as Stephen Skowronek has written, he engaged in "mawkish truisms," but his courage and good cheer in responding to an assassination attempt ("Honey, I forgot to duck," he told his wife) rallied the nation to him, and throughout his eight years, during crises like the dreadful *Challenger* disaster, he performed admirably his role as comforter of the people. Reagan, with his view of "morning in America," said *Time,* was a "magician who carries a bright, ideal America like a holograph in his mind and projects its image in the air." His successor, George Bush, failed to win a second term in part because, unable to equal Reagan's mastery of "the vision thing," he could not match Bill Clinton's more positive message.

Numerous commentators, however, have been maintaining both that Clinton has undermined respect for the Oval Office and that his impeachment and trial have permanently impaired the presidency. Democratic senator Bob Graham of Florida, who voted against Clinton's removal, stated, "History should—and, I suspect will—judge that William Jefferson Clinton dishonored himself and the highest office in our American democracy." Furthermore, the institution of the presidency has been damaged by the unwise unanimous decision of the Supreme Court in the Paula Jones case to permit private suits while a president is in office on the patently absurd premise that they will not distract a chief executive from his duties and by other court rulings making it more difficult for a president to confer in confidence with his counsel or rely on the discretion of the Secret Service.

From the very beginning, the republic has struggled with the conundrum stated at the constitutional convention by Gouverneur Morris as the delegates struggled with how much authority to give the president: "Make him too weak: the Legislature will usurp power. Make him too strong: he will usurp the Legislature." The president, wrote Clinton Rossiter nearly two centuries later, is "a kind of magnificent lion who can roam widely and do great deeds so long as he does not try to break loose from his broad reservation." Over the years, a number of institutions and forces—Congress, the courts, an entrenched bureaucracy, pressure groups, among others—have served to constrain the presidency, but without ever fully resolving Gouverneur Morris's dilemma.

There is no reason to anticipate that the presidency is going to diminish significantly in the twenty-first century, for the White House has continued to be the focus of the nation's aspirations. Commenting on the Lyndon Johnson era, a British journalist observed that "it was now . . . to the President, far more than to the Congress or to any other agency, public or private, more even than to the courts, that Americans looked for the carrying out of their ideals." In 1970, Daniel Patrick Moynihan gave expression to that perception in saying, "I am one of those who believe that America is the hope of the world, and for that time given him, the President is the hope of America."

Important though the chief executive is as administrator, policymaker, and party leader, he has a role in the political culture of the United States that goes beyond any of these discrete functions. The philosopher Michael Novak has written of the American president:

> Hands are stretched toward him over wire fences at airports like hands extended toward medieval sovereigns or ancient prophets. One wonders what mystic participation our presidents convey, what witness from what other world, what form of cure or heightened life. . . . His office . . . evokes responses familiar in all the ancient religions of the world. It fills a perennial vacuum at the heart of human expectations.

Since the era of William McKinley, the office has magnified in importance. By the 1970s, one political scientist went so far as to say, "There can be no doubt that the President of the United States today is the single most powerful human being in the history of the world." As distinguished political scientist E. S. Corwin of Princeton concluded sixty years ago: "Taken by and large, the history of the presidency is a history of aggrandizement." He acknowledged that "the story is a highly discontinuous one. Of the thirty-three individuals who have filled the office not more than one in three has contributed to the development of its powers; under other incumbents things have either stood still or gone backward." But he added: "Yet the accumulated tradition of the office is also of vast importance. Precedents established by a forceful or politically successful personality in the office are available to less gifted successors." And if the White House is tarnished today, it still lodges a grand tradition created by a number of the holders of the office in this century, a tradition on which future presidents can build.

BIBLIOGRAPHY

Historians usually prefer to rely on the most recent books in their field, but writers on the twentieth-century presidency quickly learn that many of the most valuable works are decades, even generations, old. They include Harold J. Laski's *The American Presidency: An Interpretation* (New York: Harper, 1940), a view from the British left; Wilfred E. Binkley's highly readable *The President and Congress* (New York: Knopf, 1947); Edward S. Corwin's classic, *The President: Office and Powers, 1787–1957* (New York: New York University Press,

1957); Clinton Rossiter's often-quoted *The American Presidency* (New York: New American Library, 1960); and the prolific James MacGregor Burns's *Presidential Government: The Crucible of Leadership* (Boston: Houghton Mifflin, 1965). Richard E. Neustadt's *Presidential Power: The Politics of Leadership* (New York: Wiley, 1980), originally published in 1960, influenced John F. Kennedy. Patrick Anderson's *The President's Men* (Garden City, N.Y.: Doubleday, 1968) surveys White House assistants from FDR to LBJ.

Perhaps as a consequence of Watergate, the 1970s saw the appearance of a number of significant volumes: Arthur Schlesinger, Jr.'s alarum, *The Imperial Presidency* (Boston: Houghton Mifflin, 1973); Thomas E. Cronin's pathbreaking *The State of the Presidency* (Boston: Little, Brown, 1975); James David Barber's *The Presidential Character* (Englewood Cliffs, N.J.: Prentice-Hall, 1977), more useful for its commentary on chief executives than for its elaborate theory; Joseph A. Califano, Jr., *A Presidential Nation* (New York: Norton, 1975); and Richard M. Pious's perceptive *The American Presidency* (New York: Basic Books, 1979). Stanley Bach and George T. Sulzner, eds., *Perspectives on the Presidency* (Lexington, Mass.: D.C. Heath, 1974) is a useful anthology.

Though much of recent scholarship takes off from these earlier works, several make their own contribution. George C. Edwards III and Stephen J. Wayne, eds., *Studying the Presidency* (Knoxville: University of Tennessee Press, 1983) offers explorative essays. Donald L. Robinson, *"To the Best of My Ability": The Presidency and the Constitution* (New York: Norton, 1987) and Louis Fisher, *The Constitution between Friends* (New York: St. Martin's, 1979) both place the executive office in a constitutional matrix. Marcus Cunliffe, *The Presidency* (Boston: Houghton Mifflin, 1987) is written with characteristic panache, and Thomas E. Cronin and Michael A. Genovese, *The Paradoxes of the American Presidency* (New York: Oxford University Press, 1998) is a challenging new interpretation.

Countless books have been written about individual presidents, with those on Theodore Roosevelt, Woodrow Wilson, Franklin D. Roosevelt, Harry S. Truman, Lyndon B. Johnson, and Richard Nixon especially important for the history of the twentieth-century presidency, but readers can also draw upon volumes studying more than one president: Walter Johnson, *1600 Pennsylvania Avenue: Presidents and the People since 1929* (Boston: Little, Brown, 1960); Morton Borden, ed., *America's Eleven Greatest Presidents* (Chicago: Rand McNally, 1971); James T. Patterson, "The Rise of Presidential Power before World War II," *Law and Contemporary Problems,* 40 (Spring 1976):39–57; Fred I. Greenstein, ed., *Leadership in the Modern Presidency* (Cambridge: Harvard University Press, 1988); William E. Leuchtenburg, *In the Shadow of FDR: From Harry Truman to Bill Clinton* (Ithaca, N.Y.: Cornell University Press, 1993); Robert Dallek, *Hail to the Chief: The Making and Unmaking of American Presidents* (New York: Hyperion, 1996); Stephen Skowronek, *The Politics Presidents Make: Leadership from John Adams to Bill Clinton* (Cambridge, Mass.: Harvard University Press, 1997); and Sidney Milkis and Michael Nelson, *The American Presidency: Origins and Development, 1776–1990* (Washington, D.C.: Congressional Quarterly Press, 1990), an indispensable overview. H. G. Nicholas's appreciation of FDR, "Roosevelt and Public Opinion," appeared in *Fortnightly* 163 (May 1945). Tom Wicker's *JFK and LBJ: The Influence of Personality upon Politics* (New York: William Morrow, 1968) contrasts the styles of these two presidents.

2 | PIETY AND PROPERTY

Conservatism and Right-Wing Movements in the Twentieth Century

Lisa McGirr

Taking stock of the history of conservatism in the twentieth century, one cannot help but be struck by the staying power and vibrancy of the Right in American politics and national life. In the wake of three periods of conservative upheaval—in the 1920s, at mid-century, and in the late 1980s—liberal observers asserted that the Right was in disarray, had reached its apogee, and was in retreat. Each time, they were wrong. Indeed, conservative forces have shown a remarkable ability to thrive and flourish, despite Daniel Bell, Richard Hofstadter, and Seymour Martin Lipset's claims of the late 1950s that right-wing mobilization was fueled by a marginal group of status-anxious men and women fighting a hopeless battle against modernity. And in the past two decades, conservatives have not only entered the mainstream of respectable political life, they have also set the nation's political agenda. This resilience of the Right suggests the tenacious and deep-rooted nature of conservatism in American life. To understand the broader course of American history over the past one hundred years, then, we must take a close look at the institutions, ideas, politics, and networks that have fueled American conservatism. Conservatism has a history, a history that is central to understanding the twentieth-century United States.

If American conservatism has a history, its fortunes have ebbed and flowed over the course of the century. The story of the American Right can best be told by looking at three distinct phases of its development. First, there was the period between 1900 and 1932, a time when conservative ideas were still very much at the heart of American culture and national life. Second, there was the "long durée" of 1933 to 1980, years that in conservatives' eyes represented a trying time of displacement, marginalization, and struggle. It was a time during which they had to adjust to their new position as simultaneously insiders and outsiders to the realms of power. Eventually, their posture as "outsiders" enabled them to build a self-conscious movement to develop a critique of liberal elites. By the 1960s, this movement was cohesive and had institutions, networks, and a broad grass-roots following. While a variety of sometimes incompatible impulses fueled right-wing mobilization, for political purposes the movement has fused anticommunism, moral traditionalism, and libertarianism. And in the third stage in the history of the twentieth-century Right, between 1980 and the present, conservatives regained institutional power. Boosted into the corridors of national power by the Reagan landslide, conservatives in Washington have transformed the relationship between federal and state power, limited the regulatory capacity of the state, and altered the fundamental structure of the New Deal Order.

Before we embark on a chronological survey of the history of twentieth-century American conservatism, we need to know what it is we are talking about. How should we define conservatism? It is not easy to answer this question, considering that the Right has been far from united. Over the years it has been composed of various distinct groups whose priorities, constituencies, ideas, and policies often differed, and still do. This chapter, for example, will include discussions of individuals and groups ranging from those on the Far Right to mainstream conservatives within the Republican party. Two dominant tendencies mark what we have come to know as American conservatism: libertarianism and religion. Libertarians have sought to limit the intrusiveness of the nation-state in economic matters and to defend personal liberty (defined, at its most rudimentary level, as economic liberty). Unabashedly hostile and fearful of the powers of the central state, they have championed private property, free competition, and the impersonal mechanism of the market to maintain freedom. Thoroughly distinct from a Burkean conservatism that envisions the state as the symbolic unity of the people, libertarianism emphasizes the freedom of individuals from the fetters of obligation. Religious conservatives have opposed the expansion of centralized federal power, which they believe encourages atheism, moral depravity, and a disintegration of family and church authority. Closely linked to powerful currents within Protestant Christianity and, more recently, conservative Catholicism, this "fundamentalist" conservatism has championed a series of timeless absolutes, especially absolute moral verities and an absolute truth. The bedrock for the moral strength of the nation, according to these men and women, lies not simply in liberty but in a respect for the Christian foundations of the nation.

Obviously, these different emphases are in a philosophical sense quite contradictory. Thus, our recognizing that several tendencies and outlooks coexist within a single movement and even within the minds of individuals helps us better understand the ideological tensions within American conservatism. Yet, as importantly, all conservatives have shared a number of concerns: Libertarians and religious conservatives have been united in their opposition to liberal "collectivism"—decrying the growing tendency of the state to organize social and economic life in the name of the public good. Both tendencies have championed a virulent anticommunism, evoked a staunch nationalism, and decried what they saw as liberal moral relativism with its emphasis upon experimentation to solve social ills. Conservatives of all stripes believe that America has an organic benevolent order that would function well if not for the tampering of liberal elites.

Both elements of the conservative world view have drawn upon deep roots in American life. Indeed, in the late nineteenth century and for the first third of the twentieth century, these ideas, although aggressively contested, still occupied a central place in American culture and politics. While corporate liberals, progressives, populists, and socialists sought to regulate and curb the abuses of concentrations of private power in the face of industrializing America, conservatives championed a staunch individualism. William Graham Sumner, for example, in his influential treatise *What Social Classes Owe to Each Other,* first published in 1883, argued for the positive virtues of selfishness. Ignoring the inequities and coerciveness of private economic power, Sumner argued that competition, the market, and struggle alone would keep America strong. The state, he warned, "must be kept at bay from becoming master of the lesser beings."

In the first two decades of the twentieth century, Sumner's pessimistic variant of social Darwinist thought waned as progressivism, populism, socialism, and World War I spurred new thinking about the legitimacy of state involvement in the economy and national life. But wartime labor militancy and a postwar strike wave culminated in a severe backlash. In the wake of the Palmer Raids of 1919 and the open-shop campaigns of the early 1920s, ideas of the prerogatives of private property and laissez faire liberalism deepened once more. In the prosperous 1920s, the Republican presidencies of Warren Harding, Calvin Coolidge, and Herbert Hoover presided over the reassertion of economic conservatism. Herbert Hoover especially sang the praises of classical liberalism and business self-regulation, championing staunch individualism as the American creed.

Just as antistatist ideas were alive and well in the first third of the century, so too was a steadfast brand of normative conservatism. Impulses to regulate morality of course had a long history and had been at the heart of Victorian American culture. While in the Gilded Age laissez faire liberalism reigned supreme, its champions at times sought to utilize the powers of the state to regulate private moral behavior by, for example, supporting antiobscenity measures such as the Comstock laws (1873). In the first two decades of the twentieth century, the strength of a belief in society's right to regulate private behavior, championed by progressives and conservatives alike, was evident in the ratification of the Prohibition amendment in 1920. But the most vigorous expressions of a staunch cultural conservatism arose in the 1920s, the decade that witnessed the first offensive of a militant and defensive conservative

Christianity. Willa Cather's comment in a prefatory note to a collection of essays, that "the world broke in two in 1922 or thereabouts," dramatically captures the cultural ruptures of this decade. It was a time of deep tension between the forces of radicalism, modernism, secularism, immigration, and urbanization on the one side and the preservationist impulses of a staunch conservative Protestantism on the other side.

The rise of the Ku Klux Klan, in particular, represented a powerful expression of right-wing reaction to cultural and social change and evinced a deep-seated religious and cultural fundamentalism in American life. During its heyday in the mid-1920s, three to five million men and women joined the ranks of the hooded order, making it one of the largest and most influential grass-roots social movements in twentieth-century America. Identifying Catholicism, bolshevism, immigrants, and African Americans as threats to "100 percent Americanism," the Klan drew to its ranks a broad group of men and women throughout the Midwest, West, and South, areas where Protestant religiosity and assumptions of white racial superiority were part of the woof and weave of daily life. Mostly of middle-class and lower-middle-class background, they donned the Klan's white robes because the organization promised to stave off a national drift away from the values of small-town Protestant America that effectively had supported a set of power relations and a way of life. Railing against both the consolidation of wealth at the top and proletarians below, Klan ideology, as historian Nancy MacLean has asserted, evinced a "reactionary populism" that drew upon elements of classical liberalism, nineteenth-century republicanism, and Protestant evangelism. While the Klan was enormously successful for a brief moment, winning political power in Indiana, Oklahoma, Oregon, and a number of other states, its heyday was short lived. A series of scandals involving Klan leadership that culminated in the arrest and conviction of Indiana Klan leader David C. Stephenson for murder placed the hooded order on the road to decline. Corruption alone, however, does not explain the Klan's demise. Rather, as Leonard Moore has cogently argued, with the Klan message of discontent and Protestant dominance delivered, the Klan had served its purpose. Indeed, the issues that had propelled the Klan seemed for the moment settled in their favor. Labor radicalism and anxieties over African-American militancy declined by the mid-1920s. Passage of immigration-restriction and quota legislation of 1924 represented the triumph of nativism. And legislation supporting "old-time religion" in public schools through outlawing of the teaching of evolution stood its ground despite vociferous attacks.

The Klan, however, was not the only organized expression of cultural conservatism in the first third of the twentieth century. The twentieth century also gave birth to Protestant fundamentalism. A conjunction of theological and social crises in the early part of the century, as historian George Marsden argued, meant that American Protestantism began to split into two major strands, one of them liberal in politics as well as in theological outlook, the other conservative both in politics and theology. Reform-minded liberals sought to salvage the authority of Protestantism by reconciling it with Darwinism and scientific advances and by emphasizing the importance of Christianity as a lived faith and practice. Conservatives clung to what they saw as bedrock Christian beliefs of bible inerrancy, the virgin birth, Christ's atonement and resurrection, the authenticity of miracles, and dispensationalism. They expressed a pessimistic disdain for efforts at reform inspired by a predominantly pre-Millenialist theology and emphasized instead soul winning. *The Fundamentals,* a series of pamphlets financed by two California entrepreneurs, Lyman and Milton Stewart of Union Oil and published between 1910 and 1915, outlined the essentials of this orthodoxy. Following on the heels of the appearance of *The Fundamentals,* the United States' entry into World War I heightened tensions. The war unleashed the forces of secularism and labor militancy, bringing debates within American Protestantism to a head. Conservative Protestants organized in 1919 to combat modernism in the churches by founding the World's Christian Fundamentals Association. Thereafter, this coalition of conservative Protestants became known as the "fundamentalists" when the editor of a Baptist newspaper coined the term in 1920.

Conservative Christians not only fought "modernism" within the churches but they organized campaigns to save American society from "infidelity." Despite a theology that emphasized the futility of action to reform the world, their evangelical traditions and the urgency of their concerns led them into public battle to Christianize America. Their most vigorous campaign centered on preventing the teaching of biological evolution in the nation's schools. Darwinism, fundamentalists believed, contributed to the erosion of American morality in its implicit challenge to the creation story in Genesis. As a result, antievolution laws were passed in several states in the South and West in the first half of the 1920s. These efforts to ensure the teaching of Christian orthodoxy in the schools culminated in the famous Scopes "monkey" trial in 1925, which tested the Tennessee antievolution law. The law stood, demonstrating the formidable power of fundamentalist sentiment in Tennessee. Yet the media's portrayal of fundamentalists as rubes and hicks damaged the movement nationally. Defeated in northern denominations and ridiculed in the court of public opinion, fundamentalism faded from national view by the late 1920s. Contemporary observers (and generations of historians thereafter) assumed the movement, which they had seen as a product of backward rural culture, would disappear with the spread of modern education. But despite its defeats, fundamentalism thrived outside the mainstream of Protestant church life through evangelization in local churches in the South, Midwest, and West. Decades later, their evangelical heirs would rise again to remake the world in their image.

Indeed, this militant variant of Protestantism in the 1920s with its calls to retrieve the United States from the brink of moral bankruptcy by making

America a God-centered nation and championing "old time religion" had much in common with later religious Right mobilizations. Yet these later mobilizations were also distinct in many ways. During the 1920s, with Republican party conservatives in the White House, fundamentalist Protestants did not show the staunch antistatist ethos that would characterize their post–World War II views. In the 1920s, in effect, religious conservatives saw government as a bulwark against bolshevism and moral decline and they championed its authority. Not only their allegiance to government authority but also the animus of their attacks would shift in the decades to come. The 1920s' religious Right scapegoated Roman Catholics, immigrants, and African Americans as threats to moral righteousness and a godly nation. Their nativism was a harbinger of the virulent anti-Semitism that fueled the Protestant Far Right during the Great Depression. By the post–World War II period, however, anti-Semitism and anti-Catholicism were discredited within the broader culture and even within the ranks of the Right. While still propelling segments of the fringe Right, these ideas would not play as central a role in the later decades of the twentieth-century.

The New Deal liberal state and especially the economic, social, and cultural world it wrought in its wake drove the formation of what we have come to know as modern American conservatism. The New Deal boded the dawning of a new age. It first marginalized, then reshuffled, and eventually reinvigorated American conservatism.

As we know, during the 1930s the United States witnessed a vast expansion of the power of the federal government. The simple equation of freedom with private property and the market was thrust aside in favor of broadened definitions of freedom that included, in Roosevelt's famous words, "freedom from want and freedom from fear." Once the ideals of limited government, individual responsibility, local control, and the prerogatives of property had stamped the discourse of government officials and policymakers. Now, however, these ideals were increasingly marginalized in American political debate.

This changed political climate sparked several different kinds of rightist impulses as conservatives desperately struggled to make their voices heard. A group of prominent conservative businessmen, for example, organized the American Liberty League in August 1934 to protest what they saw as the New Deal's "creeping socialism." Wealthy supporters, representing big industries like Dupont and General Motors, sought to "protect" society from radicalism and economic reform. While the organization was highly successful in enlisting prominent businessmen like Alfred P. Sloan and John Howard Pew and raising millions of dollars, it failed to convince Americans that their liberties were endangered by the New Deal. At a time when business had been deeply discredited by the depression, their pleas smacked of self-serving economic preservationism and their organization proved an abysmal failure. It ended its activities by and large in 1936 and finally disbanded in 1940.

Organized business pressure groups were not the only conservative voices of opposition to the New Deal. At a time of economic immiseration, the 1930s witnessed a number of efforts to combine brown-shirt demagoguery with populist appeals as an alternative to the redistributive plans of New Dealers, the labor movement and the left. One such tendency on the Right in the 1930s had its roots in the fundamentalist battles of the 1920s and in conservative Protestants' growing sense of beleaguerment. Fundamentalist ministers Gerald B. Winrod and his "Defenders of the Christian Faith" as well as William Pelley and his "Silver Legion," both of whom had made their mark in the antievolution and antimodernist crusades of the 1920s, now organized to combat American radicalism. In the 1930s, they railed against an international Communist conspiracy with headquarters in Moscow whose tentacles reached everywhere, including into FDR's White House. Winrod and Pelley believed that behind the international Communists stood a Jewish international cabal. Winrod's *The Hidden Hand—The Protocols and the Coming Superman* (1932) was an example of the conspiratorial anti-Semitism of the Far Right in these years. This anti-Semitism was shared by a broader group of militant fundamentalist preachers like William B. Riley, who wrote *The Protocols and Communism* (1934). It gained sanction and legitimacy from such prominent businessmen as Henry Ford, who had circulated during the 1920s several hundred thousand copies of the *International Jew*, a four-volume text that linked international bankers, Bolsheviks, and Jews. This book, despite Ford's eventual disavowals, became the manifesto of conspiracy theorists and anti-Semites throughout the 1930s.

Informed by the severity of the economic crisis, right-wing organizing during the Great Depression evinced a statist ethos that was distinct from past and future mobilizations. Indeed, at times right-wing proponents advanced radical ideas that removed them from traditional conservative hostility to state involvement in the economy. Far-right preachers such as Pelley and Winrod embraced a pro-Nazi and pro-fascist corporatism. Pelley, for example, evoked the notion of the "Christian Commonwealth" that linked a vitriolic hatred of Jews with a unique brand of corporatism in which the United States would be formed into one gigantic corporation. Citizens received a share in the corporation at birth and would be financially remunerated according to their contributions to the corporation, with the government creating a grading scale of occupations. While a more statist vision of the economy could hardly be articulated, Pelley sharply distinguished his beliefs from those of collectivists and Communists: Christian economics, he contended, does not make "the gigantic error of assuming that all men are truly born free and equal or are entitled to equal privileges." While Riley and Pelley's shrill rantings gained them some followers in the Midwest, South, and West, they failed to capitalize seriously on the discontents of the Great Depression. Their openly fascist sympathies only hastened an already certain demise when during the war the government charged them with seditious activities.

In a similar vein, Father Charles Coughlin embraced a brand of conservative politics that linked statist ideas with a preservationist core. His ideas, however, attracted a far greater following than had the conspiratorial militant Protestantism of Winrod and Pelley. Beginning in 1930, as historian Alan Brinkley has chronicled, Father Coughlin, priest in a small parish in Detroit, secured a national radio network and offered his explanation for political and economic woes. His populist brand of conservatism linked a virulent anti-communism with attacks on monopolistic capitalists and especially international bankers. Coughlin blamed the strife and social conflicts of the depression years, evident in demonstrations of the unemployed and a strike wave in 1934, on both labor and capital. He called for renewing the health of the nation by enabling every man to achieve the American dream of home buying and property ownership. Standing in the way of fulfilling these God-given rights, argued Coughlin, was a group of decadent, fat-cat capitalists who drained the nation's resources. And behind them, he hinted, stood a conspiracy of international bankers.

Building on his huge radio following, Coughlin launched the National Union for Social Justice in 1934 to press for economic change. He advocated most consistently the nationalization of the banking industry, the abolition of the Federal Reserve, and the establishment of a central bank. His selective tirades against New Deal reforms turned to outright hostility toward the Roosevelt administration in 1935. Evoking a staunch nationalism and attacking Roosevelt's liberal internationalism, Coughlin demonstrated the influence he wielded when he called upon his listeners to inundate their senators with telegrams opposing Roosevelt's proposal for U.S. entry to the World Court. On the eve of the vote a deluge of telegrams and letters poured into Washington calling for rejection of the treaty and the next morning the proposal was defeated. While Coughlin was surely not solely responsible for the defeat, historians have credited him with helping to turn the tide against the proposal. Whereas in his early years, Coughlin balanced attacks on the New Deal with support for Roosevelt, after 1935, and particularly after his failed entry into politics in 1936, his politics became increasingly aggressive and ever more shrill. By 1938, with his support waning, he exhibited a vociferous anti-Semitism, disseminating such anti-Semitic fabrications as *The Protocols of the Elders of Zion* and praising Adolf Hitler. His movement, already marginalized by the late 1930s, met its end through wartime suppression.

As Coughlin lost influence, his staunch isolationism and pro-nationalist position was appropriated by other conservative initiatives. While opposition to American entry into World War II included progressives and pacifists, conservatives boasted a distinct variant of isolationism that linked calls for a strong defense—a "fortress America"—with concerns over government regimentation of the economy. This conservative isolationism made its impact felt through the America First Committee. Founded in 1940 and headed by General Robert E. Wood, chairman of the Sears Roebuck Corporation, American First garnered significant support, boasting a prominent group of leaders and drawing large crowds to its rallies. Opposition to U.S. participation in the European war also made itself felt on the Far Right through the "Mother's Movement," which, according to historian Glen Jeansonne, linked conservative isolationism and anti-Semitism with a maternalist ideology. These conservative isolationist organizations faded from view after the United States entered the war on December 7, 1941.

World War II effectively ended the reformist spirit of the New Deal, but it also solidified the recast world of the New Deal Order by vastly expanding the role of the federal government bureaucracy in national life. The postwar world thus posed new challenges and new opportunities for conservatives. Conservative politicians within the Republican party had since the 1930s kept up their tirades against the New Deal, struggling on the side of "liberty against socialism." In 1946, building on public resentment toward rationing, high meat prices, and the Office of Price Administration, Republicans succeeded in recapturing Congress, bringing to Washington a group of influential conservatives. The "class of 1946" included Richard Nixon of California, William Jenner of Indiana, William F. Knowland of California, Joe McCarthy of Wisconsin, and John Bricker of Ohio. Resurgent Republicans allied with conservative Democrats in seeking to roll back wartime labor gains. They successfully contained the power of organized labor through the Taft-Hartley Act (1947), with devastating implications for the labor movement in the post–World War II era. Yet if Republicans believed that their victory in 1946 represented a mandate for laissez faire individualism and hostility to the New Deal, a mandate that would herald a GOP presidential victory in 1948, they were wrong. Truman's victory in 1948 and the Democrats return to dominance in Congress that same year demonstrated that there was little electoral support for ending state benevolence. The old slogan "liberty against socialism" failed to galvanize more than a core constituency of conservatives.

The Republican party increasingly split into two factions. Its eastern internationalist wing sought containment of the New Deal, while the Republican "Old Guard," largely centered in its midwestern wing, demanded nothing less than rollback.

During these same years, right-wing intellectuals, convinced that Americans were falsely under the sway of liberal ideas, sought to alter the climate of debate. Working largely in isolation from one another, in fits and starts, these intellectuals sought to build a philosophical basis for American conservatism. They founded journals and wrote books navigating the new world that had come out of the 1930s and 1940s. No single person articulated right-wing concerns with this new order, especially the trend toward centralized state planning, as sharply as Friedrich Hayek. Hayek, an economist and émigré from Austria who fled after Hitler invaded his country, was hailed by many as the intellectual father of postwar libertarianism. Hayek's most important work, a small book named *The Road to Serfdom* (1944), argued that centralized state planning leads inevitably to totalitarianism. Lauding free competition and the market economy to maintain freedom, which in his eyes meant freedom from government constraint, Hayek argued that economic planning and social welfare in the hand of government would produce dictatorship. Journals ranging from *Human Events* (1944), *Plain Talk* (1946), and the *Freeman* (1950), while hardly influential voices, echoed Hayek's concerns and championed classical liberalism along with a virulent anticommunism.

At the same time that Hayek and libertarian conservatives developed their ideas, as historian George Nash has chronicled, Russell Kirk and a group of conservative "traditionalists" forged an ideology that was soon to become a distinctive segment in a burgeoning conservative intellectual movement. Kirk sought to debunk criticisms that conservatism in America was merely a defense of materialistic businessmen or the dogma of Manchesterian economics. In *The Conservative Mind* (1953) he argued, instead, for a philosophical conservatism grounded in religiosity, authority, traditionalism, and a rejection of liberal egalitarianism. Confined to the circles of academia, however, these intellectuals were scattered voices of protest against what seemed like a very real hegemony of vital center liberalism.

Despite the Right's sense of beleaguerment, conservatives received a boost for a moment by the rising tide of anticommunism that swept the United Stated during the 1950s. Concerns over Communist gains internationally since World War II, especially the Soviet's Union's dominance in Eastern Europe, the "loss" of China in 1949, and Russia's obtainment of the atom bomb that same year, contributed to the rise of Senator Joseph McCarthy to national prominence during the early 1950s. Right-wingers who had hawked conspiracy theories since the 1930s found new audiences for their allegation of Communist infiltration into government, the mass media, unions, schools, and other vital institutions. Their audiences, moreover, went well beyond the core base of the Republican party. Catholic ethnics still linked to the New Deal, for example, found in Joe McCarthy, with his vigorous anticommunism and attacks on effeminate liberal elites, a hero.

McCarthyism, however, represented a phenomenon that went far beyond the man for whom the red scare was named. McCarthyism was not a mass movement with membership organizations or meetings but rather a political tendency rooted in popular anxieties of the postwar years generated by the cold war and broader social and cultural change. It was, moreover, a political tendency that had grave consequences for American public life in these years. Its targets were as often liberals, progressives, and civil libertarians as Communists. California's mini-House Un-American Activities Committee, for example, cast its net so widely that at one point it declared the American Civil Liberties Union a "communist front or transmission belt organization." The same committee agitated against sex education in public schools, programs they accused of following "the Communist Party line for the destruction of the moral fiber of American youth." Yet, the all-consuming atmosphere of anti-communism in the late 1940s and particularly the early 1950s gained its strength in large part because it represented a consensus ideology shared by Democrats and Republicans alike. The marginal difference between soft and hard anticommunism was insufficient to stir the public at large to join conservative ranks and embrace its broader agenda.

Despite the stranglehold McCarthy put on the expansion of liberal goals in the 1950s, McCarthyism could not stem the historical tide that, for the moment, lay with the expansion of liberalism. The undercurrent of discontent that McCarthyism evinced with the world of the New Deal liberal state and the events of the cold war did not coalesce for political purposes. Conservatives once dominant in the halls of Washington and the nation were still playing a reactive role, seeking to stem calls for expansion of Social Security and public housing, and for civil rights and health insurance legislation. A broad segment of the American public still had a fundamental stake in New Deal social reforms.

Demonstrating the limits of conservatives' political influence even further was their loss of control over the Republican party. The political strength they had enjoyed during the early 1950s in the national Republican party through their champions Senator Robert Taft of Ohio and Senator Joe McCarthy of Wisconsin vanished by the mid-1950s. It was Dwight D. Eisenhower, not Robert Taft, who won the Republican party primary battle of 1952. Indeed, the death of Taft one year later and McCarthy's censure in 1954 left conservatives without powerful spokesmen in Washington. The triumph of liberalism was symbolically confirmed when Supreme Court Justice Earl Warren, appointed by Republican president Dwight D. Eisenhower, presided over *Brown* v. *Board of Education* in 1954. Supreme Court decisions in 1957, moreover, dismantled the remains of McCarthyism, limiting state activity against "subversion." As a result, by the late 1950s the New Deal Order with its commitment to an activist state and Keynesian economic policies seemed to be deeply embedded in the institutions of the American state and central to the nation's dominant political ideology. This seemed like a hopeless situation for the remaining critics of liberalism. Bereft of powerful spokespersons in Congress, the executive, and the media, the outlook for the Right's political success seemed bleak. It was indeed at this moment that liberal intellectuals like Daniel Bell, Seymour Martin Lipset, and Richard Hofstadter dissected those remaining conservative impulses and organizations and described them as fanatics without a future.

How is it that history turned out to be so different from what most reasonable observers expected in the late 1950s? How did these marginalized conservatives turn themselves into a viable political movement that only some thirty years later would bring Ronald Reagan to the White House? It was a combination of changing social and economic conditions fueled by the New Deal state itself and conservatives' own strategies that eventually brought them back into political power.

For one, the late 1950s and early 1960s saw a revitalization of a newly reformist liberalism. Democrats substantially increased their majorities in both houses of Congress in 1958, and John F. Kennedy's election to the presidency in 1960 symbolized the triumph of an assertive, internationalist liberalism that had a strong faith in the ability of the federal government to manage capitalism in order to solve social as well as economic problems. This newly assertive liberalism also championed a new set of individual and personal freedoms. While the student movement antiwar protests had yet to heat up, the civil rights movement made its first mark on the national scene already in the 1950s with the Montgomery bus boycott (1956) and Little Rock school crisis (1957). By the early 1960s, with sit-ins across the South and freedom riders' journeys into the heartland of segregation, change beckoned on the horizon. While the Right had already been dissatisfied with the moderate Republicanism of Eisenhower, the election of a liberal Democrat to the presidency and the deepening penetration of liberal ideas into the nation's schools, churches, and communities created a sense of urgency, encouraging conservatives to organize against what they perceived with increasing alarm as dangerous developments.

Businessmen and intellectuals were the first to act. Perceiving their weakness within the halls of power in Washington, as well as in the Republican party, they saw the need for new strategies to make their influence felt. Some sought to effect a revolution of ideas, and the burgeoning number of conservative books and journals testify to their efforts. William Buckley began publishing *National Review* in 1955 to help usher in a "new era of conservatism." Russell Kirk followed in 1957 with the more scholarly quarterly *Modern Age* to "forthrightly oppose . . . political collectivism, social decadence and effeminacy." While the journals began an effort to formulate a set of conservative ideas and policies, a spate of national organizations followed suit to translate ideas into politics. In 1958 conservative Republican party politicians and business leaders created Americans for Constitutional Action to help repeal "the socialistic laws now on our books." A group of conservatives meeting in Indiana in December of the same year founded the John Birch Society. And finally, in 1960 William F. Buckley together with a group of conservative students founded Young Americans for Freedom (YAF) in 1960 to provide a vehicle for conservative youth to work for "economic freedom," "state rights," and "the destruction of international communism." Older groups also grew by leaps and bounds. The Christian Anti-Communism Crusade, conceived in 1953, held its first week-long "Anti-Communism Schools" in 1958. On the upswing in the late 1950s and early 1960s, it doubled its receipts each year. In 1961, sparked by its successes in places in the Southwest, where sympathizers were able to back their support with money, the Crusade took in over one million dollars.

These organizations, along with the resources that backed them, invigo-rated a grass-roots movement that had begun to mobilize in local schools and communities to reverse the tide of liberalism. In the booming Sunbelt, most especially, in places like Southern California, Arizona, and Texas, middle-class men and women organized study groups, opened "Freedom Forum" book-stores, filled the rolls of the John Birch Society, entered school-board races, and worked within the Republican party, all in an urgent struggle to safeguard their particular vision of freedom and the "American heritage." The high-tech sub-urbs of Southern California, in particular, proved to be a hotbed for conserva-tive activism in the 1960s. Here, the largely white-collar, educated, and often technologically skilled women and men embraced right-wing politics not least because they saw their own lives and the booming communities where they made their homes as tributes to the possibilities of individual entrepreneurial success. Regional business leaders, moreover, promulgated a staunch libertar-ian ethos that helped to lead citizens to an unabashed celebration of the free market. At the same time, the men and women who had come to the bur-geoning Southland were often steeped in a strident nationalism, staunch moralism, and religious piety that was part of the woof and weave of the com-munities from which they haled. While this cultural conservatism had been tenored by an earlier linkage to New Deal reforms, it took on aggressive new meanings in the places they now made their home, sharpened by their new af-fluence and their discomfort with the prevalent liberalism in state and national politics in the 1960s.

The most vigorous organized expression of this conservative resurgence was the rise of the extremist John Birch Society. Its rapid growth evinced that not one but two variants of radicalism characterized the 1960s. Though de-rided by liberals and the national media, the organization gained strength, de-veloping into one of only a few conservative political vehicles concerned with developing a mass base. Candy manufacturer Robert Welch, a man long active in Massachusetts Republican party politics and in the leadership of the Na-tional Association of Manufacturers, had founded the organization in Decem-ber 1958. Disillusioned with the moderate leadership of the Republican party, Welch saw the need to build an organization to thwart the growth of "social-ism" and "communism"—which, in his eyes, included all aspects of the wel-fare state whose progress, he claimed, was rooted in Communist conspiracy. He sought to develop a national mass membership organization of dedicated anti-Communist patriots who would work to shift the political direction of the nation. Choosing the name "John Birch Society" after a Baptist missionary killed by Chinese Communists, Welch linked the society to cold war events, a link that would inform its activities throughout the decade.

The Birch Society, originally an organ of an older midwestern conser-vatism, mushroomed in the South and West and, especially, in the rising Sun-belt. Eight years after its founding, the society drew approximately 80,000 to

100,000 members (exact membership has always been kept secret). Indeed, at its height it rivaled the peak membership strength of the Communist Party U.S.A. during the Popular Front period. Moreover, like the Communist party, the John Birch Society flourished in supportive ideological waters of "fellow travelers." In 1962 Welch stated that the society was growing fastest in the Southwest, contrasting this area with his home state of Massachusetts, where it encountered much less favorable terrain. Its members, solidly middle-class men and women, were often active in broader conservative circles. They played important roles as both rank-and-file volunteer activists and leaders of the Goldwater movement.

The John Birch Society linked an older and a newer Right. Inheriting the language, targets, and symbols of McCarthyism, the society's mission was increasingly fueled by concerns over the social and cultural changes of the 1960s. The organization profited from anxieties over social and cultural change by establishing a "Task-Force on Civil Disorder," programs to "Impeach Earl Warren," and campaigns to "Support Your Local Police." Indeed the growing number of adherents by mid-decade suggests that these appeals bore fruit. Not only were the society's set of concerns or the geographic areas that fueled its growth novel, but it also embraced a pluralist religious appeal, something the old Christian Right had refused to do. In contrast to the Right prior to World War II, the John Birch Society sought to curb the anti-Semitic tendencies its members sometimes evinced. More important, the society drew not only conservative Protestants to its ranks but a significant number of Catholics. Indeed Robert Welch, the leader of the society, claimed that 40 percent of its members were Catholics.

The John Birch Society embraced a fusionist variant of conservatism that linked libertarian economic ideas, a moral traditionalism, and virulent anticommunism. Although propelled in no small part by conservative concerns with the ever more assertive civil rights movement, it distinguished itself sharply from the "racist right" of the White Citizen's councils, States' Rights parties, and Ku Klux Klan. These organizations also flourished in the wake of civil rights gains. The first White Citizen Council, for example, was established in Indianola, Mississippi, in the wake of the *Brown* decision in 1954 and expanded rapidly thereafter. Integration, in the eyes of the Citizen's councils, represented regimentation, totalitarianism, communism, and destruction. The revived Far-Right Ku Klux Klan embraced violence and terrorism against African Americans and civil rights workers to achieve its goals. These organizations tapped into a long tradition of populist racism in the South. This politics of white supremacy flourished in the Deep South where race had been a determinant marker of populist politics through the twentieth century. While these organizations mirrored northern and western conservatives', hostility to federal control and liberal elites, their overt racism, for the most part, did not resonate beyond the Deep South. Acknowledging the narrow regional appeal of the movement's shrill racist messages, the broader conservative movement, even the conspiratorial John Birch Society, wrapped its hostility toward civil rights in a language of anticommunism, opposition to federal control, and fear of collectivism. It was this more muted and thus supposedly more respectable opposition to enabling African Americans to obtain their constitutional rights that carried the day in the conservative movement during the 1950s and 1960s.

If the formation of *National Review,* Young Americans for Freedom, and the John Birch Society were signs of a revival on the Right in the realm of civil society, conservatives were well aware that to exert significant political power they would have to gain influence over the institutions of the state. And this influence could best be exerted by gaining control of the Republican party. During the 1960s, an amalgam of conservatives contributed to the effort "to take back" the party. Utilizing the networks and experiences forged in the grassroots mobilizations earlier in the decade, a new generation of conservative Republicans with a strong southern and western regional bent challenged the eastern wing for control of the party. And they won. In 1964, backed by powerful new centers of regional capital in the rising Sunbelt and by the deeply segregationist sentiments of white Southerners, they succeeded in capturing the Republican party for their standard bearer, Barry Goldwater, in 1964. This "takeover" signified a historic power shift in the party. The party of Lincoln, now captured by southern and western interests, would in the decades to follow become the party of evangelical Christians and cowboy capitalists.

Yet ironically, Goldwater's nomination almost doomed conservatism as a national movement. After all, Goldwater went down to monumental defeat in November of 1964. The election was in many ways a debacle for conservatives: Goldwater lost by 15,951,220 votes. Johnson won the greatest number of votes, the greatest margin, and the greatest percentage any president has ever drawn from the American people, confirming that most citizens in 1964 optimistically embraced the possibilities of the liberal promise in a period of national affluence. Goldwater, in effect, had failed utterly to reach beyond his core constituencies in the Deep South and the Southwest. And even in the Deep South, the strength of Goldwater's vote was due to his strong states' rights stance rather than his broader conservative agenda. In all, his strident anticommunism, pronouncements on "conventional nuclear weapons," and "low-yield nuclear bombings" shocked a nation already anxiously living under the threat of nuclear warfare. His unmitigated hostility to the welfare state and to Social Security failed to resonate in an era of affluence. Goldwater's rhetoric, indeed, not only failed to appeal to a broader constituency, it scared many people outright. "When in all our history," prominent historian Richard Hofstadter asked only weeks before the election, "has anyone with ideas so bizarre, so archaic, so self-confounding, so remote from the basic American consensus, ever gotten so far?" In a similar vein, one prominent Republican branded "Goldwaterism" a "crazy-quilt collection of absurd and dangerous positions." The respectable political spectrum in the 1960s shared a consensus that the federal government was needed to resolve problems that free-market capitalism could not. In a decade of liberal achievements, right-wing pronouncements on turning back the welfare state and conservatives' belief that the government had no place in redressing social and economic inequities were considered among liberal Democrats, moderate Republicans, and the left alike as "extremist," so farfetched and radical did they seem.

Moderate Republicans, as well as Democratic liberals and the Left, frequently characterized the conservative movement in the 1960s with reference to its most extremist component: the conspiratorial John Birch Society. Yet, it is misleading to equate the movement as a whole with the society. Conservatives within the Republican party certainly had beliefs that meshed well with those of the John Birch Society—virulent anticommunism, laissez faire economics, and a staunch moralism. But many right-wing proponents were repelled by the conspiratorial aspects of the Birch philosophy, and felt that Welch's erratic leadership of the society had damaged the movement as a whole. Whereas some conservatives criticized the society's conspiratorial vision, on the other hand, conservatives from William Buckley to Barry Goldwater and Ronald Reagan were quick to distinguish between its leader and its members whom they considered to be "some of the solidest conservatives in the country."

Still, the "Birch" or "extremist" tag hounded the conservative movement through the mid-1960s, a constant reminder that the movement's ideas lay outside the bounds of respectable political discourse. And indeed, the rhetoric of the John Birch Society and the ideas expressed in their journal, *American Opinion,* were, despite some conservatives claims to the contrary, extreme. At their more radical edge, they evinced a mixture of blood-and-soil nationalism and traditionalism with an antidemocratic free-market ethos. The Birch Society's calls to "impeach Earl Warren" moreover, its "scoreboards of Communist conquest," exposés of "treasonous networks in the state department," calls for "getting the U.S. out of the U.N.," and tirades against what one *American Opinion* writer asserted was the liberal "goal" of "one world, one race," "one world, one government," smacked of a zaniness that was easily lampooned by liberals. Taken together, it contributed to marginalizing the conservative movement in these years.

How would the Right be able to leave their ghetto behind and expand their influence? Two factors contributed to conservative ascendancy in the second half of the 1960s. First, cultural, social, and political changes played a major role. And second, the Right itself, by muting its own rhetoric and rethinking its strategies, picked up on these new opportunities, transforming itself into a viable electoral contender by decade's end.

A sign of the conservative reorientation in the wake of Goldwater's defeat and the new opportunities provided by the social and cultural upheavals came when a b-rate movie actor named Ronald Reagan ran in 1966 for the governorship of California, the most populous state of the nation. Reagan scored a clear victory for conservatives. Importantly, in the wake of Goldwater's defeat Reagan and other conservatives had refashioned their discourse, moving away from tirades on socialism and communism and toward attacks on liberal "permissiveness," "welfare chiselers," and "runaway spending." Reagan, a man attuned to package himself for his public, was able to sustain a right-wing politics while at the same time attracting a broader group of constituents whose loyalties were up for grabs.

Reagan succeeded not only by embracing a repackaged conservatism, but also because large-scale cultural and social changes made it easier for him to attract voters critical of the New Deal Order. The boiling cauldron of concerns about morality, law and order, and race generated in the two years between Goldwater and Reagan's campaign played into their hands. In effect, just as the Right was moving into the respectable mainstream, the mainstream moved toward them.

Reagan's victory exhibited most of the elements that have come to characterize conservatism since the 1960s. It symbolized, for example, the growing importance of the Sunbelt and West to modern conservatism. Moreover, it showed that conservative support came most easily from the newly affluent suburbs of the region. In these places, highly skilled men and women, many of whom worked as engineers, doctors, and dentists, fueled the right-wing upheaval. Embracing modern lifestyles, these newly mobilized men and women were far removed from the status-anxious conservatives left behind by modernity that Bell and others had described. They forwarded a virulent brand of cultural conservatism linked to a staunch economic libertarianism sustained and deepened by regional business leaders.

Importantly, the increasing tilt of the Republican party Right toward the South and West amplified the unambivalent statist posture the Right had adopted in terms of defense. An older Taftite conservatism had tenored its anticommunism with concerns over state spending, including military spending. By the 1960s, however, such qualms disappeared, not least because conservatives drew their strength from a region where lives were closely linked to the cold war military-industrial complex.

The social and cultural upheavals that benefited Reagan presaged the rise of a majoritarian conservatism that would make itself felt on the national scene in the 1968 presidential election. National political contenders like Nixon and Wallace picked up on the discourse of "morality," "law and order," "welfare chiselers," and "liberal permissiveness," and rode a tide of popular middle- and lower-middle-class resentment toward the social changes of the decade. While neither Nixon nor Wallace represented quintessential Republican conservatism—Wallace with his southern segregationist, harsh antielitist rhetoric, and Nixon with his conservative pragmatism and internationalist centrism—both put forward their own brand of conservative populist lingo that spoke to some, if not all, of right-wing concerns.

By the late 1960s, the Right had made important political gains. Ronald Reagan, an unabashed right-wing ideologue, had won a resounding victory in his run for governor. Richard Nixon, a centrist Republican who courted the Republican's right wing, had gained his party's presidential nomination with the strong backing of conservatives and had won the election through an embrace of a new middle-class conservatism. And George Wallace, a law-and-order populist, had garnered 13 percent of the national vote on a third-party ticket. In effect, by the late 1960s the Right refashioned itself and gained new political respectability. News of antiwar protests, hippie youth culture, and riots in the nation's inner cities filled the evening news, and the conservative critique of liberalism resonated with an increasing number of Americans.

Already in the 1960s, the conservative revival had been propelled in no small part by cultural and social issues. A series of Supreme Court decisions that took prayer out of schools and expanded personal rights and freedoms, a growing youth culture, and women's liberation generated anxieties among cultural conservatives about the preservation of family values. By the early 1970s these concerns became ever more prominent. In March 1972, the Senate overwhelmingly passed the Equal Rights Amendment, and in 1973 the Supreme Court legalized abortion in its famous *Roe* v. *Wade* decision.

The rise of a new social issues conservatism had an uneven impact on the Right. On the one side, older organizations that had been so critical to the mobilizations earlier in the decade experienced decline. On the other side, new conservative initiatives sprang up. These initiatives moved the center of activity away from the anticommunism that was so much a part of the mobilization in the early 1960s and instead embraced new single-issue campaigns as well as a newly politicized evangelical Christianity. As a result of this reorientation, the John Birch Society, an organization that had played such an important role in channeling grass-roots activity earlier in the decade, experienced the greatest decline. Despite the social upheavals of the decade, the society was running into trouble. In the wake of the conservative reorientation after their monumental defeat in 1964, the John Birch Society, with its apocalyptic utterances and its belief in a Communist conspiracy, turned into more of a liability than an aid to the conservative movement and it was increasingly marginalized.

Yet it was many of the men and women who had been foot soldiers in the Goldwater mobilization who now turned their wrath against "secular humanism." Phyllis Schafly, who had been a prominent Goldwater supporter in the 1960s and who wrote *A Choice Not an Echo* to generate support for his presidential run, now turned her attention to the increasingly assertive feminist movement. In 1973, Schlafly created a national network to oppose ratification of the ERA (Equal Rights Amendment). In 1975 she changed the name of her "Stop ERA" campaign to the "Eagle Forum." Her organization represented one of the opening battles of a Right increasingly focused on family and reproductive issues.

The concern over sexual permissiveness, women's liberation, homosexuality, and threats to the "traditional family" that propelled the Eagle Forum also fueled the politicization of conservative evangelical Christians and their reentry into politics. Religious conservatives saw the deep social changes of the 1960s and 1970s as an assault on their values and beliefs, propelling their reentry into politics. Yet while the new crusades of the Religious Right drew upon the ideological inheritances of their evangelical forbears in the 1920s, they were also distinct in important ways. The militant fundamentalists in the 1920s were strongest in the rural and small-town Midwest and South—but in the 1970s and beyond it was the affluent suburbs of the Sunbelt and West with their huge corporate-like megachurches that would drive fundamentalism into its newly assertive political posture.

The prominence of evangelicals in politics by the late 1970s drew strength from the growth of evangelical and fundamentalist Christianity nationally. Beginning in the mid-1960s, the number of adherents in mainline Protestant denominations declined, while theologically conservative churches flourished. Many of these churches became the organizational bastions for the Christian Right's political mobilizations. Eventually, these religious conservatives succeeded not least because they built powerful institutions that disseminated their message. The Moral Majority, the Christian Voice, and Concerned Women for America, all of which were established in the late 1970s, brought their vision of religious traditionalism and a staunch economic conservatism to the halls of Congress and the White House.

The Religious Right's new prominence in Republican party politics was also boosted by a group of politically experienced conservatives who saw the social conservatives as natural allies in building a broad-based electoral coalition. A small coterie of influential conservative political operators including Richard Viguerie, Howard Phillips, and Paul Weyrich sought to capitalize on the importance of new social issues. In doing so, they tried to distinguish themselves from traditional Republican conservatives who had emphasized economic issues and anticommunism. This group, which adopted the "New Right" label, exaggerated the newness of their politics for strategic purposes. Their mobilization represented a repackaged fusion of anticommunism, libertarianism, and traditionalism. Its core organizers, moreover, had first delved into politics in the conservative revival of the 1960s. Indeed, it is interesting to note that the term *New Right* had first been used by Lee Edwards in 1962 when he proposed a conservative platform for Young Americans for Freedom. Still, the New Right's use of the term did reflect the new prominence of the organized Religious Right within the conservative coalition. Indeed, Kevin Phillips popularized the term to refer to the new prominence of social conservatives on the Right in 1975.

But the success of the Right in the 1970s cannot only be explained by the preferences, aims, and aspirations of its rank-and-file constituency nor by a group of politically savvy conservative operators in Washington, D.C. At least as essential for the new prominence of the Right in American life in the 1970s was the reorientation of American business. A segment of conservative business leaders had long been central to conservative causes. Among them, wealthy millionaires like J. Howard Pew backed such policy organizations as the American Enterprise Institute, in the early 1960s, at a time when few businessmen offered such support. He also provided significant backing for the evangelical flagship journal *Christianity Today* and journals of opinion ranging from *Human Events to National Review.* But in the 1970s, driven by sweeping economic changes, a much broader segment of the business community mobilized to assert their recast political interests. New conservative think tanks such as the Heritage Foundation began their work, and older ones like the American Enterprise Institute and the Hoover Institution saw vast infusions of money. The AEI, for example, which had a budget of less than 300,000 dollars in 1960, expanded dramatically in the 1970s. By 1977 it boasted a budget of five million dollars, and four years later that number had doubled, backed by six hundred corporate donors.

This new expansion of conservative institutions earned the Right increasing visibility and helped to bring antistatist ideas into the mainstream of American intellectual life and policy discussions. Additionally, a broader middle-class economic preservationism, symbolized best by California's Proposition 13 tax revolt, encouraged an increasing number of Americans to move away from an embrace of the liberal project and to search for a new political home. Suddenly, laissez faire ideas seemed to make as much "common sense" to many Americans as the New Deal Order had during the 1950s and 1960s.

The reorientation of the conservative movement, then, along with the social, cultural, and economic changes that marked the 1960s and 1970s, transformed conservatism from a marginal movement preoccupied with communism into a viable electoral contender. As a result, by 1980 conservatives were able to bring their vision of national identity and their prescriptions for a free and just society to the White House. Twenty years later, a vision that once had been outside the bounds of respectable discourse and was so contrary to postwar liberal conceptions of the American past and its future, has become the dominant discourse in the halls of Congress and the nation.

Since their rise to national power in the early 1980s, conservatives have seen both successes and failures. Indeed, their new position of dominance in itself has opened rifts in places where conservatives had once been united against a common enemy. Free marketeers, the senior partners in the conservative coalition, have been at the cutting edge of recent historical change. Religious conservatives, while obtaining new access to the corridors of power, are still waiting to see their concerns over abortion, homosexuality, and obscenity reflected in public policy. Indeed, some politically oriented religious conservatives' disillusionment with their ability to "Christianize America" has led to a reconsideration of their political activism and a proposal to withdraw once more from politics. Even if a segment of the Religious Right does retreat, however, the history of the past one hundred years should assure us that such a retreat would be momentary and incomplete. If the past is any guide to the future, then the deep and tenacious roots of conservatism in this country over the past one hundred years suggests that we can expect the Right to have a continued and vital presence on the national stage as we enter the new millennium.

SUGGESTIONS FOR FURTHER READING

Among the accounts of the Ku Klux Klan in the 1920s, the best are Nancy MacLean's *Behind the Mask of Chivalry: The Making of the Second Ku Klux Klan* (New York: Oxford University Press, 1994), Leonard Moore's *Citizen Klansmen: The Ku Klux Klan in Indiana, 1921–1928* (Chapel Hill: University of North Carolina Press, 1991), and Kenneth Jackson's *The Ku Klux Klan in the City* (New York: Oxford University Press, 1967). The more important analyses of religious fundamentalism in its early years are Ernest Sandeen's *The Roots of Fundamentalism: British and American Millenarianism, 1800–1930* (Chicago: University of Chicago Press, 1970); and George Marsden's *Fundamentalism and American Culture: The Shaping of Twentieth-Century Evangelicalism: 1870–1925* (New York: Oxford University Press, 1980).

There are a number of useful studies on the Right from the Great Depression through World War II. Alan Brinkley traces Coughlin's career in *The Voices of Protest: Huey Long, Father Coughlin and the Great Depression* (New York: Vintage, 1982), and Leo Ribuffo traces the fundamentalist Right in *The Old Christian Right: The Protestant Far Right from the Great Depression to the Cold War* (Philadelphia: Temple University Press, 1983). For an understanding of the post–World War II Republican Right, see David W. Reinhard, *The Republican Right since 1945* (Lexington: University of Kentucky Press, 1983). George Nash has skillfully chronicled the conservative intellectual movement in *The Conservative Intellectual Movement since World War II* (New York: Basic Books, 1976). See Richard M. Fried, *Nightmare in Red: The McCarthy Era in Perspective* (New York: Oxford University Press, 1990), and Ellen Schrecker, *Many Are the Crimes: McCarthyism in America* (Boston: Little Brown, 1998).

The classic study of the social basis for McCarthyism and the "radical Right" in the 1960s is Daniel Bell, ed., *The Radical Right* (New York: Doubleday, 1963). While the essays are marred by an interpretation that sees conservatives suffering from a kind of clinical psychosis, the book is an important starting place for understanding how social scientists have understood the movement. Despite its interpretative frame, it provides fruitful information about the sources for right-wing support. Seymour Martin Lipset's *The Politics of Unreason: Right-Wing Extremism in America, 1790–1970* (New York: Harper & Row, 1970), despite its tendency to lump together all segments of conservatism under the "extremist" label, does provide a useful chronological survey of right-wing mobilization in the twentieth century.

For the 1960s there is a growing literature on the conservative movement. See, for example, John Andrews, *The Other Side of the Sixties: Young Americans for Freedom and the Rise of Conservative Politics* (New Brunswick, N.J.: Rutgers University, 1997), Mary Charlotte Brennan, *Turning Right in the Sixties: The Conservative Capture of the GOP* (Chapel Hill: University of North Carolina Press, 1995), and David Goldberg, *Barry Goldwater* (New Haven, Conn.: Yale University, 1995). My own book examines the Right in the 1960s from a social movement perspective. See Lisa McGirr, *Suburban Warriors: The Origins of the New American Right* (Princeton, N.J.: Princeton University Press, 2001).

On gender and the Right in the 1970s, see Rebecca Klatch, *Women of the New Right* (Philadelphia: Temple University Press, 1987) and Kristin Luker, *Abortion and the Politics of Motherhood* (Berkeley: University of California Press, 1984).

For the rise of a "populist conservatism" in the late 1960s and the 1970s, see Michael Kazin, *The Populist Persuasion* (New York: Basic Books, 1995), Jonathan Rieder, *Carnasie: The Jews and Italians of Brooklyn against Liberalism* (Cambridge, Mass.: Harvard University Press, 1985), and Ronald Formisano, *Boston against Busing: Race, Class, and Ethnicity in the 1960s and 1970s* (Chapel Hill: University of North Carolina Press, 1991).

A number of works have chronicled the rise of the national Right since 1945. See Jerome Himmelstein, *To the Right: The Transformation of American Conservatism* (Berkeley: University of California Press, 1990), Sara Diamond, *Roads to Dominion: Right-Wing Movements and Political Power in the United States* (New York: Guilford, 1995), and Godfey Hodgson, *The World Turned Right Side Up: A History of the Conservative Ascendancy in America* (Boston: Houghton Mifflin, 1996).

3 | TWENTIETH-CENTURY LIBERALISMS
Transformations of an Ideology
CHERYL GREENBERG

I n at least one respect, liberalism resembles pornography. To paraphrase Supreme Court Justice Potter Stewart, we can't define it but we know it when we see it. Indeed, even books with such promising titles as "Liberalism and Its Discontents," "Liberalism and Its Challengers," and "Liberalism Ancient and Modern" fail to actually define their central term. (I choose these examples not to criticize them, for they are among the finest examples of the scholarly scrutiny of liberalism, but rather, since they are such important studies, to suggest the depth of the supposed consensus.) At first glance there is no problem—we all know what the authors mean, don't we? But a look at the history of liberalism, or at least liberalism as popularly understood, shows that there is a significant problem. To begin with, there is liberalism as an ideology and liberalism as a set of policies and programs, supposedly but often not very closely springing from some unified ideology. Even if one could resolve this debate between theory and practice we have a further problem—what ideology? which programs? Liberalism has meant very different—indeed sometimes conflicting—things to different people in different places at different times.

Even confining our gaze to the past hundred years in the United States, the liberalism of the Gilded Age Republican party looks very different from the liberalism of the New Deal, for example, which transformed the state from a potential agent of oppression to a potential agent for good. Liberalism is criticized in one age for undermining community and the notion of public good because of its overreliance on personal freedom, and in another for undermining "liberty"—the word as well as its emotional resonance.

Further complicating the story, much of contemporary conservatism embraces traditional liberal values, especially that of individual liberty. Indeed, many American conservatives claim they are truer to the vision of classical liberalism than are modern-day liberals. In many ways that is true. But it also means that distinguishing liberalism from conservatism in the American context is tricky and not altogether possible. Daniel Rodgers defined liberalism as "emancipation of the individual from the authority of prescribed status, custom and the needs of state; legitimation of a plurality of private interest spheres and purposes; acceptance of the barter and friction inherent in a democratic politics and a market-based economy."[1] Much of this defines American conservatism as well. But there are differences, both in how these goals are achieved and in the embrace of modernity, diversity, and state protection of the neediest that liberalism, in its noblest ideals, represents.

"Classical" liberalism first appeared in western Europe in the late eighteenth century, a product of the European Enlightenment and the Age of Revolution. It opposed despotism and aristocratic privilege as well as the coercive and invasive control of religion. In its place liberals advocated individual freedom and representative democracy. Enlightenment thinkers such as John Locke and John Stuart Mill outlined the case for the first point: all individuals had certain "natural rights" including life, liberty, and property. Not just law but also capitalism would protect those rights; Adam Smith argued that the pursuit of individual self-interest produced the closest possible approximation to the public good. Free-market capitalism also permitted the temperate enjoyment of pleasure and material goods, a value liberalism contrasted with undesirable religious asceticism. These liberal thinkers were mindful of the dangerous potential power of the state, exemplified by the despotism of so many European nations. Thus they argued that government ought to be limited to those activities (such as protection of property and mutual defense) that could not be pursued individually, and they argued for a private sphere free from government intrusion.

As for the desirability of democracy, liberals insisted that this was the only acceptable form of state control. Democracy would allow individuals to represent their needs and opinions and adjudicate conflicts. In this spirit liberals favored persuasion over force, and the rights of citizens over the preferences of elites. This liberalism was a modern impulse, rooted in optimism about human nature and a faith in science and progress.

Yet nineteenth-century liberals lived comfortably with slavery, the suppression of women, and other positions we would today consider contradictions. Individual freedom required the ability to use it wisely, to be rational and self-disciplined, something few white men believed African Americans (or Native Americans, another "dependent" population) were capable of. And the liberal insistence on a private sphere not governed by democratic rule and off limits to government scrutiny excluded those dwelling in that private sphere, women and other dependents, from enjoying liberalism's benefits. It was liberal ideology, then, that circumscribed these groups, not a failure to apply it; part of the left-liberal agenda has been to shift groups of people from the dependent class into the class of autonomous individuals whose rights liberalism defends—that is, to press liberalism toward universalism.

Given its origins in resistance to tyranny, traditional liberalism feared the state as potential usurper of rights and sought to minimize its power and reach. This distrust of government remained until Progressive-era legislation, the central planning of the world wars, and the New Deal revealed to many liberals the power of the state to do good. If universalism was the first transformation of classic liberalism, this was the second: to expand it beyond political rights to "social" rights through state action and to advance personal freedom through protection against discrimination. The state, these liberals argued, ought to provide everyone with basic resources such as food, shelter, education, and health care to ensure the liberal ideal of equal opportunity.

Our modern conception of liberalism, then, is really a recent phenomenon. It was in the 1930s and 1940s that liberalism took on a new character, chastened by worldwide economic depression and Nazi racism, emboldened by new ideas of state power emerging from the New Deal and the prosecution of the war, enthusiastic at the triumph of democracy, and fearful of communism—or what looked like communism. This modern form of liberalism, a clear descendant of the original, but not identical to it, has at its root four basic assumptions. First, and consistent with earlier forms of liberalism, the social foundation is the individual, not the group, and it is the individual's rights that must be secured. Second—and here it is most clearly distinguished from conservatism—although individuals are responsible for their own advancement, the state has a crucial role to play in guaranteeing equality of opportunity (but not, equality of outcome). Third, modern liberalism stresses reform rather than revolution, moderation and compromise rather than confrontation. Liberalism's historic commitment to democratic process remains, although the choice of strategies during the cold war was constrained by anticommunism. Thus twentieth-century liberalism has tended to sweep divisive issues under the rug so as not to disrupt the fragile consensus it has achieved. Finally, this liberalism enthrones pluralism as its goal for civil society.

Pluralism, founded in reply to early twentieth-century pressures on immigrant populations to "melt," called for the recognition of the unique cultures of different groups, who were nonetheless to conform to the prevailing public norm. Liberals viewed tolerance and inclusion as a means of acculturation; since those freed from oppression would naturally embrace society's values, pluralists did not see this as coercive or incompatible with the goals of personal liberation.

If modern liberalism has emerged from earlier forms, but with a new conception of the central role for the state, how did this occur? We turn first to a review of early American liberalisms, explore the emergence of a new liberalism wrought by the New Deal and the cold war, and finally, assess the challenges to liberalism and its resulting declension in recent decades.

NINETEENTH-CENTURY LIBERALISMS

In the United States, "classical" liberalism can be clearly seen in the values of nineteenth-century liberal Protestants, and those of the liberal Republicans of the 1870s and 1880s. Paralleling the political revolutions spurred by the Enlightenment was a spiritual revolution against traditional Calvinism. Liberal Protestants objected to the denial of human agency in the traditional view of an all-powerful and unknowable God. Instead they promoted Enlightenment ideals about human nature which led them both to a commitment to the pursuit of justice in this world and to acceptance of worldly values and commercial pleasures. For them salvation was not for the afterlife but a process in this life. If perfectability was unattainable, surely progress could be made toward that end through human will.

Reaching its fullest power in the early years of the twentieth century, liberal Protestantism produced the "Social Gospel" movement whose advocates believed that social conflicts could be resolved and the public good achieved with good-faith effort, careful administration, and the application of scientific principles. They advocated government regulation to manage social and economic evils, and professional management of economic and political institutions to ensure their efficiency and fairness. These values would come to be embraced by activists, religious or not, in the late nineteenth and early twentieth century who called themselves Progressives. These liberal Protestants, then, gave to American liberalism much of its character—faith in human progress and the usefulness of scientific tools, commitment to justice, an embrace of modernity and cosmopolitanism, and belief that seemingly conflicting and disparate agendas could be made to work together to promote a more harmonious whole. This view was neither a simple response to industrialization nor a wholesale critique of it. Instead, by seeking to mediate, reform, and regulate its worst effects, liberal Protestants (and later Progressives) encouraged and legitimated it.

In the political arena, liberal Republicans embodied the values of classic liberalism: demanding individual autonomy and political freedom while viewing the state as potential tyrant. They recognized opportunities for the state to intervene to protect individual rights, most clearly seen in the Civil War's ending of slavery, codified in the Thirteenth Amendment, and the expansion of democracy through the assertion of African-American (male) voting rights in the Fourteenth and Fifteenth amendments. The Reconstruction statutes protecting other black rights proved more vulnerable, however, as they seemed to insert the state too dramatically into private economic arrangements. Similarly, arguments for workers' rights led these business-oriented Republicans to emphasize a limited role for the state and place above it the sacredness of individual autonomy and private contract. This was the liberalism of John Stuart Mill, defended within the context of a capitalist market posited by Adam

Smith and his intellectual descendants. The market, as open arbiter of individual decisions freely made, would provide for all.

Nevertheless, government did of course play a role in shaping the marketplace, with subsidies, charters, and laws protecting the interests of these new industrialists. Indeed, these classical liberals defended the interests of property and corporations so single-mindedly that they seemed to ignore the plight of the poor and propertyless. Many of those seeking to challenge these Republicans took up other strands of liberalism, among them not only Social Gospelers but also Populists.

Scholars continue to debate the nature of populism. Nevertheless, within the contradictory and contested impulses of this farm-based movement can be found elements of the liberal agenda. Even its name reminds us that populism sprang more from a commitment to "the people" than to liberalism per se; still one cannot believe in "the people" without embracing democracy and rejecting the control of elites, two central liberal tenets. Populists (among other things) opposed monopolies and corporate power as limiting the rights and opportunities of individuals. Monopolies could set prices, determine wages and working conditions, and make special deals for themselves, all of which flew in the face of the public interest. Populists therefore opposed all centralization of power, including that of the state, seeing it as a threat to local and individual autonomy.

Much of the Populist agenda was not liberal at all; it opposed much of what the capitalist marketplace was doing and lamented the passing of old-time values and agrarian independence. Yet Populists simultaneously embraced modernity, progress, and government intervention when those forces worked in their favor. For example, they sought government-sponsored arrangements to market their produce more profitably. In their engagement with modernity, their appeal to democracy, and their demands for an end to centralized power, Populists represented one form of liberal thinking. In its reliance on the masses, its distrust of outsiders and its hearkening back to tradition, populism never fully embraced liberalism.

THE PROGRESSIVE ERA: TAMING CAPITAL

Like populism, the Progressive era was too contradictory to be placed under a single ideological banner. Nevertheless elements of liberalism can clearly be identified, some from its classical roots, others reshaped for a new age. Following traditional patterns, Progressive-era liberalism opposed monopolies and corporate power. But the embrace of state power was new. Progressives felt less concerned the state would threaten individual autonomy, since most shared the Social Gospelers' faith that in the hands of experts, policies could be set that served everyone's best interests. And unlike earlier liberals who feared government as a potential tyrant, these men and women insisted that government action was the only choice to protect the public against what they saw as the greater threat—the increasing concentration of economic power.

Thus "muckrakers," exposé-writing journalists so called because they "raked the muck" up from the bottom of society, published stories about abuses of corporate power, squalid housing conditions, violations of worker rights, and similar offenses, with the expressed intent to provoke such public outrage as to compel government to act on behalf of the public good. And act it did; Progressive-era governments, federal, state, and local, passed legislation that imposed quality controls over food manufacture, set air and space requirements for tenement houses and maximum hour and minimum wage laws for workers (struck down by the courts), challenged monopolies, granted women the right to vote, and established a graduated income tax. Although an often misplaced faith in the disinterested ability of experts meant many of these efforts were co-opted by the very elites Progressives hoped to regulate, they nevertheless reflected a belief in the power of the state to do good and the moral imperative for it to do so.

Progressives recognized the rapid and significant changes occurring around them, and the urgency to respond to the challenges they posed: the declining numbers in agricultural production, increasing industrialization and immigration and the corresponding growth of cities, the closing of the frontier, changing roles of workers, women, young people, and African Americans. By the 1920s liberals had embraced modernity and pluralism, with which they sought to respond to these changes, and the beginnings of a modern American culture these men and women were helping to shape were already visible. Materialism, prosperity, and rapid social change had produced a cosmopolitanism and a corresponding embrace of pleasure that look familiar to our eyes. This liberalism took the form of personal liberation from restrictive Victorian and religious norms, and group liberation from categorical restrictions like racism and anti-Semitism. While neither was fully articulated until the 1960s (and still not fully realized), both were visible even in the early years of twentieth-century liberalism.

Not all of progressivism followed liberal tenets; perhaps it is more accurate to say the many forms of progressivism revealed the many forms liberalism could take. (Indeed some were not liberal at all, but more socialist or communitarian.) Some were isolationist; others embraced action, even imperialism, on the world stage. Progressives could be xenophobic and racist or could embrace immigrants and African Americans as welcome contributors to American culture. Some Progressives argued that granting women the vote would expand democracy; others defended it on the ground it would help limit the impact of African-American votes. Progressives divided also over the question of women's equality, with those opposing the Equal Rights Amendment (first proposed in 1921) insisting that without special protections, women would be at the mercy of ruthless men and malevolent markets. Within the birth control movement, a desire to limit the reproduction of the poor and undesirable proved as strong a motivation as that of freeing women from unwanted pregnancies. In these debates, members of both sides considered themselves Progressives.

Progressives' attitudes toward the economy were similarly varied. There was, for example, "New Nationalism," a position articulated by Teddy Roosevelt. This view advocated active centralized planning and state supervision and regulation of the economy and of large corporations. Large structures were not evil in themselves, but needed to be monitored and regulated to ensure they operated in the public interest. Contrasted to that view was Woodrow Wilson's "New Freedom," which insisted that large structures were necessarily bad. The only response to this was a decentralized and competitive economy with firm antimonopoly legislation and a limited role for government.

Still, similar concerns and goals drove Progressives. Individuals ought to be protected from the depredations of large and impersonal forces, whether the untimely death of a breadwinner or the exploitation of an industrial employer, and the law was the proper source for such protection. Equality of opportunity was a proper goal for Americans, hence programs to assimilate immigrants, modernize education, and provide for the "deserving" poor. Certainly most Progressives were blind to other injustices such as lynching, and adhered to traditional views about women's proper role as sustainer of the family (even if many acknowledged a new, public place for women to operate in order to fulfill that role). And even the most perceptive of the Progressives insisted that the only option for immigrants and nonwhites was assimilation to white American norms. Nevertheless, such limits of vision still fit within a liberal framework that, after all, had long tolerated racism, sexism, and other forms of discrimination. Progressive-era liberals continued to draw a distinction between public and private, and many still believed there were inherent differences in the fitness of groups for full American citizenship.

While World War I was divisive for Progressives, many believed it had the potential to revitalize and extend modern ideas and institutions and bring about a new international order and a strengthened commitment to democracy. This dream died at Versailles and was buried by the postwar conservative resurgence that elected Harding and prompted nativism and antiradicalism. But the war's mobilization programs did promote the dream of a harmonious world at home—what scholars have termed a "corporatist" or "associational" economy where scientific management and a cooperative structure of labor, management, and state would serve the public interest by producing economic order and increasing production to combat scarcity. These Progressives believed the state could and should change economic institutions—destroy private monopolies, regulate corporations, and create cooperation within and between industries—to encourage more rational and efficient production and thereby lower prices for consumers. This desire to order the economy was unattainable but seductive, and it remained the dream of Progressives and some New Deal liberals.

THE EMERGENCE OF THE NEW DEAL ORDER

While the New Deal of Franklin Roosevelt shared much with Progressive-era liberalism, including faith in government activism and commitment to social legislation and to solving the problem of scarcity, it also broke with some earlier beliefs. The New Deal never looked nostalgically back to a more ordered past as progressivism and particularly populism had done. More to the point, the political landscape had changed since the early twentieth century, and new issues replaced older ones. New Dealers never challenged political machines the Progressives saw as corrupt and antidemocratic; rather Roosevelt tried to create alliances with them. Economic planning efforts declined, and there was no full engagement with the problems of monopoly. Instead, by the end of the depression policies to direct economic institutions had been replaced by less intrusive fiscal maneuvering. Finally, the New Deal drastically expanded Progressive notions of an activist state, intervening in the economy with great energy (if not always great ideological consistency). Little of this was intended; New Deal liberalism developed in fits and starts, a combination of theory and experimentation.

The New Deal economic system that emerged, called "Keynesianism" after economist John Maynard Keynes, advocated using government aid to stimulate consumption. This "priming the pump" was to be achieved through deficit spending so that in times of tight money, the state would serve as economic stimulus of last resort. This approach was not embraced suddenly or wholly, but rather by accretion. Keynesian reliance on government's fiscal rather than managerial role in the economy also came slowly. But by the middle 1940s all the elements of the new liberal economic policy were in place.

Part of any depression stimulus package had to focus on workers' earnings; liberals pressed for protections for union organizing. The first steps were small. In 1932 under Herbert Hoover, Congress passed the Norris-LaGuardia Act limiting injunctions and prohibiting "yellow dog" (antiunion) contracts. The next year, as part of President Roosevelt's active "One Hundred Days," section 7a of the National Industrial Recovery Act (NIRA) guaranteed unions' right to organize and bargain collectively. By 1935, more substantial union protections emerged in the National Labor Relations (Wagner) Act. All this helped promote a larger and more aggressive labor movement, especially within the Committee for Industrial Organization. Concerned to (among other things) improve the earning power of their workers, union officials used the depression to press their agenda. Thus it is not surprising that labor, newly energized by both the worker radicalization of the depression (limited though that radicalism may have been) and government protection of union organizing (limited though that protection may have been), enthusiastically endorsed government plans for pump priming.

Struggles over the liberal economic policy were determined both by trial and error and by pragmatic political considerations. As Progressives had, most liberals at first sought to order the economy and private industry. The NIRA contained weak but real antimonopoly and union-organizing provisions, a public works program, and a structure, the National Recovery Administration (NRA), to bring together industrial leaders to produce industrywide labor and production codes for fair competition, fair pricing, and decent working conditions. But within a year or so it had become clear that such an approach was not effective. The codes promoted centralization and concentrated power like the old hated trusts, and permitted those with power (corporations, white workers, officials) to continue to control or exclude those with less power (small producers, African Americans, rank-and-file workers).

This led other liberals to reject the model of the associational economy. Government should instead regulate industry and enter the market directly to protect the public interest. These New Dealers promoted development and created jobs with the Tennessee Valley Authority and the Works Progress Administration, which brought public investment in infrastructure. Yet while they opposed monopolies and corporate control, they sought expansion of the states' regulatory powers rather than antitrust legislation. They established new rules for banks and the stock market, and strengthened unions. In this they reflected Teddy Roosevelt more than Woodrow Wilson—the issue for economic institutions was not size but their fairness to workers and to consumers. And they argued fairness could best be achieved through increased control by the state. Unlike Progressives, these liberals believed the economy was too large and too complex to be rationalized or for all interests to be harmonized, and saw government's role as regulating the inevitable conflicts and instability. This required constant struggle and monitoring, tasks best done by an active and regulatory government.

That was no small change from Progressive-era liberalism. It challenged deep-seated American antistatist sensibilities and was therefore controversial. When a seemingly simpler solution emerged that also seemed to solve the economic crisis, many liberals jumped at it. This solution was fiscal control.

Fiscal liberals argued that government should use its monetary powers to achieve liberal goals: tax to provide revenue and redistribute wealth, spend to stimulate growth, expand consumption, and solve social problems. Like other liberals, then, they advocated an active government to sustain and expand the economy. Indeed, the link between government spending and a healthy economy was clear to them. They pointed to Roosevelt's decision in 1937 to cut government programs in light of substantial economic improvement. The result was an immediate economic collapse.

Also like other liberals, fiscal advocates recognized the problems in the capitalist economy: instability, dislocation, unequal opportunity. But they believed they had found a way to use state power to ease these problems not by ending capitalism (as many to the left of liberalism sought) or by fundamentally altering it (as planning and regulatory liberals sought). Rather, they saw economic growth as the key to expanding opportunity, and fiscal programs as the way to bring this about without the government intervening too deeply in the economy. Thus they advocated that government compensate for the weaknesses and imbalances in the economy without managing economic institutions, for example creating the Federal Reserve Board to set monetary policy. The state's role, they concluded, ought to be promoting consumption while protecting and even fostering private enterprise. Government investment in economic development was too intrusive; monetary policies would achieve the same goals with less conflict.

World War II further demonstrated the possibilities of manipulating the economy for good—hadn't government wartime production brought us out of depression? Yet the production boards confirmed the failure of older economic strategies and furthered the commitment to a compensatory rather than regulatory or coordinator role for government. Critics pointed to exploitation by corporate leaders, government meddling, and despite that, inefficiency. Meanwhile, totalitarian states in some European nations reminded liberals of the dangers of state control and led them to conclude that planned economies brought the domination of either the state or of monopolies. Either seemed a bad choice. Nevertheless, they acknowledged that the spending made a real difference. This confirmed for them that the central economic problem was not scarcity, as the Progressives had it, but rather underconsumption. All this helped persuade liberals to move from a direct interventionist state to one that worked on social policy through manipulating fiscal policy and focused on raising purchasing power through Social Security, welfare, and federal credit programs. This was the version of New Deal liberalism that triumphed and shaped policies for subsequent decades: using monetary polices and deficit spending to put money into people's hands without tampering with fundamental social or economic structures.

Fiscal liberals could argue that government could do more by pumping money into the economy than by trying to supervise or regulate it in part because significant regulatory, antimonopoly, and labor laws were already in place. That is not to say that no further protections were needed. African Americans complaining of industrial discrimination during the war, for example, turned to the government for redress. Roosevelt responded with the Fair Employment Practices Act which prohibited (to limited effect) discrimination on the basis of race, religion, or national origin. Nevertheless, even these critics of wartime production policies advocated not an expansion of economic planning but protections of individual rights within existing frameworks. Similarly, unions, pressured to keep a lid on wartime protest, gained a seat at the table by acquiescing but lost an independent voice for deeper structural change. (Not that such changes were either desired by most union members or politically feasible.) By 1945, then, the regulatory or associational liberal vision had been replaced by the fiscal and compensatory, and the goal of alleviating scarcity had been replaced by the goal of expanding consumption.

In practice, New Deal liberalism meant government commitment to providing at least minimal assistance to the needy (defined as the poor, the old, the young, the unemployed), protecting individuals' rights (defined as workers, religious minorities, and later African Americans and women), and regulating the market. It meant an expanded role for government that would compensate for (rather than challenge) the limits of capitalism. And finally, it created a new set of expectations for government, a new list of citizen entitlements. This liberalism, fundamentally reshaped by Roosevelt and the responses to the depression, was in some sense so new and so broadly defining of the era that it has come to be called the "New Deal Order."

Along with the New Deal Order came a new rationale. Government action was no longer posited as a necessary evil to save society, but rather as a positive good to further social progress. Certainly it legitimized capitalism, but it also blended the idea of economic growth with that of a welfare state. In other words, by increasing consumption, welfare programs sustained growth; growth in turn would further social progress if government ensured an egalitarian distribution of these new goods and resources. These liberals had retained liberalism's traditional concern for the individual, but adapted it to a more social democratic vision, seeking to extend rights further, and seeing that task as government's responsibility. This let drop the other component of classic liberalism, distrust of the state, which became the purview instead of conservatives.

Still, this commitment of liberals to social democracy did not make them socialists; they embraced rather than challenged the capitalism crucial to the continued expansion of their programs. Furthermore, their concern for equality had real limits. Roosevelt and other New Deal leaders did help African Americans and Native Americans, appoint some women to policy posts, and include antidiscrimination provisions in many of their policies, but never to an extent that would upset racial or gender status quo or threaten power relations—that would threaten the fragile electoral coalition these programs managed to forge. After all, the groups that supported the Democrats and the New Deal included African Americans and white Dixiecrats, urban laborers and western farmers, unions and modern consumption-oriented businesses, former Progressives, immigrants and working-class traditional families. Policies had to be limited in order not to offend one or another of these powerful constituencies, who all shared a commitment to an expanding economy and greater opportunity, but did not necessarily agree on much else. This brings us to another product of this liberal New Deal Order: it created a new political coalition whose competing interests required divisive issues to be downplayed for the sake of unity. This would have fateful consequences for liberalism. In later years many who rejected the evils liberalism tolerated would come to reject liberalism itself.

Thus the political and economic experience of the depression and the war shaped what policies and approaches were appropriate, and what postwar liberalism, or the New Deal Order, would mean. At the time this seemed not an ideological but a pragmatic debate: what programs and policies were most appropriate and politically feasible to get us where we want to go? Fiscal versus social Keynesianism, monetary manipulations versus economic planning, antimonopoly versus associational structures, a regulatory versus a compensatory government—all this suggests again how multivariate is liberalism (if not as an ideology, at least as a set of policies).

In part the debate appeared pragmatic rather than ideological because foreign examples of communism, fascism, and nazism transformed discussion of liberalism in the United States. Now enshrined as the western political tradition, standing in opposition to these more coercive and threatening forms of government, liberalism no longer seemed a legitimate subject for debate. The question was not whether liberalism was the proper ideal for society but rather how well we were living up to that ideal. Intellectuals from the 1930s through the 1950s pointed to liberal tendencies throughout our history: the absence of a feudal or aristocratic system, the hardiness of our small producers and yeoman farmers, the proliferation of voluntary societies (all first remarked on by de Tocqueville), the openness of our frontier, our rags-to-riches meritocracy, and our melting pot pluralism. Through these mechanisms all voices would eventually be heard and mistakes rectified. In other words, our society was liberal by consensus; there was no other American political tradition. Such were the arguments of Lionel Trilling's 1950 work *The Liberal Imagination*, and of Louis Hartz in *The Liberal Tradition* five years later. But how to achieve this liberal utopia was by no means as clear, as was obvious in the struggles between New Deal policymakers just described. Those battles would continue to rage, and increasingly to confront challengers on the right and the left, in the second half of the century.

POSTWAR LIBERALISM: CONFIDENCE AND CAUTION

Even after the war the triumph of fiscal over regulatory liberalism was not yet absolute. Postwar left liberals still pressed for national planning. They urged the federal government to expand consumption with programs to achieve full employment and high wages. Their position was perhaps best embodied by the proposed Full Employment Bill of 1945, which would have committed government to centralized planning and substantial spending to sustain high employment levels. The left liberals' time had passed, however. By the time of this bill's passage as the Employment Act of 1946 it had lost much of its interventionist character, subdued by more conservative forces. Truman's Fair Deal, which would have expanded health, education, and housing programs as well as civil rights protections, met with resounding defeat. Adherents of state economic intervention or planning were relegated to the progressive wing of labor and the Democratic party.

The economy had changed, as had the contours of world politics. Both consolidated the position of moderates. Now jobs were plentiful without the state having to create them; this confirmed their view that the role of government was only to ensure that the existing structure sustain the economic boom and make opportunities more widely available. Abundance legitimized an expanded role for the state to sustain it and distribute its benefits. But these liberals recognized the forces arrayed against them, and so urged that fiscal policies be used to promote that abundance, far less threatening to conservative Democrats or business and therefore more politically feasible. This pragmatism worked; the protection of individual rights within a capitalist framework of growth sustained by fiscal policies represented national Republican as well as Democratic positions. Thus even the election of Republican Dwight Eisenhower in 1952 left the basic tenets of economic liberalism in place.

Still, the postwar abundance that to moderate liberals meant a shift from intervention to compensation, from regulatory to fiscal policy, meant to conservatives that there was no further need for state involvement at all. Now the United States could return to economic freedom and limited government. Especially in the South, conservatives' and white supremacists' entrenched political power seemed unaffected by liberals' rise in federal government. If anything challenged conservatism there it was not socialism or liberalism but native-grown populism of the Huey Long variety: a fear of concentration of power that had brought antimonopoly support to the New Deal but brought as well a fierce distrust of government. The white South was Democratic but hardly liberal. Gaining power in the postwar elections, challengers of liberalism ended New Deal programs such as the WPA and Civilian Conservation Corps (CCC), opposed Truman's Fair Deal and civil rights proposals, limited the Wagner Act with legislation like Taft-Hartley (1947), and refused to make the Fair Employment Practices Committee (FEPC) permanent. Certainly some liberal measures, most notably the 1944 GI bill that provided financial and educational benefits for veterans, survived, and by helping level the playing field raised hundreds of thousands into the middle class. Nevertheless, Trilling's and Hartz's claims notwithstanding, liberalism was not as widespread a commitment as New Deal liberals had hoped, and this fact helped narrow liberal options.

The limits of postwar liberalism came not only from economic or social conservatism but also from cold war anticommunism and a distrust of mass action that placed severe constraints on how far toward the left liberalism could safely move. First, there was the danger of discrediting a position by having it labeled Communist or subversive, a tactic conservatives employed against virtually all liberal legislation. Second, liberals observed the dangers of authoritarian governments and the aroused masses. While a strong government won the war, more powerful was suspicion of strong governments like Nazi Germany, the Soviet Union, and China, each of which embarked on programs to repress their own people and conquer others. These governments were led by men whose rhetoric had transformed susceptible populations into dangerous mobs.

Nor were fears of bigotry and intolerance rooted only in examples from abroad. Demagogic leaders here from Father Coughlin, the anti-Communist, anti-Semitic radio priest of the 1930s, to the red-baiting senator Joseph McCarthy offered homegrown examples of the same possibility; many liberal intellectuals came to fear unmediated democracy as the potentially dangerous tool of demagogues. In such a climate, liberal agendas were tempered by the fear of radicalism on the one hand and the fear of mass movements on the other, and thus trod narrow and careful paths through the complex and troubling social, political, and economic issues still facing the nation. Caution, pragmatism, fear of mass action, and suspicion of ideology marked much liberal thought in this era. Even Hannah Arendt, a pioneer scholar of authoritarianism, counseled against civil rights protests, for example, as inappropriately inserting government into private decisions.

Cold war anticommunism not only tempered economic and class critiques, it also limited support for groups deemed insufficiently anti-Communist. As a result many liberal organizations expelled known or suspected Communists from their ranks and avoided taking positions that even hinted of leftist leanings. Some organizations compromised their own ideological base to pursue an anti-Communist agenda. For example, the liberal National Student Association was offered—and accepted—secret financial support from the CIA which saw it as a vehicle for anti-Communist propaganda in the international student movement. One could conclude that liberals had abandoned liberalism. On the other hand, such choices reveal liberals' optimism: theirs was a faith that society's existing structures could be reformed. This belief helped direct as well as narrow their focus to promoting pluralism and tolerance, pursued through education, law, and emphasis on the unifying elements of an American civic creed.

This optimism also underlay American liberal commitments to globalism. World War II made apparent and the cold war confirmed that the United States had to serve as both role model and policeman for the world. This was "the American century," Henry Luce proclaimed; the nation was a moral force for good, triumphant in the struggle to protect democracy and rights. This view motivated a commitment to an activist foreign policy, to promote and protect

American values around the world. While our actual motivations—advancing our material and strategic self-interest—were less altruistic, the rhetoric used to justify our actions suggest the mid-century American mind set. Appeals to liberal ideals worked to buttress support for our foreign policy initiatives in a way appeals to our physical well-being could not have. This liberal energy and optimism, which coexisted with the caution prompted by fear of radicalism and mass action, can be discerned similarly in other liberal projects of the period, including enthusiasm for technological progress and the boundless faith that through civil rights legislation and poverty programs, we could solve society's problems.

Nevertheless, cold war policies, whether promoted by liberals or conservatives, also had more negative consequences. They helped create a national security state that colluded with industry and controlled the economy—precisely what liberal policies were supposed to prevent. Furthermore, full civic equality and economic prosperity required the commitment of both intellectual energy and material resources, which were instead overwhelmingly devoted to fighting communism. Race and gender were glaring challenges to American equality, but those raising such questions were branded Communist and most narrowed their sphere of concern to civic rather than economic or structural questions so as to avoid that label. To maintain its stature internationally, government responded to civil rights challenges more often by suppressing evidence of oppression than by remedying it.

Despite these limitations, liberalism still promised equality and prosperity, and thus remained the hope of those in need. Certainly this was the case for African Americans. By virtue of their geographic location and their race, most African Americans were excluded from liberal programs. But the flight of almost two million African-American sharecroppers in the 1940s to urban areas and to the North and West, pushed by industrialization, segregation, floods, and crop failures, pulled by employment and opportunities for better education, voting rights and greater freedom, helped focus national attention on the problem of racism, and provide new vehicles for combating it.

The antecedents of what we call the civil rights movement lay in over two centuries of struggle for black equality. But in the twentieth century large portions of the civil rights movement embraced liberal ideals as their goals. Groups like the National Association for the Advancement of Colored People (NAACP) challenged segregation laws as violations of the liberal commitment to expanding democracy and individual equality of opportunity. And more public mass demonstrations for equality, while opposed by some cold war liberals as too close to mob rule, reflected a deep faith that, confronted with moral evil, whites would change. This optimistic liberal faith, embodied by African-American leaders such as Martin Luther King, Jr., and Ella Baker, and the black and white participants in Congress on Racial Equality's 1947 "Journey of Reconciliation," the 1955 Montgomery bus boycott, the sit-in movement launched in 1960, and the 1961 "Freedom Rides," would be tried by white recalcitrance. But in this period, postwar liberalism's commitment to pluralism, expanding democracy and economic opportunity, and enhancing individual freedom and opportunity, motivated most of these civil rights activists, both leaders and followers.

Government leaders and their liberal advisers also began to feel the urgency of the civil rights demands after the war. Wartime black migration brought black voters and the issue of segregation out of the South. The rhetoric of World War II helped whites draw links between nazism and racism, and pointed up the urgency of fostering better intergroup relations so the divisiveness that brought the Nazis to power could not flourish here.

The New Deal and the Fair Employment Practices Act had both put the question of race before government in a way not seen since Reconstruction and revealed the inroads African Americans had already made in making public their concerns. New Deal programs in turn raised black expectations, and the greater freedom of the North allowed for more open black activism as well as the formation of potent voting blocs. All this forced liberal leaders to reconsider their priorities: was their goal to confront only economic inequities or social ones as well?

So some white liberals agreed with African Americans that they must confront bigotry as well as the economy. The way they did so, via an integrationist pluralism, was true to liberalism's focus on the individual, and emphasized unity over diversity. Embodied in Gunnar Myrdal's magisterial analysis of the plight of African Americans, An American Dilemma, published in 1944, liberals viewed racism as a moral and attitudinal problem rather than a structural one. In other words, racism was a problem of individual moral failing and had to be challenged by education and legal restrictions on discriminatory behavior. This was, certainly, a limited vision of civil rights. By focusing on integration into white society it discouraged any ethnic or racial self-celebration. It opened the door for a greater tolerance among Americans (though obviously limited in both depth and breadth) but only toward a certain, narrowly integrationist pluralism that ultimately brought the revolt of those who saw it as destructive to their own identities. It excluded any discussion of structural racism or the racial nature of colonialism as subversive and therefore outside the bounds of legitimate discourse. And even this limited approach that in no way challenged the deeper racial and racist institutions of American society was not endorsed by all liberals. To sustain the New Deal coalition, race concerns remained at the periphery of liberal thought.

Liberalism also confronted questions about women's roles. For some, the economic crisis of the depression and the return of the victorious soldiers a decade later reaffirmed their commitment to traditional values. But for others, the fragility of male job security revealed by the depression and the economic liberation that wartime work had provided, raised troubling questions about women's proper place. Almost six million women joined the work force in World War II, many of them wives and mothers, and many in traditionally male jobs. Some chose to leave work at war's end, and others were forced out by employers or unions concerned about protecting the interests of returning male workers. But many other women remained at work, and that number rose as inflation and consumerism demanded increasing income for families to reach or remain in the middle class. Many of these women wanted to work, enjoying the responsibility and freedom it and a paycheck offered. Liberalism had accepted a private sphere out of reach of democracy's dictates, where women and other dependents safely remained. Some now questioned the validity of that public/private distinction and the appropriateness of those gendered constraints. Nevertheless, like questions about race, critiques of gender relations faced an uphill battle in their confrontation with traditional ideals held by both men and women and reinforced by national popular culture.

Postwar liberal projects were not only limited by directly excluding women and African Americans from opportunities. Sexism and racism also affected policy decisions in ways policymakers either did not recognize or did not concern themselves about. Social Security, for example, in some sense the embodiment of the liberal agenda, originally excluded from coverage the two fields in which most African Americans were employed: domestic and agricultural work. Further, Social Security, with its relatively higher benefits, went primarily to men, employed outside the home, since it was seen as a replacement for the "family wage" traditionally earned by male breadwinners. Needy women were required to rely on the far more parsimonious programs for single mothers with children. Government benefits like mortgage assistance that helped thousands achieve middle-class status were systematically denied in African-American or racially mixed neighborhoods, while colleges attended by those receiving tuition aid from the GI bill routinely excluded African Americans and limited the enrollment of Jews. Most, of course, were also all male.

Both the promise and the limits of postwar liberalism manifested themselves in the Supreme Court. Especially following the appointment of Earl Warren as chief justice in 1953, Americans saw a shift from judicial restraint to judicial activism. Neither restraint nor activism is inherently liberal, of course; *activism* simply refers to the willingness of judges to move beyond precedent to rule on new social and cultural issues. If activist judges act to limit reform or overturn new programs, as the Supreme Court did in the Progressive and early New Deal eras, they are activist without being liberal. But in this era liberal judges were the ones overturning programs and precedents, and doing so in the name of liberal values such as tolerance, equal opportunity, and civil liberties. The most famous of these cases, *Brown v. Board of Education of Topeka, Kansas* (1954), overturned the 1896 *Plessy v. Ferguson* decision permitting racial segregation. But there were dozens of other such liberal decisions, including *Baker v. Carr* (1962) and *Reynolds v. Sims* (1964), which upheld the principle of one person/one vote. *New York Times v. Sullivan* (1964) advanced freedom of the press by making it more difficult for political figures to sue for libel. *Griswold v. Connecticut* (1965) permitted the dissemination of information about birth control, and posited a constitutional right to privacy. *Roe v. Wade* (1973) legalized abortion. The courts protected the rights of accused criminals, with cases like *Gideon v. Wainright* (1963) guaranteeing legal representation and *Miranda v. Arizona* (1966), immortalized by police shows, requiring that every arrested person be read his or her rights.

At the same time, conservatives on the Court tempered its liberalism much as conservative legislators hampered liberals in Congress. The Court showed caution, for example, in requiring school desegregation not immediately but with "all deliberate speed." It pulled back free speech protections in *Konigsberg v. State Bar of California* (1957) and *Barenblatt v. U.S.* (1959) and upheld the constitutionality of anti-Communist prosecutions under the Smith Act in *Scales v. U.S.* (1961). When in doubt, the justices deferred to the decisions of elected officials. The Court, like the other branches of government, reflected a largely optimistic and energetic liberalism, tempered by caution and pragmatism.

Postwar liberalism, then, embodied both caution and confidence. It endorsed civil rights for those persecuted by race or religion, so long as those rights were pursued legally, were focused on the individual, and did not fundamentally challenge economic relations. Culturally, liberalism embraced what scholars have termed "cosmopolitanism": elevating tolerance, relativism, and rationalism over parochialism or provincialism. The liberal political economy provided for most middle-class workers a consumer paradise of leisure goods and services that fostered a buying spree that shaped American culture. For many, liberalism thus came to be equated with individual freedom, consumption, privacy, and secularism.

Yet there remained gaps in this New Deal Order or cold war liberalism: between rights for some and rights for others, between those able to enjoy the booming economy and those excluded by poverty, sex, or race. The liberalism of this era accepted the contradictions of a democratic order at home that we often refused to honor abroad, and despite its supposed embrace of individual rights, pressed conformity to an increasingly bureaucratic corporate culture and rigid and homogeneous social life.

A more left-leaning liberalism might have helped resolve these tensions, but they could not be articulated in the 1950s because those on the left had been silenced by anticommunism. The labor movement had become increasingly concerned with wages and job security at the cost of larger questions about the nature of work and of profits—not that there was much possibility of radical economic change in this cold war era. Any talk of full employment or structural (as opposed to individual) racism was branded communist and therefore beyond the pale. Instead, liberals in government mediated between the competing interests of different constituencies in what has been termed a "broker state." They had little choice given that they were challenged at every turn by a variety of economically and socially conservative institutions and individuals who did not support liberals' values. Still, while understandable for an electoral coalition too fragile to exert more direction and too reluctant to interfere more directly in the economy, the implication of this choice meant relinquishing the ideological high ground for more pragmatic political terrain.

SIXTIES LIBERALISM AND BEYOND: THE CHALLENGES OF LEFT AND RIGHT

Thus in the more activist 1960s when "Great Society" and civil rights programs emerged, it was impossible within established political discourse to fully discuss the class-, race-, and gender-based stratification of economic and political power. As a result, civil rights programs aiding black people appeared to do so at the expense of whites, and antipoverty programs lost funding to the war in Vietnam. When the American economy finally slowed, it challenged the faith that fiscal policies were all that was needed to ensure economic health. An even greater consequence of that economic downturn was that no longer could an ever-growing pie make expanded opportunities painless. A backlash against an apparently overgenerous and unruly liberalism thus emerged. Alongside it, leftists in the civil rights movement, the New Left, feminism, and the counterculture launched their own critiques of a liberalism they argued was morally bankrupt. By the 1970s these competing critiques had dethroned liberalism as the unquestioned political order. How did this come about?

The balance between cautious and active liberalism had already begun to tip in favor of the latter by 1960. John F. Kennedy, with his energy and youth and his discomfort with the "politics of drift," perhaps best embodied this new dynamism even if, in hindsight, his image and his legacy were more liberal than his actions. That liberal energy took us to Vietnam and brought civil rights legislation and the "War on Poverty" (aided, of course, by activists to the left of liberals, and by the assassination of Kennedy himself). We now doubt our ability to solve the problems of poverty and inequality, or at least that government can. But in the 1960s liberals held fast to their faith that government could and should. And they were convinced they could do it easily—theirs was a sense of an unbounded future, with limitless possibilities. Kennedy vowed to put a man on the moon by the end of the decade, and the country succeeded.

Despite this new energy and optimism, many on the left—including those originally motivated by liberal ideals—criticized liberalism for doing too little to achieve true equality. African Americans pointed to the failure of liberals to protect their bodies in the freedom rides and civil rights marches, or their voting rights in places like Mississippi or Alabama. They accused liberals of supporting institutions over principles. The Mississippi Freedom Democratic Party held elections for an integrated state delegation to the 1964 Democratic convention, and argued that it, rather than the traditional whites-only Mississippi Democratic party, should represent the state. Even staunch liberals like Hubert Humphrey resisted that demand and instead offered to seat two members of the MFDP as "at large" members while leaving the Dixiecrat slate to represent Mississippi, thus placing party support over the civil rights ideal. (The MFDP refused the compromise and left the convention.)

Women pointed to the entrenched sexism and paternalism of liberals and of liberal laws such as welfare. They pointed as well to gaps in the law, noting that liberal ideas about the private sphere allowed men to cover up domestic abuse and leave sexist gender roles unchallenged.

Critics of the poverty programs pointed to the limits of health care, the parsimony of welfare and distrust of its recipients, and the persistent underfunding of education and antipoverty initiatives. They noted the unwillingness of poverty workers to follow the legislative mandate of "maximum feasible participation" by the poor in shaping poverty programs. Together, antipoverty workers and the New Left pointed to the enormous power and control of corporations, the persistently unequal distribution of wealth, and the disproportionate political power held by wealthy white men.

At the same time intellectuals questioned the usefulness of the liberal ideal, not just how well Americans were living up to it. Because liberalism placed the individual at the center, it provided no room for critiques of power allocated on the basis of group membership. Furthermore, an individualist focus led to an impoverished sense of civic society or community as simply the meeting place of autonomous individuals. Some argued that postwar liberalism's goal of ever-increasing consumption inevitably produced a commodified and empty vision of the good society where image replaced substance and where happiness was defined as the pursuit of material goods.

All this broke the majority position of the Democratic party, long liberalism's political home, and offered an opportunity for Republicans and conservatives to dominate politics and challenge the liberal social order. These conservatives made principled arguments of their own in opposition to what liberalism had become. Unlike traditional liberalism, defined by its distrust of government, postwar liberalism committed government to act everywhere. These conservatives countered with a claim first raised by the earliest liberal thinkers: increasing the power of the state inevitably threatens individual rights and liberties. Nor would it help to limit state intervention to the economy. Economic control directly extended to political and social control, they contended, and pointed to the examples of Nazi Germany and the USSR. Classical liberal antistatism was now closer to the position of these conservatives than to that of liberals.

Other conservatives supported government activism, but in order to promote traditional values. Like liberalism, conservatism encompassed those who embraced individual freedom and those who desired government intervention to promote their own agenda. These contradictory impulses within both ideologies remind us that neither was monolithic. Both interventionist and individualist conservatism joined the chorus of those criticizing liberalism.

Now those beneficiaries of liberalism's largesse but uncomfortable with liberalism's cosmopolitan and secular style or its apparent capitulation to the demands of minority groups had a political alternative. In other words, those to the left of liberalism were not its only critics. Feminism upset many who saw an impending social crisis for the family and for society. Civil rights advances coupled with black criticism of white society upset traditionalists further. An increasing number of former liberals, or at least members of the Democratic coalition who had considered themselves liberals, came to resent government as too impetuous, too interfering, too threatening to their own position.

The first powerful sign of the backlash was the election of Richard Nixon in 1968. Even he, however, embodied much of the liberal agenda from his visit to China to his establishment of the Environmental Protection Agency and his proposal for a negative income tax to provide an earning floor for all families. Between 1968 and 1980 local agendas and politics, what Jonathan Rieder has called the politics of space, continued to erode liberalism's traditional coalition. Most pronounced in the previously "solid" South, political defections were apparent everywhere. In neighborhoods like Canarsie and Yonkers, in cities like Boston and Chicago, in states like Texas and California, issues of school integration, crime, the environment, neighborhood integrity, industrial relocations, and low income housing continued to polarize the previously at least loosely allied liberal electorate.

Local politics became increasingly marked by arguments over "reverse racism" and by laments about "limousine liberals" or "bleeding hearts," elite liberal leaders whom they claimed abandoned their concern for the working or middle class, for law and order, for merit, rules, or morality. Lower-middle-class and middle-class whites resented what they saw as the special treatment African Americans received, the undermining of the ethnic integrity of their neighborhoods and the quality of their schools produced by various forced integration or shared funding plans, and the willingness of government officials to impose on them what those officials were unwilling to accept for themselves and their more affluent neighborhoods (what social critics called "NIMBY" or "not in my back yard"). They saw the revolt of young people; the increased danger and social problems of cities; challenges to the nation's foreign policy directions (especially in Vietnam); the undermining of traditional morality in the greater access to pornography, birth control, and abortion; rising divorce rates; growing numbers of women in the work force; changes to traditional school curricula; expanded rights and protections for criminals; and greater sexual and social openness. In these struggles for the future of America, liberalism appeared to have sold out its values, and moved from commitment to individual equality, political rights, and mitigation of the worst of capitalism to wasteful spending, sanctimoniousness, irresponsibility, and favoritism.

And they endured the first prolonged slowing of the economy since World War II. The rise of the Japanese and European economies, spending on the Vietnam War, OPEC oil embargoes, and similar developments destabilized the American economy and raised both inflation and the unemployment rate. This reinforced dissatisfaction with liberal leadership and limited the money available for social programs. With the economy closer to a zero-sum game, advances for some became setbacks for others.

While much of the fear and anger came from nonliberal sources, it is also true that liberal political structures like the Democratic party had moved to the left. This is perhaps best illustrated by the selection of George McGovern as the Democratic candidate for president in 1972. Not only did he advocate what seemed to moderates too much like appeasement in Vietnam, not only did he seem unconcerned about law and order and welfare dependency and too sympathetic to radical agendas, he was nominated because the party's selection mechanisms had been revised to give activists far more power and the traditional power brokers far less. In other words, not only his candidacy but also the means of his selection demonstrated to these erstwhile liberals that the party of their liberalism no longer represented them.

These disgruntled former liberals increasingly withdrew their support from a liberalism that seemed to them to have abandoned its legitimacy and instead listened more closely to conservative social critics who sought a return to what now seemed simpler times. In the South this return took the form of reassertion of states' rights and traditional values, particularly resistance to neighborhood integration and expansion of African-American voting rights. In the Sunbelt it took the form of nationalism and antiunionism; in the West cutting benefits to immigrants and the needy and fighting economically limiting environmental policies; in the Northeast resistance to school integration and generous welfare programs. By the election of Ronald Reagan in 1980, the repudiation of postwar liberalism seemed complete. Both Left and Right had lost faith in the possibility of achieving equality and justice while maintaining current institutions and norms (although the two sides differed in what equality and justice would look like and who were the neediest recipients). The Left advocated justice at the price of the system. The Right favored preserving institutions and middle-class values against leftists who sought to destroy them. Liberals, apparently with little to contribute to the debate, were marginalized in this struggle over the soul of the culture.

LIBERALISMS

Late nineteenth-century liberalism, concerned with property rights and entrepreneurial opportunities, remained deeply individualist in its vision of society and limited in the role it envisioned for government. Its foreign policy was generally nationalistic and, beyond the Western Hemisphere, isolationist. The Progressive era challenged this with social welfare legislation and the insistence that the United States had global interests. Still, many Progressives sought an individualist, competitive society, and retained earlier blinders about the limited reach of liberalism's ideals, especially in the case of race. The New Deal changed our understanding of liberalism. Still endorsing individual competition, New Deal liberals placed it within a welfare state and shifted attention to consumption and opportunity. World War II and the cold war internationalized this new liberal vision by providing a new global role for the United States: to promote liberty and democracy.

This new liberalism of reform at home and activism abroad, created by Roosevelt and consolidated by Truman, emerged as a national consensus under Eisenhower, and strained to the breaking point under Johnson. Although its outlines were accepted even by Nixon, the beginning of the end had come. Liberalism had succeeded in opening the democratic process, guaranteeing legal rights and protecting against the worst ravages of capitalism. Within its ideology it could do no more. Yet the failures and limits of liberalism had also become clear. Bureaucracy, waste, paternalism, bloated budgets, the intrusion of government—and yet the stubborn persistence of social problems liberalism promised to end. By the elections of Ronald Reagan and George Bush, liberalism had come to mean license, and liberals meant a privileged elite out of touch with and unconcerned about the needs of ordinary people.

If before the 1960s liberalism was limited by the injustices it ignored, after the 1960s it was limited by cynicism and disillusionment from the Left and by backlash from the Right. As a result, liberalism seemed to have lost its momentum. Since the 1940s liberalism, for all its limits, was energetic in its confidence in American goals and what liberals perceived as uniquely American core values. By the 1960s liberals' energy and confidence had extended to the conviction that they could end injustice without fundamental changes in American institutions or social structures. By the 1980s that fervor, that confidence, that commitment to activism had been lost. As a result, there was little left to defend when critics weighed in. Even President Clinton, the only Democrat to serve since 1980, made shrinking the role of government a priority and proclaimed, "The era of big government is over."

Some have made the opposite argument, that even the triumph of conservatism continues to reflect liberal values. George Bush's "new world order" defined American interests abroad as the liberal ideals of democracy and freedom. His promise of a "kinder, gentler" America hearkened back to traditional welfare state liberalism. Nevertheless, if liberalism has left its mark on politics, it is because liberalism can be construed so broadly as to encompass much of American conservatism. Both contain a commitment to individual rights, to democracy, and to internationalism. To claim the persistence of more than this level of liberalism in politics today after the end of welfare, the slashing of aid to legal immigrants, and retrenchment on civil rights, is simply not credible.

Ultimately, twentieth-century liberalism did not, and perhaps could not, adequately address pressing problems of race, class, gender, or social or economic structure. As a result, tensions festered until they exploded both to the right and the left, and brought liberalism down with them. Today even Democrats look as conservative as Republicans. A new order is emerging; not liberal or conservative but rich and poor, elite and mass. Political power is increasingly concentrated in a few wealthy and corporate hands, and policies increasingly favor the well off at the expense of the poor. One result has been a renewed interest in—and even defense of—liberalism as a way out.

These more recent defenses of liberalism have had to broaden its ideas, locating within it a fuller commitment to democracy, for example, or embracing the moral energies of social reformers. Others have pushed liberalism toward a more communitarian ideology that would nurture stronger and more participatory communities, or pushed it to close the gap between the public and private sphere, thereby challenging patriarchal and other debilitating hierarchies. Still others press liberalism to embrace more inclusive notions of virtue and citizenship to expand the reach of justice and encompass a richer notion of diversity.

Will we see a rebirth of classical liberalism, a new liberalism for our post–cold war, post–New Deal Order age, or move on from a political system too discredited and outdated to be useful? The answer must await those who, perhaps a hundred years from now, will assess the twenty-first century.

NOTE

1. Daniel Rodgers, "Republicanism," in *A Companion to American Thought*, edited by Richard Wrightman Fox and James T. Kloppenberg (Cambridge, Mass.: Blackwell, 1995), p. 585. He contrasted liberalism, which focused on individual rights and interests, with republicanism, which placed devotion to the public good at the center.

BIBLIOGRAPHY

A listing of books on each historical period under scrutiny would fill an encyclopedia. Even keeping within the ostensibly narrower field of liberalism, one is faced with such an array of works that it is possible here only to skim the surface. Among the best books dealing with liberalism as an overall theme are Alan Brinkley, *Liberalism and Its Discontents* (Cambridge,

Mass.: Harvard University Press, 1998); Alonzo Hamby, *Liberalism and Its Challengers*, 2nd ed. (New York: Oxford University Press, 1992); Patrick Neal, *Liberalism and Its Discontents* (New York: New York University Press, 1997) and for an older view, Leo Strauss, *Liberalism, Ancient and Modern* (New York: Basic Book, 1968). There are many social and philosophical explorations and critiques of liberalism. Some of the best include John Rawles, *Political Liberalism* (New York: Columbia University Press, 1993); James Hoopes, *Community Denied: The Wrong Turn of Pragmatic Liberalism* (Ithaca, N.Y.: Cornell University Press, 1998); Michael Sandel, *Liberalism and the Limits of Justice*, 2nd ed. (New York: Cambridge University Press, 1998); Peter Berkowitz, *Virtue and the Making of Modern Liberalism* (Princeton, N.J.: Princeton University Press, 1999); Ellen Paul, Fred Miller Jr., Jeffrey Paul, eds., The *Communitarian Challenge to Liberalism* (New York: Cambridge University Press, 1996). (The same editors also explore the liberal economy in *Liberalism and the Economic Order* [New York: Cambridge University Press, 1993].) One of the best defenses of liberalism is James Kloppenberg, The *Virtues of Liberalism* (New York: Oxford University Press, 1998). The New Deal Order and its reshaping of classical liberalism is complex; some of the best work in this area has been collected in Steve Fraser and Gary Gerstle, eds., *The Rise and Fall of the New Deal Order* (Princeton, N.J.: Princeton University Press, 1989). Full-length works dealing well with this subject include Alan Brinkley, *The End of Reform: New Deal Liberalism in Recession and War* (New York: Knopf, 1995); Steven Gillon, *Politics and Vision* (New York: Oxford University Press, 1987); and David Plotke, *Building a Democratic Political Order* (New York: Cambridge University Press, 1996). Post–New Deal developments are discussed in Brinkley, *The End of Reform*; Gareth Davies, From *Opportunity to Entitlement: The Transformation and Decline of Great Society Liberalism* (Lawrence: University Press of Kansas, 1996); and Paul Gottfried, *After Liberalism: Mass Democracy in the Managerial State* (Princeton, N.J.: Princeton University Press, 1999). An important study of the post-1960s northern white disenchantment with liberalism is Jonathan Rieder, *Canarsie: The Jews and Italians of Brooklyn against Liberalism* (Cambridge, Mass.: Harvard University Press, 1985), and Adolph Reed has edited a provocative collection about race and liberalism called *Without Justice for All: The New Liberalism and Our Retreat from Racial Equality* (Boulder, Colo.: Westview Press, 1999). Many fine studies of individual liberals and their struggles to reshape or preserve liberalism have been produced, such as William Chafe's *Never Stop Running: Allard Lowenstein and the Struggle to Save American Liberalism* (New York: Basic Books, 1993) and Allida Black's *Casting Her Own Shadow: Eleanor Roosevelt and the Shaping of Postwar Liberalism* (New York: Columbia University Press, 1996). For an excellent study of liberalism and labor see Kevin Boyle's *The UAW and the Heyday of American Liberalism, 1945–1968* (Ithaca, N.Y.: Cornell University Press, 1995); for a discussion of the Supreme Court, see Laura Kalman, *The Strange Career of Legal Liberalism* (New Haven, Conn.: Yale University Press, 1996) For fuller bibliographic discussion of liberalism and women, African Americans, unions, immigrants, and presidents, see other chapters in this volume.

4 | THE REPUBLIC AS EMPIRE

American Foreign Policy in the "American Century"

ROBERT J. MCMAHON

The dawning of the twentieth century coincided with the emergence of the United States as a player of increasing prominence on the world stage. The Spanish-American War of 1898—or, more properly, the Spanish-American-Cuban-Filipino War—heralded not just America's emergence as a fledgling world power but the advent of the globe's newest empire as well. By humbling a horribly outmatched Spain in a three-month non-contest that Secretary of State John Hay lauded as "a splendid little war," the United States positioned itself to gain direct, or indirect, control over all of Spain's former colonies. And that is exactly what Washington did. In the immediate aftermath of the war, it seized outright possession of the Philippines, Puerto Rico, and Guam while establishing de facto control over Cuba's political and economic affairs—and insisting upon the unilateral right of intervention in that long-coveted island.

For good measure, the United States also annexed Hawaii at this same time. That strategically and economically valuable Pacific outpost had to all intents and purposes fallen under American sway well before the William McKinley administration sought its formal annexation. Congressional approval of the administration's annexation proposal, in July 1898, formalized the arrangement.

Just five years later, President Theodore Roosevelt negotiated a treaty with Panama, Colombia's breakaway province, that allowed the United States to construct, oversee, and defend an isthmian canal. Panama also relinquished to U.S. control at that time a strip of territory that became the Panama Canal Zone, an area over which the United States would long exercise all the rights of sovereignty.

Those events, compressed into a breathtakingly brief period of time at the turn of the last century, mark an important break in the history of American foreign policy—and in the history of the American republic more broadly. They form the essential backdrop for the following reflections on the course of American foreign relations during what has come to be called the "American century." It will be my contention that applying the concept of empire to America's world role throughout the *whole* twentieth century—a concept that until fairly recently discomfited scholars of American foreign relations and the general public alike—can illuminate much that is critical about the U.S. engagement with the broader world over the past one hundred years.

Although the United States became an empire in the formal sense only at the close of the nineteenth century, it bears emphasizing that Americans were hardly strangers to territorial or economic expansion prior to that point. Indeed, much of American history in the years between 1776 and 1898 was the story of a nation once bounded by the Atlantic Ocean and the Appalachian Mountains expanding across the breadth of the North American continent, subjugating in the process the indigenous and other peoples who had the misfortune to lay in its path. Aggressive commercial expansion into much of what today is commonly referred to as the Third World also constitutes a critical part of that preimperial story.

But the imperial surge of the 1890s represented a turn, perhaps even a watershed, in U.S. history. In the wake of that surge, the United States found itself exercising sovereignty over noncontiguous territories for the first time. They were territories, moreover, not likely ever to be incorporated into the union as states for an amalgam of political, constitutional, and not least, racial reasons. Observers and interested participants at the time—both supporters and opponents of territorial expansion—well recognized the momentous issues involved in the republic's evolution into an empire. We should as well.

The American empire matured, grew, *and* contracted, and assumed very different guises during a century in which the global power and influence of the United States ascended to ever loftier heights. During a century punctuated by two world wars, the cold war, and a massive wave of decolonization that sounded the death knell for most types of formal colonial rule, the United States metamorphosed into one of history's mightiest empires. From the position of a rising but still second-rate power in the early 1900s, the United States became the global hegemon after World War II, a position it has maintained, and solidified, over the past half century. Today the United States stands not only as the world's sole remaining superpower militarily *and* the engine of the global economy, but culturally supreme as well, with the symbols of its consumer culture—from movies, television programs, and popular music to fast food franchises, styles of clothing, and computer software—ubiquitous in virtually every corner of the planet. If the Roman, Ottoman, and British empires at their respective peaks boasted sovereignty over far more square miles of territory, the modern American empire dwarfs all its historical predecessors in terms of its military strength vis-à-vis other nation-states, its economic dominance, the complete absence of serious rivals, and an impact on the world community in every realm from the political-ideological to the military to the commercial to the cultural, that is simply without parallel.

The concept of America-as-imperium, a notion once employed only by scholars of a decidedly revisionist bent or by radical activists pursuing their own political agendas, has achieved a surprising amount of respectability of late. Even a historian as traditionally minded as John Lewis Gaddis readily concedes that the modern United States has been a globe-straddling empire, even if his dubious assertion that it proved more an empire of attraction than any of its historical forerunners is intended to minimize the negative connotations of the term. Gaddis's broad definition of empire offers an excellent reference point for the present essay. Empire implies, in his words, "a situation in which a single state shapes the behavior of others, whether directly or indirectly, partially or completely, by means that can range from the outright use of force through intimidation, dependency, inducement, and even inspiration." Drawing a useful distinction between formal (territorial) empires and informal empires, Gaddis adds: "One need not send out ships, seize territories, and hoist flags to construct an empire: 'informal' empires are considerably older than, and continued to exist alongside, the more 'formal' ones Europeans imposed on so much of the rest of the world from the fifteenth through the nineteenth centuries."

This chapter aims, appropos of the sweeping scope of the present volume, simply to sketch some of the broader contours of the enormous topic—America's role in the world over the past century—that has fallen under my purview. My remarks will be arranged primarily around this theme of empire. I will argue that the concept of America-as-empire is fundamental to an appreciation of America's world role in the twentieth century, and especially so for the post-1945 period when American power and influence reached their zenith. I will contend, furthermore, that the concept of empire provides an excellent entree into three of the most important, most intriguing, and most controversial questions about U.S. foreign policy in the American century. First, what have been the principal forces driving U.S. foreign policy? Idealism? Material needs? Strategic interests? Fear of external enemies? Ideology? Politics? Second, what have been the principal continuities or discontinuities in American foreign policy over this one-hundred-year period? And, finally, what impact has the United States had on the wider world? If one takes a broad, global perspective on this past century, then what difference has the United States made in and to that world? In what specific ways, in short, might this century appropriately be termed the *American* century?

My central arguments run essentially as follows. First, despite the idealistic language in which its foreign policy has so frequently been couched, the United States—like other great powers—has always acted primarily out of its own perceived self-interest. Grandiose conceptions about how American foreign policy serves the interests of all the world's people have, however, coexisted with and reinforced the headlong American determination to advance its own material and security needs. Second, prior to World War II, commercial ambitions largely drove U.S. foreign policy making. With no powerful enemies or prospective enemies in sight, Americans were free to concentrate on exploring and exploiting overseas opportunities for increasing national wealth and power.

Third, during and after World War II, security concerns rose to the fore. Deep-seated fears about the need to fend off external dangers—both geopolitical and ideological—came to dominate American diplomatic and defense policies at that time, and continued to do so right up until the end of the cold war. Fourth, since the end of the cold war Americans have remained wary of any and all potential external threats. Yet those threats have proven much more diffuse and far less acute in the 1990s than in the preceding half century. American policymakers of the post–cold war era have, consequently, placed as much, or more, weight on the economic dimension of international affairs as they have on the security dimension.

Since the foundation of the republic, Americans have drawn attention to what they considered the uniqueness of their civilization, their history, their character, their motives. Many even found divine sanction for the conceit that America had a global mission to share its superior values, institutions, and culture with others. The United States was the "world's best hope," Thomas Jefferson proclaimed in his 1801 inaugural address, the "last, best hope of earth" in Abraham Lincoln's famous rephrasing. Just before U.S. entry into World War I, Woodrow Wilson articulated that missionary imperative with even greater fervor. "We created this nation not just to serve ourselves," he declared, "but to serve mankind." In a similar vein, at the height of the cold war Harry S. Truman publicly professed his conviction "that God has created us and brought us to our present position of great power and strength for some great purpose."

More recently, George Bush, reflecting on the foreign policy achievements of his administration—and his generation—explained what he referred to as "America's purpose in the world" in almost identical terms. The then lame-duck president hailed the cold war victory of the United States as a triumph for "the forces of freedom." "Amid the triumph and the tumult of the recent past," he proclaimed grandiloquently, "one truth rings out more clearly than ever: America remains today what Lincoln said it was more than a century ago, 'the last best hope of man on Earth.'" It continued to serve, he said, "as a beacon for all the peoples of the world."

To Jefferson, to Lincoln, to Wilson, to Truman, to Bush, as to virtually all national leaders throughout its history, the United States was not just another nation among nations. It was unique, special, annointed. Its foreign policy encompassed more than the mere pursuit of national interest. U.S. statesmen convinced themselves that their country's engagement with the world also advanced such universalistic goals as democracy, economic development, individual liberty, and social justice. That U.S. national interests often happened to coincide—or seemed to coincide—with the promotion of such exalted goals simply served for them as confirmation of their nation's special purpose. Ever since the era of the founding fathers, most American decision makers have simply taken for granted that what was best for the United States was best for the world as a whole. "The United States was the locomotive at the head of mankind," as Secretary of State Dean Acheson liked to say, "and the rest of the world was the caboose." Secretary of State Madeleine Albright has more recently, but with just as much arrogance, annointed the United States the world's "indispensable nation."

That messianic vision cannot be dismissed as purely elite cynicism. Presidents, to be sure, are not elected, nor secretaries of state appointed, on the basis of their commitment to global reform. It is their presumed ability to protect the United States from prospective enemies while promoting domestic harmony and prosperity that typically bring them to power. Yet one of the keys to twentieth-century American foreign relations can be found in the connections American leaders have invariably made between the opportunities, and problems, presented by the world beyond the home shores and the advancement of core domestic needs and values.

A keen appreciation for how engagement with the wider world could advance the interests of the republic has always undergirded the idealistic-sounding pronouncements of American statesmen. President Bill Clinton's espousal of a global "enlargement" strategy to supplant the cold war era's containment strategy stands as an excellent contemporary illustration of this phenomenon. The enlargement concept calls for the United States to actively encourage the expansion of democratic values and practices throughout the world. It is predicated on the theory, backed by a substantial body of social science literature, that democracies rarely fight each other. Hence, promoting the spread of democracy abroad should help safeguard world peace while enhancing the security of the United States. This is but the most recent echo of a venerable notion: namely, that American interests would best be served if the external world evolved in certain, specific ways. The enlargement strategy, in short, is part of a long-standing search for the international environment most conducive to the flourishing of the American system.

The emergence of the United States at the turn of the last century as both world power and empire is best understood within this wider framework. America's imperial surge of 1898–1903 was a consequence, primarily, of the domestic needs identified by American elites at that time. Those needs derived especially from the economic depression-cum-political crisis of the 1890s and the social and labor unrest that followed on its heels. War with Spain, and the opportunistic seizure of colonies that war permitted, was the McKinley administration's response to those deep societal problems.

It was decidedly *not* a response to perceived external threats. American leaders of that era were agreed that the United States, with a two-ocean barrier and with generally friendly, and much weaker, neighbors in Canada and Mexico, enjoyed an enviably large margin of physical safety. Certainly if compared with European countries of that era, the United States was remarkably free from serious external dangers. Genuine threats to the physical safety of the United States had, in fact, largely evaporated a century earlier—with the 1815 peace settlement that brought an end to the War of 1812, to be precise. That settlement ushered in a long era of "free security," in historian C. Vann Woodward's apt phrase. Unlike European powers of the nineteenth and early twentieth centuries, the United States did not have to worry about maintaining large standing armies to protect its borders from potentially hostile neighbors. If foreign policy for most nations at most times typically revolves around the effort, on the one hand, to advance national interests and, on the other, to ensure security from potential external dangers, then what is most striking about American foreign policy right up to the Second World War is that it focused mostly on the former consideration—and that the second was largely taken for granted.

American political and business elites of the late nineteenth century looked to the diplomatic realm primarily for how it might contribute to domestic needs, particularly for how it might help promote economic prosperity and foster social harmony at home. To that end, they devoted steadily increased attention to the importance of overseas markets, raw materials, and investment opportunities to the health of the burgeoning U.S. economy. "I wish to declare," said Secretary of State James Blaine in 1890, "the opinion that the United States has reached a point where one of its highest duties is to enlarge the area of its foreign trade. . . . Our great demand is expansion. I mean expansion of trade with countries where we can find profitable exchanges. We are not seeking annexation of territory. . . . At the same time I think we should be unwisely content if we did not engage in what the younger Pitt so well termed annexation of trade."

Blaine, like so many of his contemporaries, worried about the periodic economic downturns that beset the rapidly industrializing American economy and saw expanded foreign trade as the most effective solution to the root problem of overproduction. Overproduction was not just an economic problem, moreover, since depression brought unemployment, strikes, social unrest, and political upheaval. With the depression of the 1890s, unemployment rose to 16.7 percent in 1894, and remained at between 12 and 14 percent right up to the eve of the Spanish-American War. A record number of strikes occurred during that period, including the paralyzing nationwide Pullman strike that President Grover Cleveland suppressed with federal troops. The swelling tide of labor violence and class conflict, the rise of the Populist movement, the angry march of "Coxey's Army" of the unemployed—all drove home to Amer-

ican elites the direct connection between economic failure and domestic upheaval. Walter Q. Gresham, Cleveland's secretary of state, worried that those
developments seemed to "portend revolution." He confided to a friend his fear
that "there probably would be a revolution in the U.S., with a great leader
emerging and then there would be a quest for empire."

President McKinley's call for war with Spain in March 1898 is directly
traceable to the concerns expressed by Blaine, Gresham, and so many other
political and business leaders of this period about the unsettled state of the
American social and economic order. Although historians have debated—
often vehemently—the precise hierarchy of factors that influenced McKinley,
virtually all agree that domestic causes were paramount. The careful and calculating McKinley became convinced that only war could restore American
property interests in Cuba, end the uncertainty over the civil war in that island
that plagued the business community and hence stalled economic recovery at
home, and put the United States in a position to help establish an open door
for trade and investment in a rapidly crumbling China. Those specific concerns were connected more broadly to the American drive to expand access to
overseas markets, raw materials, and investment opportunities. The health of
the domestic economy and the preservation of the nation's social order,
McKinley and most other political and business leaders had become convinced, demanded nothing less.

Since their solution—empire—seemed so fundamental a departure from
the nation's traditions, it sparked an unusually divisive debate at home. The
intensity of that debate should not be allowed to obscure the basic fact, however, that it focused more on the *how* of foreign expansion than the *why*. Most
opponents of imperialism, as well as its advocates, saw increased access to foreign markets and the development of strategically located naval and coaling
stations to help protect U.S. overseas investments as important national interests. The anti-imperialists rejected the formal acquisition of territories for a
curious combination of reasons: abhorrence of dominating other peoples, concern with violating the nation's anticolonial traditions, practical objections
about the likely costs and risks of territorial acquisitions, and blatant racism.
In the latter regard, the views of South Carolina's senator John McLaurin are
quite revealing. The Southerner warned that such "a mongrel and semibar-
barous population" as the Filipinos, "inferior but akin to the Negro in moral
and intellectual development and capacity for self-government" could spell
doom for the republic. McKinley and his pro-empire supporters naturally took
the high road, emphasizing the practical benefits, and purported beneficence,
that they said animated the drive for empire.

They won the debate, of course, which came to a head with the favorable,
if close, Senate vote for annexation of the Philippines in 1901. At the same
time, McKinley and his supporters made clear the circumscribed nature of the
empire they desired. They sought not a sprawling American colonial im-

perium but merely the minimum territory needed to advance their goal of conquering foreign markets, along with pinpoint bases and coaling stations to help protect the overseas markets and investments they coveted. A comparative perspective is in order here. "Between 1870 and 1900," the historian Walter LaFeber has pointed out, "Great Britain added 4.7 million square miles to its empire, France 3.5 million, and Germany 1 million. Americans, however, added only 125,000 square miles. They wanted not land, but more markets to free them from the horrors that had resulted from the post-1873 depression."

Presidents Theodore Roosevelt, William Howard Taft, and Woodrow Wilson each in turn identified the essential goals of American foreign relations much along the same lines. Eager, like McKinley, to expand America's share of international trade, each of those leaders also saw foreign policy first and foremost as an opportunity for advancing national interests. They were not, it bears emphasizing, worried about the need to protect the home shores from prospective foreign enemies; unlike their counterparts in Europe's chancelleries, they were able to take the nation's seeming invulnerability to foreign attack for granted. TR's seizure of the Panama Canal Zone, his "corollary" to the Monroe Doctrine, and his mediatory efforts following the Russo-Japanese War; Taft's "dollar diplomacy"; Wilson's interventionism in the Caribbean and his efforts to contain the more radical elements of the Mexican, Chinese, and Russian revolutions—all those initiatives stemmed from basic calculations about the likely benefits to be derived for America's economy and society from a more powerful, assertive, and economically expansionist United States. When these presidents did identify potential "threats" overseas—and the distinction here is crucial—they invariably recognized them as threats to U.S. *interests* rather than as threats to U.S. *national security*.

Bolder than any of his predecessors, Wilson took a near missionary stance toward world politics. He visualized the United States as the key historical agent in what he confidently believed would be the world's transformation from chaos, imperialism, and revolution to liberal rationality and order. The stable, orderly, and peaceful world Wilson envisioned was to be governed by the principles of free trade, self-determination, collective security, and respect for international law. In such a world, Wilson was convinced, the American economic and political system could prosper and flourish. His commitment to the liberal transformation of the world, so evident in his famous fourteen points address during World War I and in his subsequent efforts to bring that vision to fruition at the Versailles Peace Conference, merged his idealist convictions with his hardheaded sense of American self-interest.

Wilson's deep humanitarian-religious convictions can hardly be doubted. Yet they coexisted with an eminently practical strain that was sharply attuned to the relationship between foreign developments and the health of the domestic system. Wilson had a deep appreciation for the complex needs of a national economy already beginning to dominate the global marketplace; he was convinced that world interdependence compelled the United States to play a commanding role in international affairs, or suffer for its failure to mold the external environment in the manner most conducive to U.S. needs. He believed that the technological efficiency and superiority of Americans made U.S. preeminence the most likely outcome of any fair international competition. Given a chance, Wilson once predicted, "the skill of American workmen would dominate the markets of all the globe." One of America's chief purposes, consequently, was "to enrich the commerce of our own states and of the world with the products of our mines, our farms, and our factories, with the creations of our thought and the fruits of our character."

What was best for the material well-being of the United States, in short, needed to be pursued aggressively. And what was best for the United States was what was best for the world as a whole. Idealism in Wilsonian thought thus merged seamlessly with realism: the pursuit of a better world with the pursuit of a more prosperous and peaceful American domestic order.

Wilson's decision to bring the United States into World War I in April 1917, although triggered by Germany's decision to launch unrestricted submarine warfare earlier that year, chiefly stemmed from those broader considerations. It bears emphasizing that this decision did not derive from fears about America's physical safety. Wilson did not see the Kaiser's government as a threat in that sense. How could a Germany bogged down in a draining war on the European continent, and with no realistic prospect of military success in the near future, possibly pose a serious menace to the security of the United States? Wilson's war decision was the product, instead, of several other considerations: among them, his abhorrence of Germany's violation of human rights, its flouting of basic precepts of international law, and its wholesale assault on the freedom of neutral nations to engage in legitimate commerce during wartime. Yet those concerns alone, though critical, cannot fully explain his war decision. Wilson also brought the United States into the European conflict because he identified a unique opportunity to bring the conflict to a speedy close while helping to shape the ultimate peace settlement. Only active American engagement in the war, the president realized, could earn the United States a seat at the peace table, and Wilson needed that seat if he was to play the leading role in constructing the postwar order that he desired. Above all, he sought a durable peace, a peace based on the principles most conducive to the flourishing of the American economic and social order.

Perhaps Wilson himself best expressed America's concrete economic stake in the postwar peace settlement during a May 1919 message that he sent to Congress. "Peculiar and very stimulating conditions await our commerce and industrial enterprise in the immediate future," he remarked in a forceful defense of the Versailles treaty.

> Unusual opportunities will presently present themselves to our merchants and producers in foreign markets, and large fields for profitable investment

will be opened to our free capital. . . . I believe that our business men, our merchants, our manufacturers and our capitalists will have the vision to see that prosperity in one part of the world ministers to prosperity everywhere; that there is in a very true sense a solidarity of interest throughout the world of enterprise, and that our dealings with the countries that have need of our products and our money will teach them to deem us more than ever friends whose necessities we seek in the right way to serve. . . .

Of course, Wilson lost the treaty vote in the Senate, having foolishly gambled his dwindling political capital on a treaty that allowed no further modifications or reservations. That tactical blunder cost him, and his new world order, dearly. Yet the epic ratification struggle that blocked U.S. entry into the League of Nations, the centerpiece of Wilson's program, should not be allowed to obscure the fundamental points of agreement between treaty proponents and treaty opponents. Aside from a handful of old-fashioned isolationists—the so-called irreconcilables—there was a remarkable degree of consensus among Democratic and Republican senators about the need for the United States to assume a position of full engagement with, and leadership of, the wider world. The vast majority of senators were internationalists who recognized, as fully as did Wilson, that the American economic and social order was dependent upon the preservation of a peaceful, stable, predictable world open to the penetration of American capital. The health of the domestic system demanded nothing less.

The key difference was between those who agreed with Wilson that American interests would best be served by involvement in a League of Nations that the United States could mold and control in its own interests, and those who feared that the league represented too great a risk since *it* might actually control the United States. Put in other terms, both sides wanted an American empire—informal, to be sure, but an empire nonetheless. Wilson's version of empire, however, seemed to call for greater sacrifices, and greater risks, than most Republicans thought necessary.

Their most articulate spokesman, Charles Evans Hughes, who fittingly became secretary of state and the nation's chief diplomatic strategist at the inception of the Republican ascendancy of the 1920s, envisioned a different role for the United States: a role that leavened Wilsonian internationalism with a strong dose of American unilateralism. It was to be, in the apt characterization of historian Warren Cohen, an "empire without tears."

It was not an empire in the classic sense of formal territorial acquisitions and direct rule over other peoples. Rather, it was an empire that sought markets, influence, and control through nonmilitary instruments of power; military muscle was to be used only as a last resort and only when and where it could be used effectively and at minimal cost—such as in Latin America. Clearly American political, economic, and cultural power and influence continued to spread in the interwar period. In virtually every sense, the United

States was the world's premier power throughout the 1920s and 1930s. By the end of World War I, it had become the world's leading creditor nation; New York had by then supplanted London as the financial capital of the world capitalist system. Between 1914 and 1929, the value of U.S. exports more than doubled, and U.S. private investments abroad grew fivefold. In fact, the United States so outdistanced its chief economic rivals during these years that by 1929 American national income was substantially greater than that of Great Britain, France, Germany, Canada, and Japan *combined*.

Republican statesmen of the 1920s and early 1930s sought to use American economic clout and political influence to bring about what one called "a commercial and non-military stabilization of the world." In 1931, the State Department's John Carter summarized the dominant strand in American thinking thusly:

> Our world policy could be summarized as "prosperity and peace" were it not that this oversimplification disguises the perfectly solid self-interest involved in such a policy and suggests hypocrisy rather than national common sense. Prosperity abroad aids prosperity in America, and general international peace both prevents the economic waste of war and precludes the necessity for piling up economically wasteful armaments.

Much of what the United States focused its diplomatic energies on in the 1920s—from the disarmament agreements negotiated at the Washington Conference of 1921–1922 to the various efforts designed to encourage European territorial settlements and help restore economic productivity in Europe to the initiatives aimed at easing the complex debt-reparation tangle left by the Versailles treaty—served the larger goal of world peace and prosperity.

By working toward that goal, American leaders were convinced that they could both expand and protect America's foreign trade, thus contributing to prosperity at home and defusing, in the process, the social turmoil sure to follow an economic contraction. "The nations of the world must be reestablished on a sound financial basis if our surplus products are to find an export market," explained Secretary of the Treasury Andrew Mellon in 1928.

> Only in this way can business compute in advance the price it must pay for raw materials and figure more accurately on the price which can be secured for finished products. If this can be done, business can operate on a larger scale and increase its foreign purchases, which means a greater demand for our surplus products and an expansion in business here and in other countries as well.

But the Republican administrations of the 1920s and early 1930s, agreed though they were on the value of foreign trade, were even more fixated on the rapidly growing domestic market for American goods. Many believed that the home market was far more important to American prosperity than markets overseas. Hence American political and business elites believed that their various efforts aimed at promoting a global equilibrium, though certainly important, were not vital to the protection and flourishing of the domestic social and economic order.

Given the absence of any genuine security threats to the United States during the interwar era, it should not be surprising that Washington assumed a lowered profile in world affairs with the onset of the Great Depression. Democratic president Franklin D. Roosevelt, who saw domestic rather than foreign economic measures as the key to American recovery, furthered the trend toward relative international disengagement during his early years in office. The qualifier "relative" is crucial, though, since the United States remained the world's most powerful nation throughout the interwar years—even if an "empire without tears" appeared increasingly more problematic with the breakdown of the post–World War I peace structure during the mid- and late 1930s.

Only with the emergence of militarist regimes in Japan, Germany, and Italy, regimes willing to challenge the status quo in fundamental ways, were questions of security thrust to the fore. And even then, it was not until *after* the outbreak of World War II that American elites were truly forced to rethink the "free security" assumptions that had governed so much of U.S. foreign policy since the early nineteenth century. American diplomatic and military experts expected that a European war, if and when it did occur, would be a rerun of World War I, with static lines and with neither side able to gain the upper hand. Thus as late as the summer of 1938, Hugh Wilson, the U.S. ambassador in Germany, was advising the State Department: "Twenty years ago we tried to save the world and now look at it. If we tried to save the world again, it would be just as bad at the end of the conflict. The older I grow the deeper is my conviction that we have nothing to gain by entering a European conflict, and indeed everything to lose." Wilson's unusually blunt appraisal was based on the common assumption among American analysts that a European conflict, although highly undesirable, would not jeopardize the security of the United States.

The stunningly rapid advance of Germany and Japan during the first half of 1940 forced a fundamental rethinking of that complacent assumption—and compelled a fundamental reconceptualization of the potential dangers that external powers might pose to the physical safety of the United States. By mid-1940, Hitler's forces stood in control of much of western Europe and were knocking on the door of Britain, the chief remaining holdout. Japanese forces, long ensconced in China, were threatening to gain control over much of Southeast Asia as well; with the Nazi occupations of colonial overlords France and the Netherlands, opportunity beckoned. With a great sense of urgency, the Roosevelt administration commissioned a series of studies to assess how American interests might be adversely affected, in the short term and in the long term, by a Nazi-dominated Europe and a Japanese-dominated East Asia. The results of those efforts were hardly encouraging to FDR. As the historian Melvyn P. Leffler has emphasized, Roosevelt and his top planners worried that if Hitler maintained, and consolidated, his hold on the continent he could dictate the terms of trade between the United States and Europe while bringing the raw material producing states of Latin America to heel in a greater German-dominated trading bloc. To compete, the United States might need to impose unprecedented governmental controls over the export sector, interfering with market mechanisms and limiting the traditional freedoms enjoyed by private capital within the American political economy.

Changes of that magnitude were anathema to Roosevelt. "The logic of such implications," he declared,

> Would lead us to embark upon a course of action which would subject our producers, consumers, and foreign traders, and ultimately the entire nation, to the regimentation of a totalitarian system. For it is naive to imagine that we could adopt a totalitarian control of our foreign trade and at the same time escape totalitarian regimentation of our internal economy.

Roosevelt insisted that the United States could not become "a lone island in a world dominated by the philosophy of force. Such an island represents to me . . . a helpless nightmare of a people without freedom—the nightmare of a people lodged in prison, handcuffed, hungry, and fed through the bars from day to day by the contemptuous, unpitying masters of other continents."

The president's firm opposition to the Axis powers and his liberal provision of aid to the allies in the pre–Pearl Harbor period was inspired, as Leffler so trenchantly puts it:

> by his recognition that Axis domination of Eurasia would demand a reconfiguration of the American and Western Hemisphere economies, an unprecedented role for government, a huge increment in defense expenditures, and eternal vigilance against internal threats from fifth columnists as well as against external aggression from Axis powers themselves. In such a context, personal freedoms and individual liberties would have difficulty surviving.

Since Germany appeared to be growing stronger rather than weaker as it absorbed additional territory—a frightening reversal of the World War I pattern—FDR realized that time was not necessarily on America's side. Hitler's Germany, in a formal, tripartite alliance after September 1940 with Italy and Japan, was gaining the potential for unprecedented military/industrial strength. Unless Germany and its allies were defeated, Roosevelt and his top strategists feared, American military/industrial power would soon be dwarfed by that of the Axis powers. The physical safety of the American homeland would then be endangered. America's core political and economic values, moreover, would be gravely compromised by the countermeasures needed to compete with the Axis powers.

A fundamental lesson emerged here that has continued to shape American thinking about foreign policy through the World War II and cold war eras right up to the present: namely, that no potential adversary or coalition of adversaries should ever again be allowed to gain preponderant control over the territories, resources, military base sites, and industrial infrastructure of the Eurasian heartland. For if that occurred, the international system would be badly destabilized, the balance of world power dangerously distorted, and the physical safety of the United States put at grave risk.

Such thinking carried over to the postwar era and lay behind the expansive national security requirements that shaped U.S. cold war strategy. A National Security Council paper of March 1948 warned, for example, that

> between the United States and the USSR there are in Europe and Asia areas of great potential power which if added to the existing strength of the Soviet world would enable the latter to become so superior in manpower, resources and territory that the prospect for the survival of the United States as a free nation would be slight.

Imbued with the lessons of World War II, U.S. policymakers during the late 1940s thus came to see the Soviet Union as much the same kind of threat that Germany had been earlier in the decade. The widely divergent ideological underpinnings of the two states concerned U.S. officials much less than the power potential, manifest and latent, that each represented.

The problem that the Soviet Union posed for the United States in the early postwar period was not exclusively, or even primarily, a function of the aggressive actions undertaken by the Stalinist regime—or of that regime's military capabilities, for that matter. Rather, American apprehensions derived largely from the instability inherent in an international system reeling from global depression, the massive destruction and dislocation caused by world war, and the wave of anticolonial rebellions sweeping the Third World. Those conditions gave the Kremlin countless opportunities to expand its power and influence without resorting to military force. The positive appeal of communism's promises, coupled with the seemingly miraculous transformation of the Soviet Union in a mere generation from a backward country to a military-industrial powerhouse, captured the imagination of nationalists and revolutionaries across the globe. That powerful ideological attraction was especially unsettling to American leaders since it proved so difficult to combat. U.S. analysts, moreover, assumed that Communist parties and movements everywhere would be subservient to the Soviet fatherland. By any reasonable standard, the United States stood at the high-water mark of its power in the early postwar era. American decision makers were, nevertheless—however paradoxically—haunted by a sense of their nation's vulnerability.

In response to this newly discovered sense of vulnerability, and in furtherance of its long-standing desire to forge an external environment conducive to American interests and values, the United States pursued a twofold strategy throughout the cold war. On the one hand, it adopted the celebrated containment policy. Containment's hallmarks included many of the seminal defensive initiatives of the early postwar years: the Truman Doctrine, the Marshall Plan, NATO, the economic resuscitation of Germany and Japan, the anchoring of those former enemy states in the western alliance system, the buildup of a huge nuclear arsenal to deter Soviet aggression, and much more. Those initiatives were designed especially to contain and constrain the Soviet Union, thereby precluding the emergence of another set of circumstances by which a hostile power might gain direct or indirect control over the Eurasian heartland.

At the same time, the United States pursued a more positive strategy, using its power to help reform the world capitalist system along lines most compatible with America's material needs. It is what National Security Council document NSC-68 of April 1950 rather disingenuously referred to as building "a healthy international environment." The push for a global open door for trade and investment, for the free covertibility of currencies, the pegging of the dollar to gold, the enshrinement of the dollar as the pillar of the world economy, the establishment at the Bretton Woods Conference of the World Bank and the International Monetary Fund as central instruments of a new, presumably more stable world economic regime—all stemmed from the U.S. determination to create a vibrant, depression-proof, international economic order. Such an order, American elites were convinced, was essential to the peace, prosperity, stability, and predictability that the American political economy needed. The alternative, moreover, looked to be chaos, revolution, and conflict; and after a horrific war that had claimed as many as fifty-five million lives, no American policymaker considered such an alternative acceptable.

The two strategies—containing the Soviet Union and forging a stable, American-dominated world economic order—became inseparably linked throughout the cold war era. Each, it bears emphasizing, meant empire; and each led to conspicuous policies of empire building on the part of the United States. Historians have spilled quantities of ink debating whether American postwar expansion was dictated more by security needs or more by the needs of the American political economy. My aim is not to resolve that debate by pinpointing the precise ratio of each that went into American cold war decision making. That would be an impossible task under any circumstances. Rather, it is to call attention to the convergence between the strategic and material goals pursued by the United States, while emphasizing that the *new departure* for the United States during the postwar period was its security fixation. For the first time since the early nineteenth century, American elites, together with the American people as a whole, were confronted with what seemed to be a very real danger to the physical safety of the American homeland. The rapid buildup of a Soviet nuclear arsenal from 1949 onward just deepened that sense of vulnerability, as did the establishment that same year of a communist regime in China that was closely allied to the Soviet Union. Americans had always looked to the diplomatic realm for ways to increase domestic prosperity and harmony. After 1940, they looked overseas also—even primarily—for ways to help fend off potential dangers. That, I submit, represents the critical discontinuity in American foreign relations when one takes a long view spanning the entirety of the twentieth century.

The inexorable logic of empire led to a far-reaching transformation of the United States after 1945. A national security state was forged, and the American people mobilized, to wage permanent warfare against the communist menace and the threat it seemed to pose to the American way of life. In the event, the United States became an increasingly militarized state and society. As historian Michael Sherry has shrewdly observed:

> Militarization reshaped every realm of American life—politics and foreign policy, economics and technology, culture and social relations—making America a profoundly different nation. To varying degrees, almost all groups were invested in it and attracted to it—rich and poor, whites and nonwhites, conservatives and liberals . . . Certainly, all were changed by it.

By the end of the 1950s, the United States occupied approximately 450 military bases in some thirty-five different countries. It had binding security pacts with virtually every Latin American country and with twenty additional countries outside the Western Hemisphere. By that time, approximately one million Americans were stationed overseas in forty-two different countries. The United States had become by then, as it has remained, a determining force in world affairs and a critical influence in the political, economic, and social horizons of scores of countries and hundreds of millions of people around the world.

The cold war initially focused on Europe, of course, the traditional cockpit of great power rivalry and ideological contestation. But by 1949–1950, with the division of Europe into American-led and Soviet-led spheres of influence largely complete, an uneasy stability prevailed there that has actually led some scholars to dub the postwar era "the Long Peace." Elsewhere, of course, the world was anything but peaceful. In fact, most of the major East-West crises of the cold war erupted not in Europe but in the Third World, including nearly all that threatened to escalate into direct Soviet-American confrontations. As well, the vast bulk of the armed conflicts that have broken out since the end of the Second World War have been fought in the Third World. It is particularly telling that all but two hundred thousand of the estimated twenty million people who died in wars fought between 1945 and 1990 were felled during conflicts that raged across various parts of Asia, Africa, and Latin America.

The cold war impelled American strategists to view virtually the entire world, even areas way beyond the Eurasian heartland, as potentially vital to the national security of the United States. A series of perceived interconnections made it difficult for America's cold warriors to differentiate between areas of vital importance and those of peripheral value. First of all, the resources and markets of much of the Third World were considered essential to the health of the world economy, the economic recoveries of Western Europe and Japan, and America's own commercial and military requirements. If certain economically and strategically valuable Third World countries fell under Soviet control, moreover, the Kremlin could strengthen its military-industrial power while that of the West would be correspondingly weakened. In addition, the political exigencies of America's two-party system made the "loss" of any additional territory to communism, from the Truman administration onward, a political liability of potentially catastrophic proportions.

The psychological underpinnings of power, best captured by the frequently invoked concept of America's credibility, further elevated the stakes at play for the United States in the Third World—even in its distant periphery. Washington policymakers reflexively viewed any Soviet intervention, threatened intervention, aid offer, or diplomatic initiative anywhere across the globe as a test from which other states, large and small, would derive important lessons about the power and resolve of the respective superpowers. The United States, consequently, vested enormous significance in each and every Third World challenge or hot spot—from South Korea, Vietnam, Laos, and Indonesia to Egypt, the Congo, Angola, and Nicaragua—regardless of the intrinsic strategic or economic value of the territory in question. A State Department White Paper on Laos of 1959, for example, insisted that that landlocked country of three million people actually constituted "a front line of the free world." Similarly, President Ronald Reagan, in his various appeals for additional aid to the Nicaraguan *contras*, emphasized that the security and welfare of the United States could be grievously compromised by developments in Central America. "If we cannot defend ourselves there," he warned in one speech, "we cannot expect to prevail elsewhere. Our credibility would collapse, our alliances would crumble, and the safety of our homeland would be put in jeopardy."

The abiding need of the United States to demonstrate, to allies and adversaries alike, its strength, resolution, determination, and dependability thus led to a blurring of distinctions between vital and peripheral interests. It was a pattern familiar to other empires throughout history, as was America's consequent overextension—or "imperial overstretch," in the phrase made famous by the historian Paul Kennedy.

The American empire did, indeed, undergo a spectacular expansion throughout the postwar era. Most of America's empire building derived, as noted above, from the heightened sense of vulnerability that formed so instrumental an element of the cold war mind set. The deeper reasons for America's fixation with its presumed vulnerability, at a time when its power was actually at a historic peak, probably lie more within the realm of social psychology than within the realms of geopolitics or political economy. Regardless of the precise origins of American fears, though, they were quite real to a whole generation of U.S. policymakers. In that regard, it bears emphasizing that the national security interests that Americans identified in Western Europe, East and Southeast Asia, Central America, the Middle East, and virtually everywhere else on the planet did not derive from self-aggrandizing territorial ambitions. Nor did they emerge primarily from America's economic ambitions. The American cold war empire was essentially a defensive empire. Built to contain Moscow, Beijing, and the indigenous revolutionaries who might ally with one or the other of the communist powers, it was the product of America's fears rather than its greed. But it was, nonetheless, an empire, and it contained the inherent pitfalls and tensions traditionally associated with all imperial projects.

The Vietnam War brought home to Americans the high costs of empire. It triggered a wrenching domestic debate about the price of American globalism, a debate that raged fiercely throughout the United States during the late 1960s and early 1970s. Spurred by the steadily mounting social, economic, and political costs of the Vietnam conflict, it touched virtually every corner of American society, dividing ordinary citizens, political leaders, government officials, and nongovernmental elites alike. Not since the Civil War, a century earlier, had Americans found themselves polarized so profoundly over a single issue. But the Vietnam War was, of course, not really a single issue; it served, rather, as a uniquely potent symbol of the global interventionism—and overextension—of the cold war era. As such, the conflict in Southeast Asia became the touchstone for a long-delayed national debate about the meaning, purpose, and price of empire.

The public's repudiation of the war forced a disengagement and retrenchment in Southeast Asia and other areas. It also compelled a sober reexamination of the limits of American power after the mid-1970s. Some historians have labeled this period a "retreat-from-empire." But that term, however useful, oversimplifies a process that involved more readjustment to changing realities than actual retreat.

Since Vietnam, of course, the cold war itself has come to an abrupt end, and America's chief postwar rival has imploded. That has left the United States as the planet's sole remaining superpower. Scholars will long debate the precise melange of causes that led, by the late 1980s, to the demise of the cold war and the concomitant collapse of the Soviet Union. According to George Shultz, secretary of state throughout much of the Reagan administration, the United States in the end won the "titanic struggle" with Soviet communism partly as a result of adept leadership and partly as a result of the superiority of American values. Shultz's perspective may amount to little more than a simplistically self-serving gloss on a most complex historical process. Yet the veteran diplomat's emphasis on the critical role played by values, ideas, and culture in America's cold war victory commands our attention. Arguably, the widespread appeal and attraction of American culture has contributed mightily to America's contemporary global preeminence, perhaps as much as its military strength and nuclear arsenal have.

By culture I mean here not just America's traditional espousal of democratic values, individual rights, and free markets, but the influence of American consumer capitalism and popular culture—in all their various guises. "The hegemony of American popular culture in Europe could hardly be more total," observed American writer Susan Sontag from her villa in Italy in May 1999. "One has to go back to the Roman Empire for a similar instance of cultural hegemony," observed the German political analyst Josef Joffe two years earlier. "Actually, there is no comparison," he quickly added. "America's writ encircles the globe, penetrating all layers of society. Modern mass culture, for better or worse, is American."

Some, but hardly all, of the security fears that earlier proved so dominant have faded in importance in this new era. No longer, presumably, do American policymakers lie awake at night fretting about the prospects of a hostile power gaining sway over the Eurasian heartland. Nor can many now be haunted by the possibility that the global power balance might tip suddenly against the United States. Although enemies abound—from Iraq and Libya to Serbia and North Korea—and the future direction of both Russia and China remain highly uncertain, no other country in the foreseeable future seems likely to acquire the combination of military capabilities and ideological appeal that made the Soviet Union so formidable a foe throughout the cold war era. American security may not be "free" in the pre-1940 sense, but the security environment of the post–cold war epoch appears much closer to that of the early twentieth century than to that of the cold war period.

As security threats have receded, economic interests have reemerged as America's principal diplomatic focus. President Bill Clinton's influential secretary of commerce, Ron Brown, well captured the shift in priorities when, in 1993, he proclaimed: "Commercial interests are now on an equal par with security in the world of foreign policy." Clinton himself has made this point repeatedly. "Building a new structure of opportunity and peace through trade, investment and commerce," the president emphasized in 1995, ranked as the cardinal objective of U.S. foreign policy in the post–cold war era. The United States still seeks to mold the world beyond its shores in its own image, of course, but it pursues those efforts now as much to make the world receptive to American products and values as to protect the nation from perceived outside dangers.

Is the United States, then, still an empire? Does the framework sketched at the outset of this chapter still hold on the eve of the new millenium? I believe so. But it is a very different kind of an empire once again: not the modest territorial empire of the early twentieth century; not the defensive cold war empire that reached its zenith during the 1950s and 1960s; not the empire-in-(partial)-retreat that followed the Vietnam debacle. Rather, America now stands as the world's dominant power, in "hard" and "soft" terms. It is a power without serious rivals, exercising, in the view of U.S. authorities, a form of "benign hegemony" for which the rest of the world should be grateful—Albright's "indispensable nation."

In the view of many non-Americans, however, the United States is simply the bully that acts unilaterally to get its own way because it can. "One reads about the world's desire for American leadership only in the United States," a British diplomat recently sneered. "Everywhere else one reads about American arrogance and unilateralism." But that, too, is hardly new.

Whatever one's perspective on America's exercise of global leadership in our own times, though, there can be little doubt that the appellation "American empire" remains a fitting one. The United States has been an empire throughout the twentieth century. And that, I would hazard to guess, is what it is likely to remain for a very long time to come.

SUGGESTIONS FOR FURTHER READING

Becker, William H., and Samuel F. Wells, Jr. *Economics and World Power: An Assessment of American Diplomacy since 1789.* New York: Columbia University Press, 1984.

Cohen, Warren I. *Empire without Tears: America's Foreign Relations, 1921–1933.* New York: Knopf, 1987.

———. *America in the Age of Soviet Power, 1945–1991.* Vol. 4 of *Cambridge History of American Foreign Relations.* New York: Cambridge University Press, 1993.

Costigliola, Frank. *Awkward Dominion: American Political, Economic, and Cultural Relations with Europe, 1919–1933.* Ithaca, N.Y.: Cornell University Press, 1984.

Gaddis, John Lewis. *Strategies of Containment: A Critical Appraisal of Postwar American National Security Policy.* New York: Oxford University Press, 1982.

———. *We Now Know: Rethinking Cold War History.* Oxford: Clarendon Press, 1997.

Garthoff, Raymond L. *Detente and Confrontation: American-Soviet Relations from Nixon to Reagan.* Washington, D.C.: Brookings, 1985.

Hogan, Michael J., ed. *America in the World: The Historiography of American Foreign Relations since 1941.* New York: Cambridge University Press, 1996.

———, ed. "The American Century: A Roundtable (Part I)." *Diplomatic History* 23 (Spring 1999): 157–370.

Iriye, Akira. *The Globalizing of America, 1913–1945.* Vol. 3 of *Cambridge History of American Foreign Relations.* New York: Cambridge University Press, 1993.

Kolko, Gabriel. *Anatomy of a War: Vietnam, the United States, and the Modern Historical Experience.* New York: Pantheon, 1985.

LaFeber, Walter. *The American Search for Opportunity, 1865–1913.* Vol. 2 of *Cambridge History of American Foreign Relations.* New York: Cambridge University Press, 1993.

Leffler, Melvyn P. *A Preponderance of Power: National Security, the Truman Administration, and the Cold War.* Stanford, Calif.: Stanford University Press, 1992.

———. *The Specter of Communism: The United States and the Origins of the Cold War, 1917–1953.* New York: Hill and Wang, 1994.

Levin, N. Gordon. *Woodrow Wilson and World Politics: America's Response to War and Revolution.* New York: Oxford University Press, 1968.

Lundestad, Geir. *The American "Empire" and Other Studies of U.S. Foreign Policy in Comparative Perspective*. New York: Oxford University Press, 1990.

McCormick, Thomas J. *America's Half-Century: United States Foreign Policy in the Cold War*. Baltimore: Johns Hopkins University Press, 1989.

McMahon, Robert J. *The Limits of Empire: The United States and Southeast Asia since World War II*. New York: Columbia University Press, 1999.

Paterson, Thomas G. *On Every Front: The Making and Unmaking of the Cold War*. Rev. ed. New York: Norton, 1992.

Sherry, Michael S. *In the Shadow of War: The United States since the 1930s*. New Haven, Conn.: Yale University Press, 1995.

5 | WORK PLACES
The Economy and the Changing Landscape of Labor, 1900–2000

KEVIN BOYLE

The economic history of the twentieth-century United States is written in the countless places where Americans have worked and lived. It is written in the shuttered mines of West Virginia, the abandoned sharecroppers' shacks of the Mississippi delta, and the empty steel mills of northern Indiana. It is written in California's strawberry fields and Alaska's oil fields, Detroit's auto factories and Seattle's aerospace plants. It is written in the skyscrapers of New York City and Chicago, the technology parks of North Carolina's research triangle, and the shopping malls of the nation's suburbs. It is written in the graceful homes of Oak Park, Illinois; the curving streets of Levittown, New Jersey; and the sun-baked barrio of south-side San Diego.

This chapter traces the economic transformations that have swept across the United States in the twentieth century. The story could be told in the terms favored by economists and policymakers: movements in the gross national product, changes in the balance of trade, alterations in the money supply. I will certainly draw on such terms; they are too important to ignore. The centerpiece of this story, however, will be the world of work, all those places where Americans made goods, made money, made homes, made lives for themselves and their families.

The story comes in three parts. By the dawn of the twentieth century, the United States had become the world's greatest industrial nation, its economy driven by a vast complex of mines, factories, rail lines, and shops that had not existed a half century earlier. Though immensely powerful, the industrial system was also very unstable, undermined by structural weaknesses and sweeping injustices. The rise and fall of the industrial system from the late nineteenth century to the Great Depression constitutes the first part of the story. The second part tells of that period, roughly from 1933 to 1970, when Americans at last seemed to conquer the system's instability, to make the system

101

work. The success was far from complete; many Americans continued to suffer from poverty and economic fear. Millions of others did benefit from the system, though, including many who had borne the burdens of industrial life earlier in the century. Then, in the final three decades of the century, the industrial system cracked. That dramatic event shifted the center of the economy, a shift detailed in the third part of the chapter. Thus Americans end the century as they began it, struggling to adjust to a new economic system, a system at once extraordinarily powerful and frighteningly insecure.

THE WORKSHOP OF THE WORLD

Three years before the new century began, Ramsey MacDonald, the future prime minister of Great Britain, visited Chicago. He was appalled at what he saw. The city was "like a demented creature," he wrote, "harum scarum, filthy from top to toe." It was a fair characterization. Perhaps more than any other place in America, Chicago had benefited from the great wave of late-nineteenth-century industrialization, which had made the frontier cow town into one of the world's great cities. But Chicago, like the rest of the nation, had also suffered from the unsystematic, uncontrolled nature of the industrialization process, which left its scars upon the land and its people.

Since the early years of the nineteenth century, the nation's most innovative and aggressive businessmen had committed themselves to building mass-production industries. By 1900 they had succeeded. Once overwhelmingly an agricultural nation, the United States' economy was now defined by the ability of its factories to produce a staggering quantity and array of goods. "We have long been the granary of the world," a banker exulted in 1898. "We now aspire to be its workshop. . . ." Many of the goods businessmen produced were basic consumer items: cloth, clothing, shoes. Others were luxury goods, from cigarettes to bicycles to pianos, some of which had not even existed a few decades before. Still other manufacturers devoted themselves to making products, such as machine tools, necessary to create the consumer goods flooding into the marketplaces. Production was not distributed evenly across the country. Eighty-six percent of the nation's goods were made north of the Mason-Dixon line and east of the Rocky Mountains, essentially in a broad, and ever-expanding, urban complex stretching from New England to Baltimore, Philadelphia to St. Louis. But industrialization reached everywhere. Miners, lumbermen, and oilmen across the West and Southwest labored to supply the raw materials necessary to keep the factories running and the cities heated. Farmers, sharecroppers, and farm laborers, 38 percent of gainfully employed Americans in 1900, grew the food that fed the cities, or the crops, such as tobacco and cotton, that fed the factories. And the web of rail lines, almost 200,000 miles of track in 1900, brought the flood of goods into the small towns and rural backwaters that had once seemed so distant from the big cities. Historian Edward Ayers captures the novelty of the trains' cargo in the rural south. "Parcels contained fashions from New York or patterns from Butterick," he says, "shoes from Massachusetts or suits from Philadelphia. No matter its content, each box carried more than an inert product. It brought an implicit message: this is the new way of the world."[1]

All of this had been made possible by what the Sears, Roebuck catalogue called "wonderfully ingenious machines." Throughout the nineteenth century, businessmen had spent massive sums to develop machinery capable of making goods that heretofore had been produced by craftsmen, and could do so, moreover, at a much more rapid pace than craftsmen could manage. Once in place, the machinery made American workers much more efficient. Between 1870 and 1900, per-capita output increased every year, on average, by 2.1 percent, almost a percentage point higher than the pre–Civil War high. Productivity gains were not restricted to manufacturing. New equipment on the farms, particularly on the Great Plains, made American agriculture more more efficient. Aided by generous government grants, businessmen had also constructed a technologically sophisticated transportation network that linked factories and customers from coast to coast.

As it spread across the nation, the industrial system generated massive numbers of jobs. A quarter of American workers in 1900 held jobs as factory operatives or laborers, a far higher percentage than had done so a few decades before. Eleven percent more worked as craftsmen and foremen, and another 18 percent worked in white-collar jobs—the vast army of salespeople, clerical workers, managers, shopkeepers, and nondomestic service workers—that the industrial system generated. To fill the factories and the offices, employers had to push up wage rates: manufacturing wages, for instance, increased 50 percent between 1860 and 1900.

In response, millions of people poured into the industrial heartland. Perhaps five million of the newcomers in the last four decades of the nineteenth century came from the American countryside. Many more came from abroad. Over three million immigrants arrived in the United States between 1900 and 1905 alone, part of a great global stream of people whose lives had been fundamentally altered by the industrialization process not only in the United States but in other parts of the world as well. The industrial system immediately absorbed them: by the turn of the century, immigrants dominated industrial labor in many cities. In Pittsburgh's great steel plants, for example, 89 percent of the unskilled workers were foreign born. "The work is heavy, but I don't mind," an immigrant wrote his wife. "Let it be heavy but let it last without interruption."

For all its vitality, though, the turn-of-the-century economy was also deeply troubled. Some of the problems were systemic. Businessmen needed huge doses of investment capital to maintain the pace of technological innovation. The American financial system, underdeveloped, unpredictable, and unstable, could not consistently meet the need. Business' rigid adherence to the gold standard added to the problem by limiting the amount of money in circulation. Manufacturers were also harmed by their own limits. In many cases, company officials were much more adept at producing goods than they were at matching the goods with market demand. As a result, manufacturers repeatedly found themselves producing more than the public was willing or able to consume. In combination, the weaknesses of the financial system and of company management caused repeated and intense economic downturns, the scourge of late-nineteenth-century American capitalism. When inventories piled up, manufacturers cut production and employment, in the process triggering recession. Financial and monetary shortcomings then transformed recession into depression, most terribly in 1873 and 1893. The problem was even greater than that, though. Even in prosperous years, industrial workers could count on weeks, perhaps even months, of unemployment as their bosses cleared their warehouses of stockpiled goods.

Intense competition added another layer of problems. Determined to control a larger share of the market than their competitors, manufacturers continually tried to cut their prices. The only way to do so was to cut costs. Individual farmers, likewise caught in competition's grip, produced more and more each year in hopes of pushing up their profits. The competition had its bright side: in the late nineteenth century the nation's price level actually fell. But the brutal competition put intense pressure on the production process. Industrialists ruthlessly exploited the environment, squeezing it for raw materials, filling it with debris from the production process. Those Americans, typically workers, who were unlucky enough to live near factories or mines therefore had to endure vile conditions: the smell of the stockyards, the poisons of the chemical plants, the soot that settled on clothes and food.

Worse yet, competition also led employers to relentlessly push their machinery and their workers to maximize output. In the cotton South, where wage labor had not taken complete hold, landlords ruthlessly exploited the sharecroppers who actually worked the land. The shortage of labor in industry prevented manufacturers from cutting wages, though some certainly tried. In some industries, employers filled their factories with women and children, whom they could pay less than men. More commonly, manufacturers demanded that their employees, male or female, work long days under dangerously unsafe conditions, precautions being too expensive to consider. Foremen enforced owners' demands, sometimes by cajoling their workers, often by intimidating them. The results were predictable. Turn-of-the-century factories, mines, and railroads were deadly places. "In Braddock, it was an exceptional month which didn't see a man crippled or killed outright," Thomas Bell wrote in his 1941 novel of working-class life in the Pennsylvania steel town, *Out of This Furnace.* "American industry, for all its boasting, was still crude and wasteful in its methods; and part of the cost of its education . . . was the lives and bodies of thousands of its workers." Bell knew his subject. In the early days of the new century, he had lost two uncles, both Slovak immigrants, one killed in a fight with a foreman, another gassed to death in an accident at the famous Edgar Thomson steel mill.

The instability and brutality of the system fostered profound conflict at the point of production. In the West and South, farmers afflicted by falling prices and mounting debts launched a massive political revolt—the Populist movement—against tight money and corporate interests. On the shop floor, skilled workers fought to beat back the deskilling process the machine age had wrought and thus to preserve the power they once had had over the production process. For their part, semiskilled and unskilled workers struggled to defend long-standing work and political traditions and to combat oppressive conditions. Many such confrontations took place outside the public's notice, a worker squaring off against his or her foreman, say, amid the clatter of the factory. Other confrontations were epic affairs, hundreds or thousands of unionized workers taking to the streets in dramatic strikes. Strike waves rolled across the nation as the nineteenth century closed: 600,000 workers went on strike in 1886, 700,000 in 1894. Working-class activists followed no single model of unionization; instead, they struggled to find organizational forms and political goals that could stand up to capital's power. The Knights of Labor tried mass mobilization in pursuit of a "corporate commonwealth"; the founders of the American Federation of Labor (AFL) focused more narrowly on craft unionism that sought a fairer share of capital's bounty; fledgling industrial unions like the Western Federation of Miners, the forerunner of the Industrial Workers of the World (IWW), embraced more radical visions of a restructured political economy. No matter what the form, though, farmer and worker movements faced withering opposition. Populism collapsed in the waning days of the 1890s. Though AFL unions enjoyed some success, a phalanx of employers, judges, and government officials beat back most union campaigns, at times doing so in brutal ways. By 1900, only 3.1 percent of workers were unionized. But the cost of victory had been high. Sensitive observers understood that the conflicts of the late nineteenth century had cut deeply into the body politic and that unless treated the wound would continue to fester.

Americans thus began the new century with an economic system that was both profoundly powerful and profoundly troubled. Addressing those problems became the great national project of the first half of the 1900s. Businessmen themselves took up part of the burden. To put an end to the competitive pressures they faced, industrialists launched a massive wave of mergers in the first decade of the twentieth century. The resulting corporate giants—U.S. Steel, DuPont, International Harvester, and Standard Oil, to name but a few—were designed to control their markets. And so they did. By 1904, a single firm accounted for at least 60 percent of total output in each of fifty industries. The largest corporations also instituted new, complex management systems capable of coordinating and controlling from central offices the production and flow of goods, thus bringing a greater degree of stability to the marketplace. Again, new technologies, such as the typewriter and the telephone, made the new systems workable, in the process changing the work routines for millions of white-collar Americans.

A coterie of investment bankers, meanwhile, assumed responsibility for bringing order to the financial markets, particularly the market for industrial securities. Those efforts were intimately linked to the corporate merger and reorganization movements. In fact, the greatest of the investment houses, J.P. Morgan and Company and Rockefeller's National City Bank, were the driving forces behind the most important corporate consolidations, such as U.S. Steel, whose management systems they then remade. "In short," economic historian W. Elliot Brownlee explains, "the investment bankers became the first organizers of the modern industrial economy, as they sought to establish system and regularity in the interests of protecting their investments." Centralization was never complete; there were still many producers in at least some important industries, such as textiles, that did not join the merger mania. But the trend was unmistakable. In the first few decades of the twentieth century, competition gave way to consolidation.

Government officials in the early part of the century likewise joined the search for stability, often over the bitter objections of corporate America. From the municipal level upward, progressive activists tried to overthrow the laissez faire orthodoxy that had dominated public policy in the late nineteenth century. Inspired by an array of political influences, from Bismarck's Germany to the Social Gospel, progressives embraced no coherent ideology. But they agreed that the state needed to use its power to ameliorate what they perceived to be the worst abuses of the industrial system. In state after state, progressives thus fought to outlaw child labor, to improve urban housing, to launch workmen's compensation and unemployment insurance schemes, and to limit the hours women worked in a day. In Washington, meanwhile, progressive policymakers sought to reshape pivotal parts of the economic system. The apogee of those efforts came in 1913, when in a stunning burst of political energy progressives created the federal income tax and Federal Reserve systems. Like so many other progressive reforms, the new mechanisms were limited in their reach. Only a minority of Americans were actually required to pay taxes under the first tax codes, and the Federal Reserve's power was divided among twelve regional banks rather than centralized in a central body. These limitations should not, however, obscure the great leap the progressives had taken. For the first time since the Civil War, the federal government had assumed the power to restructure personal incomes and to maintain and manipulate a national currency.

Together, the structural changes in the economy gave early-twentieth-century industry a much more secure base than it had had in the waning days of the 1890s. Prices moved upward as competion declined. Recessions still occurred, but they were less intense than they had been. Most importantly, with financial markets more stable, entrepreneurs and manufacturers were able to push the industrial system to new heights. The gross national product soared from $19 billion in 1900 to $97 billion in 1928, while productivity continued to increase at its already rapid pace. Much of the increase resulted from businessmen using the system's well-honed production techniques to make a host of new consumer items. Entrepreneurs and inventors often developed the new products. But in keeping with the trend toward consolidation, major corporations soon took control of their production. By the 1920s, industrial giants churned out many of the accoutrements of modern life: radios, washing machines, refrigerators, toothpaste, all products that virtually no American had owned in 1900. Life would never be the same.

The greatest of these new products, the automobile, illustrates the transformation. In 1900, cars were luxury items, handcrafted by skilled workers. Then a handful of brilliant entrepreneurs—Ransome Olds, the Dodge brothers, and of course Henry Ford—developed machines and processes that could do the craftsmen's jobs at a much faster rate. When Ford inaugurated his famous assembly line in 1914, his workers, now largely semiskilled and unskilled, were able to produce a car in one-sixth the time it had taken skilled auto workers just a few years before. The auto manufacturers then relentlessly marketed their products, creating a demand that seemed insatiable. By 1928, there were 20 million cars on the road; there had been fewer than 200,000 just twenty years earlier. The industry's success transformed the automakers into huge firms. In its early days, the industry seemed a throwback to nineteenth-century capitalism. There were a plethora of firms, many of them family owned, all of them competing for a share of the market. But in short order the industry began to consolidate. The pivotal point came in the 1910s, when the investor William Durant, using DuPont money, created the great conglomerate General Motors. Within a decade, GM dominated the auto market.

Social historians have rightly noted the great transformations in American culture the auto industry triggered. Its effects on the economy were no less profound. The industry's exponential growth made it an insatiable consumer of other industrial products, such as steel and glass. It also consumed a massive amount of labor. All told, the auto industry employed 400,000 workers by the mid-1920s, with the greatest auto plant, Ford's sprawling River Rouge complex, alone offering 100,000 jobs. The industry's ratchet effect was even greater. By one estimate, by 1929 one of every six Americans owed his or her job, either directly or indirectly, to the auto industry.

The new consumer industries did not just create jobs; they also altered the nature of work for millions of Americans. Some of the changes were positive. Many workers were able to move into white-collar jobs as industry generated hundreds of thousands of new positions for engineers, accountants, managers, clerks, secretaries, and salespeople. Pay for these jobs ranged widely: in 1929, a typical engineer received $3,468 a year, the equivalent of $30,908 today, whereas the typical salesperson earned only $1,594, $14,206 in today's dollars. Even the lowest paying white-collar job, though, was safer than factory labor and less back-breaking than farm work. Even the latter jobs improved in some important ways. Rising prices in the first three decades of the twentieth century eased the burden for many farmers, particularly in the West. Blue-collar wage rates likewise continued to rise: on average, a manufacturing worker earned 55 percent more in real wages in 1929 than he had in 1900. Many factory hands also worked shorter days than they had in the late nineteenth century, as their bosses became convinced that exhausted workers were not efficient workers. Even the steel industry, the most demanding of employers, had embraced the eight-hour day by the 1920s.

In other ways, however, the world of work remained as harsh as it had been. Southern farmers struggled as cotton prices fluctuated wildly. Tenants and sharecroppers, already desperately poor, saw their incomes plunge. In response, thousands of croppers, black and white, fled the South for the urban North. On the factory floor, foremen continued to push and intimidate workers. Though shortened hours helped reduce the accident rate, factories continued to be extremely dangerous places. New industries were little better than more established ones. Auto workers called Detroit the "eight finger city," so many of its residents having lost digits to the rapid-fire machinery of the assembly line. New production techniques created other problems as well. New machines and more centralized management systems further undermined the power of skilled workers to control the shop floor. Semiskilled and unskilled workers in many consumer industries complained bitterly about the relentless pace of work, a pace made possible by assembly lines that managers could speed up at will. "You could drop over dead," a worker in an electrical plant said, "and they wouldn't stop the line." Given the circumstances, it is not surprising that labor conflict continued to flare. This was particularly the case in the first two decades of the twentieth century: the level of strike activity was higher in the years from 1912 to 1915 than it had ever been before. Progressives responded by trying to promote a system of orderly collective bargaining, managed by government authorities. But their efforts were plagued by problems. Though progressives managed to draw some important working-class activists into their circle, others kept their distance. The leaders of the AFL, the nation's most powerful labor organization, feared that state power, no matter how well intentioned at the start, could be used to destroy workers' freedom to represent their own interests. Far to the AFL's left, the radical IWW rejected progressives as tools of the capitalist class. The more important rejection came from the capitalist class. To be sure, a few sophisticated business-men agreed with the progressives that collective bargaining could reduce class conflict. But most employers continued to see unionization as an unadulter-ated evil. The new conglomerates were particularly virulent in their anti-unionism. The Rockefeller-owned Colorado Fuel and Iron Company was so determined to break a 1913 strike by its workers, for instance, that it triggered a virtual war in the coalfields, during which sixty-six people lost their lives. This was not the stuff of interclass harmony.

Then, when the United States entered World War I in 1917, the balance of power seemed to tip. Desperate to avoid strikes that would cripple military production, the Wilson administration established a federal agency, the Na-tional War Labor Board (NWLB), to promote and supervise collective bar-gaining. What's more, the NWLB seemed willing to sanction union demands that gave factory workers not just better wages but also significant control over their work lives. To settle a series of strikes by machinists in Bridgeport, Con-necticut, for example, the NWLB agreed that workers be allowed to establish shop floor councils that could challenge management control over work pace. Not surprisingly, union membership skyrocketed in the war years, two million new workers signing union cards between 1917 and 1920.

But it was not to last. Almost as soon as the war ended in late 1918, cor-porate America and its conservative political allies launched a massive coun-teroffensive. They forced the Wilson administration to scrap the NWLB. Trad-ing on middle-class fears of radicalism, businessmen also crushed a series of postwar strikes. The union movement reeled under the onslaught. By 1923, the labor movement had lost most of the members it had gained during the war, while some of the largest unions, such as the United Mine Workers, teetered on the edge of collapse. Trapped in the postwar maelstrom, progres-sivism likewise lost its hold, its advocates pushed to the margins of American politics. Thoroughly cowed, the labor movement went into a decade-long re-treat. In the 1920s, strike activity never came close to matching the level it had reached in the first two decades of the century.

Many businessmen thus looked on the 1920s as a golden age for industrial capitalism. The consumer revolution was in full flower; the progressives' in-terference in business affairs had been beaten back; and workers seemed qui-escent. Productivity and profits reached record levels. But the corporations' victories in the late 1910s had come at a very high price. Without government or labor pushing them to do so, businessmen had no reason to share their bounty with the working class. The average worker's wages continued to rise; market pressures saw to that. But they did not rise fast enough to allow them to participate fully in the consumer economy their labor was creating. That was a recipe for disaster.

Sections of the national consumer base had been soft throughout the 1920s: farmers, for example, had suffered from falling prices since the end of

World War I. Many working-class families earned enough to buy lower priced consumer goods, such as radios, but big-ticket items remained beyond their reach. A study of Ford workers, well paid by working-class standards, showed that only 47 percent owned cars in 1929. Middle-class consumption was great enough to offset these weaknesses for much of the 1920s. But by 1928 markets were becoming saturated. The late-nineteenth-century cycle thus reappeared. Inventories began to pile up in warehouses. Employers began laying off workers. In 1929 the economy slid into recession.

In the best of worlds, the Federal Reserve system should have acted to counterbalance the downswing by expanding the money supply. But Federal Reserve officials, obsessed with sustaining the strength of the dollar, did exactly the opposite. Again, the nineteenth-century pattern played itself out. The recession quickly deepened into depression. Factory production dropped off dramatically, the GNP falling 44 percent between 1929 and 1932. The banking system essentially collapsed, while the unemployment rate skyrocketed to 25 percent. Fear spread across the nation as the crisis deepened. "I don't want to steal," a desperate Pennsylvanian wrote his governor, "but I won't let my wife and boy cry for something to eat. . . . How long is this going to keep up? I cannot stand it any longer. . . ." For all intents and purposes, the workshop of the world had shut its doors.

AN ALMOST PERFECT MACHINE

Nestled in the foothills of the Appalachian Mountains, Oak Ridge, Tennessee, was a rural place in the early twentieth century, its rolling land dotted by family farms and tiny villages. Then the federal government arrived. In the 1930s the Tennessee Valley Authority (TVA) built the great Norris Dam just a few miles up the Clinch River, which cut through the region. The dam brought electricity to the region, lighting homes and holding out the promise of economic development. But no one expected the intensity of the development to come.

A few weeks after the bombing of Pearl Harbor, federal officials began buying up the area's homesteads. Contractors then began constructing three sprawling manufacturing complexes, the largest of which covered more area than any building had ever covered before. The area soon swarmed with workers, over thirty thousand by 1943. Nondescript industrial sites from the outside, the complexes were, in fact, production centers for uranium isotopes, pivotal for the production of atomic weapons. Oak Ridge had become a major manufacturing site, a center for the most complex of technologies, and one of the most powerful places on earth.

The federal government's power to foster such transformations stemmed from the brutalities of the Great Depression. As the economy spiraled downward year after year in the early 1930s, many Americans became convinced that it could not be saved without dramatic intervention. From the pulpit and the street-corner soapbox, the editorial page and the seminar room, flowed a stream of proposals for changes in the nation's economic life. Some of the proposals called for minor alterations—little more than tinkering, really—while others envisioned radical change. Then, in March 1933, the new president of the United States, Democrat Franklin D. Roosevelt, took control of the discussion. He would not surrender it for twelve years.

Steeped in the progressive tradition, Roosevelt and his advisers, the New Dealers, assumed that the government must take responsibility for correcting the industrial system's shortcomings. They understood that the shortcomings were great; the depression proved that. But, unlike the era's radicals, they insisted that the essentials of the system could and should be preserved. Thus they applied government power on an unprecedented scale to reinvigorate the system that lay prostrate before them, not to create a new economic order on the remains of the old. The New Deal followed no coherent plan. It was a haphazard project, constructed under the most dire circumstances, shaped by political calculations, and full of false starts and dead ends. Any generalizations thus run the risk of making it far simpler than it was. In the main, however, the Roosevelt administration believed that large-scale capitalism could best be preserved—and the depression most effectively ended—if the federal government shifted power and resources within the system and by so doing made the system more equitable and more just.

Those efforts took far longer than Roosevelt had hoped. By the end of the 1930s FDR had pushed through a number of dramatic reforms, but the most important of these were still not secure. The nation was still mired in depression, albeit a less severe one than when FDR had taken office. Only with World War II would the federal government complete the transformations Roosevelt had envisioned in 1933. Two efforts illustrate the process: the New Dealers' struggle to promote mass unionization, particularly in the largest industries, and their work to promote economic development in those parts of the country that had lagged behind the industrial Northeast and Midwest. The war emergency did not simply bring the New Deal to fruition, however. It also added a new central goal to the government's responsibilities, as Washington took up the task of making the United States the dominant power in world capitalism. The federal government's efforts thus took fifteen years to complete. But in the end the New Dealers succeeded to a degree unimaginable in the dark days of the early 1930s.

Unionization proved to be a brutal battleground. Like his progressive predecessors, Roosevelt believed that a government-supervised system of collective bargaining would foster stability in the work place. Creating such a system, however, was not high on FDR's list of priorities in the early days of his administration. Other liberal Democrats, most notably New York senator

Robert Wagner, were much more committed to the union cause. Wagner and his allies saw unionization as a matter of justice, a way for workers to check the awesome power their employers had over them. They also believed unions could serve as a mechanism for solving the depression. Unionized workers, they reasoned, would force industries to pay higher wages, thus giving the working class the purchasing power they needed to participate in the consumer economy their labor had made. It took two years and a series of bloody strikes to bring Roosevelt around to Wagner's point of view. When he did so, he threw his support behind Wagner's landmark National Labor Relations bill, passed into law in the summer of 1935. The Wagner Act, as it immediately came to be known, guaranteed the right of workers to form unions of their own choosing without employer interference. It also created a permanent government agency, the National Labor Relations Board (NLRB), to enforce the law. At last, the progressive model of collective bargaining was on the statute books.

But it was not yet in operation at the nation's work places. Cautious by nature and experience, the leaders of the AFL had refused to spearhead a drive to organize the mass of American workers. Armed with the Wagner Act's promise of government protection, other unionists took up the cause. Eight union presidents, led by the United Mine Workers' John L. Lewis, broke with the AFL in late 1935 and formed a new labor federation, the Congress of Industrial Organizations (CIO). They then drew to their side a wide array of working-class activists—traditionalists and militants, conservatives and Communists—all pulled together by the promise of a unionization campaign that would cut through the heart of industrial America. And so it did. In one extraordinary year, beginning on a bitterly cold December day in 1936, the CIO launched a frontal assault on the greatest manufacturing corporations in the nation. One by one, they fell before the union onslaught. By the end of 1937, the workers at General Motors, U.S. Steel, and General Electric, all militantly antilabor firms, were organized into CIO unions. In all, the CIO claimed three million members. Large-scale unionization had come to industrial America.

The CIO's success was truly stunning, so stunning that the radicals within its ranks believed it could now push its agenda beyond organizing and toward the reconstruction of the economic order. But for all its new-found power, the CIO remained, in Robert Zieger's phrase, "a fragile juggernaut." Its position depended on the support of the federal government, support it risked the more radical its agenda became. The AFL, stung by the CIO's triumphs, was now undertaking its own organizing drive, which threatened to undercut the CIO's momentum. The workers in some critically important firms—the Ford Motor Company, for example—remained unorganized. And even many of those who had been brought into the CIO remained wary of an organization that had yet to prove its staying power. As the New Deal entered its final days, then, administration officials still could not be sure that their hopes of a permanently unionized industrial work force had been fulfilled.

Then came World War II. To secure extremely lucrative defense contracts, many of the major manufacturers that had avoided unionization in the late 1930s finally conceded their workers' right to organize. In return for a promise not to strike during the war, federal authorities promised that the flood of new workers moving into unionized defense industries would be required to join unions. Together, these breakthroughs pushed union rolls to new heights: by 1945 unions represented 22 percent of the work force and 35 percent of nonagricultural workers. Now more secure, unions had the leverage to deliver better wages, benefits, and working conditions to their rank and file. Despite wartime wage freezes, the average weekly earnings in manufacturing rose by 70 percent. These victories carried a cost. Union militants then, and many labor historians today, contend that organized labor's commitment to the American war effort undermined its ability to criticize industrial capitalism. From Washington's point of view, that was not much of a price to pay. The New Dealers had never seen unionization as a means of attacking the existing economic order. They had seen it as a way of bolstering the system by giving working people a greater sense of justice and a greater ability to participate in the consumer society. By 1945, they had achieved their goals.

The New Dealers could also take pride in the extraordinary geographic redistribution of resources they had wrought since assuming power in 1933. At the onset of the depression, it was commonplace for Westerners and Southerners to complain that their regions were economic colonies of northeast and midwest capital, exploited for their natural resources and prevented from industrializing themselves. The complaint was not really justified; southern underdevelopment, in particular, stemmed less from northern oppression than from southern elites' exploitation of their own region's people. But it captured an essential truth: the West and South were less industrialized, more dependent on agriculture, and much poorer than the the northern industrial core. That fact, the New Dealers believed, made the West and South drags on the national economy.

FDR thus entered office committed to transforming the western and southern economies. As was typical of Roosevelt, he had no plan for doing so. Some 1930s reforms were explicitly developmental. The administration spent millions, for instance, to build dams that would bring water to arid California fields and cheap power—the building bloc of industry—to the Tennessee Valley, the Pacific Northwest, and much of the Southwest. Other reforms sought to undermine long-standing practices that set the South and West apart from the northeastern standard. The 1938 Fair Labor Standards Act established a minimum wage in large part so as to force southern employers to raise their wages to national levels. Still other reforms altered the regional economies in the course of pursuing other goals. To cite the most important example, the Agricultural Adjustment Act (AAA) aimed to boost farm prices by limiting crop production. In the process, however, the act led many southern landlords to purge their plantations of their tenants, thus fundamentally undermining the southern sharecropping system. The changes were often wrenching: the AAA displaced so many croppers that Gunnar Myrdal called the act "an American enclosure movement." The advancements, in contrast, were not always obvious. At the end of the 1930s, the southern and western economies remained behind that of the Northeast. But change had surely come. "The 'outward aspects' of southern economic life had changed much less than the 'inward aspect,'" the historian Gavin Wright says. "The economic underpinnings and social glue that kept the regional economy isolated were no longer present in 1940."[2]

World War II greatly accelerated the pace of economic change in the South and West. Defense dollars poured into the two regions, underwriting the construction of new roads, new military camps, new factories, even new towns. More fundamentally, the administration used wartime spending to give the South and West the industries their newly built infrastructures could support. In the most dramatic cases, federal money made the regions centers of production for entirely new goods: Texas, for instance, was given control of the newborn synthetic rubber industry. The administration also made the South and West competitive with northeastern manufacturers in established industries, such as ship building and aircraft production. The growth of manufacturing triggered dramatic population shifts. Richmond, California, to take one example, had 23,000 residents in 1940. Then Edgar Kaiser build a shipyard there. Within years, Richmond's population had skyrocketed to 123,000. The attraction of war work reinforced the New Deal's undermining of southern agriculture; by one estimate, the South lost 22 percent of its farm population during the war years. The agricultural labor shortage became so severe that the Army assigned German prisoners of war to harvest the cotton crop in some parts of the South. Many Southerners were shocked at the changes the war had brought. "We no longer farm in Mississippi cotton fields," novelist William Faulkner lamented. "We farm now in Washington corridors and Congressional committee-rooms." And so they did. Through the power of war, the South and the West had become pivotal parts of the nation's industrial machine.

American industry, in turn, had assumed a much greater power in the world by 1945 than it had had in 1933. The United States had already become the world's greatest manufacturing nation by the turn of the century. But American businessmen and policymakers did not assume the power on the international stage that the nation's position offered them. They supported protectionist trade policies that prevented U.S. goods from dominating world trade. They did not accept responsibility for maintaining international financial markets, even after Britain, traditionally the world's banker, could no longer do so. They were even wary of international agreements that might have given the United States the means to exercise greater influence abroad.

The depression reinforced the traditional American attitude toward world affairs, as the domestic crisis overwhelmed international concerns. But World War II changed everything. U.S. policymakers became convinced that the global economic instability of the 1930s had helped to push the nations of the world into the abyss of total warfare. The war itself had destroyed the ability of other industrial powers to foster the stability necessary to prevent another such cataclysm. Japan lay in ruins, while Europe, in Winston Churchill's words, had become a "rubble heap, a charnel house." The American economy, meanwhile, had never been more robust. The GNP had risen in real terms by 70 percent between 1939 and the end of the war; industrial production had more than doubled; and the unemployment rate had plummeted to 2 percent. Thus only the United States was in a position to assume responsibility for building a stable global economic order. Policymakers decided that they could not let the moment pass.

They did not. In the course of the 1940s, American officials created a series of economic mechanisms stunning in their sweep. The creators of the International Monetary Fund (IMF) set out to use the strength of the American dollar to create and maintain stable currency rates across the globe, thus fostering secure financial markets and vigorous international trade. The World Bank was designed to expand industrialization's reach by providing poorer countries with the capital they needed to undertake economic development. And the Marshall Plan targeted the battered economies of Europe for billions of dollars in aid to underwrite their recovery. The onset of the cold war narrowed the scope of these efforts, as the communist nations chose not to participate in the American-led global financial arrangements. Even so, the Americans had an extraordinary sphere of influence. From the Australian outback to Iraqi oil fields, from Manila to Manchester, the American economy had become the bedrock upon which the noncommunist world rested.

Franklin Roosevelt did not live to see the results of his administration's efforts. Within a few years of his death, though, it was clear that the New Deal had triumphed in its central goal of strengthening and stabilizing the industrial system created in the early years of the century. Unionization, virtually complete in the central industrial firms by 1950, decreased the degree of conflict on the factory floor. Managers still controlled basic corporate decision making, as they always had, but unionized workers now had a work-place rule of law that afforded them greater protection than ever before. Many workers revelled in the change. "When we talked to the foreman, we talked to the foreman on an equal basis: 'This work's too hard; this man can do the job; this man's got seniority . . . ,'" auto worker Nick DiGaetano recalled of life on the shop floor in the postwar era. "We did not have to stand up like the Italian boys. They tell me in Italy when they go to speak with management . . . they stand up with their hat in their hand."[3] Workers still went on strike, of course, but the collective bargaining system made walkouts less confrontational and more easily resolved. Finally, widespread unionization boosted workers' wages. Average annual wages in manufacturing, for example, were 65 percent higher in real terms in 1950 than they had been in 1925. Unions were not responsible for all of those gains; the demand for labor certainly played a role. But there is no doubt that unions did force employers to pay their workers more—sometimes much more—than they had earlier in the century. With more money in their pockets, working people could become the consumers the New Dealers had hoped they would be.

The policies established in the Roosevelt years ensured that in the postwar era a greater percentage of American workers received the higher wages manufacturing offered. A number of traditionally low-wage sectors had been fatally weakened by the end of the 1940s. In the most dramatic change, only 4 percent of Americans in 1950 worked as farm laborers, down from 18 percent at the turn of the century. The percentage of American workers in factory jobs, in contrast, climbed to 20 percent in 1950, up from 13 percent in 1900, while another 14 percent worked as foremen or craftsmen. Continued defense spending—driven by the cold war—accounted for part of the increased demand for factory workers. In 1951, the defense budget stood at $22.5 billion, much of that money pouring into factories that made tanks, missiles, and planes. The new international order also helped to boost the demand for industrial labor inside the United States. Stable currencies made it easier for American companies to sell their goods around the world. The Western European nations proved to be particularly reliable customers, as they used their Marshall aid to buy the American goods they needed to rebuild their economies. High manufacturing wages also generated more factory jobs. As working people spent their income on cars, refrigerators, and other items, the factories that made those goods hired more workers, who then added their dollars to the consumer boom.

Working-class Americans were not the only beneficiaries of the upward economic spiral of the 1950s and 1960s. As the industrial system expanded, white-collar opportunities increased as well. By 1950, 9 percent of American workers served as managers or proprietors, up from 6 percent in 1900, and 12 percent held clerical jobs, up from 3 percent at the start of the century. Much of the growth came within major corporations: General Motors alone employed 100,000 front office workers in the mid-1950s. Corporations anxious to develop and promote new products hired legions of engineers, advertising people, accountants, and other professionals, who by 1950 accounted for 8 percent of the work force, double their percentage in 1900. Not all white-collar jobs were high paying; clerical workers—mostly women—often earned less than unionized factory workers. But in general the growing number of white-collar Americans had salaries sufficient for them to enjoy the consumer society even more fully than their working-class counterparts. Their demand for goods thus pushed the economy to even higher levels. The GNP grew by 25 percent between 1953 and 1961; corporate profits soared to record levels; and per capita income grew by almost 10 percent. Historian Melvyn Dubofsky was referring to the postwar collective bargaining system when he wrote of "an almost perfect machine." But he could have been referring just as easily to the American economy as a whole in the two decades after World War II.

"Almost perfect" falls short of perfection, however. Those Americans who worked in dying sectors, such as the sharecroppers who remained in the Mississippi delta, continued to experience crushing poverty. Facing higher wage bills than ever before, officials in some thriving industries fell back on the tried and true practice of investing heavily in new technologies that could replace workers with machines. Auto industry managers, for example, mechanized a large part of the engine assembly process in the early 1950s, while the major electronics firms put in machines that could complete wiring operations formerly done by hand. The effects were felt almost immediately. Despite high consumer demand, the percentage of Americans doing factory work fell slightly between 1950 and 1960, an ominous portent for that pivotal center of the work force. Workers in older industrial cities—many of them African Americans drawn there by the promise of work—were particularly hard hit. Rather than update old plants, corporate officials generally preferred to shift production to new facilities, often building on the southern and western infrastructure the federal government had built. Cities such as Detroit, Cleveland, and Bridgeport were rapidly stripped of industrial jobs; Detroit alone lost 140,000 such jobs between 1947 and 1963. Northern inner cities thus began to decay, victims of deindustrialization in a land of plenty.

Shifting power relations, meanwhile, laid the basis for challenges to the industrial system. As industrial employment flattened out, the labor movement found it difficult to maintain its membership. Unions represented 25.5 percent of the work force in 1955, the year before the AFL and CIO merged; from that point on, the percentage began to slide. At the other end of the economic spectrum, corporate America initiated another merger movement in the 1950s, this one so great that by 1960 the top 5 percent of U.S. corporations earned 90 percent of all corporate income. The resulting firms were of such size that they had the power to transcend national boundaries. At the same time, the federal government found itself straining under the ever-growing costs of its international obligations. The outflow of dollars necessary to maintain the U.S. military abroad, for instance, made it increasingly difficult for the nation to sustain its commitment to stable exchange rates. In 1962, the Kennedy administration had to beat back an investors' run on U.S. gold reserves that threatened to unravel the international edifice built twenty years before.

So the postwar industrial machine had its problems. But those problems were far outweighed by the machine's tremendous performance. In the bitter winter of 1933, Franklin Roosevelt had promised to restore the industrial economy to health. The actions his administration had taken did just that. The postwar generation reaped the rewards.

THE POSTINDUSTRIAL REVOLUTION

Shortly after 1 p.m. on February 1, 1999, the power plant of the Ford River Rouge complex in suburban Detroit burst into flames. The fire began with a gas buildup in boiler No. 6, a 60-foot high coal fire furnace. Something sparked, triggering an explosion so powerful it ripped through the boiler's inch-thick steel hull. One worker, a 57-year-old father of six, was killed instantly by the blast. Four other workers suffered fatal injuries, while thirteen more were terribly burned by the heat and the boiling water that sprayed through the plant. No one saw the disaster coming, a survivor said. "Boom. That was it."

But the disaster did not come out of nowhere; it had been building for years. When the power plant opened in 1920, it was a technological marvel. Six stories high, its massive boilers generated enough energy to light a city the size of Boston. They needed to be so powerful, since the Rouge was itself a great manufacturing city. Staffed by almost 100,000 workers, it was the world's greatest industrial complex. Among its numerous buildings were the world's largest foundry, a major steel mill, a paper mill, an auto body making plant, and an assembly plant of unprecedented size. By the last year of the twentieth century, though, the Rouge had become a shell of what it once had been. The company had sold off portions of the complex and had moved most of its production elsewhere. Only seven thousand workers remained employed in the complex, which produced just one car line for Ford's far-flung empire. Four hundred workers staffed the power plant, now an aging hulk, "running on bubble gum and bobby pins," as one of the victims explained. " . . . the place was an accident waiting to happen." Now, as the smoke curled into the gray February sky, the once great Rouge ground to a halt. Thus in a moment of tragedy did the Rouge, once the symbol of American manufacturing might, become a symbol for the system's decay.

It is surprising just how quickly the American industrial system went into decline. Trouble began in the second half of the 1960s, when the United States' place in the world suddenly shifted. Their economies at last restored, Japan and the nations of Western Europe finally had the ability to challenge American manufacturers' share of the U.S. and world markets. Lyndon Johnson's escalation of the Vietnam War, meanwhile, dramatically accelerated defense spending, which pushed up the inflation rate at home and exacerbated the American balance of payments/problem abroad. Those problems undermined investors' faith in the U.S. dollar. The doubt became so great that in 1971 government officials were forced to concede that the dollar could no longer serve as the anchor for international exchange rates, which from that point on would float freely. The global financial system U.S. policymakers had built in the 1940s had been destroyed.

The problems deepened in the course of the 1970s. Foreign-made goods, often cheaper and better made than comparable American goods, claimed more and more of the American market, particularly in core industries such as steel, automobiles, and electronics. A series of unpredictable events—a disastrous wheat harvest in the Soviet Union, the Arab oil embargo—drove up prices on basic goods, further fueling inflation. The combination was devastating. At the end of the decade, unemployment stood at 7 percent, as companies facing declining market share and laid off workers. At the same time, inflation had soared to 13 percent. Corporate profits fell from a high of nearly 10 percent in 1965 to below 5 percent in 1979. Here was the stuff of revolution.

Of course, revolutions do not just happen; they are created. The postindustrial revolution was no exception. As profits fell, businessmen and bankers took up the vanguard role, promoting fundamental changes in the system that seemed to be failing them. By the late 1970s, corporate officials had begun shifting resources within their firms: shutting down plants to reduce capacity and costs; moving production to low-wage regions, often outside the United States; shifting their businesses away from lower-profit manufacturing and toward the less capital intensive service sector; refocusing their investments from production to speculation. But businessmen understood that corporate restructuring was not enough. If profit margins were to be improved, the vanguard insisted, the government also had to abandon its willingness to redistribute resources down the economic scale and instead had to support the corporate strategies already under way. In other words, the government had to reject the core of the New Deal system and put something entirely new in its place.

To that end, the business elite allied themselves with the growing conservative movement of the late 1970s. Like turn-of-the-century progressivism, 1970s conservatism defied easy categorization. It was an amalgam of groups: tax rebels, free marketeers, supply-siders, a polyglot of religious and cultural conservatives, and aggressive cold warriors, among others. Their varied commitments pulled the movement in ostensibly conflicting directions. Supply-siders demanded less government spending, for instance, while cold warriors insisted on boosting defense appropriations. But for all their differences, the conservatives shared an overarching goal of reversing what they believed to be the excesses of liberal governance. That goal pulled the corporate vanguard into the conservative camp, a move that strengthened the movement considerably. By the end of the 1970s, the vanguard and the conservative forces stood ready to attack the political order that had stood for half a century.

This was no simple task. Parts of the New Deal had become deeply entrenched; rooting them out would take time and a great deal of political capital. Launched in the waning days of the Carter administration, the conservative transformation of public life has stretched over two decades and is still not complete. Ronald Reagan made the conservative program the nation's agenda; George Bush sustained it; Bill Clinton gave it the imprimatur of the Democratic party. Despite all the effort, portions of the New Deal remain. Indeed, the conservatives of the 1980s and 1990s found part of the old order much to their liking. Reagan, for example, poured billions of dollars into defense industries, in the process helping to complete the industrial transformation of the South and West that FDR had begun. Statistics show just how much the regional balance has tipped: between 1980 and 1990, the Northeast and Midwest lost 1.5 million manufacturing jobs; the South and West gained 450,000 such jobs. But even if conservatives have not completely reversed the New Deal, they have given the corporate vanguard the victories it had most sought.

Most obviously, the federal government no longer is committed to mechanisms that redistributed power and money away from the corporate center. It is possible to cite any number of examples, such as the Reagan administration's abolition of public housing programs or the Clinton administration's destruction of the welfare system. Nothing more clearly illustrates the transformation of government, however, than the great reversal of its labor policy.

Union power had already been waning when conservatives took power. Built to bring representation to industrial workers, the labor movement had eroded as factory work forces shrank. In 1980, only 20 percent of American workers belonged to unions, down from 25.5 percent in 1954. Then the Reagan and Bush administrations, convinced that high union wages served as a drag on corporate profitability, turned government policy against unionization. Ronald Reagan signaled the shift during the famous PATCO strike of 1981, when the president fired 11,500 striking air traffic controllers. The more significant change resulted from Reagan and Bush appointing conservatives to the National Labor Relations Board, the New Deal agency that enforced labor law. The appointees greatly widened management's power to resist union organization and demands, stripping away many of the protections the Wagner Act had provided. Many corporations with unionized work forces used their new power to demand that their workers accept wage cuts and reduced fringe benefits. Some employers went further, breaking the unions in their firms. Companies without unions, moreover, felt free to intimidate those workers who dared to consider organizing or to complain about working conditions. According to one study, one of every twenty workers who demanded union representation in the 1980s lost his or her job. Little wonder that by 1995 only 15 percent of American workers belonged to unions, the lowest percentage in the industrial world.

As the conservatives undid the redistributive functions of the New Deal, they created new policies that supported corporate restructuring. Again, the examples are legion. The deregulation of finance facilitated speculation; international treaties, most notably the 1993 North American Free Trade Agreement, made it easier for corporations to move production outside the United States; tax code changes and lax enforcement of antitrust law allowed for yet another wave of mergers. These and similar policies, in turn, gave corporations the ability to accelerate the pace of change. The experience of General Electric (GE) is indicative of the larger trend. In the course of the 1980s, GE sold off its consumer electronics division, its small appliances division, and its semiconductor division. At the same time, the company acquired the entertainment giant RCA (which included the television network NBC), the investment house of Kidder Peabody, the Montgomery Ward credit company, Travels Mortgage, the Burton Group Financial Services, and the Employers Reinsurance Corporation. Thus one of the nation's greatest manufacturing firms divested itself of much of its industrial production and became a conglomerate of service sector companies.

The corporate tradition of product innovation did not cease, of course. High-technology companies flourished in the 1980s and 1990s, flooding the market with new goods that, like the auto earlier in the century, have transformed the way Americans live. But even these companies, as new and vibrant as they are, conform to the new economic order. Many high-tech firms kept only their technical and managerial staffs in the United States; their production plants went overseas. The most powerful new firms, such as Microsoft, ruthlessly suppressed competition. And fledgling firms—many Web servers, for instance—were more vehicles for speculation than for production. The high-tech sector, then, is not the new incarnation of the old industrial sector that it is often portrayed to be. It is another part of the postindustrial revolution.

Government policy, finally, has facilitated the globalization of capital markets. When the United States abandoned its commitment to sustaining exchange rates in the early 1970s, investors were free to speculate in currencies. The result was a major change in the world monetary system: now investment houses, rather than national governments, have the power to set most exchange rates. At first, the U.S. dollar suffered terribly under the new rules, its value dropping by 20 percent between 1977 and 1979. Then federal government policy changed. From 1979 to the present, the Federal Reserve has made its major priority the maintenance of the dollar's value, whatever the cost to the economy as a whole. The Reagan administration then deregulated the banking industry in a way that gave the largest American banks the ability to dominate currency speculation. The Rockefeller-owned Citibank, in particular, claimed preeminence in such trade, which now amounts to a trillion dollars a day. Policymakers, meanwhile, have pushed American investors to pour dollars into foreign markets. The Clinton administration, in particular, has helped American businessmen and bankers to place billions of dollars in emerging markets in Asia and South America, funding new factories, mines, housing developments, and pure speculation from Bangkok to Brazil.

Put together, the economic changes of the past two decades fundamentally altered the nature of work in the United States. The transfigured economy demanded more high skilled workers: in 1997, 18 percent of workers held professional or technical positions, up from 11 percent in 1960. At the other end of the spectrum, low-skilled work had virtually disappeared. Only 4 percent of workers in 1997 were laborers, 1 percent were private household help. The biggest changes came in the broad middle range of jobs. There, corporate restructuring devastated industrial employment. At GE, 300,000 employees lost their jobs as the corporation transformed itself. GE's experience was hardly unusual. Only 10 percent of American workers labored in factories in 1997, compared with 19 percent in 1960. Clerical work has also begun to decline with the growth of computerization. The service sector, in contrast, has boomed: 25 percent of workers were employed in sales or service jobs in 1997, which had employed only 15 percent of workers in 1960. The great American industrial machine, the wonder of the twentieth century, no longer drives the nation's economy.

The benefits of economic restructuring have been profoundly skewed. Corporations, not surprisingly, have done very well, their profits soaring in the 1980s and 1990s. Conservative government policies ensured that the well-to-do, but not the majority of Americans, would share in the boom. The wealthiest 5 percent of families earned a larger share of the national wealth in 1994 than did the poorest 40 percent, a situation that did not exist in 1980. The wealthy also outstripped the middle class: in real terms, the median family income has stagnated since 1980, while the income of the top 1 percent of American families has increased by over 100 percent. The wages of manufacturing workers serve as perhaps the most dramatic demonstration of the new economic order's effects. As factories have shut and union power has collapsed, industrial wages have tumbled. The average worker in manufacturing now earns less, once inflation has been factored into the equation, than he or she did in 1960.

The postindustrial revolution has also made more insecure the economic lives of a great many Americans. The economy has twice plunged into severe recession since 1980; the first time, in 1981 and 1982, the unemployment rate reached 9.5 percent, its highest point since 1941. Even in flush times, the insecurity has persisted. Millions of workers, from factory operatives through middle managers, have lost their jobs in the course of mergers, as newly enlarged companies trim their work forces. Many Americans are counting on pension plans whose safety rests on the shaky health of developing economies. Industrial workers who once held union jobs now struggle to make do without the protection of seniority agreements and grievance procedures, while the poorest Americans battle to get by without the safety net the welfare system once provided.

Despite its costs, economic restructuring has not reversed the great progress the American economy has made in the last hundred years. By virtually every economic measure—wages, working conditions, poverty rates, standard of living—Americans are better off today than they were at the dawn of the century. Many of the economic scars that cut into the land in 1900 have healed. Factories have become safer; working-class tenements have been razed; sharecroppers' shacks have been shuttered. The successes of the century are everywhere to be seen: in the stunning skyscrapers that corporations have built; in the suburban houses that the sons and daughters of working people have made their homes; in the international development that American dollars have fueled. But the successes have been tempered by a troubling continuity. A hundred years after the United States became the world's greatest industrial power, the American economy still does not provide many of its people with the security they seek for themselves and their families. That scar remains as raw as it was when the century began.

NOTES

1. Edward L. Ayers, *The Promise of a New South: Life after Reconstruction* (New York: Oxford University Press, 1981).

2. Gavin Wright, *Old South, New South: Revolutions in the Southern Economy since the Civil War* (New York: Basic Books, 1986), p. 236.

3. Quoted in David Brody, *In Labor's Cause: Main Themes on the History of the American Worker* (New York: Oxford University Press, 1993), p. 245.

SUGGESTIONS FOR FURTHER READING

Primary sources are the best starting points for tracing economic change in the twentieth century. *Historical Statistics of the United States, Colonial Times to 1970* (Washington, D.C.: Government Printing Office, 1975) contains a wealth of information. *Statistical Abstract of the United States,* published annually, brings economic data to the present. W. Elliot Brownlee, *Dynamics of Ascent,* 2nd ed. (New York: Knopf, 1979) is a readable overview of the economy that covers most of the twentieth century. David Hounshell, *From the American System to Mass Production, 1800–1932* (Baltimore: Johns Hopkins University Press, 1983) is a very informative history of technological change. Peter Fearon, *War, Prosperity and Depression* (Oxford: P. Allan, 1987) is a fine general account of the interwar economy. Herman Van Der Wee, *Prosperity and Upheaval* (Berkeley: University of California Press, 1986), though dense, puts the postwar economy in a global perspective. On recent economic changes, see Bennett Harrison and Barry Bluestone, *The Great U-Turn* (New York: Basic Books, 1988); Howard Wachtel, *The Money Mandarins* (New York: Pantheon, 1986); and Michael Bernstein and David Adler, eds., *Understanding American Economic Decline* (New York: Cambridge University Press, 1993).

There is a vast literature on work and unionization. Bruce Laurie, *Artisans into Workers* (New York: Hill and Wang, 1989) traces the transformation of labor in the nineteenth century. David Montgomery, *The Fall of the House of Labor* (New York: Cambridge University Press, 1987) is a magisterial study of working-class Americans in the early twentieth century. Robert Zieger's *The CIO* (Chapel Hill: University of North Carolina Press, 1995) is the best study of that pivotal organization. There still is no single study of the labor movement in the post–World War II era.

The beginning point for understanding the New Deal is David M. Kennedy, *Freedom from Fear: The American People in Depression and War, 1929–1945* (New York: Oxford University Press, 1999). Bruce Schulman, *From Cotton Belt to Sun Belt* (New York: Oxford University Press, 1991) is a first-rate study of the federal government's attempt to shift resources to the South and West. On the federal government's labor policy, see Melvyn Dubofsky, *The State and Labor in Modern America* (Chapel Hill: University of North Carolina Press, 1994).

6 | THE HISTORY AND POLITICS OF POVERTY IN TWENTIETH-CENTURY AMERICA

JACQUELINE JONES

P overty has a history, but it also has a politics. As a historical reality in twentieth-century America, poverty is grounded in the material circumstances that shape the everyday lives of men, women, and children—the absence of adequate food, shelter, clothing, and medical care—and in the tangible struggles and strategies among the poor to provide for themselves and to root out the sources of their own deprivation. The social configuration of poverty—who is poor when, where, and why—reflects readily identifiable and measurable structural transformations related to several factors, including economic change, the growth of state power, the development of social-welfare policy, and patterns of immigration and migration.

In contrast to this material reality, however, the politics of poverty reveals ever-shifting debates over the definition of the term and the larger meaning of the reality. Indeed, by the end of the twentieth century, the subject of poverty has become a political Rorschach test of sorts: Conservatives tend to see less of it and minimize its significance within the grander scheme of American prosperity, while liberals tend to see more of it and emphasize its significance as a measure of social injustice. It is this tension—between the hard reality of twentieth-century poverty on the one hand and the various fluid ideologies surrounding it on the other—that is the subject of this chapter.

Not surprisingly, the problem of poverty within the world's richest nation carries with it a number of apparent paradoxes. Throughout the twentieth century, technological innovations have been heralded as an indicator of progress, and yet the effort to streamline and rationalize production has often led to the displacement of certain groups of workers; hence in the 1920s consumers enjoyed lower prices with the invention of the mechanical coal cutter, while the men (especially African-American men) who had mined the coal by hand lost their jobs. In the 1970s, New England fishermen benefited from federal government policy that kept foreign trawlers out of their territory and invested their windfall profits in radar, sonar, and other sophisticated kinds of tracking devices; twenty years later these men were victims of their own success, deprived of the means of their livelihood now that the rich reserves of cod and flounder had been depleted by overfishing. Within the context of (specific type of) technological change, then, progress produced poverty.

By the late twentieth century, this pattern of ongoing innovation had culminated in a so-called high-technology economy, in which cars were being made by robots and bank transactions were being processed by computers; yet this economy depended on ever-increasing numbers of exploited workers, from Mexican strawberry pickers in California to Chinese garment-sweatshop workers in New York City. The modern cleaning lady—a woman of color laboring in a downtown skyscraper or an edge-city shopping mall and trying to support her children on six dollars an hour—had become emblematic of the contradictions embedded in the shape of the postindustrial work force.

Meanwhile, some observers chose to ignore these contradictions and suggest that the United States had at this point in its history managed to defy the biblical injunction, "The poor are always with you." For example, in a report entitled "The Myth of Widespread American Poverty," Heritage Foundation senior policy analyst Robert Rector claimed that, since 97 percent of the so-called poor owned a television, they were not really poor at all. By that standard, neither presumably were the homeless folks temporarily lodged in a shelter equipped with a TV. According to this view, poverty was less a real problem and more of a cynical political ploy manipulated by leftists who sought to call into question the whole free-enterprise system.

And too, it is an ironic fact of American life that on the one hand over the last generation or so we have become so intolerant of political inequality—for example, few would argue today on behalf of the machinations that deprived so many rural, southern African Americans of the right to vote until well into the 1960s—and on the other hand we as a nation have become so tolerant of economic inequality. In the late 1990s, Microsoft chairman Bill Gates's net worth (upward of $30 billion) was equal to the net worth of the bottom 40 percent of the population, yet this disparity prompted little or nothing in the way of public outrage, little or nothing in the way of meaningful policy initiatives from politicians. As their own stock portfolios swell, the white middle class becomes even more fierce in their resistance to proposals to equalize public school funding among suburban, urban, and rural districts. Indeed, with the increasing concentration of wealth have come state-sponsored efforts to deprive the nonelderly poor of the meager aid that they receive from government transfers in the form of medical care, food stamps, and monthly cash subsidies. This paradox suggests that the poor serve a larger political function in the late twentieth century, that their very existence is integral to postindustrial America.

Today, even an agreed upon definition of poverty remains elusive. Those whom demographers classify as poor might be the first to argue with the whole notion, and to remind us that the term itself carries with it certain patronizing attitudes toward those who subsist on the margins of American affluence. Are people poor if they do not consider themselves poor, or if they do not know that they are poor by certain objective standards? At times, men and women who have grown up in straitened circumstances understand that, while they were accumulating fond memories of a childhood in a large, loving family, their parents were making desperate, even heart-breaking efforts to keep hunger and want at bay. Remembering his childhood in the coalfields of Pike County in eastern Kentucky during the 1940s, Jim Vernatter fondly remembered playing with his neighbors and siblings, making up games using an old tire and swimming in the local swimming hole. In the absence of commercialized forms of leisure, there was a lot of "socializing with your neighbors." Though poor, the Vernatter family was a close one, and "when you have that in a home, the other things are secondary," he claimed. At the time, the young boy was oblivious to the cares of his father, who eventually succumbed to long hours spent in the mines, and to the anxieties of his mother, who worried where the next meal was coming from.[1] Thus poverty played itself out differently in the lives of these two generations.

At times some observers (wrongly) conflate or confuse the material reality of poverty with a particular kind of culture, an emptiness of the spirit. Interviewed in the early 1970s, a white man named Richard Jackson, a native of Henderson County, in western North Carolina, spoke about a lost vision of the good life in Appalachia. Time was, he asserted, when people in the mountains could tell the difference "between wealth and money. . . . They aren't the same thing. . . . Wealth was having enough land to feed you and tools to work it. Now we talk about [wealth] in terms of money. That's a lousy salad; coins are not chewable at all." Jackson made a distinction between the hardship associated with physical deprivation, and the satisfaction associated with a freely chosen, physically arduous but plain life, outside the culture of consumerism. He noted, "There is nothing beautiful [or] romantic about an enforced marginal existence. There is something beautiful about people who have decided that in order to live in a pretty good place [in this case, the Blue Ridge Mountains] they are willing to make some sacrifice in terms of convenience."[2] Jackson and others would dispute the notion that poverty could be measured in money or things at all.

Nevertheless, as scholars we do try to measure poverty, and over the course of the twentieth century the data we have collected and the uses to which we have put those data have become ever more sophisticated. Using a fixed number—an annual income of $15,595 for a family of four—the U.S. Census Bureau reports that, in the late 1990s, about 13 percent of all Americans are poor. Predictably, this figure is disputed by both the Right and the Left. According to some, poverty is a relative concept, and we must locate today's poor within a historical as well as an international context. About two-thirds of those classified by the census as poor own at least one of the following: a microwave oven, a VCR, an air-conditioned house or apartment. According to this view, compared with the poor a generation ago, and the poor today in Africa and India, America possesses a group of less-well-to-do people, but they are hardly impoverished.

At the same time, other observers argue that the census figure is much too low—for example, that regional variations in the cost of living render such a fixed benchmark meaningless. In 1998, the Boston-based Women's Educational and Industrial Union established "self-sufficiency standards," defined as "the amount of money required to meet basic needs without public or private subsidies, such as public housing, food stamps, or free babysitting by a friend or relative." By this measure, a single person in Boston would need an annual income of $15,642 just to survive. The addition of two children to this household—one preschool and one school age—would raise the self-sufficiency standard to $38,563. Considering the number of American families that find themselves with "too much month at the end of the money" (in the words of sociologist Kathryn Edin)—that is, families that are just a health-care crisis away from complete and utter disaster—the American poverty rate escalates to 25 percent of the total population. This figure includes a substantial number of people who work.

Obviously many of the kinds of data that demographers and policymakers rely on to analyze poverty in the 1990s are not available to historians who want to chart the trajectory of poverty over the course of the twentieth century. Today for example we are able to calculate the shift in the relationship between economic growth and poverty, to distinguish those mired in intergenerational or chronic poverty from those who are poor for a short amount of time, to classify the poor according to race and family size and structure, to correlate poverty with an individual's formal education as well as earnings, and to highlight the plight of children within various groups. And so, by using the Census Bureau definition of poverty, policy analysts can draw several conclusions about the nature of poverty at the end of the twentieth century: The decade of economic recovery in the 1980s failed to reduce poverty (to the extent that growth in the 1960s and 1970s helped to reduce rates). Blacks are twice as likely to be poor as whites (the poverty rate of the former is 24.6 percent), almost one-third of Hispanics are poor, and families with no workers, or with a female head, are disproportionately likely to be poor. About one-quarter of all rural children are poor. Over the last fifteen years or so, the percentage of the poor in "deep poverty" (their incomes at or below 50 percent of the poverty line) has increased from less than one-third to about two-fifths of the total number of poor people. Among the most significant factors affecting poverty rates over the last twenty years or so are the shift to a more vulnerable (i.e., female-headed) family structure, decreasing government benefits and transfer payments for the poor, and decreasing wages for the working poor (especially men). The decline in the percentage of workers who belong to labor unions—from an all-time high in the early 1950s of about one-third the work force, to about 10 percent today—has played a role in this overall wage decline.

Although we cannot hope to match this sort of statistical and demographic precision in our historical analysis, it is possible to make certain generalizations about the history of poverty in the twentieth century, and to explore the issue according to the following criteria: first, the groups disproportionately at risk throughout the one-hundred-year period—those with specific ethnic and age characteristics, and those residing in specific regions of the country; second, the factors that produced poverty-stricken populations, including patterns of immigration and migration, technological innovation, and federal and state policy (concomitant with the rise and fall of charitable aid); and third, the variety of strategies employed by the poor to challenge the root causes of their plight, including welfare rights organizations, labor unions, and grass-roots living-wage campaigns. I shall conclude the chapter with a discussion of the political implications of poverty, specifically the larger economic and ideological functions served by poor people within a rich, dynamic industrial society.

Here it is worth at least acknowledging the expansiveness of the subject and lamenting the fact that the space available in a single chapter is not enough to deal with it adequately. It is not difficult to offer a laundry list of topics relevant to the history of poverty—the history of private and public charity, and its up-scale sister philanthropy; the history of American public education; the history of labor unions; crime and law enforcement; prisons, orphanages, and other institutions populated by the poor; homelessness; housing patterns; stereotypes and other perceptions of the poor as expressed explicitly in the mass media and implicitly in public policy debates over various social-welfare issues; the gender, racial, and age dimensions of economic marginalization; the tactics of middle-class advocates for the poor; racial ideologies as a means of perpetuating and justifying poverty; and the ways in which the poor have sought to speak for themselves via literature, song, and radical political activity. At the same time, I would like to point out that the history of poverty is very much embedded in the larger history of twentieth-century America, and that we can learn much about material deprivation by studying its counterpoints—the spread of affluence and the rise of a consumer society, economic growth and the onward march of suburbanization. Poverty and wealth exist in symbiotic relation to each other, and it is not possible to understand one without understanding the other.

We can begin by noting that certain groups have been overrepresented among the poor throughout the twentieth century, and each of these groups has a unique history. The relatively high rates of poverty among African Americans constitute a bitter legacy of slavery, though that legacy is more complex than most scholars acknowledge. It is true that, during the Civil War era, black men and women embraced freedom with little in the way of material resources. Die-hard southern rebels and Yankee radical Republicans alike resisted any plan that would enable the black population to achieve self-sufficiency thorough land ownership, but for different reasons. The unreconstructed rebels were determined to preserve their supply of dependent black agricultural labor. For their part, the Yankees assumed that blacks might temporarily return to a condition of neoslavery (as sharecroppers and tenant farmers) and yet gradually accumulate enough money to enter the ranks of modest landowners. Denied credit, bereft of job opportunities elsewhere, and in any case rooted to the land of their forebears, the majority of southern black people continued to toil on the land of white people, paid in promises rather than cash, until well into the twentieth century.

In too many instances scholars have drawn a straight line between the hardships associated with slavery on the one hand and the hardships associated with late twentieth-century African-American populations on the other. Yet the current subordinate condition of nearly a quarter of all blacks (and more than half of all black children) was not a foregone conclusion in 1865. First of all, between the Civil War and the "Great Migration" (beginning in 1916), the rural southern black family was just as stable (characterized by two parents), as its poor white counterpart. The family dislocation and joblessness associated with late-twentieth-century African-American communities were functions of the process of ghettoization, a political process that rendered northern blacks in particular confined to poor neighborhoods and deprived of quality public education. Moreover, white people in a variety of capacities—qua employers, workers, and consumers, colluded to exclude black people as a group from "modern" jobs—those associated with retail sales, new communications technology, and machines in the manufacturing sector. For example, not until the 1970s did southern textile mills hire black men and women—and then only when competition from foreign imports mandated low wages and ultimately produced a depressed domestic industry. Black people remain disproportionately poor today because so many whites profited from enslaved labor for so many generations; but after emancipation, political and economic marginalization assumed new and ever-changing forms.

The story of twentieth-century Native American poverty has demonstrated certain constants until very recently. Confined since the nineteenth century to reservations that denied them the opportunity to provide for themselves, as late as the 1990s groups like the Sioux of Pine Ridge, South Dakota, and the Navajo Nation of Arizona showed consistently high rates of poverty (two-thirds among the Sioux, for example) and unemployment (85 percent among the Navajo, for example). Their communities were characterized by all the social indicators that accompanied such distress—alcoholism, depression, suicide, divorce. And yet by this time of course it was possible to juxtapose the plight of these groups to the apparent success of others that had instituted legalized gambling on their reservations. The Foxwoods Casino, operated by the Pequots in Ledyard, Connecticut, was among the most profitable of all gambling resorts in the United States in the 1990s, providing members of that group (individually and collectively) with a handsome income. Yet the Pequots' prosperity came at a price; throughout the United States, casinos served to extract a regressive tax on poor people residing in surrounding communities. In depressed areas especially, like the Mississippi River town of Vicksburg, Mississippi, gambling resorts exacerbated the problem of poverty by profiting from the people who could least afford to part with the little money they had. In the history of twentieth-century Indian prosperity and poverty, then, are encapsulated some of the contradictions of regional economic "development."

Over the last century, the divergent fortunes of children and the elderly suggest the possibilities and the limits of federal policies affecting the poor. Throughout much of American history, old age brought with it declining resources and increased dependency—on younger family members, on the charity of churches and neighbors. In the colonial period, elderly farmers lacked physical strength and the ability to maintain their farm homesteads, and in the early twentieth century, elderly assembly-line workers lacked the manual dexterity necessary to keep their jobs. The Social Security Act of 1935, buttressed later in the century by Medicare and other medical services for the elderly, wrought a dramatic revolution in the lives of older Americans. For example, by 1995, fully half of the elderly were still poor before taxes and government transfers; but after receiving such aid their poverty level was cut to 10 percent—two-thirds of the average rate and one-fifth of their pretransfer rate.

It is not difficult to account for this dramatic reduction in the poverty rate among the elderly; Social Security and related programs are "rewards" to men and women who have participated in the paid labor force. In contrast, children do not work, and the offspring of able-bodied, nonelderly, non-wage-earning parents are, predictably, particularly vulnerable to poverty. Indeed, a single parent (usually a woman) who lacks a high school degree, plus the presence of children in her household, make for an especially lethal combination: In 1994, among single heads of households living alone, about a tenth of all whites and about a quarter of their black and Hispanic counterparts were poor; but add children to these households and the percentages jumped to 63.3 percent, 73.0 percent, and 71.2 percent, respectively. In the cruel parlance of twentieth-century poverty, adults who earned wages for all or part of their lives have been deemed the "worthy poor," and children (especially minority children) have been deemed "the unworthy poor."

At the risk of digressing from this brief overview of the demographic characteristics of the twentieth-century poor, we should note that most policymakers, politicians, and academics have relied upon an extremely narrow definition of work in assessing which groups were entitled to various forms of aid over the years. Within the last half century or so, many Americans have been quick to glorify the unwaged labor of mothers at home, but few Americans in positions of political power have been willing to accord that kind of labor the same status accorded paid employment. Living in dangerous neighborhoods with few material resources at their disposal, poor women understand full well that caring for their children is a form of productive labor, no matter how little it earns them in terms of money or the respect of the larger society. In the words of Denise Turner, a welfare recipient in Wisconsin, "I mean if you got a family, what're you talkin' about lazy?! . . . in today's economy a woman is considered lazy when she's home taking care of her children. And to me that's not laziness. If she's doing a good job at that, she has to use a lot of skills . . . a woman is not lazy when she's taking care of her family."[3]

Inherent in these distinctions are obvious class, racial, and gender biases. In his 1992 book, *The End of Equality,* Mickey Kaus calls for a new standard of American citizenship—one based on the premise that all able-bodied adults must and should work for wages. However, he conveniently ignores middle-class, fulltime homemakers who remain dependent on their husbands for their livelihood. Like poor women dependent on programs such as the former Aid to Families with Dependent Children, these housewives do not participate in the paid labor force; yet Kaus assumes it is right that they appropriate the status of their husbands and thus (presumably) avoid the responsibility of working outside the home. The unresolved questions of "Who works?" and "What activities constitute work?" thus remain central to our understanding of the politics of poverty in the twentieth century.

Certain readily identifiable groups, including African Americans, Indians, single household heads, and children, have suffered disproportionately high rates of poverty throughout the twentieth century; yet their historical experiences have been neither fixed nor static during this period. Similarly, we must appreciate the significance of poor places, and at the same time recognize that those places have changed over time. Northern central cities, the hills and hollows of Appalachia, the Mississippi delta, Indian reservations—these sites contained large numbers of poor people in the early part of the twentieth century, and the poverty persists today.

And each of these places has its own history. The center cities have been transformed from enclaves of newly arrived immigrants from Eastern Europe, and newly arrived migrants from the South, to communities of a variety of poor groups of color—African Americans as well as newly arrived people from Southeast Asia and Latin America. The Mississippi delta used to be home to thousands of African-American sharecroppers who labored in cotton fields; today the delta is home to blacks who piece together a living through foraging, wage work (in catfish and poultry processing plants, for example), and government assistance. During the first part of the twentieth century, Appalachia supported hard-scrabble farmers and struggling workers in lumbering and coal mining; by the 1920s, the depletion of lumber reserves, combined with mechanization of coal production, left the population with few opportunities to earn a living wage. The incursion of the tourist industry into that region has not provided the firm economic foundation that would lift the region out of poverty.

Other areas of the country have followed a different historical trajectory and arrived at a similar point today—they are all distressed communities that lack good jobs for people who possess little in the way of specialized skills or formal education. These are communities with poor schools (relative to their computer-rich counterparts in the suburbs), places where people rely on underground economies of various kinds. Thus areas as seemingly divergent as South Central Los Angeles and Waterloo, Iowa, have converged in some respects, because both lost good blue-collar jobs in the manufacturing sector in the 1970s and 1980s, and those jobs have not been replaced. In fact, the idea of place goes a long way toward illuminating the demographic characteristics of poor people in modern American history. While the country as a whole grew and prospered, some places were left behind; by the 1990s these places included enclaves of migrant agricultural workers like Belle Glade, Florida; fishing villages on the New England coast; "stranded" rural communities formerly dependent on a single kind of enterprise that had ceased operations or moved its production facilities elsewhere; crowded ports of entry for Asian and Central American immigrants; and towns that had evolved in tandem with cold war industries (defense plants and military bases).

This discussion alerts us to the larger historical forces that have contributed to the creation of impoverished communities. Large-scale population movements have both exacerbated and alleviated the sources of poverty in the course of the twentieth century. Indeed, it is difficult to generalize about the fate of migrant and immigrant peoples who found their way to the Northeast, Upper Midwest, and West Coast during this period. Certainly a focus exclusively on the wretched material conditions endured by immigrants in New York's Lower East Side around the turn of the century would highlight their long work hours, low wages, and crowded and unhealthful living conditions. But this type of poverty was not necessarily enduring or intergenerational, at least partly because the New York regional economy provided plentiful employment opportunities to a wide variety of people during this period. Similarly, the refugees who fled the Oklahoma dust bowl in the 1930s and found their way to Bakersfield, California, began to prosper during the World War II–era boom in that area of the country. By the 1960s and 1970s, working-class whites in that area discovered that their way into the middle class was eased by the arrival of immigrants from South America, who joined the agricultural work force and thus allowed native-born whites to rise within local economies. A similar dynamic pertained in relation to the Appalachian migrants who settled in the Lower Midwest during the 1940s and 1950s; though initially clustered in poor communities like Uptown, Chicago, and Lower Price Hill, Cincinnati, these rural folk gradually ascended ladders of internal occupational mobility within various work places, leaving others (and especially African-American migrants from the South) to do the most menial kinds of work.

In contrast, the Cambodians and Guatemalans who made their way to the United States in the 1970s and 1980s entered an entirely different kind of national economy—one that allowed for little mobility (either residential or social) among people who could not speak English or understand a computer language. In fact, we have reached a point where one of the traditional solutions to the problem of poverty—geographic mobility—no longer pertains in any meaningful way. Gone are those destinations that promised (and in at least some cases delivered) so much to people who had so little—New York City at the turn of the century, California in the 1940s and 1950s, the Sunbelt in the 1970s. Today the best jobs are reserved for those who have accumulated the most impressive educational records, and more and more of the rest are relegated to service positions that provide little in the way of good pay or benefits.

Just as population movements have affected patterns of poverty within the last century, so have patterns of business consolidation and technological development. In the 1980s the national news media highlighted the unanticipated, devastating consequences of the new global economy, when these developments began to affect the white middle class. Yet these processes have a long history. In his classic study, *The Philadelphia Negro* (published in 1899), W. E. B. DuBois outlined the ways that the city's changing economy spelled disaster for the African-American caterers who had once operated thriving enterprises for the benefit of wealthy white customers. In the 1890s, as an emerging consumer economy necessitated new standards of customer service, the "application of large capital to the business" of catering meant that some entrepreneurs were now in a better position to respond to cues "as to propriety and fashion from New York, London, and Paris." Under these conditions, a business that originally depended upon the "talent and tact" of its owner now increasingly relied on economies of scale; and "with this new and large clientele that personal relationship between the caterers and those served was broken up, and a larger place for colored prejudice was made." In effect, a whole class of workers—black caterers—fell prey to shifts in consumers' tastes, and the entire Philadelphia black community registered the baneful effects of "progress."

To cite two other examples: the automation of the auto industry began to displace large numbers of lower-level workers as early as the 1950s, and around this time the introduction of the mechanical cotton-picking machine in the South drove an impoverished population northward. Steel workers in Pittsburgh and Gary, textile workers in the North Carolina Piedmont, and rubber workers in Ohio—all of these groups fell on hard times in the 1970s. The choices that they are their families faced were cruel ones—to sever ties to kin in the area and move and seek work elsewhere; to remain in the community and find low-wage jobs in fast food restaurants, all-night drugstores, or nursing homes; or to apply for government assistance and rely on the help of friends and neighbors.

The state has played a key role in shaping patterns of poverty in twentieth-century America, in terms of both reducing poverty and increasing it among certain populations. Convinced of the inadequacy of local and private relief efforts, the architects of the New Deal–sponsored welfare state built upon early twentieth-century state experiments in the area of social-welfare policy (minimum wage laws and workers' compensation) and on previous federal efforts to alleviate hardship among the widows of army veterans. During the 1930s, these policymakers initiated sweeping programs designed to smooth the raw edges of the capitalist system, characterized as it was by periodic downswings in labor demand and by the permanent problem of poverty among the elderly. On paper at least, these legislative initiatives promised to cushion the blows felt by millions of workers in a chronically unstable economy, and to enable those workers to protect themselves against rapacious employers—programs guaranteeing an income for the elderly (Social Security), aid for those thrown out of work temporarily (unemployment compensation), federal protection for workers who joined a union and bargained collectively with their employer, minimum wages and hours for workers, an end to child labor.

From the very beginning, however, it was clear that the so-called social safety net woven by New Dealers contained large holes. In the South, local administrators refused to extend the benefits of Aid to Dependent Children to African-American women and their offspring; official Democratic party policy decreed that these women should work in the cotton fields and the kitchens of white men and women, for starvation wages, rather than receive federal "largesse." In general, policymakers conceived of social-welfare legislation primarily as a form of insurance for industrial workers and for elderly workers who had worked at regular jobs; part-time and seasonal laborers, including domestic servants and field hands, were excluded from the provisions of programs like Social Security, unemployment compensation, and minimum wages and hours. And too, when blue-collar workers successfully won union recognition from the largest steel and auto companies in the late 1930s, they demanded health insurance as part of their employment benefits. This pact lessened the pressure on the federal government to implement a universal health-care system, leaving millions of workers who were outside of these large companies—and outside of the paid labor force altogether—vulnerable to the costs of ill health and long-term medical problems.

In the mid-1960s, a series of policy initiatives called the "War on Poverty" targeted a broader spectrum of poor than the factory workers who constituted the primary beneficiaries of the labor legislation of the New Deal. The Model Cities and Head Start programs, legal services for the poor, and the Community Action Program together represented the first significant infusion of federal money into poor communities in thirty years. Other aspects of President Lyndon Johnson's "Great Society," including Medicare and Title VII of the Civil Rights Act of 1964, sought to provide a broad range of safeguards for poor people, from health insurance for the elderly to increased job opportunities for white women and African Americans. Yet these measures represented forms of government-sponsored social welfare, rather than meaningful challenges to an economy that proved incapable of providing good jobs at high wages to everyone who wanted to work.

Moreover, social-welfare legislation intended to benefit the nonelderly poor remained highly susceptible to political influences. Thus in the 1950s, southern welfare administrators began to concoct a new threat to the fabric of civil society—the African-American unwed mother who, it was claimed, produced large numbers of children and then enjoyed herself at the expense of hard-working taxpayers. In 1963, a new group, the National Welfare Rights Organization (NWRO), composed primarily of poor women in northern cities, launched a campaign to publicize welfare benefits among women who were eligible for such benefits but either unaware of their existence or unaware of the complicated application procedures necessary to secure them. (Declared Johnnie Tillmon, first chairwoman of the NWRO, "an AFDC mother learns that being a 'real woman' means being all the things she isn't and having all the things she can't have.") Nevertheless, the southern stereotype of predator African-American women had become a national preoccupation by the 1980s, when President Ronald Reagan began to denounce the high-living "welfare queen" as a threat to the country's moral fiber.

Reagan's presidency launched a new generation of policymakers and academics who claimed that entitlement programs for the poor actually increased poverty levels by discouraging able-bodied individuals from working and providing for their families. By the mid-1990s, prejudice against the poor had reached such a fevered pitch that a self-proclaimed liberal president, Bill Clinton, could preside over the dismantling of the welfare safety net and, as mandated by the Temporary Aid to Needy Families Act (passed in 1996), hand over welfare policy to state legislators and big-city mayors, politicians notoriously unsympathetic to the poor. Within six years of taking office in 1993, Mayor Rudolph Giuliani had cut the welfare rolls of New York City by 40 percent (from 1 million recipients to 600,000) and created a workfare program that put 30,000 of the city's poor to work. Relatively easy to skim off the top of the rolls were the women who had the skills and the support systems that would allow them to seek gainful employment (no matter how poorly paid); harder to place were the majority of recipients who were hobbled by the language barrier, chronic health problems, substance addiction, or any number of debilitating personal circumstances. These women and their children were the casualties of an insidious numbers game, a game played by politicians who courted middle-class voters with the latest statistics of poor people shed from government assistance programs.

Over the last one hundred years, federal, state, and local governments at times worked at cross-purposes with themselves. As we have seen, in the 1930s Congress's social-welfare policies contributed to the immiseration of groups excluded from those policies, including African Americans, nonindustrial workers, and the rural poor in general. These men and women faltered to the extent that full-time manufacturing employees benefited. In the 1940s, the federal government responded to the pleas of large agricultural enterprises—from cotton planters in Texas to fruit and vegetable growers in California—and approved the "Bracero" program, which allowed large numbers of Mexicans to enter the United States in search of work. This policy had the effect of helping to keep agricultural wages low among native-born workers. The federal tax deduction for homeowners' mortgage payments helped to stimulate the growth of all-white suburbs in the 1950s, while ignoring African-American renters who languished in the inner cities, hostage to discriminatory bank lending policies, segregated public housing, and so-called suburban neighborhood improvement associations.

Other government initiatives harmed the poor in both a relative and absolute sense. In the 1970s, when cities began to restrict and regulate flophouses and states began to deinstitutionalize their mentally ill populations, the number of homeless people increased dramatically. The North American Free Trade Agreement, passed in 1993, promoted a policy that provided for the unfettered movement of goods and capital across international borders, while workers remained immobilized within low-wage regional and national economies. In the late 1990s, New York City "workfare" recipients toiled at below-minimum-wage pay, displacing large numbers of the working poor—janitors, street cleaners, and office workers—and weakening the union of public employees in the process. At the same time, Mayor Rudolph Giuliani began to crack down on a whole host of workers—taxi drivers, food peddlers on the city streets—enforcing tough new licensing codes and making life ever more difficult for the least fortunate residents of the city. And too, throughout the twentieth century, state and federal taxation policies have contributed to the growing inequality of public schools in rich and poor areas; today those policies have disastrous consequences for the future economic possibilities of poor children.

With the exception of the Social Security program, governmental initiatives have done little to root out the structural causes of poverty. In order to locate meaningful challenges to the political economy that produces poverty, we must look to the history of the poor themselves, and to a range of activities, from the mundane to the radical. Like the poor throughout human history, residents of distressed communities in this country in this century have worked to pool their modest resources and to engage in cooperative activities calculated to sustain families, kin groups, and neighborhoods. They have foraged, hunting and fishing and tending gardens in rural areas, and stripping abandoned buildings of wood and other materials that could be used or sold in urban areas. Throughout this century the poor have exhibited high rates of geographic and residential mobility, ever on the move for a better job and more reasonable landlord, a safer street or better school for their children. (As noted above, however, today that mobility is more likely to be intraregional, as the cost of relocating becomes ever higher and the opportunities for good entry-level jobs recede.) And by their whole-hearted embrace of consumer culture, many poor people declare their intention to partake of the blessings of American Society, to join with the middle class in claiming that nice clothes, CD systems, cars, and credit cards are key to current definitions of American citizenship. In the process, though, impoverished young people in particular (like their middle-class counterparts) become vulnerable to the manipulative blandishments of advertisers; global capitalism promotes the ideal of material luxury without providing economic opportunities commensurate with achieving that ideal.

Historically, labor unions have exerted a powerful force against wage decreases and in favor of wage increases; and even today, joining a union is arguably the most effective step that any worker can take to escape a life of poverty. In the early twentieth century, the American Federation of Labor, with its emphasis on skilled, white male workers, dominated the landscape of labor organizing, easily fending off challenges from groups like the Industrial Workers of the World (founded in 1905) with more expansive visions of workers' rights. Labor leadership was lodged in the hands of white men, even within industries that relied upon women workers. Thus women activists in the garment industry, like Rose Schneiderman and Clara Lemlich, had to contend with the antifemale bias of the male heads of the International Ladies Garment Workers Union. Until the late 1930s, with the founding of the Congress of Industrial Organizations, most unions were highly exclusive organizations, and even after World War II (until the 1970s), many trade and a considerable number of industrial unions retained institutionalized forms of discrimination against white women and men and women of color. The laboring classes remained fractured along racial, age, gender, and regional lines, constantly reconfiguring themselves in response to emergency situations, but failing to coalesce around a single political strategy or ideology. Likewise, groups of poor people in general continued to be estranged from one another, and that estrangement helped to stifle the unified, collective voice of dispossessed peoples.

In a dramatic reversal, by the late twentieth century people of color, and especially those employed in the service sector, began to take the lead in labor organizing. By the late 1990s, the Service Employees International Union (SEIU) was the fastest growing union in the nation, and locals in Las Vegas, Nevada, were in the forefront of militant labor organizing. Waitresses, janitors, bartenders, and chambermaids recognized the power of a union not only to counter the trend toward depressed wages, but also to protect them against arbitrary firings and layoffs. President of the 40,000-strong Culinary Workers Union Local 226, Hattie Canty (a 60-year old African-American widow and mother of ten children) told a reporter in the mid-1990s, "I am blessed to live and work in Las Vegas." She explained: "My house is paid for. I bought cars while I was a maid. I bought furniture. I bought the things I needed for my family while I was a maid. And the way I did it was through organized labor."[4] The SEIU drew upon the confrontational tactics invoked by industrial unions earlier in the century—sit-down strikes and noisy public protests, tactics that continued to bolster the power of union locals in a postindustrial era. In February 1999, 74,000 Los Angeles home health care workers voted to become part of the SEIU, joining 600,000 of their counterparts throughout the nation.

The poor have used other means as well to challenge the machinery of private and public institutions that support the status quo. In the 1960s, with the beginning of the Legal Aid program, farm workers in California and public-housing tenants in New York, among other groups, sought redress in the courts, with the help of lawyers subsidized by the federal government. Like unions, free legal services serve to upset the balance of power between the rich and poor, and thus prove to be potent (if politically unpopular among the middle class) weapons in the fight against poverty. In the late twentieth century, some elderly immigrants have rushed to embrace American citizenship, not necessarily out of purely patriotic motives, but to ensure they will not lose the government benefits that are becoming increasingly restricted to the native-born.

Thus the ground war on poverty continues to evolve. In 1995, a coalition of labor unions, community groups, and religious organizations created the living wage movement, an effort to increase the pay of city workers throughout the country, especially those affected by the increasingly common policy of out-sourcing city services to private firms. The guiding principle behind the movement is, "If private firms want city contracts, they must pay their workers substantially better than the subsistence poverty wage of the national minimum." By 1999, this campaign had been successful in seventeen cities (the first was Baltimore), and twenty-four other cities had similar campaigns under way. In Los Angeles, the director of that city's Living Wage Coalition, Madeline Janis-Aparcio, noted that the drive was "a tool for union organizing, for confronting the problem of wage inequality and for expressing a certain level of dignified treatment of workers."

Too often over the last century the public discussion of poverty has relied on stereotypes of the poor themselves, stereotypes both rhetorical and iconographical. In 1890, anticipating the significance of the documentary photographer in the twentieth century, the journalist Jacob Riis combined images of what appeared to be the wretched denizens of New York's Bowery district with his own pointed analysis about the baneful effects of both heredity and environment in creating impoverished populations (most of which happened to possess a clearly identifiable racial or ethnic identity). Here in black and white was the "everyday dismal dreariness" of life among the cellar dwellers, the addicts and the urchins, the tramps and the bootleggers, whether they were Italian or Chinese ("born gamblers" all), or Jews ("money is their God"). During the Great Depression, Farm Security Administration photographers illustrated the collective experience of the rural poor, black and white, Midwest and South, a group viewed by other Americans as somewhat exotic and marginal to industrial society. In their impact, these photos were uneven, for some emphasized hopelessness and despair among the men, women, and children they portrayed, while others focused on the grim determination of activists like members of the Southern Tenant Farmers' Union and the United Mine Workers.

In the 1960s, pictures of the gaunt faces of children in Kentucky, paired with those of children playing among the glass-strewn empty lots of the inner city, provided the backdrop for the War on Poverty. The book *The Other America*, by Michael Harrington, likewise brought the plight of the poor—whites as well as blacks, children as well as adults, rural folk as well as city residents, to the attention of the mass media and policymakers. However, by the 1970s, these relatively sympathetic images had been eclipsed by one that illustrated the alleged irresponsibility of the poor—the overweight African-American woman with her large brood of children. This theme—the inability of the poor to care for themselves or their children—emerged in the 1980s in the form of sensationalistic news stories focused upon drug addicts and "packs" of predatory youths. As a nation we saw what we wanted to see, and what we saw confirmed what we already believed to be true.

During the last century, a central question has framed the debate over poverty: "What are the civic responsibilities of large corporations, governmental entities, nonprofit organizations, and individual citizens to the body politic?" The Sixteenth Amendment to the Constitution, providing for a federal income tax (passed in 1913), represented an initial, tentative answer to these questions, an answer that found renewed expression during the New Deal of the 1930s and the Great Society of the 1960s. Today both Medicaid and the Earned Income Tax Credit (the latter a federally sponsored subsidy) are modest but effective means of taking the edge off economic distress for certain groups of poor people.

The voluntary redistribution of money to the poor—through private efforts—is a constant theme throughout twentieth-century American history, but the dimensions and politics of that aid have shifted over time. Charity—funneled through churches, soup kitchens, homeless shelters, and voluntary societies—has tended to be localized and direct, offering tangible services to impoverished men, women, and children within specific neighborhoods. These efforts have never been sufficient to meet the needs of the poor in any particular place or time. In contrast, philanthropy—usually expended via foundations or other mediating institutions—has tended to be indirect and diffuse, from the libraries founded by Andrew Carnegie and the medical research funded by John D. Rockefeller early in the century, to the computers donated to schools and libraries by Bill Gates one hundred years later.

The recent history of charitable food distribution efforts suggests the complexities surrounding private donations to the poor. Beginning in the 1970s, local food pantries and soup kitchens managed to coordinate their collection efforts, and came to rely on massive donations of surplus food from the country's largest food producers; these donations consisted of damaged cans, mismarked packages, and other products that could not be sold in the retail market. In the early 1980s, a recession, combined with Reagan's cuts in the federal social-welfare budget, led to increased demand on such reserves, and organizations like Second Harvest helped to supplement the federal food stamp program. However, by the late 1990s, large food corporations had become more efficient in the way they processed food, and they began to make use of damaged goods (by selling them at wholesale outlets or flea markets, for example); consequently the supply of food available to the poor declined dramatically. In just three years, the amount of food donated by the largest companies had dropped from 285 million pounds to 259 million pounds. Meanwhile, cities and states worked hard to cut the number of people eligible for food stamps, and so at the same time that the supply of food was dropping precipitously, the demand was increasing enormously.

The relative overall ineffectiveness of charity in the twentieth century suggests that private citizens resist the notion that they are ultimately responsible for providing cash and services (a "handout") to the poor, regardless of the extent of government transfer payments. What about the role of the country's largest corporations in addressing the need for good jobs at good wages for all citizens? Here the answer is clear: The system of industrial capitalism exists to produce goods and satisfy shareholders, not to right the social wrongs that might or might not flow from this system. For example, when confronted with the mandate to integrate black men and women into their workforces or lose their government contracts, World War II defense contractors balked, pointing out that corporations are not social-welfare institutions. In 1943, officials in the railroad industry (which was well known for its discriminatory hiring practices and tolerance of violent attacks by whites upon blacks), released a statement:

> Railroads do not operate in a vacuum, or in a theoretical utopia. They have to operate in and serve the civilization in which they find themselves and must adopt [sic] their operations and employment practices to the social solution of racial questions as worked out by the prevailing mores and legal systems of the states they serve.[5]

Over the last hundred years, businesses of various kinds have shaped their work forces—thereby bolstering some communities and impoverishing others—in response to any number of factors, including the prejudices of their white workers and white customers. Beginning in the mid-1960s, some companies diversified their work forces in response to federal legislation outlawing racial or gender discrimination in the work place. Yet ultimately the rationale for such policies was that they were "good for business," and not necessarily that they served a wider social function.

The dismantling of the New Deal welfare system (the Aid to Families with Dependent Children program) in 1996 thrust responsibility for the poor not just back to the states but back to the poor themselves. Nevertheless, it is not uncommon to hear commentators debate whether or not middle-class suburban blacks should play an active role in alleviating the economic distress of poor inner-city blacks. Yet rarely are we treated to a discussion of the responsibility of the white middle class for poor whites; presumably that sort of discussion might release a whole host of unpleasant truths about the fractured state of civil society in America today. Robert Reich terms late-twentieth-century America a new "Gilded Age," suggesting that we as a nation are hearkening back to the time of the robber barons, when the wealthy (and near-wealthy) regarded those less fortunate with studied, almost principled, indifference, if not contempt.

The hard truth of the matter is that the poor serve a larger political function in America today; they are too useful to banish from the scene altogether. In the rural South, well into the twentieth century, landed whites derived satisfaction from the presence of disenfranchised black field hands. These whites defined themselves accordingly; they were not black, not field hands, and not poor. Similarly, today, affluent "information managers" of various kinds measure their own success and status according to a very long yardstick—the widening gap between the rich and poor. Meanwhile, the middle class keeps an anxious eye on those beneath them, for the plight of the poor serves as a constant reminder of the fate that might eventually befall them if the turbulent job market once again takes a turn for the worse.

What conclusions can we draw about transformations in the shape and nature of poverty over the last century? Certainly some aspects of poverty have not changed much at all; newly arrived immigrants—those with little in the way of formal education or job skills—cluster at the bottom of the job ladder. Women and children remain vulnerable to the vicissitudes of the economy, and to the fates of the individual men they are supposed to be able to depend upon, fathers and husbands. People of color suffer from both the legacy and the perpetuation of racial and ethnic prejudice, and the structure of the economy exacerbates those forms of prejudice. In many cases extended families strive to help mitigate the harshest features of poverty among the least fortunate, with mixed results. Technological change continues to render whole categories of workers superfluous, even within an expanding, dynamic economy.

At the same time, it is clear that the new global marketplace, combined with an ever-evolving domestic political economy, has wrought profound effects on the shape of American poverty over the last hundred years. Today poverty tends to be more concentrated, with whole neighborhoods characterized by few or no good jobs, failing school systems, deteriorating housing stock, and underground economies characterized by a wide range of strategies, from neighborly cooperation to violent drug dealing. The late-twentieth-century concentration of poverty stems at least in part from the fact that it is more difficult for the poor to move out of distressed areas, due to the lack of meaningful opportunity within an increasingly credentials-conscious national economy.

Moreover, modern consumer society—and its attendant pervasive, seductive images of material abundance, glamour, and luxury—tends to highlight the deprivation of the poor, in contrast to the early part of the century; at that time too economic inequality was a fact of American life, but many people of modest means tended to evaluate their own situation in relation to that of their neighbors, rather than a transcendent consumer consciousness. Further, more than ever before, the fate of the poor is linked to that of workers overseas; the opening of an American shirt factory in the Dominican Republic signals the closing of a shirt factory in Maine. (What is absent here, of course, is the mechanism by which the working poor might forge ties with their foreign counterparts.) And too, in contrast to the turn of the last century, education or the lack of it constitutes a key factor in the spread and persistence of poverty today. The future belongs to an aristocracy of sorts—those people who live in the wealthiest communities with the best schools, public or private, and thereby pass their status on to their offspring.

Finally, the history of governmental action or inaction in the realm of poverty has demonstrated complex twists and turns over the years. Some might argue that we have reverted to the place we were in 1900, when private charity was a key component of aid to the poor, when unions claimed the allegiance of only a small percentage of the work force, when individual states engaged in social-engineering "experiments" designed to affect the behavior of the poor, and when the federal government played little or no part in addressing the root causes of the problem. This theme of social reversion, or regression, reached its fullest expression in 1984, with the publication of *The Bell Curve* by Richard Herrnstein and Charles Murray. In this book, the authors argue that it is the unintelligent who are poor (presumably destined to remain so) and that furthermore, there is nothing that anyone or anything can do to change that essential fact (with the possible exception of distributing vitamins to poor women who are pregnant). In this view, when poor people demand their rights, they challenge the "natural" order of things, including their own biological "destiny."

Nevertheless, beneath the surface of the social Darwinian rhetoric that pervades our policy discussion of poverty today, a number of vital, grass-roots campaigns continue to demonstrate real potential to reduce poverty rates (but by and large only within very specific locales). The decisions of city governments to enforce strict affirmative-action guidelines; the living-wage movement that is spreading to more and more metropolitan areas; and the renewed energy of organized labor, especially within the service sector, the domain of the working poor—together these efforts seek to expand job opportunities to the poor, and to ensure that these opportunities will allow workers to support their families on decent wages. Therein lies the hope for the future.

Today, at the end of the twentieth century, we are in danger of allowing poverty to become a postmodern phenomenon. By that I mean that it is possible for us to analyze and scrutinize the poor out of existence, so that the lives of poor people are read as a "text" by detached "readers" who see in those lives only irony and contradiction. The "text" or "discourse" of poverty reveals more about the observer, or reader, than it reveals about the poor themselves. If poverty is ultimately only subjective and relative, then any number of different interpretations must have validity, and who is to say which ones are right or wrong? If we follow this logic, of course, we shall choose to ignore the flesh and bones of poverty, and we will fail to heed the voices of men and women who understand that what is at stake here is not scholarly or political interpretation, but social justice.

NOTES

1. Interview with Vernatter in Richard Feldman and Michael Betzol, eds., *End of the Line: Autoworkers and the American Dream* (New York: Weidenfeld and Nicolson, 1988), p. 178.

2. Interview with Jackson in Laurel Shackelford and Bill Wineberg, eds., *Our Appalachia: An Oral History* (New York: Hill and Wang, 1977), pp. 273–76.

3. Turner quoted in Mark Robert Rank, *Living on the Edge: The Realities of Welfare in America* (New York: Columbia University Press, 1994), pp. 122–23.

4. Sara Mosle, "Letter from Las Vegas: How the Maids Fought Back," *New Yorker,* February 26/March 4, 1996, 148, 151.

5. Alexa B. Henderson, "FEPC and the Southern Railway Case: An Investigation into the Discriminatory Practices of Railroads during World War II," *Journal of Negro History* 61 (April 1976): 184.

BIBLIOGRAPHY

DuBois, W. E. B. *The Philadelphia Negro: A Social Study.* 1899. Reprint. New York: Schocken Books, 1967.

Edin, Kathryn. *Making Ends Meet: How Single Mothers Survive Welfare and Low-Wage Work.* New York: Russel Sage, 1997.

Harrington, Michael. *The Other America: Poverty in the United States.* New York: Macmillan, 1962.

Riis, Jacob A. *How the Other Half Lives: Studies among the Tenements of New York.* New York: Dover Publications, 1971.

7 | CITIZENS AND CONSUMERS IN THE CENTURY OF MASS CONSUMPTION

LIZABETH COHEN

A s we look back on the twentieth century and take stock of what has changed most in the hundred years since the last "fin de siecle," it is tempting to point to *things:* automobiles and air conditioning, television and computers, fast food and shopping malls. Not only are these different from the kinds of things Americans lived with a century ago—almost uniformly machine made, more technologically advanced, less dependent on human labor to operate—but they are better distributed among Americans than their nineteenth-century equivalents. "Mass" consumption of the abundant fruits of mass production has marked America in the twentieth century more obviously than almost anything else. As critics and scholars have sought to take measure of this new "world of things" that has transformed American life, moreover, they have expanded their sight lines to include the multiple contexts surrounding objects of consumption—their production, distribution, acquisition, and use. We have learned, for example, how mass retailing and residential suburbanization have restructured capitalist supply and demand, and how new desires fed by new mass venues for popularizing consumer fantasies—such as advertising, popular magazines, and motion pictures—have made mass consumption as influential over the American psyche as the American salary.

What we are just beginning to understand, however, is that mass consumption has deeply shaped the most central dimensions of life in the twentieth century, our political economy and our political culture. Although people's identities as "citizens" and "consumers" are often presented as opposites, the former implying an embrace of the larger public interest in the political sphere and the latter concerned with indulging individual wants in the economic sphere, it is becoming clear that no such simple distinction held true over the course of the century. Rather than isolated ideal types, "citizen" and "consumer" were ever shifting categories that sometimes overlapped, often were in tension, but always reflected the permeability of the political and economic arenas in twentieth-century America. This chapter will attempt to sketch out an emerging map of the way people as citizens and consumers have redrawn the boundaries of public life over the last century.

I will focus on three watershed periods when,I argue, the connection between citizen and consumer became restructured and hence the place of consumers in American political culture was reconceived. Those three eras include the Progressive era of the late nineteenth and early twentieth century, the New Deal from the early 1930s through World War II, and the post–World War II period. Although these eras are standard chapters in any history of the twentieth century, rarely if ever are they considered as stages in the evolution of a consumerist vision of citizenship and the state.

The consumer burst on the American political landscape as a social category with the rise of progressivism, and from the 1890s to 1920 most of the ways that consumers would later figure into mainstream political discourse got at least an airing. Progressivism established the centrality of consumers to civic life, even if it failed to secure them a permanent place in public policy. Most crucial was the emergence of a century-long tension between two conceptions—what I call *citizen consumers and customer consumers*—the former, consumers who take on the political responsibility we usually associate with citizens, to consider the general good of the nation through their consumption, and the latter, consumers who seek primarily to maximize their personal economic interests in the marketplace.

The rise of citizen consumers as a new category of the American citizenry can be seen everywhere in the Progressive movement. As David Thelan has demonstrated, turn-of-the-century Wisconsin Progressives identified consumers as an ideal, broad-based constituency for political reform, as all men and women suffered unfairly from high prices, defective products, and unresponsive politicians. Progressive political reformers campaigned for more direct democracy—primaries, initiatives, referenda, recalls, and female suffrage—and specific remedies to protect consumers and taxpayers from exploitation, such as municipal and consumer ownership of utilities and fairer tax policies. Kathryn Kish Sklar and others have introduced us to the social reformist National Consumers' League and its state chapters, which organized women consumers to orient their purchasing power toward "ethical consumption" that would pressure employers and the state to improve wages and working conditions for employed women and children. Through its symbolic "Consumers' White Label" campaign, the league urged consumers to buy only white muslin underwear bearing a label testifying to its manufacture under morally acceptable and sanitary conditions, both to protect themselves from injurious goods and to lobby for protective labor legislation, child labor laws, and improvements in retail and factory work environments. Lawrence Glickman has traced a shift among American workers in their conception of full citizenship, from a view emerging out of the artisanal age that rejected wage labor as slavery depriving workers of their freedom as citizens, to a new perspective accompanying the rise of industrial work that championed "a living wage" adequate to provide an American standard of living for working-class consumers. A fair shake at consumption—through the eight-hour day, government-regulated minimum wages, and union labels—now seemed to promise workers full rights as citizens. And Michael Sandel has elucidated one powerful thrust in the drive for antitrust legislation, most identified with reformer Louis Brandeis, as an attack on monopoly in order to preserve an America where consumers were best served by small, local, independent, self-governing businesses dedicated to a republican civic ideal. Whether in the political, social, or economic spheres scrutinized by Progressives, consumption became a new stage and consumers new actors for adapting age-old concerns with morality, good government, and the public interest to the new conditions of twentieth-century life—potentially exploitative industrial capitalism, more national political constituencies, and corruptible government.

The other effort evident in the Progressive era but not fully developed until the 1920s, when mass consumption really took off, aimed at maximizing the market-oriented interests of customer consumers. Sandel identifies this other thrust in Progressive era antitrust legislating as "consumerist," as it sought to regulate monopoly out of a commitment not to republican civic ideals but to concerns for cheaper and more efficient production and distribution to benefit consumers. During the prosperity of the 1920s customer consumers took even more central a stage, as hardly anyone worried anymore about protecting consumers from producers and, in fact, the general acceptance of a doctrine of "voluntary compliance" further weakened the already limited regulatory authority of the Federal Trade Commission and the Federal Drug Administration, both creatures of Progressive reform fervor. Rather, a Republican-dominated Washington felt that the consumers' and manufacturers' joint interests were best served by allowing business to pursue unfettered technological innovations and economic efficiencies; the free market would do the rest to deliver the best quality goods at the cheapest price to customer consumers. During the 1920s, Americans engaged in mass consuming more extensively than ever before, with the expansion of a middle class with more time and money to spend, the extension of consumer credit and installment buying, and the burgeoning of advertising. Manufacturers, distributors, and advertisers essentially enjoyed free rein in the twenties, but so long as exciting new products like automobiles, radios, and household appliances kept arriving on the market, and more and more Americans seemed able to afford them, few challenged the status quo. A rumbling of consumer discontent began in the mid-1920s with the publication of such best-selling books as Stuart Chase's *The Tragedy of Waste* in 1925 and his *Your Money's Worth* of 1927, coauthored with Frederick J. Shlink, who would soon thereafter found a national consumers' organization, Consumer's Research. But a real resurgence of citizen consumers would await a crisis on the scale of the Great Depression.

The second phase in the evolution of a consumerist political culture emerged over the long reign of the New Deal from the early 1930s through World War II, as citizen consumers became increasingly viewed as the embodiment of the public interest. In a more sustained way than in the Progressive era, policymakers and the general public grew to consider consumers as a self-conscious, identifiable interest group on a par with labor and business whose well-being required attention for American capitalism and democracy to work. Roosevelt forecast the change in his presidential campaign of 1932: "I believe we are at the threshold of a fundamental change in our popular economic thought, that in the future we are going to think less about the producer and more about the consumer." By the end of his presidency in 1945, Roosevelt would preside over a recalibration of the balance between consumer and producer interests thought necessary to keep a democratic society and capitalist economy viable, through two basic strategies. The first, a political one, involved the empowerment of citizen consumers in the institutional infrastructure of the New Deal. The second, an economic one, turned consumers' aggregate purchasing power into the vehicle for pulling the nation out of grave depression. Throughout, while New Deal policymakers experimented with different ways of recognizing consumers, consumers themselves mobilized around what was a new public identity for most of them in making political and economic demands of those in power.

The incorporation of citizen consumers as a voice of the public interest into New Deal agencies began with the National Recovery Administration (NRA), the keystone of the first New Deal's program for economic recovery, whose basic premise was that codes of fair competition setting minimum prices and wages and maximum working hours would strengthen the buying public. In recognition of consumers' key role in recovery, the NRA called for consumers to be represented along with labor and business on NRA code authorities, as well as through a Consumer Advisory Board and later, a specially appointed consumer representative. Although members of the Consumer Advisory Board often expressed frustration with the business orientation of the code authorities and NRA administrators, they succeeded in "making consumers' wants known" in the corridors of power. As sociologist Robert Lynd, who served on the board, noted, "It was no secret around Washington as the NRA episode wore on that the consumer representatives . . . embodied this 'public interest' in their proposals day in and day out far more nearly than did either of the far bigger and better supported advisory boards representing industry and labor."[1] Other New Deal agencies also acknowledged consumers as a distinct constituency. The Agricultural Adjustment Administration (AAA) created an Office of the Consumer Counsel that became one of the most effective consumer advocates within a New Deal agency. The Tennessee Valley Authority and particularly the Rural Electrification Administration organized and financed cooperative associations to bring electricity to rural America, so poorly served by private power companies that as late as 1935, nine out of ten rural homes were not electrified. The Federal Housing Administration and the Home Owners' Loan Corporation offered consumers dependable, low-cost home financing; the Federal Deposit Insurance Corporation guaranteed bank deposits; and the Securities and Exchange Commission protected investors by regulating public offerings of corporate securities. Roosevelt justified his new attention to consumers as "a new principle in government" that consumers have the right "to have their interests represented in the formulation of government policy. . . . Never before had the particular problems of consumers been so thoroughly and unequivocally accepted as the direct responsibility of government. The willingness to fulfill that responsibility was, in essence, an extension and amplification of the meaning and content of democratic government." Attentiveness to the consumer also led Congress in the late 1930s to pass the first substantial regulatory legislation since the Progressive era, the Food, Drug, and Cosmetic Act and the Wheeler-Lea Amendment to the Clayton Antitrust Act of 1914.

The second way that consumers came to figure more centrally in the New Deal resulted from the growing conviction that consumers held the present and future health of the American capitalist economy in their hands. As government policymakers increasingly embraced Keynesian economic theory, particularly after the nose dive brought on by the "Roosevelt depression of 1937–1938," government spending to expand consumer demand became the prevailing strategy for hauling the United States out of depression toward renewed economic growth. With the Keynesian revolution, mass consumers through their spending became responsible for high productivity and full employment, whereas a decade earlier that role had belonged to producers. Keynesian attention to consumption, moreover, was expected to breed greater political democracy and economic egalitarianism. As capitalism revived, it promised to bolster democracy as an alternative to communism and fascism. And because dynamic consumer demand was thought to depend on a wide distribution of purchasing power, capitalist prosperity for the nation promised greater economic equality for all its citizen consumers.

As policymakers and economists in Washington were paying more attention to consumers, consumers also were asserting themselves as citizen consumers cognizant that their own well-being and the nation's were inseparably intertwined. Most dramatically, the New Deal's sudden attention to consumers as the voice of the public interest offered otherwise underrepresented groups—in particular women and African Americans—the opportunity to make new claims on those wielding public and private power in American society. With all the attention to the rise of the labor movement during the

1930s, the impressive organizing efforts of consumers have been unfairly lost in the shadow cast by mobilized producers.

With the exception of the consumer cooperative and product testing wings, women made up much of the consumer movement's leadership and rank and file during the 1930s. Through existing and newly created organizations that energized tens of thousands of women, they lobbied New Deal agencies and Congress demanding that the federal government provide greater consumer representation and stronger legal protections against corporate abuse. They expanded consumer education programs in schools and communities, mounting exhibits, organizing fact-finding missions, and running conferences. And most visibly, they orchestrated impressive boycotts and other buyers' actions to protest unfair prices and other forms of market exploitation to retailers, distributors, manufacturers, and government policymakers, most notably through massive meat boycotts in 1935. Through all these avenues female citizen consumers established themselves as the new protectors of the public interest. An early chronicler of the consumer movement claimed, "Not since the demand for suffrage have women been drawn so closely together on a common issue." Confirming that view, Dr. Kathryn McHale, the general director of the American Association of University Women, asserted that although all Americans were consumers, "no matter what our other interests," women had the prime responsibility to shape the nation's standards for production, purchase, and consumption. Women had mounted buyers' strikes before against high prices, such as the cost-of-living protests of Jewish women in New York City around the time of World War I. But women's consumer actions in the 1930s went far beyond prices and were coordinated on a citywide and even national level, crossing narrow subcommunities of ethnicity, race, and class. Whether picketing outside their local butcher shops or lobbying Congress for stricter regulation of cosmetics, women had anointed themselves creators of a safer and more equitable marketplace for the good of the nation.

African Americans in the urban North also mobilized as consumers, but they did so in ways unique to their racial situation. By boycotting some merchants while favoring others, organizing cooperatives, and undertaking other kinds of consumer activism, African Americans asserted themselves in the retail marketplace on an unprecedented scale. Faced with devastating economic hardship wrought by the Great Depression, northern blacks—most of them relative newcomers to the region's cities—had little recourse. They were already enthusiastically exercising the franchise long denied them in the South, and had in fact shifted a majority of their votes by 1936 from the party of Lincoln to the party of Roosevelt. And as they were losing jobs in the private sector in record numbers, giving them the highest unemployment rates in many northern cities, organizing at the work place had limited impact until they could join the CIO's larger offensive later in the decade. The Communist party offered some immediate help against tenant evictions and relief discrimination, but full-fledged membership appealed to only a small minority of blacks. The remaining, and most promising, avenue was African-American spending power, which—if properly channeled—could be a powerful club for demanding jobs and fairer treatment from white store owners and for favoring black-owned businesses and cooperatives, whose greater profits would then circulate within black communities. Black residents of every major northern city and racial leaders of diverse political persuasions, ranging from "conservative" spokesmen of the National Negro Business League to the more "radical" NAACP founder and well-known Socialist W. E. B. DuBois, civil rights activist Ella Baker, and the National Negro Congress, recognized over the course of the thirties the benefits of politicizing African-American consumers on a mass scale. From the "Don't Shop Where You Can't Work" campaigns that mobilized black consumers against job-discriminating white store owners in a chain of cities, to broader drives against bus companies, public utilities, landlords, and movie theaters, to support for alternative black-owned cooperatives, blacks looked to the "double duty dollar" to advance the race while they purchased.

Whereas women consumer activists sought to secure rights as consumers, ranging from lower prices to protective legislation, blacks primarily used consumer power to secure other rights, especially the right to be employed in their own communities. Blacks, too, aimed less at representing some general public interest and winning the federal government's support for their demands than at improving concrete economic conditions in northern black communities. But like consumer activists more generally, African Americans felt part of their own national effort that put the individual's purchasing power to the service of some broader social good.

The Great Depression kept in check the alternative urge of customer consumers to satisfy individual wants regardless of the public interest. But as war production fueled new prosperity, consumers' desire to spend freely threatened dangerous inflation and shortages, particularly as more and more products became needed for military use. The government's remedy was to encourage savings through war bonds, to expand vastly the reach of the income tax, and to create official wartime agencies, most notably the Office of Price Administration (OPA), to ensure that responsible citizen consumers willing to sublimate disruptive private interests to the public interest prevailed over self-indulgent customer consumers. And for the most part it worked. Despite corporate objections to price controls (for regulating profits), most American consumers supported them as fundamental to mobilizing fairly for war. Hoarding was relatively controlled, inflation contained, and crucial military materiel found its way to the front. The OPA itself developed into an expansive bureaucracy run by paid staff in Washington, regional offices, and localities and supported by legions of citizen volunteers serving on municipal war price and rationing boards and consumer interest committees. Within a month of taking over the OPA in

November of 1943, new head Chester Bowles also appointed a twenty-six-member Consumer Advisory Committee—a virtual "who's who" of the thriving wartime consumer movement—to steer the OPA as much as possible toward pro-consumer policies, such as improved product grading and labeling. Citizen consumers patriotically upholding price control and rationing not only overshadowed black-market-patronizing customer consumers on the home front, but within individuals the commitment to cooperate loyally with wartime restrictions usually won out over the desire to avoid the restrictions so as to indulge pent-up consumer appetites. The remarkable redistribution of income due to wartime employment and market regulation, moreover, only reinforced the sense that the war emergency was promoting the long held ideal of greater equality in America. Between 1941 and 1944, family income rose by over 24 percent in constant dollars, with the lowest fifth gaining three times more than the highest fifth, essentially doubling the size of the middle class. Even *Business Week* labeled the war a "great leveler."

As this tension played out from the national policy stage to the family circle, women became even more pivotal on the home front than they had been in the 1930s when they first agitated on behalf of "the consumer interest." Suddenly, women's ordinary responsibilities as chief household purchasers put them in the eye of the storm of war: their recycling of metals made ammunition plentiful, their limited consumption of sugar and shoes fed and dressed the army, their adherence to price controls kept hoarding and inflation down and morale up. Even beyond their responsible behavior as buyers, rationers, and salvagers, moreover, women staffed—and in many places directed—a massive regulation of the retail marketplace that reached into every household and every retail outlet in every municipality. As new rituals for proving patriotic citizenship emerged around obeying and enforcing OPA price, rent, and rationing regulations; participating in recycling, scrap, and waste-fat drives; and planting victory gardens and "putting up" the home harvest; women presided and became the embodiment of a gender-specific definition of the "good citizen." From the OPA's Consumer Advisory Committee in Washington to the "Little OPA's" and other state and local consumer regulatory agencies down to individual block organizations and households, women—perceived as the power behind purchasing—shaped and implemented policies that linked the viability of a nation at war to the responsible action of female citizen consumers. A popular slogan like "Lady, it's your war, win it!" was an invitation to women to assert new female political authority, not just a line on government posters. Even the *Women's Home Companion,* a magazine steeped in traditional gender roles, credited women with "the job of Economic Director of the Homefront . . . a man-sized job."

The realm of consumption became so pivotal to the success of the war effort, in fact, that to an even greater extent than during the 1930s it provided a crucial arena in which African Americans would experience—and contest—

the discrimination they met in their efforts to participate fully in American life. Although historians have generally rooted the black struggle for "Double V[ictory]"—freedom at home as well as abroad—in the demand for equality in defense jobs and the military, many of the frustrations voiced by African Americans in wartime revolved around their exclusion from sites of consumption: restaurants, bars, hotels, movie theaters, stores, pools, buses, and other so-called public accommodations (so identified because they supposedly catered to all, whether privately or publicly owned). As African Americans embarked on proving themselves loyal Americans on the home front by heeding the regulations of the OPA or by journeying to new territory north and west as soldiers and defense workers, they constantly met discrimination as consumers. And in a wartime atmosphere where good consumer and good citizen increasingly were intertwined, that unfair treatment in the marketplace took on new political significance. Whereas in the 1930s asserting their rights as consumers was part of a strategy to achieve economic power, in the context of war African Americans recognized that their political equality as citizens was at stake as well. Every time that blacks were kept off the very OPA price boards that they valued as protection against white storekeepers' arbitrary pricing, or were refused service at stores or restaurants even when wearing a military uniform and carrying Uncle Sam's green money in their pockets, they found the assumed universality of citizenship as well as the supposed freedom of the free capitalist marketplace violated. As war administrators increasingly moved consumption into the civic realm, African Americans—like women— made it a new ground upon which to stake their claim to fuller political participation. Citizenship came to be defined more broadly during World War II to encompass new kinds of political rituals beyond traditional voting and military service, and in the process the potential for political discontent and the grounds for mobilizing against racial discrimination grew. Roy Wilkins of the NAACP articulated how much blacks' rejection in the realm of consumption symbolized for them the full depth of their exclusion when he recounted that "It is pretty grim . . . to have a black boy in uniform get an orientation lecture in the morning on wiping out Nazi bigotry and that same evening to be told he can buy a soft drink only in the 'Colored' post exchange!"

The end of war and reconversion to peacetime brought the suppressed conflict between the ideals of citizen consumer and customer consumer to a head and inaugurated a third period when the relationship of consumer to citizen was reconfigured. The immediate postwar struggle over ending or extending price control became the line in the sand that each side—business and its congressional allies on the one hand and a broad coalition of consumer activists on the other—drew as critical to achieving their respective visions of postwar America. Whereas the corporate champions of customer consumers pushed for the full return of free enterprise, functioning in a free market and free of government intervention, the defenders of citizen consumers—

consumer activists, women, African Americans, organized labor, and some veterans' groups—agitated for a postwar order where the state would continue to play a role in regulating the consumer marketplace through price and rent controls, and where the good citizen would continue to be defined as one who consumed responsibly with the general good in mind. By the fall of 1946, what OPA chief Chester Bowles, fighting for his agency's survival, called "the battle of the century" came to a close and price control was definitively defeated.

In the wake of that defeat, a new vision of the postwar order began to emerge supported by a consensus of business, labor, and government interests, all of whom sought a reconversion strategy that would protect the nation from feared postwar depression and deliver postwar prosperity. Despite vicious fighting over the extension of price controls in 1946, and struggles thereafter over the balance of power in industrial relations, the tautness of government regulation, and the extent of income redistribution through taxation, minimum wage, and other policies, a surprisingly wide cast of characters came to settle on the same postwar script. They agreed that economic salvation lay in a vital mass consumption-oriented economy where good customers devoted to consuming "more, newer, and better" were in fact good citizens. Out of the wartime conflict between citizen consumers, who reoriented their personal consumption to serve the general good, and customer consumers, who pursued private gain regardless of it, emerged a new postwar ideal of the customer as citizen, who simultaneously fulfilled personal desire and civic obligation by consuming. As *Bride Magazine* told the acquisitive readers of its handbook for newlyweds, when you buy "the dozens of things you never bought or even thought of before, . . . you are helping to build greater security for the industries of this country. . . . [W]hat you buy and how you buy it is very vital to your new life—and to our whole American way of living." Labor leader Walter Reuther echoed the same message when he exhorted the 1946 CIO convention: "We make this fight in the CIO not only because Joe Smith needs more money to buy his kids food and get them adequate clothing and provide decent shelter, but in the aggregate millions of Jones and Smiths throughout America need this greater purchasing power because the nation needs this greater purchasing power."

Faith in a mass consumption-driven postwar economy came to mean much more than the ready availability of goods to buy. Rather, it stood for an elaborate ideal of economic abundance and democratic political freedom, both equitably distributed, that became almost a national civil religion from the late 1940s into at least the 1970s. Despite its ubiquity in the policies and discourses of the postwar era, however, this paradigm bore no specific label at the time, so for convenience sake I have dubbed it the Consumers' Republic. For at least a quarter century, the ideal of the Consumers' Republic provided the blueprint for American economic, social, and political maturation, as well as for export around the globe. The Consumers' Republic had many appeals. It promised great prosperity through yoking employment and economic growth to high consumer demand, and it provided a ready weapon in the political struggles of the cold war, helping the United States to justify its superiority over the Soviet Union both at home and abroad. But perhaps most attractive was the way it promoted the socially progressive end of greater economic equality without requiring politically progressive means of redistributing existing wealth. Rather, an ever-growing economy built around the interconnected dynamics of increased productivity and mass purchasing power, it was argued, would expand the overall pie without reducing the size of any of the portions. When President Truman challenged Americans in 1950 to "achieve a far better standard of living for every industrious family" within a decade, specifically to ensure everyone "an income of $4,000 a year," he characteristically reassured them that "raising the standards of our poorest families will not be at the expense of anybody else. We will all benefit by doing it, for the incomes of the rest of us will rise at the same time."

As the public good increasingly seemed to rest on Americans buying new cars, homes, appliances, and furnishings, activists in the consumer movement that had flourished through the economic doldrums of the Great Depression, the war emergency, and its immediate aftermath found themselves and their organizations increasingly marginalized. A combination of factors converged to stall consumer activism after the failed effort to protect price control. Although consumers were still very much on activists' minds, emphasis was more on the power of total consumer spending than on the need to protect the rights and interests of individual consumers, the traditional mission of consumer organizations. Consumers, moreover, felt much less vulnerable to burdensome shortages, spiking prices, and inadequate product labeling than they previously had, whereas the ascetic side of the consumer movement that had promoted government regulation and consumer restraint seemed out of step with more bounteous times. Consumer organizer Caroline Ware's call for the replacement of "conspicuous consumption" to "keep up with the Joneses" with "an American standard of decent living" premised on "keeping down with the Joneses" did not excite enthusiasm. Finally, the resuscitation with the war of business's depression-scarred reputation and the red-baiting of consumer activists and their organizations with the anti-Communist hysteria of the late 1940s both contributed to muddying the picture of an epic moral struggle between exploiting corporations and vulnerable consumers. Progress did continue during the 1940s and 1950s to update congressional legislation protecting consumers from new pesticides, additives, and drugs and unsafe conditions, but many new initiatives languished, until the mass of Americans again perceived threats to their health and safety in the 1960s and 1970s and the consumer movement revived. Meanwhile, though, the moral claim previously asserted by the consumer movement—to represent the general good— had shifted to the Consumers' Republic itself, which promised that consumers' purchasing power would improve the lives of all Americans.

As the Consumers' Republic evolved in the postwar period, it brought with it new "rules of the game" that redefined gender and racial norms. The battle over the survival of the OPA in 1946 set the stage. Pro-price control forces—overwhelmingly female, black, working class, and reformist—were painted by the victorious opposition as weak, dependent, and feminine, while the proponents of ending governmental regulation of the consumer market-place portrayed themselves as strong, independent, and masculine. From there, other structures of the Consumers' Republic continued reshaping gen-der roles to delegitimate the civic authority that women had gained on the home front in World War II. More took place than simply firing women from the well-paying defense jobs that they had held in wartime. In particular, two key pillars of the Consumers' Republic's infrastructure—the GI Bill of Rights and fine-tuning of the mass income tax that had first emerged with the war emergency—favored men over women, bolstering a male-directed family economy where men disproportionately had access to career training, prop-erty ownership, capital, and credit, as well as control over family finances. Men thereby became the embodiment of the postwar ideal of customers as citizens, limiting their wives' claims.

The chief policy instrument favoring men over women was a powerful new Keynesian program, the GI bill (officially the Servicemen's Readjustment Act of 1944) that fulfilled multiple postwar goals at once through a trio of ben-efits—unemployment pay while looking for a job, tuition and subsistence al-lowances for further education or training, and loans to purchase homes or farms or to start a business. It also aimed to avoid the economic disruption, massive unemployment, and political unrest that had followed World War I. And it jump-started the postwar economy by expanding purchasing power, by injecting new capital into existing institutions ranging from colleges to banks to the housing industry, and by creating higher earning and home-owning consumers who would make secure credit risks for future buying. Despite a powerful mythology surrounding the GI bill that celebrates its universality, in fact these tickets to upward mobility—higher education, home mortgages, and capital to found a business—were available only to those who had served in the war, which excluded all nonveterans, but particularly most women. The 2 percent of military personnel in World War II who were female took less ad-vantage of GI benefits than their male counterparts, and discovered the bene-fits were inferior to men's when they did claim them. Even women who prof-ited through their veteran husbands, sons, and fathers did not share benefits equally with the men in their families. So whether in veteran or nonveteran households, women in postwar America found themselves deprived of the GI bill's backing and thereby forced into new dependencies that limited their life options.

The other major federal policy that set new gender rules for the Con-sumers' Republic was the institutionalization of the mass income tax that had debuted during World War II. The demands of financing the war and restraining inflation had moved the government to broaden the taxpayer base far beyond the wealthy few who had been paying since the income tax's adoption in 1913. Whereas only 7 million Americans filed income tax returns in 1940, by 1945 more than 42 million did. In 1948, and less dramatically in 1951 and 1954, Congress passed amendments to the tax code that adapted wartime tax policies to postwar normalcy, articulating the fiscal underpinnings of the Consumer's Republic. Less progressive than in wartime, when the income tax contributed to the general narrowing of the income gap, revised postwar tax codes reflected the general commitment of the Consumers' Republic to spread affluence through a prospering economy, not through extensive redistribution of income. In terms of establishing new gender norms, the Internal Revenue Code as amended in the late 1940s reinforced the GI bill in favoring the traditional male breadwinner-headed family and the male citizen within it. Congress's adoption of the income-splitting joint return in 1948 favored traditional married couples in which the wife did not work outside the home, as here the benefits from income shifting from husband to wife were greatest. Although women's participation in the labor force would gradually climb back up after its fall at the war's end, the joint income tax return offered little incentive to wives to push beyond part-time and low-paying clerical and sales jobs. In allowing deductions for mortgage and other interest payments, the tax code further reinforced patriarchal privilege, as loans and credit were very difficult for women to secure until the 1970s. As the federal government bestowed advantages on male veterans and male taxpayers, it helped create the male customer as citizen who dominated his household as chief breadwinner, homeowner, credit borrower, and taxpayer.

African Americans' experience within the Consumer's Republic was complicated. On the one hand, they encountered even more insidious discrimination than women in claiming their fair share of GI benefits. Whereas most women were excluded by virtue of not being veterans, black veterans were legitimately entitled but often suffered from the way the GI bill was structured. In choosing to channel federal dollars to veterans through existing private institutions like colleges, banks, and building and loans, and thereby not expand the public sector's presence, Congress reinforced rather than challenged the discrimination that black ex-GIs routinely encountered whenever they applied to colleges or vocational training programs, and for a house mortgage or loan to start a business. On the other hand, the firm connection that the Consumers' Republic established between citizenship and consumption gave African Americans a vehicle to direct pent-up frustration from wartime discrimination into concrete action following it. In state after state beginning in the late 1940s, blacks mounted a civil rights movement challenging discrimination and exclusion from public accommodations, many of them sites of consumption and leisure. Battles to gain access to downtown restaurants and hotels, movie theaters and swimming pools, bowling alleys and skating rinks, and to buy everything from a beer to a house wherever one wanted, led to the passage of new civil rights legislation in many northern states. Even in the South, the ten years between the war and the Montgomery bus boycott of 1955 saw rumblings of protest around black exclusion from parks, theaters, and department store lunch counters alongside more celebrated efforts at voter registration. The federal Civil Rights Act of 1964, barring discrimination in all public accommodations throughout the nation, emerged out of—rather than launched—a grass-roots movement for, literally, an equal place at the table.

The benefits of the early civil rights movement aside, the Consumers' Republic—and its magic wand of mass consumption more generally—led not just to some increase in democracy and equality created by greater prosperity, but also to new kinds of stratification and inequality. A case in point is the evolution of the postwar residential landscape. The United States came out of World War II faced with an enormous housing crisis. After a decade and a half of severe depression and war, somewhere between three and a half and five million new homes were required immediately to house all the individuals and families in need, and by some estimates as many as 50 percent of existing homes needed replacement or major repairs. The remedy was mass housing construction of single-family homes, many of them in new suburban areas, a solution intended not only to shelter Americans but also to stimulate the demand economy undergirding the Consumers' Republic. By turning "home" into an expensive commodity for purchase by many more consumers than ever before and by increasing demand for related commodities like cars, appliances, and furnishings, new house construction became the bedrock of the Consumers' Republic. One of every four homes standing in the United States in 1960 went up in the 1950s, and by the same year 60 percent of Americans could claim that they owned their own home, in contrast to 40 percent as recently as 1940, the biggest jump in homeownership rates ever recorded. The democratizing of home ownership through the mass consumption market embodied the essence of the Consumers' Republic, as did the public-private partnership that supported it. Private interests carried out and profited from the home building, subsidized by the federal government's insuring of mortgages though the Veterans Administration and the Federal Housing Administration, granting mortgage interest deductions on income taxes, and constructing federal highways to link these new suburban communities to the metropolis.

But bringing housing more centrally into the mass consumption marketplace contributed to privileging some social groups over others. Access to mortgages, credit, and tax benefits favored men over women, whites over blacks, and the middle class over the working class. In addition, the extensive suburbanization of the metropolitan landscape that accompanied mass home building created new inequalities as whole communities soon became stratified along class and racial lines. While home in the Consumer's Republic became a commodity to be traded up like a car, rather than an emotional investment in a neighborhood or church parish, "property values" became the new mantra. Of course, people still chose the towns they lived in, but increasingly they selected among homogeneous, home-ruled, suburban communities occupying different rungs in a hierarchy of property values, with the quality of services varying much more than they previously had for people living within larger units of cross-class and interracial cities. In particular, education, widely recognized as the best ticket to success in postwar America, became captive to the inequalities of the new metropolitan landscape, given that local communities substantially provided, and paid for, their own schools through local property taxes. The wealthier the community, the more it had to spend. By putting its faith in the potential of the private mass consumption marketplace to deliver opportunity rather than in expanding state provisions or redistributing wealth, the Consumers' Republic contributed to growing inequality and fragmentation. Despite an early confidence in the universal benefits of selling to the "mass," before very long a postwar economy and society ostensibly built on "mass consumption" created a reality of economic and social segmentation that was only reinforced by marketing and advertising which simultaneously discovered the greater profits to be made in segmenting the market into distinctive submarkets based on gender, class, race, ethnicity, age, and lifestyle. Residential suburbanization, the engineering of a social landscape that served property values more effectively than people, became one of several arenas in which Americans shared less and less common physical space and civic culture. This has contributed to the fractured and inequitable public sphere we are struggling with today.

The shift in the center of postwar commercial and often community life from urban downtowns to suburban shopping centers that accompanied residential suburbanization, moreover, only reinforced this trend toward social fragmentation and inequality. Suburban shopping centers became another setting where customers as citizens found themselves segmented into submarkets and deprived of full and equal legal rights. Space that had been public in the urban centers became legally the private property of shopping center owners, and hence constitutional rights once guaranteed in the town square— such as freedom of speech and assembly—were not automatically protected unless state courts upheld them, and even then the poor, the black, and the young were often marginalized.

Few would dispute the evidence that over the past fifteen years or so, inequality of income and wealth in the United States has increased. Ubiquitous are the exposés lamenting the growing gulf between two Americas—one whose citizens have steady jobs, fringe benefits, and homes in the suburbs, the other whose citizens move between welfare and minimum-wage jobs, have no health insurance, and live in inner-city neighborhoods or deteriorating first-ring suburbs. Analysts point the finger at such factors as the loss of good work-ing-class jobs with deindustrialization, an increasingly less progressive tax structure, growing inequities in education, and the gap between single-parent, often female-headed households and high-earning, two-income professional ones. Undoubtedly, these all matter, but missing is the larger, longer view that acknowledges how deeply entrenched economic inequality is in the route we chose to achieve postwar abundance. In expecting the private marketplace, in what was assumed to be an ever-expanding economy, to solve the nation's so-cial and economic problems, the ideal of the Consumers' Republic has con-tributed to its own demise.

At the end of the twentieth century, "citizen" and "consumer" remain per-meable categories in our political culture, much as they were as the century began. As just one example, the Clinton-Gore National Performance Review Report aimed at "reinventing government," entitled *From Red Tape to Results: Creating a Government That Works Better and Costs Less* (1993), listed among its top goals "Putting Customers First." But rather than consumers defending the public interest as they first did in the Progressive era and more systemati-cally during the New Deal and World War II, the half-century reign of the Consumers' Republic has recast the consumer as the embodiment of more nar-rowly defined self-interest. When the Clinton-Gore report envisioned a new-style government, it modeled it after the efficient retail business: "Effective, entrepreneurial governments insist on customer satisfaction. They listen care-fully to their customers—using surveys, focus groups, and the like. They re-structure their basic operations to meet customers' needs. And they use mar-ket dynamics such as competition and customer choice to create incentives that drive their employees to put customers first." The idealized postwar cus-tomer as citizen is still alive and well, but in the latest twist, the watchdog citizen consumers of the 1930s and 1940s have been replaced by the self-interested government customers of the 1990s, who bring a consumer men-tality to their relations with government, judging government services much like other purchased goods, by the personal benefit they derive from them. Over the last half century, our confidence that an economy and culture of mass consumption could deliver democracy and equality—that it was in fact the best way to secure them—has led us from the Consumers' Republic to the con-sumerization of the republic, where politicians and their customer-voters re-ject whatever doesn't pay. A century that began with the consumer inspiring the expansion of government for Progressive reform is ending with the con-sumer inspiring government's retrenchment.

NOTE

1. Robert S. Lynd, "Foreword," in Persia Campbell, *Consumer Representation in the New Deal* (New York: Columbia University Press, 1940), p. 11.

SUGGESTIONS FOR FURTHER READING

For more in-depth treatment of themes discussed in this chapter, see the following secondary sources. My discussion of the consumer orientation of reform during the Progressive era makes reference to David P. Thelan, *The New Citizenship: Origins of Progressivism in Wisconsin, 1885–1900* (Columbia: University of Missouri Press, 1972); Lawrence B. Glickman, *A Living Wage: American Workers and the Making of Consumer Society* (Ithaca, N.Y.: Cornell University Press, 1997); and Michael J. Sandel, *Democracy's Discontent: American in Search of a Public Philosophy* (Cambridge, Mass.: The Belknap Press of Harvard University Press, 1996). For the organization of consumers for social reform, see Kathryn Kish Sklar's article, "The Consumers' White Label Campaign of the National Consumers' League, 1898–1918," in Susan Strasser, Charles McGovern, and Matthias Judt, *Getting and Spending: European and American Consumer Societies in the Twentieth Century* (Washington, D.C.: German Historical Institute; New York: Cambridge University Press, 1998). On the decline and then rise of the consumer interest during the 1920s and 1930s, see Dana Frank, *Purchasing Power: Consumer Organizing, Gender, and the Seattle Labor Movement, 1919–1929* (New York: Cambridge University Press, 1994); Lizabeth Cohen, *Making a New Deal: Industrial Workers in Chicago, 1919–1939* (New York: Cambridge University Press, 1990); and Ronald Edsforth, *Class Conflict and Cultural Consensus: The Making of a Mass Consumer Society in Flint, Michigan* (New Brunswick, N.J.: Rutgers University Press, 1987). For the best treatment of the shift in economic policy toward a Keynesianism that put consumers' purchasing power at the heart of recovery and prosperity, see Alan Brinkley, *The End of Reform: New Deal Liberalism in Recession and War* (New York: Alfred A. Knopf, 1995). Two extremely helpful studies of the consumerist orientation of the home front during World War II are Amy Bentley, *Eating for Victory: Food Rationing and the Politics of Domesticity* (Urbana: University of Illinois Press, 1998) and Meg Jacobs, "'How About Some Meat?' The Office of Price Administration, Consumption Politics, and State Building from the Bottom Up, 1941–1946," *Journal of American History* 84 (December 1997): 910–941. Issues related to consumption during the postwar reign of the Consumers' Republic are well treated in Thomas Hine, *Populuxe* (New York: Alfred A. Knopf, 1986); Kenneth T. Jackson, *Crabgrass Frontier: The Suburbanization of the United States* (New York: Oxford University Press, 1985); Lizabeth Cohen, "From Town Center to Shopping Center: The Reconfiguration of Community Marketplaces in Postwar America," *American Historical Review* 101 (October 1996): 1050–1081; and Robert Weems, *Desegregating the Dollar: African American Consumerism in the Twentieth Century* (New York: New York University Press, 1998). Two general sources that shed helpful light on consumption over the full reach of the twentieth century are Olivier Zunz, *Why the American Century?* (Chicago: University of Chicago Press, 1998) and other essays in the volume *Getting and Spending: European and American Consumer Societies in the Twentieth Century* already cited for Sklar's article, particularly those by Charles McGovern ("Consumption and Citizenship in the United States, 1900–1940"); Lizabeth Cohen ("The New Deal State and the Making of Citizen Consumers"); and George Lipsitz ("Consumer Spending as State Project: Yesterday's Solutions and Today's Problems"). The ideas I have presented in this essay are further developed in my own forthcoming book, *A Consumers' Republic: The Politics of Mass Consumption in Postwar America* (New York: Knopf, forthcoming).

8 | AMERICAN WOMEN IN THE TWENTIETH CENTURY

Sara M. Evans

I n 1900, our foremothers predicted that the twentieth century would be the "century of the child." It might be more accurate, however, to call it the "century of women." Among the many dramatic changes in American society, it is hard to find an example more striking than the changes in women's lives on every level.

At the beginning of the twentieth century, women were challenging the confines of an ideology that relegated them to the private realm of domesticity. Despite the reality that thousands of women could be found in factories, offices, and fields—not to mention in a wide variety of political and reform activities—those ideas still held powerful sway both in law and in dominant notions of propriety. Over the course of the twentieth century, however, women in America emerged fully (though still not equally) into all aspects of public life—politics, labor force participation, professions, mass media, and popular culture. As they did so, they experienced a transformation in the fundamental parameters of their private lives as well—marriage, family, fertility, and sexuality. In complex ways, women transformed the landscapes of both public and private life so that at century's end we are left with a deeply puzzling conundrum about just what we mean by the terms *public* and *private*.

Women, of course, are part of every other social group. Deeply divided by race, class, religion, ethnicity, and region, they don't always identify with one another, and as a result women's collective identity—their sense of solidarity as women—has waxed and waned. Twice in this century, however, there has been a massive wave of activism focused on women's rights. We can trace the surges of change in women's status that accompanied each of these, one at the beginning and another near the end of the century.

Changes in women's lives were certainly driven by large structural forces such as the emergence of the postindustrial service economy, rising levels of education, and the exigencies of two world wars. Yet they have also been due to women's own self-organized activism in two great waves and in numerous ripples in between. In some instances women fought for the right to participate in public life. In other instances, already present in public spaces, they struggled for equity. As a result of these struggles, American political and public life has undergone a series of fundamental transformations. Not only are women in different places at the end of the century then they were at the beginning, but also all Americans enter a new century shaped by the complexities of women's journey.

1900—DAWN OF THE TWENTIETH CENTURY

At the beginning of the twentieth century, women's lives were defined primarily by their marital status, linked to race and class. If we take a snapshot (understanding that we are capturing a moment in a dynamic process of change), the normative adult woman—both statistically and in the images that pervaded popular culture—was married, middle class, and white. On average, women lived to 48.3 years; they married around age 22 and bore approximately four children. The vast majority of households consisted of male-headed married couples and their children.

In 1900 women's legal standing was fundamentally governed by their marital status. They had very few rights.

- A married woman had no separate legal identity from that of her husband.
- She had no right to control of her reproduction (even conveying information about contraception, for example, was illegal); and no right to sue or be sued, since she had no separate standing in court.
- She had no right to own property in her own name or to pursue a career of her choice.
- Women could not vote, serve on juries, or hold public office. According to the Supreme Court, Women were not "persons" under the Fourteenth Amendment to the Constitution that guarantees equal protection under the law.

These realities reflected an underlying ideology about women and men that allocated the public realms of work and politics to men and defined the proper place of women in society as fundamentally domestic. Confined to the realm of the home, women's duty to society lay in raising virtuous sons (future citizens) and dutiful daughters (future mothers). Over the course of the nineteenth century, however, women had pushed at the boundaries of their domestic assignment, both by choice and by necessity. They invented forms of politics outside the electoral arena by forming voluntary associations and building institutions in response to unmet social needs. In the 1830s, when women like Sarah and Angelina Grimké began to speak publicly against slavery, the mere appearance of a woman as a public speaker was considered scandalous. By 1900, however, women appeared in all manner of public settings, setting the stage for change in the twentieth century.

Signs of Change

A closer look at women's status in 1900 reveals trends that signal imminent change particularly in the areas of education, labor force participation, and sexuality. The coexistence of new possibilities alongside ongoing restrictions and discrimination laid the groundwork for challenges to the norms of female subordination.

Education Women in 1900 had achieved a high degree of literacy. In fact, more girls than boys actually graduated from high school, probably because boys had access to many jobs that did not require significant education. When it came to higher education, however, women were seriously disadvantaged. They were overtly excluded from most professional education: only about 5 percent of medical students were women, and women's exclusion from legal education shows up in the fact that in 1920 only 1.4 percent of lawyers in the United States were female.

It is crucial to note, however, that in 1900 women constituted about 30 percent of students in colleges and universities, including schools for the growing female professions of nursing, teaching, librarianship, and social work. In the long run, this was a potent mix, as thousands of middle-class women embraced the opportunity to pursue higher education, which in turn generated new expectations. Education was a crucial force in creating the key leadership as well as a highly skilled constituency for the feminist mobilizations at either end of the century.

Labor Force Participation In 1900, though wage labor was defined as a fundamentally male prerogative, women could be found in many parts of the labor force. Women's work outside the home, however, was framed by their marital status and overt discrimination based on race as well as sex.

- Approximately one in five women worked outside the home, a figure that was sharply distinguished by race: 41 percent nonwhite; 17 percent white.
- The average working woman was single and under age 25.
- Only 11 percent of married women worked outside the home (up to 15% by 1940), though the proportion among black women (26%) was considerably

higher because discrimination against black men made it much harder for blacks to secure a livable income from a single wage.

- Available occupations were sharply limited. Most women who worked for wages served as domestics, farm laborers, unskilled factory operatives, or teachers. In fact, one in three women employed in nonagricultural pursuits worked in domestic service.

- Some new female-dominated professions, such as nursing, social work, and librarianship, were emerging. In addition, the feminization of clerical work, linked to the new technology of the typewriter and the record-keeping needs of growing corporate bureaucracies, signaled a dramatic trend that made the "working girl" increasingly respectable. By 1920 the proportion of women engaged in clerical work (25.6%) had surpassed the number in manufacturing (23.8), domestic service (18.2%), and agriculture (12.9%).

Sexuality and the Body Late Victorians presumed (if they thought about it at all) that female sexuality should be confined entirely to marriage. Compared with today, there was very little premarital sex, and women were understood not to have much in the way of sexual desire. It was illegal to transmit information about contraception, though women clearly conveyed it anyway through networks of rumor and gossip. Within the dominant middle class even the simplest acknowledgments of female sexuality were suppressed into euphemism and other forms of denial. Body parts could not be named in polite company, so chicken "legs" and "breast," for example, became "dark meat" and "white meat." Female attire covered women's bodies with clothing that revealed some shape but very little skin.

Yet, as the twentieth century dawned with its emerging consumer culture, sexuality could no longer be so easily contained. Popular culture included vaudeville, dance halls, and a growing variety of public amusements (such as the brand-new movie theaters). In the past, women who frequented such places risked having a "bad reputation." Yet the growing popularity of public amusements within the "respectable middle class" was beginning to challenge such perceptions.

Women's bodies were also finding new visibility in athletics. In the wildly popular arenas of public competition such as baseball and boxing, athletics were virtually synonymous with masculinity. And yet women were beginning to play lawn tennis, field hockey, and gymnastics. Some even rode bicycles.

Race, Class, and Gender Ideals Within the gender ideology of the urban middle class that emerged over the course of the nineteenth century, the "good woman" (and her antithesis) took on distinct characteristics associated with race and class. "Good" (white, Protestant, middle class) women embodied private virtues. They were chaste, domestic, pious, and submissive. "Bad" women were "low class"—immigrants, racial minorities—presumed to be promiscuous, bad mothers, and improper housewives largely on the basis of their presence in previously male-only public spaces (factories, saloons, dance halls). Such perceptions multiplied in the case of southern black women subjected to a regime of racial/sexual domination that included the constant threat of rape and the public humiliations of segregation. Yet, the denigration of lower-class and minority women on the basis of their presence in public was getting harder to sustain as growing numbers of supposedly "respectable" women showed up in the same, or similar, spaces.

The First Wave

This brief sketch of women's condition at the beginning of the century points to several forces for change that would bear fruit in the first few decades. The growth in women's education, their move into a wide variety of reform efforts as well as professions, laid the groundwork for a massive suffrage movement that demanded the most basic right of citizenship for women. The claim of citizenship was in many ways a deeply radical challenge to the ideology of separate spheres for men and women. It asserted the right of the individual woman to stand in direct relation to the state rather than to be represented through the participation of her husband or father. The growing power of the women's suffrage movement rested both on women's collective consciousness, born in female associations, and on increased individualism among women in an urbanizing industrializing economy.

While a small but crucial number of upper-middle-class women attended college, where they developed a transformed awareness of their own potential as women both individually and collectively, working-class immigrant and African-American women experienced both individualism and collectivity in very different ways. Forced to work outside the home in the least-skilled, lowest paying jobs, both they and their employers presumed that women's labor force participation was temporary. Unions objected to their presence and blocked them from apprenticeship and access to skilled jobs. Despite these obstacles, when wage-earning women organized their own unions, often in alliance with middle-class reformers, they exhibited awesome courage and militancy. In the garment district of New York, for example, the "uprising of the twenty thousand" in 1909 confounded the garment industry and led to a new kind of industrial unionism.

By 1910, middle-class white reformers had formed increasingly effective alliances with black and working-class women around the issue of women's suffrage. The massive mobilization of American women in the decade before the Nineteenth Amendment was ratified in 1920 included rallies of thousands of "working girls" and the organization of numerous African-American women's suffrage clubs. Shared exclusion from the individual right of civic participation symbolized their common womanhood. Following their victory, leaders of the National American Woman Suffrage Association joyfully dismantled their organization and reassembled as the newly formed League of Women Voters. Their new task, as they defined it, was to train women to exercise their individual citizenship rights.

Such a reorientation seemed congruent with the popular culture of the 1920s, which emphasized individual pleasures along with individual rights. The development of a consumer economy, emphasizing pleasure and using sexuality to sell, offered women other paths out of submissive domesticity and into more assertive forms of individualism, paths that did not require solidarity, indeed undermined it. The female subculture that relied on a singular definition of "woman" eroded. Female reform efforts remained a powerful force in American politics—laying much of the groundwork for the emergence of a welfare state—but a broad-based movement for women's rights no longer existed after 1920. The pace of change in areas like education and labor force participation also reached a plateau and remained relatively unchanged for several decades after 1920. Modern women were individuals. And "feminism" became an epithet.

The loss of female solidarity meant that women's organizations in subsequent decades drew on narrow constituencies with very different priorities. Professional women, lonely pioneers in many fields, felt the continuing sting of discrimination and sought to eradicate the last vestiges of legal discrimination with an Equal Rights Amendment (ERA). The National Women's Party, one of the leading organizations in the struggle, first proposed the ERA in 1923 for the vote. But they were opposed by former allies, social reformers who feared that the protections for working women, which they had won during the Progressive era, would be lost. Though fiercely opposed to the ERA, reformers continued to advocate a stronger role for government in responding to social welfare. Many of them—with leaders like Eleanor Roosevelt—assumed key positions in the 1930s and shaped the political agenda known as the New Deal. In particular, their influence on the Social Security Act laid the foundations of the welfare state. Even among female reformers, however, alliances across racial lines remained rare and fraught with difficulty. As the progressive female reform tradition shaped an emergent welfare state, African-American voices remained muted, the needs of working women with children unaddressed.

The Second Wave

By mid-century the conditions for another surge of activism were under way. During the Second World War women joined the labor force in unprecedented numbers. Most significant, perhaps, married women and women over age 35 became normative among working women by 1950. Yet cold war culture, in the aftermath of World War II, reasserted traditional gender roles. The effort to contain women within the confines of the "feminine mystique" (as Betty Friedan later labeled this ideology), however, obscured but did not prevent rising activism among different constituencies of women. Under the cover of popular images of domesticity, women were rapidly changing their patterns of labor force and civic participation, initiating social movements for civil rights and world peace, and flooding into institutions of higher education.

The President's Commission on the Status of Women, established in 1961, put women's issues back on the national political agenda by recruiting a network of powerful women to develop a set of shared goals. They issued a report in 1963, the same year that Friedan published The Feminine Mystique. That report documented in meticulous detail the ongoing realities of discrimination in employment and in wages, numerous legal disabilities such as married women's lack of access to credit, and the growing problems of working mothers without adequate child care. In 1964, Title VII of the Civil Rights Act gave women their most powerful legal weapon against employment discrimination. An opponent of civil rights introduced Title VII, and many members of Congress treated it as a joke. But Title VII passed because the small number of women then in Congress fiercely and effectively defended the need to prohibit discrimination on the basis of "sex" as well as race, religion, and national origin.

The second wave emerged simultaneously among professional women and a younger cohort of social activists. Professionals, with the leadership of women in labor unions, government leaders, and intellectuals like Friedan, created the National Organization for Women (NOW) in 1966 to demand enforcement of laws like Title VII. A second branch of feminist activism emerged from younger women in the civil rights movement and the student new left. Civil rights offered a model of activism, an egalitarian and visionary language, an opportunity to develop political skills, and role models of courageous female leaders. Young women broke away in 1967 to form consciousness-raising groups and build on the legacy of the movements that had trained them.

The slogan, "the personal is political," became the ideological pivot of the second wave of American feminism. It drove a variety of challenges to gendered relations of power, whether embodied in public policy or in the most intimate personal relationships. The force of this direct assault on the public/private dichotomy has left deep marks on American politics, American society, and the feminist movement itself. Issues like domestic violence, child care, abortion, and sexual harassment have become central to the American political agenda, exposing deep divisions in American society that are not easily subject to the give-and-take compromises of political horse-trading.

From 1968 to 1975, the "Women's Liberation Movement," using the techniques of consciousness-raising in small groups, grew explosively. The synergy between different branches of feminist activism made the 1970s a very dynamic era. Feminist policymakers dubbed the years 1968 to 1975 "the golden years" because of their success in courtrooms and legislatures. These included the Equal Rights Amendment, which passed Congress in 1972 and went to the states; the 1973 Supreme Court decision legalizing abortion (*Roe v. Wade*); Title IX of the Higher Education Act, which opened intercollegiate athletics to women; the Women's Equity Education Act; and the Equal Credit Opportunity Act.

Women formed caucuses and organizations in most professional associations and in the labor movement. By the mid-1970s there were feminist organizations representing a broad range of racial groups as well—African-American women, Chicanas and Hispanic women, Asian-American women, Native American women. Women also built new organizations among clerical workers to challenge the devaluation and limited opportunities of traditional women's work.

With their new strength, women challenged barriers to the professions (law, medicine), to ordination within mainstream Protestant and Jewish denominations, and to the full range of traditionally male blue-collar occupations, from carpenters to firefighters and police. They filed thousands of complaints of discrimination, mounted hundreds of lawsuits, and also built thousands of new institutions—day-care centers, shelters for battered women, bookstores, coffeehouses, and many others. The new feminism drew on women's stories to rethink the most intimate personal aspects of womanhood including abortion rights, sexual autonomy, rape, domestic violence, and lesbian rights.

The second wave of feminism also changed the American language both through its own publications (of which there were hundreds, the largest of them being *Ms.*, first published in 1972) and through pressure on commercial publishing houses and mass media. New words entered the American lexicon—"Ms.," "firefighter," "sexism"—while uses of the generic masculine (mankind, brotherhood, policeman) suddenly seemed exclusive. In Women's Studies programs, which grew rapidly in the early 1970s, young scholars rethought the paradigms of their disciplines and initiated new branches of knowledge.

The second wave provoked a strong reaction, of course, revealing not only male hostility but also deep fissures among women themselves. Antifeminism became a strong political force by the late 1970s with the mobilization of Phyllis Schlafley's Stop-ERA and antiabortion forces. In the face of widespread cultural anxiety about equality for women and changing gender roles, the Equal Rights Amendment stalled after 1975 and went down to defeat in 1982 despite an extension of the deadline for ratification. Antifeminism drew on the insecurities of a declining economy in the wake of the Vietnam War and on the growing political power of the New Right which made cultural issues (abortion, the ERA, "family values," and homophobia) central. The 1980s, framed by the hostile political climate of the Reagan administration, nourished a growing backlash against feminism in the media, the popular culture, and public policy. As public spending shifted away from social programs and toward the military, female poverty increased sharply. The Reagan boom after 1983 did not touch the poorest, disproportionately female and racial minority, segments of the population.

At the same time, the 1980s witnessed the continued growth of women's presence in positions of public authority: Supreme Court justice, astronaut, arctic explorer, military officer, truck driver, carpenter, Olympic star, bishop, rabbi. Mainstream religious denominations began to rewrite liturgies and hymnbooks to make them more "inclusive." Despite regular announcements of the "death" of feminism, it would be more accurate to say that in the 1980s feminism entered the mainstream with new levels of community activism, sophisticated political fundraisers like EMILY's List, and broad political alliances on issues like comparable worth. Experimental "counterinstitutions" started in the 1970s (battered women's shelters, health clinics, bookstores, etc.) survived by adopting more institutionalized procedures, professionalized staff, and state funding. Women's Studies took on the trappings of an academic discipline.

Feminism was broad, diffuse, and of many minds in the 1980s. Legal and cultural issues grew more complex. Feminist theorists wrestled with the realities of differences such as race, class, age, and sexual preference, asking themselves whether the category "woman" could withstand such an analysis. The multifaceted activities that embraced the label "feminist"—policy activism, research think tanks, literary theory, music, art, spirituality—signaled the fact that the women's movement had lost some cohesiveness.

The testimony of Anita Hill during the 1991 hearings on the nomination of Clarence Thomas to the Supreme Court, however, catalyzed a new round of national conversation, complicated by the deep fissures of race and sex. The sight of a genteel black woman being grilled by a committee of white men who made light of this "sexual harassment crap" mobilized thousands of women to run for office and contribute to campaigns. In 1992 an unprecedented number of women were elected to public office.

2000—DAWN OF A NEW MILLENNIUM

If we return to our original categories to describe women's situation at the end of the twentieth century, the contrast with 1900 could hardly be more dramatic. The average woman now can expect to live 79.7 years (65% longer than her great-grandmother in 1900), marry at age 24.5, and bear only about two children (if any at all). There are now decades in women's lives—both before and after the years of childbearing and child care—which earlier generations never experienced. As a result of the second wave of women's rights activism in the final decades of the twentieth century, in politics and law, labor force participation, education, and sexuality women live in a truly different world. Yet, in each instance equity remains an elusive goal, suggesting the need for continued and revitalized activism in the twenty-first century.

Politics and Law

No longer defined by their marital status, women enjoy virtually the full range of formal legal rights. In addition to winning the right to vote in 1920, they achieved equal pay (for the same work) in 1963 and guarantees against discrimination in housing and employment in 1964 (Title VII of the Civil Rights Act). Since 1970 women have won the right to a separate legal identity; privacy rights regarding reproduction and bodily integrity; and rights to sue for discrimination in employment, to work when pregnant, to equal education, and to equal access to athletics. Whole new bodies of law have developed since the 1970s on issues like domestic violence and sexual harassment. Nonetheless, the failure of the Equal Rights Amendment (ERA) in 1982 means that women still have no constitutional guarantee of equality.

In the last twenty-five years we have also seen a dramatic growth in the numbers of female elected officials. In 1997 there were 60 women in Congress (11.2%)—14 of them women of color; 81 statewide executive officials (25%); 1,597 state legislators (21.5%); and 203 mayors of cities with population over 30,000 (20.6%). There are two women on the Supreme Court, 30 female circuit court judges (18.6%), and 107 female district court judges (17.2%).

Education

At the end of the twentieth century, 88 percent of young women ages 25 to 34 are high-school graduates. The transformations in primary and secondary education for girls cannot be captured in graduation numbers, however. They also reside in the admission of girls to shop and other vocational classes (and boys to cooking and sewing courses), in girls' participation in athletics, in curricula that—at least sometimes—emphasize women's achievements in the past, and in school counselors who no longer single-mindedly socialize girls for domesticity and/or nonskilled stereotypically female jobs.

In the arena of higher education women are closing in on equity. Today, 54 percent of all bachelor of arts degrees go to women; 25 percent of women aged 25 to 34 are college graduates. Most striking, the proportion of women in professional schools is now between 36 and 43 percent. The revolution of the late twentieth century is evident in these figures, as most of the change occurred in the last three decades. Compare current numbers with those of 1960, when the proportion of women in law school was 2 percent (today 43%); medicine

6 percent (today 38%); MBA programs 4 percent (today 36%); Ph.D. programs 11 percent (today 39%), and dentistry 1 percent (today 38%).

Labor Force Participation

In stark contrast to a century ago, more than 61 percent of all women are in the labor force, including two-thirds of women with preschoolers and three-fourths of women with school-age children. Though African-American women continue to work at a higher than average (76% overall), the gap is clearly shrinking as the patterns that they pioneered are becoming the norm. With overt discrimination now outlawed, women practice virtually every occupation on the spectrum from blue collar to professional.

Yet alongside change, older patterns persist. Women remain concentrated in female-dominated, low-paid service occupations despite their presence in many professions and in traditionally male blue-collar occupations such as construction or truck driving. Although the exceptions are highly visible (tracked in the popular media frequently as interesting and unusual phenomena), 70 percent of women work either in the services industry (health and education) or in wholesale or retail trade. Women's median weekly earnings are still only 75 percent those of men—though there has been a dramatic gain since 1970 when they were 62.2 percent. (Note, however, that this change represents a combined gain for women of 17% and a 3% decline for men.)

Sexuality, Fertility, and Marriage

The late twentieth century has witnessed a sharp increase in single motherhood even as overall fertility has declined. One birth in three is to an unmarried woman; in 1970, that proportion was only one in ten. Sixty-nine percent of children live with two parents; 23.5 percent with mother only (for African Americans this is 52%).

Some of this single parenthood is due to divorce, something that was relatively rare in 1900 and today affects nearly one in every two marriages. The divorce rate seems to have peaked in 1980, however, and has declined somewhat since that time (in 1980 there were 5.2 divorces/1,000 population; today there are 4.4). Single motherhood is not the source of shame that it was in 1900, but it remains highly correlated with poverty.

If female sexuality was suppressed in 1900 (even though incompletely), at the end of the century sexual references and images saturate American culture. It was not until the 1930s that birth control became legal in most states. In 1961 the birth control pill introduced the possibility of radically separating sexual experience from the likelihood of procreation. Then in 1973, the Supreme Court's Roe v. Wade decision legalized abortion. Today, premarital sex is common, even normative. According to the Alan Guttmacher Institute, in the early 1990s 56 percent of women and 73 percent of men had sex by age 18.

As dramatic, homosexuality has become an open subject of public discourse, and lesbians—once completely hidden, even to one another—are creating new public spaces and organizations, fields of intellectual inquiry and theory, and families that rely on voluntary ties in the absence of any legal sanction. Lesbians have been a major constituency and source of leadership in the second feminist wave. Twenty years of visibility, however, is just a beginning. American society remains deeply, and emotionally, divided on the issue of homosexuality. Opposition to gay rights marks a key issue for the religious right, and open violence against lesbians and gay men continues.

Race and Class

The second wave grew directly from and modeled itself on the civil rights movement in the 1950s and 1960s. That movement, itself, relied heavily on the grass-roots (if relatively invisible) leadership of African-American women. In the last decades of the century, the voices of minority women have become increasingly distinct and powerful. Diversity among women, as in the society at large, has taken on new dimensions with a surge of immigration since the 1960s from Southeast Asia, East Africa, Central America, and other parts of the Third World. Predictions based on immigration and fertility suggest that by the middle of the next century whites will be only half the U.S. population. Women of color will become the new norm. Women remain deeply divided on racial grounds, but race is no longer defined as black and white.

Challenges to traditional conceptions of gender have also shaken the previous consensus on what constitutes a "good woman" (except perhaps to the right-wing traditionalists who still hold to a set of ideals quite similar to those that dominated American culture a century ago). Yet discomfort with women's move into public life is still widespread, and race and class stigmas remain. The massive growth of a welfare system whose clients are disproportionately women and children combines racial and gender stereotypes to create a new category of "bad women": single, minority, poor mothers. And wherever women appear in previously male-dominated environments, they remain suspect. In particular, the sharply polarized emotional response to Hillary Rodham Clinton during her time as first lady illustrates the undercurrent of anger at powerful, professional women. Radio talk shows have filled thousands of hours with hosts and callers venting their hostility toward this woman who, in their view, did not stay "in her place." But, of course, that is the open question at century's end: just what is "woman's place"?

CONCLUSION

This brief discussion of women in the twentieth century does not trace a smooth arc from the beginning of the century to the end. It is not simply about "progress" toward "equality." But it is, indeed, about a kind of sea change with unanticipated consequences and with dramatic acceleration in the last thirty years.

In the nineteenth century women created much of what today we call civil society. In the twentieth century they used that layer of society—which lies between formal governmental structures and private familial life—in an amazing variety of ways to reshape the landscape of American life. Virtually all of the public spaces previously presumed to belong properly to men—paid labor, higher education, electoral politics and public office, athletics—now incorporate a large and visible proportion of women. This theme of participation in public life, and the concomitant politicization of issues previously considered personal, runs through the entire century.

Such spectacular shifts have clearly been driven by large structural forces: the emergence of a postindustrial service economy, rising levels of education, two cataclysmic world wars, global power and national wealth on a level never imagined, changing patterns of marriage, fertility, and longevity. Yet the most dramatic changes can clearly be traced in equal measure to two large waves of women's activism.

The suffrage movement, by the 1910s, involved hundreds of thousands of women, branching out both tactically with the use of massive public parades and street corner speeches (females occupying public, political spaces) and in composition as it reached out to working women, immigrants, and minorities. That movement won for women the fundamental right of citizenship, the right to vote. And the Progressive movement on which it built laid the groundwork and provided many key players for the subsequent emergence of the welfare state. The impact of the second wave shows up in the astonishing acceleration of change in the last three decades of the century.

Each of these waves continued to surge forward in the decades after cresting. But each was also followed by a period in which the multiplicity of women's voices reasserted itself along with debates over the real meaning of equality. And each left much work undone for subsequent generations that face new issues and new dilemmas.

In the twenty-first century women will have choices that have never before been available, but they will not be easy. The twentieth century challenged our very definitions of male and female. Many of the signs of manhood and womanhood no longer function effectively. Work is no longer a manly prerogative and responsibility. Families are no longer constituted around a male breadwinner, a wife, and their children. More often they are two-income households (same or different sexes) or single-parent households. Large numbers of single men and women live alone. Yet "family values" have become a political code for attacks on welfare mothers, homosexuals, and nontraditional families (which, in fact, far outnumbered traditional ones). In the absence of significant societal or governmental support for women's traditional responsibilities, women assume a double burden. They participate in the labor force almost to the same degree as men, and yet work outside the home is still organized as though workers had wives to take care of household work, child care, and the myriad details of private life. Work outside the home makes few accommodations to the demands and priorities of family life.

The pioneering work of the twentieth century—as women made their way into hostile, male-dominated public spaces—remains unfinished. Most of the barriers have been broken at least once. But equity remains a distant goal. Achieving that goal is complicated by the fact that for the moment women are not a highly unified group. The contemporary struggles within feminism to deal with the differences among women are the essential precursor to any future social movement that claims to speak for women as a group. The very meanings of masculinity and femininity and their multiple cultural and symbolic references are now overtly contested throughout the popular culture.

Another legacy of the feminist movement that proclaimed that "the personal is political" is an unresolved ambiguity about just where the boundary between the personal and the political properly lies, and the dilemmas resulting from politicizing private life. At the end of the century, Americans faced a constitutional crisis rooted in the strange career of personal politics. For an entire year virtually everyone in the United States was riveted by the scandal concerning President Clinton, Monica Lewinsky, Kenneth Starr, and the American Congress. Behaviors that once would have been considered purely private (and gone unremarked by political reporters, for example) became the basis for impeachment. Who defended the distinction between public and private and who assaulted it? The tables seem to have turned with a vengeance as the right wing pried into intimate details about the president's sexual activities in a consensual relationship while the liberals (including feminist leaders) protested. The politicization of private life is indeed a double-edged sword. This should be no surprise, as conservative backlash since the 1970s has evidenced a clear willingness to use the power of the state to enforce its vision of proper private relationships on issues such as abortion, homosexuality, divorce, prayer in the schools, and the content of textbooks.

The recent history of feminism calls to our attention a number of dimensions in this crisis that should not go unnoticed. First, there have always been many members of society (racial and sexual minorities, welfare recipients, and women, to name only the most obvious) whose private behaviors have been scrutinized and regulated by those in power. By forcing these issues into public debate and evolving laws that might protect such groups (for example laws against sexual harassment) feminists have also removed the cover of silence that protected powerful men from public scrutiny for their private behaviors. That such laws were subsequently used in a campaign to unseat a president whose election was directly due to the votes of politically mobilized women resonates with irony.

Women's solidarity has waxed and waned across the twentieth century. It will certainly continue to do so in the twenty-first. The next wave of feminist activism will no doubt take a shape we cannot envision, just as no one at the dawn of the twentieth century could have imagined the battles that awaited them. That there will be another wave, however, is a safe prediction, given the unfinished agendas of the last century and the still unforeseen contradictions that future changes will create. The next wave will shape the new century.

BIBLIOGRAPHY

William H. Chafe, *The American Woman: Her Changing Social, Economic, and Political Roles, 1920–1970* (New York: Oxford University Press, 1972), laid the groundwork for subsequent studies of twentieth-century women. Peter Filene examines the implications of changing definitions of womanliness and manliness on both sexes in *Him/Her Self: Sex Roles in Modern America*, 2nd ed. (Baltimore: Johns Hopkins University Press, 1986). Sara M. Evans, *Born for Liberty: A History of Women in America*, 2nd ed. (New York: Free Press, 1996) provides a general overview of women in American history.

The "first wave" of women's rights activism in the twentieth century is chronicled by Nancy F. Cott, *The Grounding of Modern Feminism* (New Haven, Conn.: Yale University Press, 1987), and Mari Jo Buhle and Paul Buhle, eds., *The Concise History of Woman Suffrage: Selections from the Classic Work of Stanton, Anthony, Gage, and Harper* (Urbana: University of Illinois Press, 1978). On women's role in the New Deal see Susan Ware, *Beyond Suffrage: Women in the New Deal* (Cambridge, Mass.: Harvard University Press, 1981). The critical eras of the 1940s and the cold war are examined in Susan Hartmann, *The Homefront and Beyond: American Women in the 1940s* (Boston: Twayne Publishers, 1982) and Elaine Tyler May, *Homeward Bound: American Families in the Cold War Era* (New York: Basic Books, 1988). There is a growing literature on the "second wave" of feminism. Some starting points would be Sara Evans, *Personal Politics: The Roots of Women's Liberation in the Civil Rights Movement and the New Left* (New York: Vintage, 1980); Alice Echols, *Daring to Be Bad: Radical Feminism in America, 1967–1975* (Minneapolis: University of Minnesota Press, 1989); and Donald Mathews and Jane De Hart, *Sex, Gender, and the Politics of ERA* (New York: Oxford University Press, 1990).

For more depth on the history of sexuality see John D'Emilio and Estelle B. Freedman, *Intimate Matters: A History of Sexuality in America* (New York: Harper & Row, 1988); on education see Barbara Solomon, *In the Company of Educated Women: A History of Women and Higher Education in America* (New Haven, Conn.: Yale University Press, 1985); on women in the labor force see Julia Blackwelder, *Now Hiring: The Feminization of Work in the United States: 1900–1995* (College Station: Texas A&M University Press, 1997. Some excellent starting points on racial minority and immigrant ethnic women include Vicki L. Ruíz, *From Out of the Shadows: Mexican Women in Twentieth-Century America* (New York: Oxford University Press, 1999); on African-American women see Jacqueline Jones, *Labor of Love, Labor of Sorrow: Black Women, Work, and the Family from Slavery to the Present* (New York: Basic Books, 1985), and on Chinese women Judy Yung, *Unbound Feet: A Social History of Chinese Women in San Francisco* (Berkeley: University of California Press, 1995); Donna Gabaccia, *From the Other Side: Women, Gender, and Immigrant Life in the U.S., 1920–1990* (Bloomington: Indiana University Press, 1994).

For the most recent descriptions of women's status in all aspects of American life, see the series sponsored by the Women's Research and Education Institute in Washington, D.C., *The American Woman* (New York: W. W. Norton). This series has been updated biannually from its inception in 1987.

9 | "YOU DUH MAN!"

African Americans in the Twentieth Century

CHARLES PAYNE

IF I AM NOT WHO YOU SAY I AM, THEN YOU ARE NOT WHAT YOU THINK YOU ARE.

—James Baldwin

AS A METAPHOR, THE COLOR LINE IS NOT . . . REPRESENTED BY A SINGLE, SHARPLY
DRAWN LINE, BUT APPEARS RATHER AS A SERIES OF RAMPARTS LIKE THE "MAGINOT LINE"
EXTENDING FROM OUTER BREASTWORKS TO INNER BASTIONS. OUTER PORTIONS OF IT MAY
BE GIVEN UP ONLY TO HOLD FAST TO INNER CITADELS.

—Herbert Blumer

A currently popular beer commercial has as its punch line one white man
saying to another, "You duh Man, you duh *Man*!!" No doubt many listeners will recognize the phrase as a part of African-American folk idiom, but
I suspect few will reflect on the historical irony of one white man using that
phrase to another white man. In traditional usage "The Man" means the white
man, all of them, Mister Charlie. In effect, the character in the commercial is
saying "You the Oppressor! You the Oppressor!" A phrase that began as ironic
commentary on the structure of American inequality, on the fact that in this
country only white men are supposed to be men, has been appropriated by
Madison Avenue, reinscribed as a joke, and passed into popular culture shorn
of historical resonance. That process is a reminder of how deeply, if often un-
consciously, our racial history is embedded in our taken-for-granted behavior.
It is a reminder, too, of the fact that the struggle over race in twentieth-century
America has been, in large part, a struggle for the ownership of the collective
symbols of worth, often understood as "manhood," a struggle between The
Man and those who wanted to be "men" themselves. That the struggle was

often led by women just adds irony; the struggle women did so much to shape gets defined in ways that negate women.

The twentieth century began with the formal triumph of white supremacy. Wilmington, North Carolina in 1898 offered a harbinger of how the new century would unfold. By this time, freed men and women had been stripped of the right to vote in much of the South, but they were still a political force in Wilmington, a majority-black town governed by a coalition of black and white Republicans and Populists. This was an intolerable situation to many whites, especially supporters of the Democratic party, the proud party of white supremacy. In November 1898, after an election in which Democrats successfully intimidated many blacks from voting, white vigilantes, including some organized militia units, one of them armed with a Gatling gun, went on a rampage, shooting blacks in the streets, burning black homes and businesses, driving hundreds of people into the nearby swamps, running black political leaders and their white allies out of town or forcing them to resign at gunpoint or with the threat of hanging. The mayor, aldermen, and police chief, all forced to resign, were replaced by leaders of the mob. Estimates of the dead varied widely, from as few as seven to as many as several dozen. Perhaps one thousand blacks fled the town in the next month. "Approval, not condemnation, thundered down on the city's vigilantes from white pulpits, editorial pages, and political podiums across the United States," according to David Celcelski and Timothy B. Tyson. There was much talk about how "manly" the vigilantes were, about how they had restored Anglo-Saxon "manhood" to its rightful place. "Even Democrats uneasy with racial violence took pride in 'white manhood' and made no apologies for Wilmington," says historian Timothy Tyson.

Celebrating electoral victories by killing black people was almost a kind of sport at the turn of the century. When white supremacists won an election in Atlanta, four days of lynching and murdering followed. In Louisiana in 1900, white mobs rampaged through New Orleans for three days, "assaulting blacks, looting, burning and shooting." "We have done our best," said Pitchfork Ben Tillman, governor of South Carolina, "we have scratched our heads to find out how we could eliminate the last one of them; we stuffed ballot boxes. We shot them. We are not ashamed of it."

Tillman just about sums it up. By violence, by fraud and intimidation, by grandfather clauses, poll taxes, and white primaries, blacks in the South, where more than 90 percent of them lived at the turn of the century, were systematically disenfranchised. For blacks, hardly a generation from formal slavery, white supremacy meant the loss of the right to vote, the loss of any protection from the courts or the law, the loss of the ability to profit from one's labor. It meant decades of marginal governmental services, even as judged by the then-low standards of the South. It meant constant exposure to racist violence and insult. It meant that blacks were not going to be citizens in any useful sense of the term. In 1896, Louisiana had over 130,000 registered black voters; by 1904, barely 1,300. In 1900, only 3 percent of the blacks in the South were registered to vote, a figure that would not change until the Second World War.

The triumph of white supremacy actually meant the triumph of only some white people. Sociologist Carole Marks notes, "The disenfranchisement of black labor created, in effect, a disenfranchisement of white labor. By agreeing to vote on one issue, [the race issue] . . . the development of a working-class consciousness against class and privilege was abandoned." Poor whites got their manhood entitlements, they were allowed to feel superior to blacks, but in the same process they created a pool of superexploitable labor that kept wages low for blacks and whites. Poorer whites bought into a racial mythology that spited their own best interests.

Political disenfranchisement was accompanied by economic disenfranchisement. If wealthy whites were not able to maintain the structure of slavery, they created an economic system that retained its essential spirit. In the main, economic options for blacks were severely limited and the jobs they were allowed to do entailed a frustrating, humiliating, lack of control over the conditions of work and the fruits of one's labor. In 1910 62 percent of blacks in the South were in agriculture, 18 percent in domestic work. Agriculture overwhelmingly meant some form of tenant or sharecropping arrangement, work that rarely allowed more than a subsistence existence despite the backbreaking labor required. Typically, sharecroppers could not call on the courts to enforce contracts, could not call on the law in cases of physical abuse, had to buy supplies at prices dictated by their landlords, and had to accept their landlord's word as to what they had earned when settlement time came. In her study of the Mississippi delta in the 1930s, Hortense Powdermaker estimated that no more that 25 to 30 percent of sharecroppers got an honest settlement at the end of the year. Some people were just broken in spirit behind endless toil that produced only more toil. Alabama sharecropper Nate Shaw describes his father as a man who was repeatedly stripped of all he owned by landlords. Shaw himself was eventually able to "come up off the bottom" economically but only because of the timely intervention of white patrons.

Women as well as men walked behind a plow, and as arduous as that work was, many women preferred it to the only other option most of them had, domestic service. "Domestics work long hours, longer than those in industrial employment, receive the lowest wages, and work in isolated settings," notes the sociologist Carole Marks. Beyond that, there was the constant potential for degradation. There is a kind of degradation built into being closely and constantly supervised. There is a deeper humiliation in being constantly exposed to sexual harassments from male employers or older sons, to lewd comments and unfunny sexual jokes, to fondling, to actual rape. We automatically and appropriately associate lynching with the period of white supremacy, but at the level of collective psychology, the prolonged vulnerability of black women, going back to slavery, may be far more important. In a sense, the inability of black men to protect black mothers and wives and daughters is the deepest stain on the honor of the race, a humiliation so complete that nothing can remove the sting. No matter what else a black man might do, his claim to manhood was always contradicted by his inability to do anything about the vulnerability of black women. (And we may be quite sure that stripped of one traditional way to justify patriarchal domination over women, some black men reacted by overcompensating on other justifications.)

The threat of lynching, like the threat of rape, served to remind people that they were beyond the normal protections of civilized society. It was not until after World War I that lynchers made much effort to conceal their identities, an indication of how little they feared being brought to justice. While the South justified its barbarity as the only way to control mad-fiend black rapists, the NAACP found that rape was alleged—let alone proven—in only one lynching in five between 1889 and 1935. The most common offense was murder. "But the record abounds in lynchings for lesser affronts," writes Neil McMillen, "'insubordination,' 'talking disrespectfully,' striking a white man, slapping a white boy, writing an 'insulting letter,' a personal debt of fifty cents, an unpaid funeral bill of ten dollars, a $5.50 payroll dispute, organizing sharecroppers, being 'too prosperous,' 'suspected lawlessness,' horse killing, conjuring." That list leaves out "reckless eyeballing," or being too assertive in returning the gaze of a white person.

The list's absurdity implies that the murders weren't fundamentally a response to particular offenses. Lynching is best understood as a form of state-sanctioned terrorism. As a white resident of Oxford, Mississippi, said in 1938, "It is about time to have another lynching. . . . When the niggers get so they are not afraid of being lynched, it is time to put the fear in them." At the same time, it served some psychological functions for whites that we only dimly understand. McMillen finds that in Mississippi the number of killings went down after the turn of the century, but the mobs became more sadistic. Simple hanging "gave way to the faggot and to varied and often highly inventive forms of torture." There was more mutilation—chopping off fingers, toes, and ears for souvenirs, sometimes from living victims, gouging eyes out, pulling strips of flesh out with corkscrews, burning off arms and legs a section at a time, keeping victims conscious as long as possible while they were being burned. Simple killing would have done the essential job of terrorism. Perhaps we can understand the gratuitous desecration as a ritual way of proclaiming that blacks were not human. No one would treat humans that way, so if it was happening to blacks, it proved they were other than human. At the same time, some of this is almost certainly a ritual of manhood, a pattern by which each generation of southern white men proved themselves worthy of their forefathers, no less arduous in their defense of southern civilization.

Segregation policies themselves represent another attempt to humiliate black people. Some, like the frequent requirements that blacks be out of town by sundown or remain indoors after a certain hour, represent rational instruments of control. Others—the prohibitions against blacks and whites looking out of the same window, or playing checkers; Florida's requirement that black and white schoolbooks be separated even in storage; Oklahoma's requirement of separate phone booths; the custom in Atlanta's courtrooms of using separate Bibles to swear in witnesses—seem primarily to have served the function of constantly reminding whites of their presumed superiority while constantly degrading blacks.

Historians still argue over the exact nature of the social and psychological damage caused by slavery, but there is not much doubt that a great many slaves came out of the experience with a remarkably optimistic and forward-looking attitude. If Elsa Barkley-Brown is right, one expression of this was their attitude to civic participation. That first generation out of slavery was especially acute in its appreciation for democratic practice, enough that women and youngsters were expected to play a much larger role in African-American public discourse than would have been the case in the white society around them. That pattern did not change, according to Barkley-Brown's research on Virginia ex-slaves, until near the end of the century.

Similarly, it would be hard to overemphasize the importance of education to the newly freed. "They rushed not to the grog shop but to the schoolroom," wrote Harriet Beecher Stowe in 1879, "They cried for the spelling-book as bread, and pleaded for teachers as a necessity of life." Booker T. Washington observed that "Few people who were not right in the midst of the scenes can form any exact idea of the intense desire which the people of my race showed for education. It was a whole race trying to go to school. Few were too young, and none too old, to make the attempt to learn." Within a year of the war's end, ex-slaves had created at least five hundred schools of their own, "native schools," as they were called. During the brief period when ex-slaves had political power, their ardor for education was largely responsible for the establishment of free schooling in the South. As things were to work out, of course, other Southerners profited more from those schools than did the descendants of the blacks who fought for them. In 1916, per capita expenditure for education in the South averaged $10.32 for whites—itself an inadequate figure—but only $2.89 for blacks.

That story could stand for many. The optimism and ebullience of the first flush of freedom ran headlong into a half century of white supremacy, debt peonage, and legalized murder. Time and again, blacks found their best collective or individual efforts undermined. It should not be particularly surprising that many came away from that experience with doubts about whether they could improve their lot in life, distrusting white economic institutions, distrusting white law enforcement, with an acute need to assert "manhood" in a way that no one could misunderstand. I don't find anything at all surprising that the historical experience should produce enduring pockets, at the least, of anger, alienation, confusion, and resentment.

Racial anger is not so hard to understand, but the fact that not everyone succumbed to it is more interesting. Most of us are reduced to the anecdotal when the question is posed that way. Certainly, the absence of bitterness is related in some ways to traditions of the African-American church, and there are many stories from the civil rights movement that illustrate this. In 1963, Fannie Lou Hamer and several other civil rights workers, all women, were arrested in a small town and beaten virtually senseless by sheriff's men and by trustees. Afterward, when the jailer's wife and daughter brought water to her cell, Mrs. Hamer told them:

> "Y'all is nice. You must be Christian people." The jailer's wife told me she tried to live a Christian life. And I told her I would like for her to read two scriptures in the Bible, and I tol' her to read the 26th Chapter of Proverbs and the 26th Verse. She taken it down on a paper. And then I told her to read the 7th [sic] Chapter of Acts and the 26th Verse. [The two verses read: "Whose hatred is covered by deceit, his wickedness shall be showed before the whole congregation." And: ". . . Hath made of one blood all nations of men for to dwell on all the face of the earth . . ."] And she taken that down. And she never did come back after then.[1]

Annell Ponder, another one of the women beaten, understood evils like these as "examples of man's separation from God and from his own truest self." It followed that people like the ones who beat her weren't hopeless but they did, in her words, "need training and rehabilitation." That is, Mrs. Hamer and Ms. Ponder were able to use Christianity in ways that created a common moral community between themselves and men who had just abused them.

There were secular paths to the similar moral vision. In the evolution of African-American culture, the most influential form of sustained and complex interaction with whites may have involved black women domestic workers. Domestics acquire enormous amounts of information about their families. They are in the position that Patricia Hill Collins calls "outsider-within," forced to see the world from two very different social perspectives. It can be hard to mystify white people when you know them that well, but it can also be hard to hate them.

One of the people sociologist Robert Blauner interviewed for his study of American racial attitudes was Florence Grier, a black woman who began doing domestic work at the age of 11 during the depression. She got plenty of chances to see how racial contempt was nurtured:

> I've seen youngsters that I've taken care of until they got three or four years old, I've seen the youngster gradually withdraw . . . He would be just as sweet as he wanted to be when I came in the back door, but then when I went

to town that would be a different little boy! Now this little boy had been sitting in my lap, this little boy had been sleeping in my bed . . . but when we would get to town he would have to change his whole attitude. And this is the way that they teach these youngsters prejudice and selfishness. He learns by the time he is five years old that "Florence is a nigger."

That level of knowledge about how prejudice is manufactured, shared by millions of black women across the years, doesn't lend itself to hating. As I understand traditional African-American folk culture, one of its essential tenets was that white people were generally crazy but they couldn't help that. If you had been raised like white people, you'd be crazy, too. It was a position of moral superiority, which suggested that blacks understood more than whites and were thus obligated to regard whites the way adults regard children. I don't think that norm is nearly as much in evidence today as it was a few decades ago, in part perhaps because the contemporary ghetto seldom allows the richness of social experience that blacks had under white supremacy, however strange that may seem.

The ghetto—"the land of rats and roaches," Langston Hughes called it, "where a nickel costs a dime." Take that literally: housing in the ghetto can be twice as much as comparable housing outside of it. As much as sharecropping, the ghetto is an instrument of subordination. In the nineteenth-century north, blacks and whites tended to live in very mixed neighborhoods. The trend of the twentieth century, however, was for blacks to be penned into uniquely segregated racial reservations. Other ethnic groups spent some time in ethnic enclaves, but these were never as homogeneous as the black ghettoes and they were temporary. In the 1930s when Chicago was a city of ethnic enclaves, in none of the ethnic ghettoes did the ghettoized group constitute a majority of the people in the neighborhood, with the exception of Poles, who made up 50 percent of the Polish neighborhood. Blacks made up over 82 percent of the black ghetto. More, the normal pattern was for the ethnic enclave to be temporary. Jewish concentration on the Lower East Side peaks at 73 percent in the 1880s and is down to 23 percent by the 1920s. The figures on black concentration get higher in each decade. The average level of black spatial isolation doubled between 1930 and 1970.

The ghetto has not been a matter of blacks living where they choose. In polls, the overwhelming majority of black respondents express a desire for racially integrated neighborhoods. The ghetto has been defined by restrictive covenants, discrimination in property rental and sales, white flight, the refusal of white parents to allow their children to attend schools with blacks, mob violence, and worse. Between 1917 and 1920, there were fifty-eight cases of blacks moving into white neighborhoods having their homes bombed, a bombing every twenty days.

Bombings subsided after the 1920s but national housing policy often had the same underlying aim. The postwar flight to the suburbs was subsidized by the federal government in several ways, including a variety of practices of the Federal Housing Authority and the Veterans Administration, which systematically refused to allow mortgage monies to go to black neighborhoods, or, as cities became increasingly black, to cities at all. Between 1934 and 1970, for those areas where we have data, suburban areas received from six to eleven times more mortgage money per capita than contiguous cities, accelerating a downward spiral of physical decline. Public housing complexes were systematically located in ways that reinforced rather than challenged existing patterns of segregation. (And local governments manipulated the location of new schools in the same way.) Many housing projects became ghettoes within the ghettoes, extremely isolated from the social worlds around them, increasingly home to only the poorest of the poor.

More affluent blacks, unlike their counterparts in other ethnic groups, have traditionally not been able to move away from their poor:

> For blacks, high incomes do not buy entree to residential circumstances that can serve as springboards for future socioeconomic mobility; in particular, blacks are unable to achieve a school environment conducive to later academic success. In Philadelphia, children from an affluent black family are likely to attend a public school where the percentage of low-achieving students is three times greater than the percentage in schools attended by affluent white children. . . . Because of segregation, the same income buys black and white families educational environments that are of vastly different quality.[2]

The isolation of the ghetto almost guarantees that its inhabitants will develop an oppositional consciousness, defining themselves against the world that rejects them. Schoolchildren who dismiss academic success as "acting white" are one particularly unfortunate example, quite a contrast with their ancestors for whom freedom meant education. The oppositional stance may help people adjust to the ghetto, but it can also help keep them there. At the extreme, "By confining large numbers of black people to an environment within which failure is endemic, negative role models abound and adherence to conventional values is nearly impossible, segregation has helped to create a nihilistic and violent counterculture . . ." in the words of sociologists Douglass Massey and Nancy Denton.

Slavery may have been a terrible thing to endure, but a case can be made that the African-American social system that developed under it was pretty high-functioning when slavery ended. Family patterns among ex-slaves in the late nineteenth century, for example, roughly parallel those among poor white families. It is not until after the Jim Crow experience and the migrations into the ghettoes that one finds evidence of distinctive levels of social demoralization in African-American families, reflected in rising numbers of births to teenage mothers and rising numbers of female-headed households.

Movement out of rural areas was a mixed blessing, at once liberating and destabilizing. It created new economic and political opportunities but it also removed some of the communal traditions of rural life that had put some limits on the degree to which African Americans could react to their oppression self-destructively. A volatile mix was being drawn together: black men with a particularly sharp need to assert a long-suppressed manhood; a social context in which they were relatively free of white control but also less subject to the social control of rural areas, controls of kinship, tradition, and church; a limited legitimate opportunity, increasingly so when working-class jobs began leaving central cities; an always available and increasingly lucrative illegitimate opportunity structure; an increasingly intrusive popular culture that defined worth in terms of commodity consumption, irrespective of how you got in a position to consume; a reflexively oppositional culture in parts of the ghetto.

One of the consequences of that mix was a bending of the nature of masculinity in some parts of the African-American community, a process sometimes captured more convincingly by artists than by social scientists. Lorraine Hansberry's portrait of Walter Lee Younger, for example, corresponds very well with what we know of how African-American conceptions of masculinity collided with the cities. An ambitious and intelligent man, Walter Lee makes his living as a chauffeur, work in the tradition of black servility. In order to provide—barely—for his family, he has to kiss a white man's behind, and his anger over that sometimes spills onto the family he loves. At other times, it just expresses itself as big talk and a self-proclaimed manhood. To one of his sister's college-educated boyfriends he says: "What the hell you learning over there? Filling up your heads—with the sociology and the psychology—but they teaching you how to be a man? How to take over and run the world? . . . Naw, just to talk proper and read books and wear them faggoty-looking white shoes." The braggadocio is the least of it. The more tightly he seems bound to a dead-end existence, the more his behavior tends toward irresponsibility and self-destructiveness, the more he needs to find some way to assert his manhood.

Hansberry's Walter Lee Younger can be juxtaposed to the lower-class men Elliot Liebow studied in Washington, D.C., in the early 1960s, "streetcorner men" as he called them, naming them by the social milieu in which they were most comfortable. Liebow, an ethnographer, tried to understand them as breadwinners, fathers, husbands, lovers, and friends, and part of what he learned is that their failure in the first category leads to failure and confusion in all the others. These men want, almost desperately, to be good family men but they cannot make it work. The jobs available to them do not pay enough to support a family, and no matter how well the men do them, they do not lead to better jobs. Failing at the key masculine role of provider introduces constant tension into the marriage, no matter how understanding the wife tries to be. The longer he stays married, the more he is reminded of his own inadequacy.

Some respond by losing themselves in the bottle but, more profoundly, many respond by creating an alternative social world where the rules allow them to recapture some masculine pride. Indeed, they tell themselves, their relationships fail not because they are inadequate men but precisely because they are too much man for any one relationship. They are just too easily attracted to too many women to long remain loyal to any one. It is their hypermasculinity that accounts for their failure. A flaw is transformed into a bragging point. In fact, it is not a very plausible story but in this world it is in everyone's interest not to examine it too closely. At the same time, their sense of inadequacy undermines even their relationships with one another. Liebow paints a portrait of the ghetto in the early sixties in which some men were responding to their marginalization by losing the capacity to form deep human attachments of any kind, hastening the development of the meaner, harder ghetto we are faced with now.

Nonetheless, the migration out of the rural South and the wars that hastened it were liberating in some fundamental ways. A case might be made that no single event in this century had as much impact on the status of black Americans as World War II. Between 1939 and 1945, the average income of African-American families doubled. In 1940, 3 percent of southern blacks could vote, a figure essentially unchanged since the century began. In 1947, it was 12 percent; in 1950 20 percent. Blacks were beginning to move back into southern political life and the continuing migrations out of the South meant that blacks were already meaningful actors on the national political scene. Simultaneously, as cotton declined in importance, as African Americans in the South urbanized, as the South became less isolated from the rest of the nation, racial violence as a means of controlling black behavior became less common and less effective, making possible forms of activism that could never have been sustained earlier.

Americans think of the "civil rights movement" as something that happened between the middle 1950s and the middle 1960s. As we have already seen, the definitive changes actually seem to be those coming during the war or just after it. In 1947 the blacks of Clarendon County, South Carolina, to take one more example, decided to ask the school superintendent for a bus for their children. In a pattern that would be repeated many times, the superintendent refused and the black community decided to launch a fight for the complete equalization of schools. The man they chose to lead them was a Methodist minister, J. A. Delaine. In his history of *Brown v. Board*, Richard Kluger says of Delaine:

> Before it was over, they fired him from the little schoolhouse at which he had taught devotedly for ten years. And they fired his wife and two of his sisters and a niece. And they threatened him with bodily harm. And they sued him on trumped up charges and convicted him in a kangaroo court and left him with a judgment that denied him credit from any bank. And they burned his

house to the ground while the fire department stood around watching the flames consume the night. And they stoned the church at which he pastored. And fired shotguns at him out of the dark. But he was not Job, and so he fired back and called the police, who did not come and kept not coming. Then he fled, driving north at eighty-five miles an hour over country roads, until he was across the state line. Soon after, they burned his church to the ground and charged him, for having shot back that night, with felonious assault with a deadly weapon, and so he became an official fugitive from justice.

The struggle in Clarendon, which eventually became part of *Brown v. Board*, illustrates much of what was important about postwar activism. Black communities, even some rural communities, were willing to push the system in ways that would have been almost unthinkable a few years earlier. The leaders of those communities had to face a full array of repressive tactics. Some were killed, some were driven out of the South or out of activism; others, Delaine among them, held on long enough to see the South begin to change.

Brown v. Board, decided in May of 1954, is taken to be among the most crucial of those changes. In retrospect, we might wonder. As the century ends, segregated education is still the norm in this country. That would not have surprised Ella Baker, another activist whose life illustrates the connections between what we call the civil rights movement and earlier periods of struggle. She thought that legislative and judicial victories were very much overrated. The powers that be can grant them today and withdraw or undermine them tomorrow. What's important is that the movement creates people who are always capable of fighting for themselves.

Her opinions were based on a lifetime of experience and reflection. A product of rural North Carolina, by the depression she was in Harlem teaching black history and organizing domestic workers, economic cooperatives, and adult education programs. In 1941, she became an assistant field secretary with the NAACP, the most important civil rights organization of the period, which meant spending half the year traveling through the South, organizing new branches and advising established ones. That eventually led to a position as national director of branches, a position she held during the organization's most dynamic period of growth.

Philosophically, she was a radical democrat, which meant she had her misgivings about the organization for which she was working. The NAACP, she thought, was overly committed to a legal strategy that left most of its membership—400,000 by 1944—little meaningful role in the development of policy and program. Like many of the leaders with whom she had worked in the Deep South, she was increasingly impatient with the organization's conservatism. The leadership was putting too much energy into worrying about how much recognition they were getting from important white people, a concern that helped prevent the organization from taking a confrontational stance even when that would have made tactical sense. The program was overly middle class, not strong enough on the kinds of economic issues that meant most to working-class black people. Perhaps above all, she found the organization too centralized; too many decisions were being made in New York instead of by the people closest to the problems.

In 1946, she left the NAACP, working for a variety of causes over the next decade. In 1957, when the Southern Christian Leadership Conference was formed, a cadre of older activists formed around the young and inexperienced Martin Luther King. Ella Baker became SCLC's first full-time executive director. On the one hand, she brought the advantage of her extensive contacts among southern activists. On the other hand, she was an outspoken woman in an organization that didn't appreciate that from women; she was impatient, to put it mildly, with ministerial conservatism and did not personally believe in the nonviolence the organization was espousing. Perhaps most of all, she was not a great fan of charismatic leadership, and SCLC was largely built on Dr. King's charisma. She recognized that charisma has its uses, but she also thought it had an enormous downside if relied upon too much. It was unhealthy, she thought, for the movement to be reduced to something where a few big leaders were going to lead the singing masses to freedom. People, she thought, had to learn to lead themselves: "My basic sense of it has always been to get people to understand that in the long run they themselves are the only protection they have against violence or injustice. . . . People have to be made to understand that they cannot look for salvation anywhere but to themselves." What we need, she argued, is people "who are interested not in being leaders as much as in developing leadership in others." If you can give them the light, people can find their own way.

Her relationship with SCLC was thus unstable from the beginning but it put her in position to do some very important things. In February 1960 four freshmen at North Carolina A and T sat in at their local Woolworth's, protesting lunch-counter segregation. Within weeks, hundreds of students across the South had followed suit, taking the movement to an entirely new level of intensity. Ella Baker was able to call a meeting of the students, from which emerged the Student Nonviolent Coordinating Committee, which then provided the movement with many of its shock troops for the next five years, going into tough rural counties, honoring Miss Baker's deeply democratic way of thinking about leadership. She may not have been an advocate of nonviolence, but they were. In their statement of purpose, they spoke of "nonviolence as the foundation of our purpose, the presupposition of our faith, and the manner of our action. . . . Love is the central motif of nonviolence. Love is the force by which God binds man to himself and man to man. Such love goes to the extreme; it remains loving and forgiving even in the midst of hostility."

Ella Baker frequently invoked the name of her colleague, Harry T. Moore. Moore, of Mims, Florida, was a schoolteacher, described as a shy, teetotaling sort of man, president of the state NAACP, known for his persistent agitation for the equalization of the educational resources given to black and white youngsters. In 1951, he campaigned for the prosecution of a sheriff who had shot two Negro youth, killing one. Shortly after he and his wife had retired on Christmas Eve that year, a bomb destroyed their bedroom. He died immediately and his wife a few days later. In the prewar years, southern blacks typically laid low after a racial killing. It was a sign of changing times that blacks from across the state packed his funeral, paying homage to a man who was for them the kind of symbol of persistence and integrity that Medgar Evers would become for blacks in Mississippi. The black press saw another sign of change in the fact that the murder was one of a wave of bombings across the South in the early fifties. The fact that the most dangerous defenders of racism were hiding behind bombs in the night rather than rallying lynch mobs in the open suggested that killers saw a need to be more cautions. It was a measure of progress, however grim.

Charismatic leaders like Martin Luther King and Malcolm X came to symbolize the civil rights movement for most Americans, but long before either of them stepped in front of a camera, people like Delaine and Baker and Moore were risking their lives to create the political networks and organizations that would become so important in the 1960s. Until recently, civil rights scholarship concentrated on national leadership to the exclusion of the people who built the movement on the ground. Over the last decade, a new scholarship has emerged, taking a more bottom-up approach, illustrating the wide range of men and women who played historically important roles, dating back to the world war or earlier.

By way of example of illustrating the difference in the approaches, we can look at the Montgomery bus boycott, perhaps our most familiar origin myth about the movement. What we are usually told is that a tired woman refused to give up her seat on the bus, an eloquent, nonviolent prophet rose up to lead the grateful masses, and the Supreme Court eventually saw the justness of their cause. That version is better theater than history.

In fact, the people who made the boycott happen had long activist backgrounds. They included E. D. Nixon, a railroad porter with a sixth-grade education, probably the most influential black man in town. Nixon had organized the state branch of the Brotherhood of Sleeping Car Porters in 1928. He organized farm workers in the thirties and he organized a committee to make sure that Alabama blacks got their fair share of benefits from federal programs; in 1940 he helped organize the Montgomery Voters League; in 1944 he led a march of 750 people on the registrar's office; from 1939 to 1951 he headed the Montgomery NAACP, and from 1951 to 1953, the state conference.

Mrs. Parks was hardly some simple woman who stumbled into history. She was an activist of long standing. In 1943 she joined the NAACP under Nixon, became its secretary, and worked in voter registration campaigns; she first registered herself in 1945; she ran the local NAACP Youth Council and served as secretary to the state NAACP Conference of Branches. She had attended one of Ella Baker's Leadership Training conferences in the 1940s and had spent a week at the "radical" Highlander Folk School in 1955. From the 1940s on, she had refused on several occasions to comply with bus segregation laws, frequently enough that some bus drivers recognized her on sight and refused to stop for her. King's comment about her—"She was tracked down by the *Zeitgeist*—the spirit of the times"—is precisely wrong. She, like Nixon, had spent much of her adult life actively seeking levers of change, not waiting until the times were right.

Jo Ann Robinson, an English professor at nearby Alabama State College, was president of the Women's Political Caucus, a group of three hundred educated black women who had been concerned with voter registration and segregated public facilities since 1946. They had been agitating the city commission about segregated buses since the early 1950s, and in May of 1954 they had sent a letter to the mayor threatening a boycott if improvements weren't made.

Nixon and Robinson's group were largely responsible for the initial mobilization of black Montgomery. Mrs. Parks was arrested on a Thursday; Nixon started organizing the first meeting of Negro leadership on Friday; by Monday they had organized a boycott that was nearly completely effective among a community of over forty thousand people. That they could mobilize the black community so thoroughly so quickly is a reflection of how well people like Nixon and Robinson knew their community, knowledge acquired through long years of working in it.

Knowing just this little bit about the background of the bus boycott can change the way we think about the movement. Potentially, it broadens our conception of leadership, ranging from a woman with a college education to a man whose real education came from union organizing. It leaves an impression of women as thinking, determined activists. It restores a sense of human agency. Montgomery happened because many people worked to make it happen. Dr. King was the inheritor of momentum that other people established, but once he stepped into the role, he played it with a brilliance that was very much his own.

The sixties brought some clear victories for the movement, including the 1964 Civil Rights Act banning discrimination in public accommodations and the Voting Rights Act the following year. They were not without their price, however. Young activists had lost a good deal of faith in the federal government after years of seeing FBI agents watch while civil rights workers were beaten into the ground, after seeing many activists murdered while the federal government denied they had authority to do anything about it, after being frustrated by the tenacity of the ghetto. Nonviolent idealism seemed increasingly naive, and many activist young people began looking for more radical alternatives. In the fall of 1966, Huey Newton and Bobby Seale founded the Black Panther party in Oakland, California, intended to carry on in the spirit of Malcolm X.

The Panthers first came to public notice because of their insistence on carrying guns in public and having a series of confrontations with police. At one level, they represented a kind of macho street theater, a politics perfectly suited for the tastes of many young men in the inner cities. On another level, they were a quite complicated mixture of nationalist and Marxist thinking. They got young people who had never read anything longer than a matchbook to wade through Mao Tse Tung and Franz Fanon. In still another respect, they were sophisticated organizers. Huey Newton, for example, understood all the rhetoric about guns to be an organizing device that could capture the attention of young people so that one could then begin their political education. The idea the ghettoes are going to rise up in armed rebellion he regarded as absurd.

Newton regarded the party's survival programs as the key part of what they did. They set up free medical and legal clinics, provided free breakfasts to children, set up well-regarded community schools. The point was less to deliver services than to make people think. If the Panthers could provide for the needs of the poor, why couldn't the broader society? Clearly, the capacity was there, so what was wrong? It was a wonderful example of propaganda by deed.

In the late 1960s, Panther chapters proliferated across the country; they were out-recruiting the street gangs in some cities and winning a great deal of respect from older blacks. Six or seven years later most of the energy was gone. Part of the reason was clearly police and FBI repression. At least twenty Panthers were killed by law enforcement officials, some in shootouts and some— Fred Hampton in Chicago—in acts not much more than murder. At the same time, the FBI engaged in a campaign of dirty tricks intended to create distrust and confusion within the organization, which by all accounts was successful.

The organization had other baggage, though. Some of the leadership seemed to get caught up in the business of being celebrities. Some became involved in drug use. Street values, in the form of physical brutality within the organization or in the form of plain gangsterism, became problematic, as did the organization's chauvinism. Although officially committed to gender equality, on a daily basis women, perhaps a third of the membership, were marginalized and abused even though some of them were clearly among the best workers in the organization. Eventually, a very talented cadre of women were pushed out of leadership positions, often with disastrous effects. Nevertheless, the Panthers demonstrated the potential for organizing young people in the contemporary ghetto, the potential for the young men currently destroying their neighborhoods to be a part of the process of their resurrection.

Dr. King was not immune to the radical currents of the time. In the final years of his life, he articulated a more radical vision, putting himself constantly at odds with the press, the White House, and much of the liberal establishment. In those years he showed considerable capacity for sticking with what he saw as the principled position, even when it was clearly costing him support. He was publicly opposed to the Vietnam War when most of the country still supported it. With few exceptions, his advisers encouraged him to downplay his opposition. Instead, on April 4, 1967, a year before his death, he gave a speech that left no doubt about his position:

> We must stop now. I speak as a child of God and brother to the suffering poor of Vietnam. I speak for those whose land is being laid waste, whose homes are being destroyed, whose culture is being subverted. I speak for the poor of America who are paying the double price of smashed hopes at home and death and corruption in Vietnam. I speak as a citizen of the world. . . . The great initiative in this war has been ours. The initiative to stop it must be ours.

The press tore into him. The *New York Times* warned that "to divert the energies of the civil rights movement to the Vietnam issue is both wasteful and self-defeating." The *Washington Post* concluded that he "has diminished his usefulness to his cause, to his country and to his people." The *Chicago Tribune* warned Negroes that if they wanted to continue to make progress "they had better get responsible leadership and repudiate the Kings and the [Stokely] Carmichaels." That pretty well reflects the tone of national press coverage of King in his last year.

His criticism of the Vietnam adventure caused a deterioration of his relationship with the White House. His relationship with the FBI was already about as bad as it could get. The bureau—which had labeled the "I Have a Dream" speech "demagogic"—had long been engaged in a campaign to destroy King, taking every opportunity to feed rumors and negative information about him to opinion leaders here and abroad, even trying at one point to trick him into committing suicide. J. Edgar Hoover publicly called King "the most notorious liar in America" and privately called him "the burrhead."

King's growing radicalism meant increasing skepticism about whether the nation's conscience could be reached on economic matters, thus he put increasing emphasis on racism as a national problem, not just a southern problem, and as a problem closely tied to economic exploitation. It meant that he increasingly described problems of inequality in structural terms, not in terms of individual prejudice:

> In these trying circumstances, the black revolution is much more than a struggle for the rights of Negroes. It is forcing America to face all its interrelated flaws of racism, poverty, militarism and materialism. It is exposing evils that are deeply rooted in the whole structure of our society. It reveals systemic rather than superficial flaws and suggests that radical reconstruction of society itself is the real issue to be faced.

At the end of his life, his vision of the good society included some form of democratic socialism.

Popular images of King tend to remember his emphasis on brotherhood and tolerance while conveniently forgetting that he saw them in the context of a structural transformation of society. The "I Have a Dream" speech remains so popular and ubiquitous, we might suppose, precisely because of its apolitical character, its failure to imply that social change is going to cost anybody anything. "In death," one of his biographers wrote:

> King became a symbol of national unity, a moderate reformer from the South, a foe of irresponsible militants, a deeply "American" figure whose achievements testified to the resilience of American democratic ideals. The uncompromising opponent of the Vietnam War, the harsh judge of American racism, the scathing critic of free enterprise, the militant advocate of "poor people's power" had to be quickly forgotten.[3]

King's memory has been appropriated, reinscribed, and passed into popular culture shorn of much of its historical resonance. We might say much the same about how the memory of Malcolm X has been constructed. Indeed, if one looks at the last years of their lives, the gap between King's thinking and Malcolm's is less than one might expect. If King was an advocate of fundamental economic restructuring, so was Malcolm X, and he wasn't reluctant to talk about it bluntly: "You show me a capitalist and I'll show you a bloodsucker."

King's nonviolence is often juxtaposed to Malcolm's presumed support for violence, but that doesn't do Malcolm's position justice. Malcolm put different spins on it at different times, but the central point for him seemed to be that blacks should pursue their liberation "by any means necessary," which meant that violence was an option, but this is different from saying it was his program. "I don't advocate violence," he said in a 1965 speech, "but if a man steps on my toes, I'll step on his."

As a Muslim, he enthusiastically preached the party line about white devils, but after he left the Nation of Islam, he denied that there were fundamental differences among people based on race. "I believe, as the Koran teaches, that a man should not be judged by the color of his skin but rather by his conscious behavior, by his actions, by his attitude toward others and his actions towards others. . . . I believe in recognizing every human being as a human being, neither white, black, brown nor red."

When it came to gender, both Malcolm and Martin held rigid, traditional views. Ella Baker thought that Dr. King had difficulty relating to women as equals, and the only two women who served on the SCLC board during his tenure felt essentially the same way. During his Nation of Islam period, Malcolm's attitudes toward women were remarkably backward; he referred to women as "deceitful, untrustworthy flesh" and the like. Late in his life, Malcolm claimed that he had learned from his travels to the Middle East and Africa that societies couldn't be liberated if women weren't. Over the objections of some of his more traditional comrades, he insisted that women were going to hold positions of real power in his Organization of African-American Unity.

In the tumultuous final months of his life, Malcolm was reexamining old assumptions ("I'm not dogmatic about anything. I don't intend to get into any more straitjackets.") and we cannot know where he would have come down, but it seems clear that there is a complexity and depth in his thinking that gets lost when he is reduced to the one-dimensional, fist-shaking man at the podium.

How shall we assess the movement's overall achievement? Suggesting that it was some kind of complete break with the past, some kind of revolution, is probably going overboard. Still, at great cost, often to some of the least privileged Americans, the movement was a step toward a fuller democracy. It meant the end of systematic racial terror and it meant that for the first time since Reconstruction, most blacks had more or less the same access to the political system as most other Americans. The movement helped Chicanos, Native Americans, women, and others demand more voice in the decisions and definitions that affected their lives. Southern whites benefited from the movement that most of them fought so hard. The currently robust economies of many southern states would have been unlikely without the destruction of the South's archaic political and economic structures. The movement made it possible for the South to join the twentieth century, albeit sixty years late.

It is probably safe to say that there are few public issues to which Americans bring a great store of historical knowledge, and it is certainly safe to say that race isn't one of them. The history that we don't know continues to shape contemporary discourse on race.

The students I have taught in recent years have a particular view of racial history. The age of Jim Crow, the age of institutionalized white supremacy, is not much a part of how they see history. They know something about the civil war and emancipation, maybe something about Reconstruction—then the next awareness of race comes with the beginnings of the civil rights movement. Their selective sense of history informs the way in which they interrogate the present. Other groups came here poor, they say, other ethnic groups were discriminated against but managed to work their way up the ladder, and why haven't black Americans been able to do the same? Sometimes this is just a question and sometimes it is an accusation. Slavery was a hundred years ago; so get over it already.

In fact, discrimination, even a great deal of discrimination, is one thing, and white supremacy is quite another. One wants to say to them that if your grandfather was able to attend the state university, if he interacted with the political system in a way that made him feel that his vote mattered, if your uncles were able to get union jobs, if they could take their employers to court if they were cheated, if your parents rode to school on a bus and had textbooks to read when they got there, if your mother was made to feel socially comfortable when she went to school, if your cousins grew up thinking that police officers could be trusted, if your parents were pretty much able to live wherever they could afford, if they could get mortgage loans where they lived—all those are cumulative advantages whose consequences flow across time. They affect the attitude that people will develop toward social participation. They affect the kinds of networks one generation has access to, which in turn affects the kinds of social, economic, and political leads another generation will have access to. They affect the formation of family values and the ability of one generation to successfully pass its values on to the next. The consequences of spending three or four times as much on the education of white children as on the education of black children do not stop with the generation that experiences it.

Historical ignorance shapes contemporary discussion in important ways, and so does historically grounded fear. For blacks and liberals, that can take the form of fear of saying anything that could reinforce historical imagery about the inferiority of blacks. Conservatives want to reduce issues of social inequality to issues of character, and liberals react by constructing a dialogue in which character has no role whatsoever, everything is structure and discrimination and differential opportunities—one set of simplistic answers opposing another. That "family values" should have been co-opted by the Right is pretty strange, given the centrality of those values in many traditional streams of African-American culture.

At the end of the century as at the beginning, racial anxiety seems to deflect attention away from basic questions about the structure of inequality and the distribution of privilege. Affirmative action and "welfare cheats," the latter understood to be black, become the parallel to turn-of-the-century fear of "Negro dominination." They generate intense debate, whereas there is much less popular discussion of the increasing income inequality, the impact of globalization on working-class Americans, the decline of unions, and other issues that would seem more important.

While we are drawing parallels with the turn of the century, it is important to note that the young men terrorizing inner-city neighborhoods, no less than white supremacist mobs, explain what they do with a rhetoric of manly pride. So and so gets killed because he disrespected somebody's manhood, and since manhood is so brittle in this world somebody is getting "dissed" all the time. The tenacity of that rhetoric across time and racial lines may tell us more than that "manhood" is deeply engrained as a symbol of human worth. It may tell us of what some might call a cultural failure on behalf of African Americans, a failure to imagine masculinity in ways different from that handed it by the dominant culture, a failure to create or sustain alternative images of worth.

If one listens to or reads the speeches of Malcolm X, paradigmatic black nationalist, it is striking how many times he seems to say that the ultimate goal of black Americans should be respect, and he clearly means the respect of white people. That's a pretty conservative goal for a militant to be pursuing, yet he never seems aware of the contradiction. Mrs. Hamer took a more radical position. Why, she asked, in response to a question, should she want to be equal to Senator Eastland?, a response that suggests that she, more self-consciously than Malcolm, is refusing to judge herself by the standards of the world that oppresses her. In this sense, what is important about the pervasiveness of masculinist rhetoric in both street culture and nationalist discourse from Garvey to Malcolm, is that it suggests a certain failure of the collective imagination. Some of those oppressed by The Man can only envision being like The Man.

The underlying question—and it should be framed as a question, not a conclusion—is whether the character of African-American solidarity has changed over the century. W. E. B. Du Bois raised the question. In the spring of 1960—before the movement could be called that—he spoke to an audience of teachers at Fisk University and told them what the future held. "The American Negro," he began, "has now reached a point in his progress where he needs to take serious account of where he is and whither he is going." Legal equality was clearly coming and it would bring new problems. Formal equality:

> brings not as many assume an end to the so-called Negro problems, but a beginning of even more difficult problems of race and culture. Because what we now must ask ourselves is when we become equal American citizens what will be our aims and ideals and what will we have to do with selecting these aims and ideals. Are we to assume that we will simply adopt the ideals of Americans and become what they are or want to be and that we will in this process have no ideals of our own?

So long as the structure of oppression was perfectly clear, it provided a perfectly clear rationale for racial solidarity. In the absence of a threshold consensus about core values, the removal of overt structures of oppression became disorienting. Similarly, James McPherson thinks that "the process of assimilation, for us, was so abrupt and so chaotic that many of us did not have the time to tease apart the many delicate distinctions between those values affirmed by the group out of the necessities imposed by legal segregation and those values which were essentially our own."[4] The failure to sort through that distinction means "a great many of our young people now operate in a moral vacuum, improvising identities around whatever value content is available." Maybe that says something—not everything, something—about the attraction of the more chauvinistic forms of Afrocentricity or hip-hop culture and what Robin Kelley calls ghettocentricity.

Desegregated college campuses are one of the easiest places to see how the past intrudes on our contemporary discussion of race. Professor Raymond Mack at Northwestern University used to teach a lecture class entitled "Race, Class and Power." Each time he taught it, on a given day he would come to class and peer out at the large audience as if noticing something for the first time. Then he would ask the white students, Why in the world are you sitting together? Were they trying to send some kind of message? Didn't they realize how socially retrograde that was? It typically took white students a while to get his point, so accustomed were they to taking their own behavior for granted while constructing the behavior of black students as problematic.

Significant numbers of white students do see black students as problematic, and some would go so far as to say black students are the primary cause of "racism" on campus. (The loose way that term is used in these conversations is a part of the problem.) It is the black students who cluster together in the lunchroom, the black students who overreact to innocent remarks or who can't accept a joke as a joke, the black students who insist on all-black organizations where all-white organizations would never be tolerated. The white students could understand if there were still antiblack racism, but they regard that as something in our ugly past—a past they are more than willing to denounce. As to the present, though, they are sure that racism is no longer a serious social problem, they are certain that they themselves are not racist and absolutely certain that if they were they would know. Under the circumstances, black clustering together is an insult, a failure to recognize how enlightened contemporary white students are. Separation is experienced as accusation, coming from a spoiled and privileged group, some of whom wouldn't even be on campus if it weren't for affirmative action. One of the things that has not changed in the American racial conversation in this century is the tendency of white Americans to perceive themselves as the aggrieved party.

The tone of this discourse is as important as the content. It's often a tone of exasperation, impatience: Why can't they be reasonable? After all we've done for them. It is the tone one uses when someone is being deliberately difficult, and its use in this context suggests that white students have a difficult time thinking that black students might have perfectly good reasons for behaving as they do.

Black students are experiencing a different reality. Presumably, most enter college with some of the traditional African-American skepticism about white-controlled institutions and their intentions. They may not be sure exactly how welcome they are. The idea that they are invited guests seems pervasive, the idea that they are not really qualified seems pervasive—and they may worry that whites have these ideas when in fact nothing of the sort is going on. In his very useful study of race at Rutgers in the middle 1980s, Michael Moffat suspected that only 10 percent or so of white students were bluntly antiblack but they had influence far beyond their numbers. Black students were never sure of which white students were which, a dilemma that could be resolved by having minimal contact with any of them. At the same time, interaction with the self-consciously liberal white students was not always reassuring, since they objectify black students in their own well-meaning way. Black students are more than a little mystified by the idea that having lunch with their friends is widely read as an act of racial hostility.

Not surprisingly, the two groups often bring different underlying paradigms to the discussion. If white students overwhelmingly understand race in interpersonal terms, black students are much more prone to understand it partly in terms of the relative privilege between groups, so they are often proceeding from very different assumptions about what constitutes "good" race relations. Their small numbers on most campuses make black students vulnerable—the lack of nonwhite people in positions of power, the Eurocentric quality of the curriculum—all of this they may find marginalizing. The admonishment that they should just stop thinking of themselves as black, just think of themselves as individuals, is hardly reassuring. They may doubt that the campus police think of them as individuals. They know that in classes they will be expected to speak for the race, they know that if not for the previous collective struggle of blacks they wouldn't be on these campuses, and they may suspect that their ability to stay hinges upon the continued solidarity of the racial community.

Black students may need an environment where their right to be there isn't subject to question, and they can find this environment among themselves, but they may have equally vexing issues to deal with in the racial enclave. One issue may be most sharply felt on the more elite campuses—the tendency to feel uncomfortable with the idea of being or becoming middle class. This is a common dilemma of the ethnic experience, but it may be sharper in the African-American case. Black students can be very unclear on how to separate becoming middle class from becoming white, which sounds like some sort of betrayal. At the extreme, this can lead to denial of one's background or aspirations. None of us are middle class, I was once told by a roomful of black Harvard undergrads, and none of us ever will be.

Black students are going through a double integration: trying to figure out how to fit into a black world that may be very different from what they are used to at the same time as they try to fit into the larger white campus. Black students typically enter college with little experience thinking about intragroup social diversity, so that becomes something else to be negotiated in college. Watching over this process on most campuses are self-appointed groups of black students who look for violations of racial orthodoxy among other black students—BlackWatch, they are called in some places, the Soul Patrol, in others. I have seen black students read out of the congregation of the righteous for skiing, for listening to rock music, and for drinking herbal tea ("Black people drink Lipton's"). It is the kind of behavior that bespeaks group insecurity. The very triviality of the underlying conceptions of racial identity suggests people who are no longer sure of their core values.

Notice that it would be a very different situation if black students just didn't care about white folks' opinion, if they had some functional equivalent to the idea that white folks are crazy. To whatever degree, their separation is defensive, it is a cry for inclusion, to be accepted under the existing criteria of worthiness, which again means they typically don't have any critique of the existing standards, any critique of congealed privilege in this case. The affirmative action accusation loses its sting when one decides that the narrow criteria of worthiness embedded in it are not to be taken seriously.

Perhaps what is most resonant in all of this is the low intellectual level of the conversation. The "ahistorical individualism"—Moffat's phrase—of many white students, their lack of awareness of how their racial dialogue parallels that of their ancestors, their inability to take seriously the validity of any viewpoint other than their own, the defensiveness of many black students, the inability to make distinctions among white people, the intragroup intolerance, the posturing attempts to assert a confident racial identity, and their inability to think reflexively. Black students may be in danger trading off much of their particular intellectual legacy, the ability to see the world as both insider and outsider, to see social structure but not be intimidated by it. White students may be buying into a mode of thinking about race—largely devoid of the concepts of structure, historical causation, and ideology—that reinforces the tendency to think shallowly about other social issues.

Where we are headed is beyond my crystal ball. It may be that African Americans no longer have the cultural or spiritual resources to respond to their marginalization without demonizing white people. Perhaps reflexive oppositional culture will come to undermine the social functioning of black women as it has black men. Perhaps the addition of new races to the discussion about race, a welcome development in many ways, will give people one more excuse to not talk about more threatening issues between blacks and whites, and we will continue to prattle about diversity in ways that separate that discussion from discussion of power and privilege. It may be that class cleavages in the African-American community—by some measures, increasing more rapidly than the parallel cleavages in the broader society—will reach a point where broad-based social action by blacks is no longer feasible. It may be that racial identity in the middle class will be reduced to narrow issues of cultural expression without reference to any broader, unifying scheme of values. Or being black may get reduced to a certain kind of status-oriented consumption. Perhaps the newly fashionable idea that race is "just" a social construction will be conflated with the idea that race isn't real. By denying the existence of race, we can ensure the continuing inequalities of race and we can do it with the best of intentions, which is where we came in, as it were.

On the other hand, maybe economic globalization will force more sophisticated social thinking, discouraging the tendency to reduce social problems to the problems of individual character. It is interesting that displaced white workers seem willing to listen to Jesse Jackson in a way that would have been unlikely in years past. Perhaps the increasing influence of African-American cultural expression on the general culture will ultimately lead to new ways of framing questions. Maybe the improving statistics on inner-city violent crime mean that the glorification of certain forms of masculine criminality has run its course. Maybe the number of black men willing to think about sexism as a serious problem has grown enough to change the nature of that conversation in the black community, which might unlock a great many others. I recently saw a former governor of Mississippi say to an audience—in Alabama—that the trouble with white people was that they didn't understand white privilege. This is a world of infinite possibility.

If we cannot say in which direction we are headed, we do know what some of the signposts of progress would be. When black people quit struggling to be The Man, quit trying to establish their worth using the tape measure of a world that despises them, when they develop ways of thinking about "manhood" that don't involve negating any one else's personhood, when white people can read the statistics on the incarceration of black youth and ask, "How can such things be happening to *our* youth?," whenever white people can assume that black behavior is normal, and if in a particular instance it's puzzling, that black people must have a good reason for what they are doing and that they, the white people, just can't see it, we will have left more than a century behind.

None of that is likely to happen, I suspect, unless a great many of us are willing to face our history with an honesty and a humility we have been unable to bring to it in the past. Without that, we are probably condemned to more of the discourse—it can hardly be called dialogue—that we have been having, shallow, self-serving, and chauvinist in ways that serve most of us badly over the long run. We are certainly more civilized than turn-of-the-century mobs, but it is not clear that we are much smarter.

NOTES

1. Charles Payne, *I've Got the Light of Freedom* (Berkeley: University of California Press, 1995), p. 309.

2. Douglas Massey and Nancy Denton, *American Apartheid* (Cambridge, Mass.: Harvard University Press, 1993), p. 153.

3. Adam Fairclough, *Martin Luther King* (London: Sphere Books, 1990), p. 119.

4. James McPherson, "Looking for a Loomo" (unpublished paper).

SUGGESTIONS FOR FURTHER READING

John Hope Franklin's *From Slavery to Freedom* (New York: Knopf, 1967) is the best-known overview of the entire period, and justly so. David Cecelski and Timothy Tyson's *Democracy Betrayed: The Wilmington Race Riot of 1898 and Its Legacy* (Chapel Hill: University of North Carolina Press, 1998) offers several viewpoints on the Wilmington riot and its context. C. Vann Woodward's *The Strange Career of Jim Crow* (New York: Oxford University Press, 1957) and W. E. B. Du Bois's *Black Reconstruction* (New York: Atheneum, 1975) are among the classic discussions of the period.

Lawrence Levine's *Black Culture and Black Consciousness* (New York: Oxford University Press, 1977) is a very convincing analysis of the cultural evolution from slavery to freedom. There are several useful ethnographies of tenantry, including Hortense Powdermaker's *After Freedom* (New York: Antheneum, 1968) and John Dollard's *Caste and Class in a Southern Town* (Garden City, N.Y.: Doubleday, 1957). Jacqueline Jones's *Labor of Love, Labor of Sorrow* (New York: Random House, 1985) is a remarkable analysis of black women's work in both agricultural and urban settings. Theodore Rosengarten's *All God's Dangers: The Life of Nate Shaw* (New York: Knopf, 1974) is valuable not only for its detailed description of the values of one sharecropper but for what it suggests about the variety of ways people coped with the system.

On migrations, see Carole Marks, *Farewell, We're Good and Gone: The Great Black Migration* (Bloomington: Indiana University Press, 1989). The essential book on black education in the South is James Anderson, *The Education of Blacks in the South, 1860–1935* (Chapel Hill: University of North Carolina Press, 1988). Neil McMillen's *Dark Journey* (Urbana: University of Illinois Press, 1989) is a detailed analysis of the age of white supremacy in Mississippi; Leon Litwack's *Trouble in Mind* (New York: Knopf, 1998) discusses the same period across the South.

On the contemporary ghetto, Douglass Massey and Nancy Denton's *American Apartheid* (Cambridge, Mass.: Harvard University Press, 1993) is crucial and can be profitably read along with Jean Anyon's *Ghetto Schooling* (New York: Teachers College Press, 1997). Donna Franklin's *Ensuring Inquality* (New York: Oxford University Press, 1997) is one of the best recent compilations of research bearing on the historical and contemporary pressures on African-American families.

My own *I've Got the Light of Freedom: The Organizing Tradition and the Mississippi Freedom Struggle* (Berkeley: University of California Press, 1995) is an introduction to the new scholarship on the freedom struggle. Richard Kluger's *Simple Justice* (New York: Knopf, 1975) may be too optimistic in its conclusions but is still a masterful history of *Brown* v. *Board*. Taylor Branch's *Parting the Waters* (New York: Simon and Schuster, 1988) is a beautifully written overview of the movement, but the best brief overview remains Harvard Sitkoff, *The Struggle for Black Equality, 1945–1980* (New York: Hill and Wang, 1980). On Malcolm's last months, see the interviews in David Gallen's *Malcolm X as They Knew Him* (New York: Carroll and Graf, 1992). On the Panthers, see both Charles Jones, *The Black Panther Party Reconsidered* (Baltimore: Black Classic Press, 1998) and Elaine Brown's graphic recollection in *Taste of Power* (New York: Anchor, 1992). On the particular importance of women in the movement, see Patricia Hill Collins, *Black Feminist Thought* (New York: Routledge, 1999); V. Crawford, J. Rouse, and B. Woods, eds., *Women in the Civil Rights Movement* (Brooklyn, N.Y.: Carlson Publishing, 1990); and Belinda Robnett, *How Long? How Long?* (New York: Oxford University Press, 1997). Joanne Grant's *Ella Baker: Freedom Bound* (New York: Wiley, 1997) is the first biography on Ella Baker. Robin Kelley's *Race Rebels* (New York: Free Press, 1994) is a good illustration of why some scholars feel the term *civil rights movement* is too narrow to describe the African-American struggle.

My students often find David Wellman's *Portraits of White Racism* (New York: Cambridge University Press, 1977) a useful reading because it analyzes the taken-for-granted assumptions embedded in contemporary discussions of race. Michael Moffat's *Coming of Age in New Jersey: College and American Culture* (New Brunswick, N.J.: Rutgers University Press, 1989) offers an anthropologist's view of the racial discussion on college campuses. The final report of Berkeley's Diversity Project (Institute for the Study of Social Change, Berkeley, 1991) is one of the more empirically detailed and theoretically informed discussions we have of race on college campuses.

10 | FROM THE BENIGHTED SOUTH TO THE SUNBELT

The South in the Twentieth Century

Nancy MacLean

I

"The South is not 'solid,'" W. E. B. DuBois discerned nearly a hundred years ago: "it is a land in the ferment of social change." Today it is easier to see the truth of that assertion. The century between us has transformed the face of the South and the region's place in the nation. The once-ubiquitous "white" and "colored" signs have come down. Across much of the South, rural scatter has been overrun by suburban sprawl. Wal-Marts and fast food outlets spill over the region's highways. In the fields, mechanical pickers churn where earlier whole families of sharecroppers stooped. A place once known for extractive industries now flaunts state-of-the-art automobile plants and fiber optics facilities. The nearly 50-square-mile "Vacation Kingdom" at Disney World draws millions of tourists each year. And a land that used to scare off immigrants and drive out African Americans now attracts large and growing numbers of Asians, Latinos, and black emigrants from the North to make their homes. All the changes notwithstanding, of course, much remains sadly familiar. The recent revival of chain gangs has produced roadside performances of the divisions of race and class that run through all of southern life, while the takeoff of prisons as a growth industry for investors shows how profitable these inequities can be. Still, the dominant impression today's South gives off is of dynamism and hope.

As arresting as the new appearance of the South is its changed position in the nation. A virtual outsider in national politics at the turn of the century, humbled and cut off from real power, in 1999 the South supplied the president, the vice-president, the Senate majority leader, and the two preceding speakers of the house, to say nothing of Kenneth Starr. Southern white conservative Republicans have remade the party of Lincoln to such an extent that some long-time northern Republicans are crying hostile takeover. Senator Trent Lott of Mississippi, for example, when asked about his comment that "the spirit of Jefferson Davis lives in the 1984 Republican platform," explained: "The platform we had in Dallas, the 1984 Republican platform, all the ideas we supported there—from tax policy to foreign policy, from individual rights to neighborhood security—are things Jefferson Davis and his people believed in." But at the same time as the white South has tipped the national scales rightward in recent years, black Southerners—finally enfranchised—have broken the long-standing white monopoly of public power and transformed politics in the South and the nation. By 1994, 5,500 African Americans served as elected representatives in the South: they accounted for 70 percent of the national total, itself about eighty times greater than the number serving in 1940. Culturally, too, the South is more and more shaping the nation. Today, the Southern Baptist Convention is the largest Protestant denomination in the country, boasting fifteen million members, and the suburban megachurches and televangelists first tested in the South have long since moved across the Mason-Dixon line. On the radio, the South's influence is ever-present: whether one tunes into the blues, country, or rock and roll, to zydeco or gospel, they are southern creations all. Muddy Waters, Little Richard, Elvis Presley, Hank Williams, Mahalia Jackson: these are the names not simply of a regional culture but of the national culture. Without them, there would not *be* what we know as American music.

How, then, can we make sense of this change—most of it since the Second World War—that has moved the South from the sidelines to the center of national life? Many possibilities have been suggested. We might, with John Egerton, see the change as the northernization of the South, and the southernization of the North. This works well as description. The very words "northernization" and "southernization" spotlight the cultural traffic before our eyes, from how McDonald's has spread through rural Georgia to how good old boys have assumed the helm in Washington, D.C. And the idea of convergence contains a healthy ethical challenge: Egerton complained that the two regions were "not exchanging strengths as much as they are exchanging sins . . . spreading the worst in each other, while the best languishes and withers." Yet, as analysis, this alternative may rely too much on regional stereotypes that can't tell us why change occurred when it did. For a more historical explanation, some have turned to the civil rights movement, or rather, to a deeper understanding of the long standing black freedom movement that eventually succeeded in the 1960s in wiping out de jure Jim Crow and disfranchisement. After all, as Ralph Ellison once observed, "southern whites cannot walk, talk, sing, conceive of laws or justice, think of sex, love, the family or freedom without responding to the presence of Negroes."[1] It only stands to reason, then, that the remaking of race relations would have much wider repercussions. Still, this interpretation takes for granted some of what needs to be explained—namely, why the movement butted up against an immovable impasse until the 1950s, and managed to triumph thereafter. That is, the earlier stalemate and subsequent success are part of what needs accounting for in the twentieth-century South. Seeking to get at the underlying long-term processes, some have turned to modernization theory, with its promise of a framework for interpreting broad patterns of economic development and social change. The problem here is that it doesn't work. Its complacent presupposition that somehow capitalist development will naturally yield democracy and personal autonomy fails utterly to make sense of most of twentieth-century southern history, as it has that of the so-called developing world. The white South had cotton mills long before it had conscience. Economic growth proved fully compatible with racial dictatorship, suppression of labor, and denial of basic civil rights for most of the century. Indeed, some have shown how the region's physical modernization grew up on the backs of barely free and often beaten black workers in an ironic contribution to Progressive-era reform: the state-sponsored chain gangs that built the South's modern network of roads for commerce and transport.

A more promising line of interpretation for the changes that have swept the South lies in the transformation of the core institution of the South's political economy: cotton plantation sharecropping, which itself was the center of the economy that separated South from North. "Cotton," wrote the radical minister turned sharecropper organizer Howard Kester in 1936, "to a greater degree than any other product of industry or agriculture rules the South." The twentieth-century story of the region, I will argue, is grounded in sharecropping's entrenchment after Emancipation, its shake-up at mid-century, and its eventual demise. As it happens, that story speaks to most others in the modern South—whether race relations, labor history, politics, religion, or culture. The blues, for example, grew up in the storm center of that plantation country, the Mississippi Delta. And it was in relation to first slavery and then Jim Crow that the white South's distinctive evangelical culture took shape. This framework doesn't address all aspects of southern life, of course, but it does help to make better sense of both changes and continuities. Above all, an interpretation focused on the evolution of the plantation system helps to clear up a central paradox: how it was that the South incubated both the most democratic movement of twentieth-century American life, the civil rights movement, and some of the most conservative, even authoritarian, organizations from the Ku Klux Klan to the Conservative Citizens' Council. Indeed, there is a real irony at the core of this story: the region's progress has come from the burying of an institution that the South's leaders spent most of the century trying to defend and preserve. The death of that institution came from forces these leaders had always pitted themselves against: the pressure of African-American Southerners for freedom, and the incursion of federal power that finally enabled those grass-roots efforts to prevail.

Contrary to the conventional wisdom, this is not a regional story. Quite the contrary. The notion that the South offers simply "local color" for the national narrative has been crippling for understanding of American life. In fact, as I will try to suggest, Southerners and southern institutions have been shaping U.S. history for much of the twentieth century without most American historians—fixed as they are on the Northeast and Midwest—ever noticing. If this is obvious in today's political economy and culture, it was equally true in the late nineteenth century, during the Great Depression, and in the early postwar years. Southerners, in short, have so often been seen as objects of national history (most often, a problem to be acted on by others), that they are too rarely appreciated as subjects shaping national life. Yet they must be so grasped, and grasped in all their diversity, to make sense of the twentieth-century United States. "To understand America" today, the Atlanta-based journalist Peter Applebome chides, "you have to understand the South." He is right.

II

Appearances can be deceptive: the plantation system found in the South of 1900 was a new institution. Not an archaic holdover from another time, sharecropping emerged after Emancipation as a compromise between contestants of grossly unmatched power. Where planters desired a virtual return to slavery, with the former slaves producing cotton for market in a centralized gang labor system on the plantations, the freed people themselves rejected this. If they couldn't work their own plots of land, then at least they wanted to labor as tenants on family plots free from landlords' close supervision. Sharecropping was the eventual outcome of this clash of wills, as it replayed over and over again across the cotton belt in the years after the war. Then, too, sharecropping seemed a reasonable way for individual plantations and households to bring land and labor together in a cash- and credit-scarce economy. The fact that there were so few alternative avenues of employment for agricultural workers—white and black, but especially black—further entrenched the system. Above all, the conditions of staple crop production necessitated labor cheaper than planters could get from truly free workers. So in varying ways over the years they turned to nonmarket mechanisms to guarantee themselves an adequate labor supply, such as emigrant agent statutes aimed at keeping out labor recruiters from other states and vagrancy laws written so loosely that planters could round up the unemployed at harvest time.

Historians have disputed the exact nature of this postwar economic regime, its internal dynamics, and the nature of the classes that peopled it. Some have posited continuity with the prewar slaveholding planter class, for example. Others have noted how Emancipation, by dissolving property in people and shifting the focus to land—in Gavin Wright's words, turning labor lords into landlords into rural employers—fundamentally recast the social and economic system. At the same time, secession and wartime defeat dislodged the planter elite from power in the national state in the formative years of America's economic development and rise to world power status. Still other historians have emphasized such developments as the growing role of furnishing merchants, and of small-town businessmen with northern backing in developing the region's mills. Some also point out that in law and custom, sharecroppers were effectively wage laborers, whereas tenants, more often white, were more akin to small farmers or tool-owning craftsmen. Yet whether historians emphasize persistence or rupture, town or country, gradations of class position or the big divide, few dispute the cotton economy's key place in southern life in these years. "The impoverishment of farmers," write Jacquelyn Hall and her coauthors in an example of cotton's reach, "was industrialization's driving force."

To concentrate on the plantation South is thus not to discount the existence of other subregions. There were many Souths, as the saying goes, and in a longer, more fleshed-out treatment they would surely command more attention. The textile South, stretching across the arc of the Piedmont from north Georgia through the Carolinas to Virginia, led the industrialization of the region. For years it was *the* manufacturing industry of the South. Generations of southern whites manned its mills and produced a complex regionwide culture whose character continues to stimulate debate among historians. Further west and south, timber and lumbering communities employed more workers than any other southern industry save farming until the 1920s. In Appalachia, yet another South arose from the dispossession of mountain people, whose men went into the coal mines and in time built one of the most powerful and militant unions in American history. Louisiana—with its rice culture, French and Spanish influences, and unusually prominent Catholicism—had its own social and cultural ecology. Cities such as Birmingham, Nashville, and Knoxville generated an emergent urban culture—and at the same time, among people who found that urban culture barren, a string of Holiness-Pentecostal churches that acted as odd islands of antinomian interracialism in the early Jim Crow South. Each of these areas offers intriguing problems and engrossing stories that in a longer treatment would demand their own chapters.

But to understand the South's overall political economy, its main axis of power and pivot point of change by mid-century, the cotton-growing South is the place to look. The influence of cotton sharecropping was especially clear among blacks and in the area of race relations, which most historians would put at the center of southern life. One in every ten blacks lived in Mississippi in 1890; what happened there shaped events elsewhere. Nine in every ten southern African Americans lived in rural areas in 1880; fifty years later, more than two-thirds still did, most as cotton farmers. Indeed, the land area planted to cotton production continued to expand from the late nineteenth century until the eve of the Great Depression. By then, according to one investigation, more than eight million Southerners in the ten leading cotton states belonged to tenant-farming families.

For all that white supremacy put them at odds, black and white working people were unwittingly bound together in this system. What tied them was not, as long thought, widespread debt peonage, for there was actually a good deal of geographic mobility within the South. Rather, it was the existence of a separate regional labor market, one isolated from the national and international labor markets of its time in a way that the West's or New England's was not. Rooted in slavery, this isolated labor market perpetuated that institution's economic consequences—one of which was separate economies north and south. As long as they could look abroad for limitless supplies of labor, northern employers were happy to comply. Low southern farm wages pulled down the floor for industrial wages, and the unskilled wage proved nearly the same for whites and blacks. In turn, the existence of plentiful cheap labor discouraged mechanization: with so many hands to hire, why innovate? What drove this economy was less growth in productivity than acreage planted to cotton. So, in effect, the regional labor market helps explain other features of the southern economy commonly taken as signs of backwardness: its low wages, its limited-skill industry, its importation of technology and machinery, its shortage of capital, and its failure to invest in education. Even though southern industry grew quite respectably by historical standards at the turn of the century (an average of 7% a year from 1869 to 1909), it was, Wright has shown, "not fast enough *relative* to *the growing regional population*" and it was not blending into the national economy.

Indeed, this isolated regional labor market, Wright has argued most persuasively, held the key to the region's political economy. Because the South was, as he says, "a low-wage region in a high-wage country," its beneficiaries had a strong interest in insulating this market from outside influence. They had little to gain and much to fear from investing in the region's labor force. As long as that separate labor market persisted, for example, southern representatives in Congress did not jockey for federal projects for their districts that might upset the low-wage status quo. State and local politicians showed a similar disinterest in providing good schooling for laboring people, or even in higher education for the few. "A high school diploma," Wright notes, "was as good as a ticket to leave the mill village." And that was the case of the relatively favored *white* manufacturing work force; for rural blacks, it was more stark. One Arkansas planter complained in 1900: "My experience has been that when one of the younger class gets so he can read and write and cipher, he wants to go to town." Such attitudes led the South to spend far less on education than the rest of the country, usually a third to half as much over the years 1890 to 1940. Schooling the black man, the demagogue and U.S. senator

James K. Vardaman once explained, "simply renders him unfit for the work which the white man has prescribed, and which he will be forced to perform . . . the only effect is to spoil a good field hand and make an insolent cook."

Wanting a submissive labor force, the region's planters and manufacturers feared popular uprisings even more than individual upward mobility. That much was clear from the determination with which the South's white Democratic elite had checked the Populist revolt in the 1890s. Determined that black men would never again hold the balance of power in conflicts where white men divided, conservative Democrats pushed through the disfranchisement of black men and many poor white men in populism's wake. Between 1890 and 1903, each of the southern states enacted legislation restricting the right to vote, legislation that knocked out virtually all black voters and many white ones as well. The new laws, one enthusiast at the time promised, "will eliminate with equal effectiveness the least intelligent and the least conservative elements among the white and black voters alike." In Louisiana, the new constitutional provisions cut the number of registered black voters from 130,344 in 1896 (including a majority in twenty-six parishes) to just 5,320 in the whole state four years later. After disfranchisement, most southern states registered voter turnouts of 15 to 34 percent for decades on end: a drop in some places from late nineteenth-century turnouts of 75 to 90 percent. The region also proved notoriously hostile to women's suffrage, in large part for the same reasons: a fear that it would empower African-American communities, fortified by an abiding gender and sexual conservatism. At the same time, the white minority in the plantation districts entrenched its hold over state governments by other means. In Georgia, for example, a country unit voting system reserved grossly disproportionate power to rural districts. All but nullifying urban votes, this system endured well into the 1950s. Tellingly, even with such an apparatus, many white Southerners felt deep uneasiness over the security of their rule. A case in point: the Mississippi state senate only narrowly defeated a measure proposed in 1940 that would have expunged any mention of voting, elections, or democracy from the civics textbooks read by black pupils.

The rise of legal segregation in the last decade of the nineteenth century and the first decade of the twentieth provides an illustrative contrast. Four decades of controversy have shadowed C. Vann Woodward's thesis in *The Strange Career of Jim Crow* that the entrenchment of legal segregation in the 1890s marked a watershed in race relations. Researchers have found that, in fact, whites customarily excluded blacks from a range of activities in the years after Emancipation and so in some areas, Jim Crow marked an ironic step forward in giving blacks access to inferior facilities in place of none at all. And yet, as Woodward insists, "the new laws were of profound significance. They rigidified practice, eliminated exceptions, and applied to all on the basis of race alone." This Jim Crow by statute, as opposed to the informal separation practiced in much of the South until then, was a product less of the countryside than of the city: its origins thus differed from those of disfranchisement. It spread over the South like kudzu vines as the white South's politicians struggled to control the pace of social change and inhibit the scale of black aspirations in town. Town life by nature was harder to regulate than rural life because blacks were freer from white oversight and better protected by larger communities. Yet, while urban whites devised the idea of Jim Crow legislation, its spirit was very much in keeping with the interests of their rural employing counterparts, for whom the effort to subjugate black labor was a daily preoccupation.

Straining to maintain control, the planter class leaned on state and local government as an essential prop of its power. Writing of southern politics at mid-century, V. O. Key reported that the black-majority plantation counties made up the "hard core of the political South" and "managed to subordinate the entire South to the service of their particular local needs." And if planters and industrialists differed on some matters, they shared a common vision as tacit partners in a low-wage coalition that united their representatives in Washington in seeking to repel federal intrusion in the South. Control of politics was all important to them, for ends ranging from trade and welfare policy at the national level, to control of police power at the local level (so that, for example, courts could be used to keep workers on the job and extralegal violence would remain immune from prosecution), to all the important state-level functions in between such as taxation, education, and roads. Sometimes, shrewd economics drove the calculations; other times, an ugly meanness did. Most times in the South, the line between the two was hard to draw. In Mississippi, for example, the white monopoly of municipal government meant that black neighborhoods went without the sidewalks, paved streets, lights, and water and sewage systems that white citizens took for granted.

It was, as many observers have noted, not only a racially repressive but also a labor-repressive system. The two aspects were intimately bound in the South's penchant for violence. Socially, whites resorted to violence because consent was impossible to obtain and other methods of control failed to work—and sometimes simply because they could. The most grisly illustration was the practice of lynching, which peaked between the end of the nineteenth century and the first half of the twentieth. In the years from 1880 to 1930, according to the best estimates, 3,220 blacks and 723 whites lost their lives to southern lynch mobs, many of which worked for hours in broad daylight without disguises before enthusiastic audiences of thousands. Until recently, none of their members was ever successfully prosecuted. Not an easy phenomenon to understand, lynching has resisted the best efforts of reductionists. It occurred in the industrial Piedmont as well as the Black Belt, sometimes took the lives of black women and white men as well as black men (who were most commonly targeted), and involved whites from all points on the social spectrum. Yet for all that variety, lynching was embedded in and expressive of the sharecropping-based social order, and subsided only with changes in the very structure of southern society. Licensed by that political economy, lynching at the same time revealed some of its inner tensions: whites' jitteriness over their inability to secure complete control over blacks, as well as the potential rifts among whites over how to stay in command that called forth such fiendish ritual performances of racial solidarity. Beyond lynching, moreover, the South bred an unusual propensity for other forms of violence as well, which also fed on the South's social system. David Montgomery has observed this of the violence directed against workers—white as well as black—who tried to organize industrial unions. As the labor organizer Fred Beal put it, commenting on a southern textile community in the 1930s where some workers lost their lives for trying to form a union, "in as far as the Bill of Rights was concerned, it was not part of America." Although almost as prone to strike at the turn of the century as their northern counterparts, southern workers rarely won. Montgomery attributes this to three barriers that also fostered violence: the grinding poverty of the countryside, whites' fierce commitment to racial hierarchy, and the determination of southern local and state governments to keep employers happy. As he concludes, "much of the violence against southern strikers and labor union activists was of the 'socially acceptable' variety . . . instigated and participated in by prominent, propertied, educated individuals from the communities in which it occurred."

From the 1890s right through the middle of the century, this social system had at least the tacit support of northern elites and voters. Whether actively collaborating with their southern counterparts or simply willing to oblige them, influential white Northerners showed time and again that they lacked the interest or the will to challenge their southern counterparts. The Supreme Court sanctioned the new southern status quo with a string of decisions at the turn of the century that condoned segregation, upheld disfranchisement, and nullified equal protection. Republican leaders followed suit. Despite their control of Congress at the turn of the century, they showed little desire to intervene in the South to guarantee the rights pledged to their one-time allies the freedmen. More interested now in overseas expansion than in internal reform, northern leaders developed a new appreciation for southern social thought, for so-called scientific racism in particular and for antidemocratic ideas in general. "As America shouldered the White Man's Burden," C. Vann Woodward noted years ago, "she took up at the same time many southern attitudes on the question of race." So uninterested was most of the white North in elementary racial justice that even legislation to fight lynching faltered repeatedly for want of majority support in Congress or presidential backing throughout the years the crime was common.

This record makes all the more important and intriguing the challenges that southern blacks and low-income whites managed to mount in the first three decades of the twentieth century. For as onerous as the South's political economy was, it wasn't strong enough to completely curb organized resistance.

Populism has already been mentioned. However much historians continue to spar over how to interpret its social vision and interracial organizing, few would deny that its activists had more of what Lawrence Goodwyn once called "democratic promise" than their adversaries. After the demise of that rural farm protest, wage-earners picked up the baton. In several different and important cases large numbers joined together across the racial divide—though usually in biracial unions of segregated locals—to defend common interests and build more democracy into their daily lives. Dock workers in Louisiana, coal miners in Alabama, and timber workers in the Southwest all learned from bitter experience to cooperate. All told, their numbers ran to the tens of thousands. Even textile workers, the most lily-white industrial group in the region, found that white supremacy was not all it was sold as. In scattered strikes from the 1880s to the South-wide general strike of 1934 (the biggest single labor dispute in American history, some 400,000 workers strong), mill workers announced that they had interests and aspirations of their own that they would fight their employers to defend. These efforts weren't always admirable. As Tera Hunter and others point out, white workers sometimes waged hate strikes to keep blacks out of their work places. And short of active hostility, most trade unions in the region accepted white supremacy; they sought less to dismantle it than to secure the best bargain within it for their members. Still, what is most historically surprising is how laboring people once in a while broke through these daunting odds and debilitating habits to join in collective action that offered the South alternative vistas of more fairness and democracy. Similarly, the black middle class not only survived but advanced slowly over this period, itself a feat given the obstacles. Its members, women very prominent among them, joined together in campaigns to secure resources for black communities and develop their internal assets, through social work, business, and above all education. So to say the plantation was pivotal in this period is not to discount resistance. Indeed, Neil McMillen has warned historians of the segregated South that "by looking for too much [we] may see too little."

Yet the overview just advanced in one way also confirms the main argument presented here. The Deep South's plantation workers are noticeably absent from this list of early twentieth-century organizing, even as its elites helped ensure the defeat of other collective action efforts. If one thinks of the kinds of enabling factors cited by students of successful social movements, the reasons rural workers held back are not hard to find. Their restraint is the more telling because rural laborers had mobilized during Reconstruction and in some cases as late as the 1880s and the 1890s. That they did not now reflected not timeless truths about country life, but rather specific features of the political economy of sharecropping in the early twentieth century. Scattered across the rural South, often miles from a neighbor; deprived of voting power and legal rights; denied police protection from retribution; lacking in powerful local institutional supports; cut off from potential allies in other regions;

marooned by the federal government; poorly taught and badly fed—of course few sharecroppers or tenants fought for social change. The most courageous simply left. Until the 1930s, the prospects for local organizing were too dismal to risk trying. The system endured, not because its workers believed it legitimate or fair, but because they saw no achievable alternative. Ironically, it took the Great Depression and world war to upset that fatalism—and to create the conditions for alternatives to emerge.

III

Beginning tentatively in World War I and in earnest with the Great Depression, that plantation system was shaken up. Faced with unprecedented new stresses and unheard of new outside resources, the South's planter elite embarked on a course of change that ultimately got beyond its control and sparked developments never anticipated. Some of these would, in time, dramatically alter the balance of forces so as to create new space and promise for initiatives from below.

The Depression hit the South with ferocity. Its impact was the worse for coming on the heels of a decade of economic trouble in the region. After all, the industries historians and economists have labeled "sick" in the twenties—farming, textile manufacture, and coal mining—made up the very core of the South's economy. The slump after 1929 made the already bad worse. A presidential commission famously declared the South "the Nation's No. 1 Economic Problem." As Morton Sosna notes, that commission's report laid the intellectual groundwork "for what amounted to a regional affirmative action program—to prop up the South through federal largesse." The sharecropping system that had once seemed so rational for individual owners now produced collective disaster, as depressed prices and soil exhaustion ate away at the very purpose of production. In Mississippi, per capita income dropped from $239 in 1929 to $117 four years later. As industries laid off workers and speeded up jobs, farms folded and savings disappeared. Starved for tax revenue, states and localities cut back on public services and public works projects. Some urban people headed to small farms in hopes of raising a better living than they could earn in the city. For their part, male household heads and sometimes whole farm families roamed the roads in droves in pursuit of work that might support a family. The scene became desolate enough to crack the legendary resistance of the South's planters to any potentially destabilizing federal intervention in their region.

Believing they would benefit and could control the outcome, the planter elite signed on to the early New Deal. A decade's worth of farm depression in the 1920s, overproduction for glutted world markets, the crash of 1929, and planters' demonstrated incapacity to work together to solve their troubles all

made them mute their antistatist ideology and look to the Roosevelt administration for help. As one historian has said, they practically wrote the codes for
the Agricultural Adjustment Administration (AAA). That effort resulted in the
removal of more than half of the region's cotton acreage from production, leaving 7.7 million acres fallow in exchange for subsidies to the landowners. But
if it brought immediate benefits, the New Deal also burrowed deep holes in the
foundation of the southern system. By paying planters to reduce their surplus,
and thus subsidizing nonproduction, the programs began leading them away
from sharecropping and toward wage labor and mechanization. In effect, the
farm programs undermined plantation tenancy. In vain did the interracial activists of the Arkansas-based Southern Tenant Farmers Union appeal to Washington to stop the evictions of sharecroppers and curb landlords' abuses of the
virtually string-free government handouts. As Pete Daniels puts it, the AAA
helped shift the region "from sharecropping to agribusiness."

While the farm programs were undercutting the old bases of the rural
economy, the New Deal's labor programs helped to recast southern manufacturing. The changes can easily be overstated here. Southern congressmen
made sure to tailor the legislation so as to exclude much of the work force of
their region, especially farm and domestic workers. Their success shows in
that 90 percent of black women derived no direct benefit from minimum wage
and maximum hour, unemployment compensation, and social security laws.
Still, these reforms upset the regional economy's base. The National Recovery
Administration and the Fair Labor Standards Act produced wage increases that
made obsolete the mills' longtime family labor system. These programs also
began to reduce the wage differential between North and South on which the
separate labor markets rested. Effectively, they inaugurated a national minimum wage, even as southern employers managed to hold on to a racial wage
differential by other names. Later, in the fifties and sixties, national minimum
wage laws would bring the South even closer to national levels by discouraging the kinds of low-wage industries in which the region had long specialized.

And then came the war. One historian has argued that World War II
proved more of a turning point for the South than the Civil War. Others might
not go that far, but all agree that the war, coming in the wake of the reorganization begun in the 1930s, stimulated profound changes as it set in motion a
process difficult to contain. "A bird's eye view of large-scale Southern industry
makes you feel that the South has rubbed Aladdin's lamp," said the chairman
of the War Production Board in 1944. The war brought money in and lots of
it, through federal contracts, shipyards, and military bases, as well as through
higher crop prices, on a scale that dwarfed everything before. All that activity
also generated new, nonplantation employment for legions of Southerners.
Culturally, it had effects that historians have barely begun to explore, as some
four million soldiers—or one-third of the nation's total—converged across regional and racial lines on military bases spread throughout the South. As

George Orwell quipped: "if the war didn't happen to kill you, it was bound to start you thinking." And, of course, because the South's Jim Crow laws had much in common with pre-1938 Nazi racial legislation, the war against fascism reverberated back on the home front. Black newspapers South and North adroitly compared the racism of Hitler's Germany with the South's white supremacy, and found little reason for patriotism in the comparison. Their arguments agitated not only the region's racial conservatives, but also its gradualist liberals; at the same time, they galvanized many blacks and some northern white liberals.

As it refueled the economy and heated up the debate on Jim Crow, the Second World War fired a pot that had been on simmer for two decades. The outmigration of labor, begun in the 1910s but slowed during the interwar years, shot up to meet the voracious wartime demand for labor in the North. Some nine million Southerners, roughly half of them white and half of them black, quite the region between 1910 and 1950; all told, their numbers amounted to one-third of the 1910 population. While World War I–era migrants have attracted the most attention, the actual numbers of people leaving were over three times larger in the years from 1940 to 1970, when the net out-migration ended. In that latter period, workers went elsewhere not only for the prospect of the higher-paying northern and western jobs newly available, but also out of desperation as southern planters and manufacturers adjusted to new conditions by mechanizing and cutting workers loose. It was, Nicholas Lemann has observed, "one of the largest and most rapid mass internal movements of people in history." The South's farm population dropped by three million people in the war years alone as more than one in every five residents headed out, whether for the military or the new jobs available elsewhere. Their impact on the North and West, in areas from labor history to politics and popular culture, is only beginning to be appreciated.

In the South, the impact of this mass movement of population was instantly felt: it delivered the coup de grace to the older economic system. In creating severe labor shortages in agriculture, the exodus abetted the mechanization that federal farm programs first made thinkable. Indeed, the migration stimulated technological innovation, for it was only with that labor shortfall that large corporations such as International Harvester, Allis Chalmers, and Deere threw themselves into producing an affordable mechanical picker. All of this is not to understate the devastating effects of the disruption on sharecroppers and farm wage laborers: once in use, the mechanical pickers turned individuals, families, and whole communities into "surplus" labor to be gotten rid of. The journalist Rick Bragg, then a child in a farm-worker family, remembered the coming of the picker: "The first time I ever saw one I stood amazed. It was big as God, and picked rows and rows at a time. I did not know it then but I was seeing a way of life disappear into the maw of the thing."[2] The change occurred with numbing rapidity: in 1950, machines picked 5 percent of the nation's cotton; ten years later, 50 percent; and ten years after that, 98 percent. In twenty years, that is to say, a whole social system was upended. "The coming problem of agricultural displacement," wrote a prescient observer in the Mississippi Delta as early as 1947, "is of huge proportions and must concern the entire nation . . . The country is on the brink of a process of change as great as any that has occurred since the Industrial Revolution. . . . Five million people will be removed from the land in the next few years." Yet no one with the power to do so, he warned, was preparing to ease that transition and avert the "enormous tragedy" that appeared to be in the making. Told individually, then, the stories of casting out and movement away contain suffering, fear, separation, and loss alongside hope. Neither planters nor the promoters of mechanical pickers troubled themselves over the human cost of the choices they were making. Yet, told collectively and with an eye to the long term, the story appears almost a second emancipation, certainly an economic leap forward for most former sharecroppers and tenants and ultimately a broader boon for the whole society. The same sequence of events was played out on smaller scale in rice and tobacco areas after the mid-1950s; coal mining, for its part, mechanized in the 1940s and 1950s.

This massive out-migration and mechanization had political consequences as well. For one, blacks established significant beachheads in the electorate outside the South. From 1940 to 1970, the proportion of blacks living outside the South grew from 20 percent to more than 50 percent. By about the middle of that period, their voting power pushed some northern politicians to action on the South. Moreover, the shake-up in sharecropping encouraged a shift in regional economic strategies, by strengthening the hands of those Southerners interested in outside investment. A losing proposition prior to 1935 with so many powerful Southerners committed to safeguarding their established system, by the postwar years the new strategy had become a region-wide trend. Southern state governments remade themselves into booster engines and recruitment agents and avidly stepped up what James Cobb calls the "selling of the South." They sweetened their appeals to potential investors with tax concessions, infrastructural improvements, so-called right-to-work laws, and other benefits. Prior to the 1950s, the South actually taxed corporate profits at comparatively high rates; between then and the late 1970s, it happily surrendered that distinction. These shifts, unthinkable before the changes in federal labor and agricultural policy, worked. Where the South gained only 17 percent of federal government per capita spending in 1952, by 1970 it was taking in almost half of those revenues. And there were other changes under way. Fearing further loss of labor as well as the prospect of desegregation, many southern states and school districts started to spend more on black schools after 1945 (not nearly as much as on white, but the gap narrowed).

The momentum could be seen in the changing characteristics of the South's black population in these years. Displaced from the farms and seeking something better, African-American Southerners headed for cities in large numbers, even as unemployment mounted in the 1950s. The number of black farmers fell from approximately 900,000 in 1920 to 540,000 by 1950. Between 1930 and 1960, the percentage of southern blacks living in urban areas almost doubled, to 58 percent. Urban life offered better job possibilities and pay as well, such that incomes among adult black Southerners, while still very low, improved over the years 1949 to 1962 with that movement. In turn, this strengthened black institutions. Church congregations grew in size and institutional strength, and in confidence to speak out on civil rights matters. Black colleges grew more remarkably. Between 1941 and 1964, enrollments leaped from about 40,000 to 105,000. The mid-century rate of increase was three times the comparable figure for whites. The NAACP also burgeoned. Its southern membership grew from about 85,000 in 1934 to some 420,000 in 1946: a fivefold jump. Branches quadrupled, with most of the new growth in urban areas. The growing appetite for change was also evident at the polls. The number of black voters multiplied four times over between 1944 and 1950, to 600,000; virtually all of the growth came from the urban South. Meanwhile, the number of lynchings declined from double digits in the 1930s to an average of three a year in the 1940s and fewer thereafter. Together, as Doug McAdam has shown, all of these factors improved the structure of opportunities for racial change, expanded outside resources, and enhanced feelings of efficacy among those who would have to take the risks change required. Said W. E. B. DuBois of such subtle changes: "These things give us hope."

And yet, it would be grossly misleading to suggest that some sort of evolutionary process was under way in which economic and social change were leading inexorably to political reform. The evidence will not support a happy story of modernization and gradual reform. Quite the contrary: as striking in this history as the mounting pace of change on some fronts is the refusal of most southern whites—above all the region's "leaders"—to acknowledge the injustice of the existing order and accept the need for democratization and desegregation. Enthused about the New Deal in Roosevelt's first term, most southern congressmen turned against it in his second, more pro-labor administration—this about face at a time when popular opinion in the South ran strongly in favor of the initiatives coming from Washington. "After 1937," Harvard Sitkoff observed, "Roosevelt faced a shifting, informal, but highly effective, conservative coalition resolved to block, or at least limit severely, all efforts to aid Negroes, labor unions, urban areas, and disadvantaged workers and farmers." It was a coalition in which southern Democrats played a disproportionately important part.

Although their region accounted for less than a quarter of the nation's population in these years, southern congressmen could choke out and defeat progressive legislation by virtue of their seniority. That seniority, which won them control of key congressional committees, resulted from the unnatural political longevity they enjoyed as representatives of a one-party region with a grotesquely shrunken electorate. A case in point is Eugene Cox, acting chair of the all-important Rules Committee, who won reelection in 1938 in Georgia with 5,137 votes—in a district with a population of 263,606. Indicting the national system as much as the Dixiecrats he described, Malcolm X would later observe: "The only reason they have seniority is because they come from states where Negroes can't vote. . . . Half the senators and congressmen who occupy these key positions in Washington, D.C., are there illegally, are there unconstitutionally."[3] By the rules of the institution, moreover, southern leaders like Cox could simply refuse to report a bill out for deliberation by the body as a whole. "All social benefit programs," recounts Jill Quadagno, "had to pass through the House Ways and Means and the Senate Finance committees, both Southern-controlled until the 1960s." Provoked to the limits of his patience, even FDR himself tried, unsuccessfully, to purge conservative Southerners from the Democratic party in the elections of 1938. Speaking of the "feudal" system of the South to a Georgia audience, he announced: "When you come right down to it, there is little difference between the feudal system and the fascist system. If you believe in one, you lean to the other." "Belatedly," the NAACP's magazine *The Crisis* commented at decade's end, "the rest of the country has come to realize that Senators and Congressmen from poll tax states menace the democratic process everywhere because they enjoy a power in Washington which they could not wield if the elections were free." The conclusion seemed simple: "the Dixie octopus strangling the rest of the country must be shaken off."

Yet no movement from below of working people for democratic social change in the South, whether the affiliated unions of the CIO or the grassroots activists of the Communist party, could expect an easy time of it. Antiunionism, James Cobb has said, is "the South's most respectable prejudice." The violent repression employers and state and local governments unleashed against the general strike in textiles in 1934, for example, is legendary. Other draconian reprisals happened too often for listing. But Robin Kelley draws out the larger implications of these acts well: "When we ponder Werner Sombart's question, 'Why is there no socialism in the United States?' in light of the South, violence and lawlessness loom large." To be a left-wing activist below the Mason-Dixon line, Kelley reminds us, "was to face the possibility of imprisonment, beatings, kidnapping, and even death."

Obviously, the only way this system would reform was if sufficient counterpower was built up to compel change. Indeed, it is worth noting that none of the changes described above emerged organically out of the system southern elites so ardently defended, nor were they intentional. "Prior to the federal civil rights pressure of the 1960s," Cobb has written, "there was little reason to conclude that the South's conservative social order was incompatible with its economic progress." Wright perhaps put it best when he pointed out that

"Southern history is not a 'case study in economic development,' it is a case of a region being forced off of one growth trajectory and onto another." In fact, when the ferment of the early postwar years gave way to the cold war abroad and the McCarthy era at home, the defenders of the South's old order gained a breathing spell, a decade-long chance to regroup and try to retake lost ground. With Truman in office, said the journalist I. F. Stone, "the fizz was out of the bottle." By weakening the influences making for change—a liberal federal government and black pressure for change—these developments helped the region's white elites stave off challenge longer than they might have otherwise. "We have such a feeling here," Virginia Durr, a white New Deal liberal from Alabama, thus wrote in 1958 (quoted in Sullivan), "that we have been abandoned by the rest of the country and by the government and left to the tender mercies of the Ku Klux Klan and the White Citizens Council." Yet, in hindsight what stands out is how the artificial hiatus bestowed by McCarthyism and the cold war made the breakdown of the old system more abrupt and dramatic when it finally came.

IV

The plantation system—and with it the South's distinctive political economy—finally gave way by the 1960s. On the one hand, the continuing shift of the economy away from sharecropping weakened rural elites' once unwavering determination to control blacks at the same time as it enhanced the power of other elite white constituencies with other, possibly rival interests. On the other hand, as a result of these changes, blacks felt more confident that the resistance kept alive in private life, humor, song, and spirituality might now, if brought into the open through collective organizing, lead to change. Seen against a broad background, the struggles that have convulsed the South over the years since the war have been over what would emerge in the wake of that moribund sharecropping system: what the outlines of the new society would be, whom it would benefit, and how. Many of the answers are not yet in.

But one thing is abundantly clear: the civil rights movement became the pivot around which all else turned. That mass, sustained mobilization fundamentally altered the trajectory of the modern South and the nation with it. If, in one sense, the civil rights movement was an effect, its work enabled by the collapse of the plantation system, once activated the movement in turn became a cause of deeper, different change, as its activists organized to ensure that the region's transformation would be not merely economic, but social and political as well. Another the civil rights movement is discussed in some detail in chapter 9 of this volume, so my observations here will be brief. It is simply impossible to imagine the transformation of the modern South without the civil rights movement as the stimulus. In emboldening ordinary African-American Southerners to make history, and ushering them into public life and politics in large numbers, the movement changed lives, ideas, relationships, and communities. By standing firm in the face of often-brutal attempts to silence and push them back, its activists shamed and further isolated the old county-seat elite that had so long opposed them, and forced the emerging metropolitan business elite to rethink its strategies of rule. "The black leaders won," David Chappell has aptly remarked, "largely because they understood the white South better than the segregationists who claimed to be defending it." "The political task," they faced "was to attack the institutions of the white South in such a way as to divide rather than unify its people." Standing on the shared symbols of the Constitution and the Bible, and playing on the emerging elite's hunger for outside investment, the movement carried its message to the nation. It also worked steadily through the courts from the 1930s on to rewrite the rules of American life, with implications for the North as well as the South. Major court decisions disallowing segregation in state professional schools, outlawing the all-white primary, mandating that separate schools really be equal, calling for desegregation of public schools, and so forth, all came about because there was a movement organizing to push for legal change and secure it at the grass roots.

Scholars and activists alike still debate the results of the movement and its significance. Some liberal observers wax rhapsodic over the extent and speed of change; conservatives agree that much changed quickly, but offer more dyspeptic appraisals. Others, more radical and conscious of how much was left undone, whether black nationalist or social democratic, are more critical and more inclined to look to the hard-core areas of rural Alabama, Mississippi, and Louisiana, where change was slower in coming and thinner in nature than in towns and cities of the Upper South and border states. Seeing the reforms won as largely cosmetic and low in cost to whites, these critics may minimize the movement's achievement. Still others acknowledge the distance yet to be traveled while emphasizing how much the movement achieved in the relatively short time it could count on vigorous external support. When Eisenhower sent federal troops into Little Rock, Arkansas, to enforce the law of the land in 1957, that act ended an eighty-year epoch of southern history that began with the withdrawal of federal troops from the region in the Compromise of 1877. No longer could the white South count on a free hand to deprive black citizens of their rights. Too rarely used, the threat of that power still hovered over all that followed. "The movement was able, in a matter of years," stresses Doug McAdam, "to dismantle a thoroughgoing system of caste restrictions that had remained impervious to change for some seventy-five years. It was also responsible, in three years' time, for the passage of more civil rights legislation than had been enacted in all the previous congressional sessions in U.S. history." And, in a fitting irony, that legislation was steered to passage by a southern white president, Lyndon Baines Johnson. Thirty years before it would have seemed unimaginable.

Key among those victories were the Civil Rights Act of 1964 and the Voting Rights Act of 1965. Yet neither of these reforms was self-enforcing. After their passage, the freedom struggle had to shift to a new level—one historians have shown too little curiosity about—as efforts moved out of the streets and into workplace caucuses and courtrooms. The great increase in black political representation, that is to say, came not automatically when the law was passed, but because individuals filed lawsuits to end the stonewalling of whites who tried one stratagem after another to defy the spirit of the law. The same was true of how many once all-white workplaces came to desegregate and hence of how blacks won access to the post-sharecropping economy. Nearly every leading manufacturer in the South eventually found itself in federal court facing actions that compelled changes in hiring and promotion practices. Title VII was a useful tool, then, but no more than a tool: actually winning a semblance of equal opportunity employment required the efforts of hundreds of organizations and thousands of plaintiffs. The story also has its share of setbacks, circumscribed victories, and even reverses. Forty-five years after *Brown* v. *Board of Education,* many southern public schools are now almost entirely black, as whites have deserted them for exclusive private academies—academies often named early on for Confederate heroes. In the South, as in the North where similar evasions evolved, the struggle has shifted to trickier terrain. Yet interestingly, by 1993 the South had more racially integrated public schools than any other part of the country.

So historic are the changes that observers, especially white ones, can become almost giddy and neglect to consider more sober ways of interpreting these events. "My God, man," one longtime labor and civil rights leader in the South told an interviewer, "when you'd given up thirty years of your life fighting for something that should have been yours to begin with, it's a little bit disheartening." So too for industrialization: it has not proved the miracle cure its boosters once promised. More than one in four Mississippians still lived beneath the poverty level in 1980, and of southern states only Virginia had a lower rate of poverty than the national average. The South's deliberate appeal to low-wage employers long discouraged most high-wage, high-technology firms from settling there—and made some southern recruiters positively fear them, especially if they were likely to import collective bargaining with their other machinery. North Carolina, the region's most industrialized state in 1980, was thus home to the lowest-paid, least-unionized workers. There is a real irony here, which Cobb has pointed out: the attributes associated with the South's backwardness—its antiunionism, poor wage and benefit levels, low taxes and emaciated public services—became causes of attractiveness to investors deserting higher-cost areas and hence became crucial to the formula for Sunbelt success. As deep a problem stemmed from the South's version of the national economic restructuring taking place. Jobs that paid a living wage to workers with limited education were fast disappearing, with devastating consequences for the South's (and the North's) unskilled labor force of both

races, but especially blacks. Textiles, steel, auto, meat packing, and coal mining have all cut jobs in large numbers over the last few decades; few well-
paying industries have taken their places. Indeed, some have wryly suggested
that the South may be looking so much better today only because the rest of
the country is doing so much worse at providing good jobs for large numbers,
sustaining racial liberalism, and preserving an ethic of access and elementary
fairness in public life.

Notwithstanding the limits of its reach, the sheer scale of economic
growth is impressive Per capita income in the region has risen at rates far
above the national average since the beginning of World War II. Freed, in a
sense, by the changes described above, southern representatives began lobbying aggressively and for the first time for military spending, whether manufacturing, shipyards, or training camps. Outsiders are at last welcome in the
South; the initiative has shifted from the keepers of the fortress to the boosters of development. Indeed, the proportion of Southerners who earned their
living at farming dropped from 43 percent in 1940 to 6.9 percent in 1970.
When adjusted for differences in cost of living, the North-South wage differential had largely disappeared as early as the 1970s. Since then, the South's
rates of economic advance, industrial development, and urbanization have all
outpaced the rest of the nation's. By the 1980s, Wright points out, it was no
longer possible to speak of a separate southern economy as a meaningful concept: what replaced it was truly a "new economy." In it, ordinary Southerners
themselves have become spurs to development whose hunger for advanced
education, mobility, and consumer goods drives the process of change onward.

Still, the nature of the South's renovation, not just its pace, has come as a
shock to many. The demise of the old system didn't take the form that those
who worked hard to bring it on expected—or that those who fought them
feared. For years, liberal and radical observers believed that the realignment
of the southern political system would remove the red herring of race and
allow the emergence of a genuine class-based, policy-oriented coalition among
low- and middle-income black and white Southerners. The idea was that in
place of the shotgun marriage between Dixiecrats and northern labor in the
old Democratic party that weighed down all reform efforts, a more "natural"
social-democratic alliance would emerge. When the realignment finally came,
it disappointed those expectations. Black voters, to be sure, rallied to the Democratic party and made it a more liberal force in the region. But not many
whites jointed them. Ordinary and elite alike headed to the Republican party
in large numbers. Harbingers of what was to come appeared in 1948 and again
in 1964, but the massive shift came in the Nixon years. In 1972, for the first
time in American history, Republicans won every southern state and 71 percent of the vote in the presidential race; virtually all of those votes were white.
Gloating at the outlook, it was a Republican strategist, Kevin Phillips, who
coined the term "Sun Belt" (as he consigned the Democrats to the "Rust Belt").

Perhaps given the long history of white supremacy, historians should keep their eyes on the almost 30 percent of whites who still voted Democratic: given the pulls of white privilege and community pressure, that willingness to cast their electoral lot with blacks may be the more amazing datum. In any event, the process is so far along today that the South's conservatives lead the nation, even if into a cul-de-sac.

The massive changes taking place have also widened the boundaries of the possible in the South in more subtle ways. In-migration is a case in point: a new family of four settles in Florida every six minutes. The figures are not nearly as high elsewhere, although by 1980 one in every five Southerners had been born outside the region. But they are dramatic in another way. The South since 1980 has been luring large numbers of blacks away from the North and West, and this alone speaks volumes about how much has changed. The widening catchment and improving quality of education in the South is another example. It appears, too, from the growing numbers of black and white working-class Southerners who have added their voices to the nation's literature through memoir and fiction since the 1960s, that there has been a freeing up of personality and subjectivity. One thinks, for example, of Maya Angelou, Dorothy Allison, Mary Karr, Alice Walker, Rick Bragg, and many others. Their works, along with the richly varied music still coming out of the South, have opened questions little explored before in public life among nonelite southerners, questions about the meanings of manhood and the powers of motherhood; about authority and abuse in families; about what some social critics once called "the injuries of class"; about how whiteness is learned and sometimes jarred to critical consciousness; and about imagination as a strategy of psychic transcendance and social mobility. This body of work reveals a diversity of voices, aspirations, and forms of social critique that simply were not visible before the transformation of the region. These more elusive shifts in southern sensibilities await their researchers. Historians could also attend to an almost opposite current in southern religious life: what Dennis Covington has described as a "victory in the loss of self" to be found in snake-handling churches that arose among people who surrendered the hills for the postwar South's towns and cities only to find them bereft of meaning. The numbers involved here are small, but the insights gained into wider themes could be large.

Recognizing the breadth and depth of the changes the South has undergone would also help us to get a better fix on its conservatives and their project. For all the paeans to the good old days, that project is not about restoring the past (no one really wants that, not with all the money and comfort at stake). It is about using the symbols of the past to shape the future. All the buzz in the air about neo-Confederacy and southern partisanship may distract, that is to say, from the card game at the table. Speaking of the Cult of the Lost Cause a hundred years earlier, Woodward once offered an insight that is equally true of that cult's modern-day echoes: "The deeper the involvements in commitments to the New Order, the louder the protests of loyalty to the Old." Even such atavistic-seeming politicians as the mid-career George Wallace might usefully be seen as variants on this theme: men self-consciously setting out to shape an emerging social order dressed up in the garb of the past, "in order," as one perceptive historian said in another context, "to present the new scene in world history in this time-honored disguise and this borrowed language." The battalions of southern whites fighting to preserve the Confederate flag as a symbol of public power are engaged in an analogous project. Perhaps, though, the best illustration is the case of Cobb County, Georgia, the home district of the former speaker of the house Newt Gingrich. The overwhelmingly white, suburban voters of Cobb County, while cheering on the Gingrich-led "Republican revolution" that preached the virtues of small government, self-reliance, and entrepreneurship, amassed more than $3.2 billion in federal aid in 1992. The county's residents enjoyed about $4,000 more federal aid per capita than New York City's—almost twice as much. More is involved here than irony or simple hypocrisy. Incongruities such as these suggest the need for a closer look at so-called conservatism in the post-sharecropping South, for an analysis that would examine its exponents less as nostalgics trying to preserve an ill-defined and in any case hardly unified past, than as people reacting to and trying to exert control over an emerging society still very much in flux. The heat with which the South's—and the nation's—cultural conflicts still simmer indicates that the outcome is far from settled.

V

The South in the twentieth century was the site of a rich variety of local cultures and cross-cutting lines of social conflict. But the culture that proved most influential in shaping the region and its relationship to the nation, I have argued, was that of cotton-plantation sharecropping. As long as it survived, those who benefited from it worked to isolate their labor force from the nation's. They were not alone responsible for the white supremacy, the widespread poverty, and the educational deprivation that plagued the region; indeed, the system could not have endured without northern aid. But without their active monitoring of the plantation economy it is hard to imagine that these other patterns would have persisted in the same way. Nor is this to deny that throughout these years important changes were afoot: among them the growth of buzzing towns and cities, the rise of a wide array of reform efforts, the spread of consumer culture, the popularization and circulation of southern music via radio, the growing variety and complexity of the region's literature, the development of southern spirituality and churches, the diversification of the South's economy, and what Jacquelyn Hall has called the modernization of gender and sex. Many of these developments reveal the South, not as a land apart, but as a place washed over by the currents of mainstream American life. "The New South," as Ed Ayers has said, "appears far newer when we measure change by paying close attention to concrete differences in people's lives instead of contrasting the region with the North's more fortunate history or the claims of Southern boosters." My argument is not that these differences don't matter. It is simply that in the kind of bird's eye view of the region's evolution possible in a brief overview, the story of the entrenchment, shake-up, and demise of the plantation looms larger. That shift offers a necessary though not sufficient explanation for many of the other changes the region has undergone. And further, my case is that two key forces prompted that reconstitution of the South's political economy: black pressure at the grass roots and outside intervention in the region—whether the jolt of the Depression or the prodding of the federal government in the New Deal, war mobilization, and civil rights enforcement.

At the outset of this chapter, I made a twofold commitment: to try to make sense of the changes within the South, on the one hand, and of the altered place of the South in the nation, on the other. Now at the end, I make a confession disguised as a call for research: it is easier to observe the latter than to argue with evidence about how it came to be and how it has affected the rest of the country. The journalist Peter Applebome tells us that the white South has managed to "redefine the [national] political center of gravity from center-left to center-right." Another journalist, Kirkpatrick Sale, has argued that the "power shift" from the North to the "Southern Rim" has been so dramatic and irrevocable that "it is a way of comprehending modern America." While both of these propositions—along with others about the postwar South's influence on labor, race relations, and national culture—are more than plausible, historians have yet to weigh in on these discussions. We lack the research that would show how these southern influences came to be felt, and why so many Northerners succumbed to them. The literature on the South's movement from the sidelines to the center is simply not there, by and large, perhaps due to the abiding assumption that the South was always and only a dependent variable in the national equation. When that notion, like once-hegemonic assumption of black passivity, is finally seen for the plain prejudice it is, the intellectual payoff is likely to be large. For as scholars seek to learn what exactly happened in the years after World War II, some may head off to earlier times to see how the South influenced other events and trends in modern American history. We may find then that the margins have been moving the center for a very long time.

NOTES

1. Ralph Ellison, *Shadow and Act,* (1964; reprint, New York: Vintage, 1972), p. 116.
2. Rick Bragg, *All over but the Shoutin'* (New York: Pantheon, 1997).
3. From the speech "The Ballot or the Bullet," reprinted in *Malcolm X Speaks,* ed. George Breitman (New York: Grove Press, 1965).

BIBLIOGRAPHY

Applebome, Peter. *Dixie Rising.* New York: Times Books, 1996.

Arnesen, Eric. "Following the Color Line of Labor: Black Workers and the Labor Movement before 1930." *Radical History Review* 55 (Winter 1993).

Ayers, Edward L. *The Promise of the New South.* New York: Oxford University Press, 1992.

Bartley, Numan V. *The New South, 1945–1980.* Baton Rouge: Louisiana State University Press, 1995.

Boles, John B., and Evelyn Thomas Nolan. *Interpreting Southern History.* Baton Rouge: Louisiana State University Press, 1987.

Brundage, W. Fitzhugh, ed. *Under Sentence of Death: Lynching in the South.* Chapel Hill: University of North Carolina Press, 1997.

Carlton, David. *Mill and Town in South Carolina, 1880–1920.* Baton Rouge: Louisiana State University Press, 1982.

Carter, Dan T. *The Politics of Rage.* New York: Simon & Schuster, 1995.

Chappell, David L. *Inside Agitators: White Southerners in the Civil Rights Movement.* Baltimore: Johns Hopkins University Press, 1994.

Cobb, James C. *Industrialization and Southern Society, 1877–1984.* Lexington: University Press of Kentucky, 1984.

———. *The Most Southern Place on Earth.* New York: Oxford University Press, 1992.

Covington, Dennis. *Salvation on Sand Mountain.* Reading, Mass.: Addison-Wesley, 1995.

Daniel, Pete. *Breaking the Land.* Urbana: University of Illinois Press, 1985.

Egerton, John. *The Americanization of Dixie: The Southernization of America.* New York: Harper's Magazine Press, 1974.

Grantham, Dewey W. *The South in Modern America.* New York: HarperCollins, 1994.

Gregory, James N. "Southernizing the American Working Class: Post-War Episodes of Regional and Class Transformation." *Labor History* 39 (May 1998).

Hahn, Steven. "Class and State in Postemancipation Societies: Southern Planters in Comparative Perspective." *American Historical Review* 95 (February 1990).

Hall, Jacquelyn, Robert Korstad, and James LeLoudis. "Cotton Mill People: Work, Community, and Protest in the Textile South, 1880–1940." *American Historical Review* 91 (1986).

Honey, Michael. *Southern Labor and Black Civil Rights.* Urbana: University of Illinois Press, 1993.

Hunter, Tera. *To 'Joy My Freedom.* Cambridge, Mass.: Harvard University Press, 1997.

Jones, Jacqueline. *Labor of Love, Labor of Sorrow.* New York: Basic Books, 1985.

Kelley, Robin D. G. *Hammer and Hoe.* Chapel Hill: University of North Carolina Press, 1990.

Kester, Howard. *Revolt among the Sharecroppers.* 1936. Reprint. Knoxville: University of Tennessee Press, 1997.

Key, V. O. *Southern Politics in State and Nation.* New York: Knopf, 1949.

Kousser, J. Morgan. *The Shaping of Southern Politics.* New Haven, Conn.: Yale University Press, 1974.

Lemann, Nicholas. *The Promised Land.* New York: Knopf, 1991.

McAdam, Doug. *Political Process and the Development of Black Insurgency.* Chicago: University of Chicago Press, 1982.

McMillen, Neil R. *Dark Journey: Black Mississippians in the Age of Jim Crow.* Urbana: University of Illinois Press, 1990.

Montgomery, David. "Violence and the Struggle for Unions in the South, 1880–1930." *Perspectives on the South* 1 (1981).

Quadagno, Jill. "Theories of the Welfare State." *Annual Review of Sociology* 13 (1987).

Sale, Kirkpatrick. *Power Shift.* New York: Random House, 1975.

Sitkoff, Harvard. *A New Deal for Blacks.* New York: Oxford University Press, 1978.

Sosna, Morton. "More Important Than the Civil War? The Impact of World War II on the South." In *Perspectives on the American South,* vol. 4, edited by James C. Cobb and Charles R. Wilson. New York: Gordon and Breach, 1987.

Sullivan, Patricia. *Days of Hope: Race and Democracy in the New Deal Era.* Chapel Hill: University of North Carolina Press, 1996.

Tindall, George Brown. *The Emergence of the New South, 1913–1945.* Baton Rouge: Louisiana State University Press, 1967.

Weiner, Jonathan M. "AHR Forum: Class Structure and Economic Development in the American South, 1865–1955." *American Historical Review* (October 1979).

Woodward, C. Vann. *The Origins of the New South, 1877–1913.* Baton Rouge: Louisiana State University Press, 1951.

———. *Thinking Back: The Perils of Writing History.* Baton Rouge: Louisiana State University Press, 1986.

Wright, Gavin. *Old South, New South: Revolutions in the Southern Economy.* New York: Basic Books, 1986.

11 | DEMOCRACY, CITIZENSHIP, AND RACE
The West in the Twentieth Century

PEGGY PASCOE

The history of the twentieth-century West began—as it looks likely to end—in a political struggle over democracy, citizenship, and race. Over the course of a century in which migration and immigration fueled forms of national and transnational capitalism that sometimes conformed to and sometimes collided with the political structures of state and nation, the U.S. West anticipated and precipitated many of the predicaments that have marked twentieth-century American history. We can trace them in the burst of imperialism that opened the century, in the progressive reforms of its first two decades, the wartime West of the 1940s, the democratic West of the 1960s, and the border-patrolled West of today.

It was not, however, until the last few decades that historians focused much attention on *this* history of the American West. For most of the twentieth century, western history emphasized frontier ideology and regional difference rather than the relationships among nature, culture, race, gender, power, and state formation that occupy so many western historians at century's end. During the last two decades, though, a wealth of "new" studies offer rich detail for a survey of twentieth-century U.S. western history that underscores five especially revealing moments in the history of western (and American) democracy, citizenship, and race.

IMPERIAL WEST

We can mark the birth of the modern, twentieth-century West in the great American debate over the future of the Philippine Islands. During the century that preceded this debate, Europeans carved Africa, South America, and Asia into colonial empires, while Americans stretched their Atlantic coast settlements across the North American continent. Hitching their longing for land to the trail of national destiny, Americans grabbed all the land they could, initially by purchase from various European powers, as in the Louisiana Purchase of 1803, and later by outright conquest, as in the U.S.-Mexican War of 1848. After the country defeated Spain in the short-lived Spanish-American War of 1898, a national debate erupted over the question of what to do with Spain's former colonies, including the Philippines.

One answer to this question came from Theodore Roosevelt, a self-styled cowboy, president-in-the-making, and enthusiastic promoter of American imperialism. Roosevelt campaigned for the United States to claim a place among the great European powers by acquiring and governing the Philippines. This imperial project dovetailed with corporate demands for overseas markets, but it was grounded in Roosevelt's tendency to see progress and civilization in terms of great racial battles. "Nineteenth-century democracy," he had written in 1894, "needs no more complete vindication for its existence than the fact that it has kept for the white race the best portions of the new world's surface." Roosevelt traced both his own and his country's strength to the heritage of western toughness embodied in the cowboy. During the Spanish-American War, he filled the ranks of his famous Rough Riders with cowboys, ranchers, and miners from Arizona, New Mexico, and the Indian Territory of Oklahoma in hopes that their frontier vitality would rub off on the New York "swells" sprinkled among them. After the American victory, he compared the acquisition of the Philippines with the conquest of American Indians. "Every argument that can be made for the Filipinos," Roosevelt told an audience in Cincinnati, Ohio, "could be made for the Apaches; every word that can be said of Aguinaldo could be said for Sitting Bull. As peace and order and prosperity followed our expansion over the lands of the Indians, so they will follow us in the Philippines."

If Roosevelt was a self-righteous imperialist, his major opponent, William Jennings Bryan, was an equally self-righteous anti-imperialist. A Nebraska politician known as the "Great Commoner," Bryan stood for a different, and competing, legacy of western history. Couching his political ambitions in the language of populism, Bryan portrayed America as a democratic republic in which farmers and workers were the personification of pioneer virtue and the epitome of democracy. "Some [may] dream of the splendors of a heterogeneous empire encircling the globe," he told fellow Nebraskans at the Trans-Mississippi Exposition in Omaha, but "we shall be content to aid in bringing enduring happiness to a homogeneous people, consecrated to the purpose of maintaining a government of the people, by the people, and for the people." Insisting that imperialism was a denial of the great American principle of the "consent of the governed," Bryan waged a fervent campaign for Philippine independence. But because he, too, conflated American democracy with whiteness, Bryan stopped short of extending the "consent of the governed" to Filipinos. "The Philippines," he explained, "are too far away and their people too different from ours to be annexed to the United States, even *if* they desired it."

Both these depictions of the western past—Roosevelt's celebration of rugged cowboys wresting the land from savage Indians and Bryan's paean to democratic farmers spreading westward across the continent—resonated among the proud citizens of a country whose government strove to put as much property as it could in the hands of its male citizens, and to protect their right to keep it. Whether the citizens in question were would-be farmers who homesteaded in the Great Plains or the captains of industry who presided over sugar plantations in Hawaii, the economic principle of private property offered a compelling rationale for government activity. Nineteenth-century Americans used it to stake liberal homestead grants and to foster massive extractive industries. They also used it to acquire the lands they needed for these ventures, filing lawsuits to transfer the titles of Spanish land grants in the Southwest to Anglo-American hands and devising an Indian policy that chopped reservations into individual parcels of land, most of which were then sold to white settlers.

Americans relied on citizenship policy to set the rules of admission to this community of property owners as well as to regulate the immigrants who flocked to the American West from all over the world. Immigrant homesteaders were required to promise to become U.S. citizens before filing their claims to land. Immigrants who became citizens quickly acquired voting rights, and used them to fight battles with mining and timber barons at the ballot box as well as on the picket line.

In these respects American citizenship was a remarkably inclusive phenomenon, but only for "white" men. Late-nineteenth-century American women were not allowed to vote, and in most other respects, their citizenship status was a function of their marital status. Racial restrictions on citizenship were at least as deeply rooted as gender restrictions. As early as 1790, American law limited the right of naturalized citizenship to "free white persons"; in the late nineteenth century, racial limitations on citizenship expanded rapidly. Well-intentioned "friends of the Indian" hoped that allotment policies would leverage Indian land ownership into Indian citizenship, but in practice both were subject to a "trust period" of twenty-five years. In California, immigrant workers from Europe blamed their misery in the panic of 1873 on immigrant workers from China, and Congress responded by declaring Chinese immigrants "ineligible for citizenship." Racial restrictions on citizenship and property ownership were soon joined by racial restrictions on marriage, an intimately symbolic means of engendering western white supremacy. By 1900, most western states had passed laws prohibiting whites from marrying African Americans. Seven of them (Arizona, California, Idaho, Nevada, Oregon, and Wyoming) also prohibited whites from marrying Chinese; three more (Arizona, Nevada, and Oregon) prohibited whites from marrying Indians, and Oregon added "Kanakas," or native Hawaiians, to the list.

It was against this backdrop that the great debate over imperialism reached its climax. Both sides of the tug-of-war gained some ground. Theodore Roosevelt's triumph was territorial. The United States did acquire the Philippines. But it was Bryan's triumph—the rhetorical one—that would be the most enduring. At the turn of the century, the U.S. West reached well beyond the North American continent, enticing immigrants from all over the world to labor in western mines and forests, and taking control of Hawaii, Guam, the Philippines, Wake and Palmyria islands, and American Samoa. Yet westerners (and Americans) continued to interpret their history, character, and economic development as the triumph of democratic expansionism rather than the consequence of conquest. Bryan had, in effect, forged such lasting connections between whiteness, democracy, and anti-imperialism that for the next half century, when westerners talked about colonialism, the colony they had in mind was the West of white farmers and white workers, and the colonizers the exploitative monied "interests" of the East.

Meanwhile, in the Philippines, conquest swallowed up all pretence of democracy. U.S. soldiers established American rule in the islands by crushing the forces of Philippine nationalism. More than 200,000 Filipinos, mostly civilians, died in the process. Soon afterward, the U.S. Supreme Court decided that Filipinos were American "nationals" but not American "citizens." Before long a steady stream of Filipino immigrants would follow in the footsteps of Chinese and Japanese immigrants before them, becoming migrant laborers on Hawaiian plantations and in California's emerging "factories in the fields."

In the end, then, the great American debate over imperialism showed Theodore Roosevelt and William Jennings Bryan pitting two nineteenth-century western discourses against each other to produce a formative twentieth-century western discourse. Both men helped expand the western obsession with Chinese exclusion into a broader form of anti-Asian racism that would be the U.S. West's most distinctive contribution to America's imperial age.

PROGRESSIVE WEST

The second revealing moment in twentieth-century western history—the next chapter in the history of democracy, citizenship, and race—was written in the fight for "the people" against "the interests" led by reformers who claimed the name "Progressive." Steering a course between greedy corporations on the one hand and radicals of the so-called dangerous classes on the other, western Progressives offered their own version of popular democracy. California lawyer Hiram Johnson rode to the California governorship on his promise to "kick the Southern Pacific Railroad out of politics." Idaho lawyer William Borah made his name by prosecuting labor radical Big Bill Haywood. Borah lost the case, but was soon elected to the U.S. Senate, where he sponsored constitutional amendments providing for a graduated income tax and the direct election of senators. Mining engineer Herbert Hoover amassed a fortune supervising international mining ventures, then became famous for his international relief work in World War I. In the 1920s, he turned his post as U.S. Secretary of Commerce into a platform from which to preach voluntary cooperation between business, labor, and government.

If anything united western Progressives, it was the belief that their reforms were in the best interests of the people. Before they were finished, they had shaped American land-use patterns, electoral politics, immigration policy, and racial thinking to fit their concept of the public good. In the name of the people, they revamped American land policy. Arguing that government-owned land should be conserved for public purposes rather than sold to homesteaders or corporate interests, they set about creating national parks and forests and laying the basis for public water development. Progressive conservation policy came to life in the proliferation of national parks and monuments, the appointment of Gifford Pinchot as the nation's chief forester, and the passage of the Newlands Reclamation Act in 1902. If, in the end, the Forest Service would work closely with lumber corporations and the Bureau of Reclamation would build monumental dams that benefited agribusiness more than family farmers, Progressives had nonetheless stemmed the century-long tide of government land sales.

In the name of the people, western Progressives gutted the power of traditional political parties, enacted a wide range of electoral reforms, and added women to the electorate. Texas Progressives were the first in the nation to replace urban political machines with city commission governments. Oregon pioneered the initiative, referendum, and recall, reforms that would become mainstays of twentieth-century American politics. California adopted a nonpartisan cross-filing system that allowed candidates to place their names on the primary ballots for more than one party at a time. In one election held under its terms, the same candidate was nominated by the Progressive, Republican, Democratic, Prohibitionist, *and* Socialist parties. In Montana, progressive political reforms like these made it possible for Jeannette Rankin, the leader of the state's successful women's suffrage campaign, to become the first woman ever elected to the U.S. Congress, in 1916.

And in the name of the people, western Progressives expanded the rights of citizenship beyond voting and property ownership to include the first hesitant government protections for working men and women. Willing to side with workers rather than corporations, yet wary of worker collectivism, Progressives lodged their defense of social justice in the emerging administrative state. A case in point is an Oregon law that limited women workers to a ten-hour day. When Portland laundry owner Curt Muller first violated the law and then challenged his conviction for doing so, women reformers mounted an appeal strong enough to overturn the U.S. Supreme Court's notorious resistance to labor legislation. Speaking for a unanimous court in 1908, Supreme Court justice David J. Brewer explained, "as healthy mothers are essential to vigorous offspring, the physical well-being of women becomes an object of public interest and care in order to preserve the strength and vigor of the race."

Yet, as Justice Brewer's words suggest, progressive visions of the public interest also laid the basis for a very modern notion of "race," one embodied in racial disfranchisement, segregation, and exclusion. Progressive electoral reforms designed to promote "direct democracy" ensured that white voters would vastly outnumber nonwhite voters. Citywide municipal elections subsumed ethnic voting districts. As "aliens ineligible for citizenship," Asian immigrants were ineligible to vote anywhere in the West. In Texas, reformers limited black and Hispanic voting with poll taxes and all-white primaries. Western school districts matter of factly segregated African-American and Mexican-American students. Housing was also widely segregated through restrictive covenants like those of southern California's Inglewood, which prohibited homeowners from selling or renting their property to "any person other than those of the White or Caucasian race." In the national parks, progressive officials worked to remove Indians from sites they preferred to present to the public as pristine wildernesses.

Blending these racial exclusions into American ideals of democracy would require all the storytelling power the newest western corporate giant—the movie industry—could muster. One of its pathbreaking directors, D. W. Griffith, provides an example. In rhetoric that could have been taken from any Progressive reformer, Griffith was fond of declaring that moving pictures were a "moral and educational force" for the good of the people. Working from this perspective, he specialized in "idea" films in which innocent young women were rescued from the evils of drink, immorality, and war. But Griffith's greatest contribution to film history, indeed the best-selling movie of its time, was *The Birth of a Nation,* issued in 1915. Retelling the story of the Civil War and Reconstruction as a tragedy of epic proportions, Griffith lingered over a scene in which a young white woman, desperate to elude a black male pursuer, jumped off a rocky summit to her death. In the film's dramatic climax, white Northerners and Southerners joined in a triumphant parade of the Invisible Empire of the Ku Klux Klan. After a protest by California African Americans failed to prevent its Los Angeles premiere, the newly formed NAACP held rallies all across the country, but audiences continued to flock to the movie. Watching the Klan reunite the divided nation of the 1870s, audiences of the Progressive era gave birth to a nation of their own, one in which white supremacy would be taken for granted.

Griffith encouraged viewers to take *The Birth of a Nation* as an accurate depiction of history, but the film revealed more about Progressive race relations than Reconstruction-era America. The battle scenes were shot in the San Fernando Valley. The Klan rode to the rescue near Orange County, California, on horses imported from western Arizona ranches. Because Griffith had decided to have "no black blood among the principals," the major black roles were played by white actors in blackface. The hundreds of black extras Griffith hired for group scenes were California African Americans hoping to break into the movie industry; during the film's production, they were housed in segregated barracks. Only a few of them had (minor) speaking parts, and none of their names appeared in the credits.

The link between American nationalism and white supremacy celebrated in *The Birth of a Nation* also formed the basis for Progressive immigration policy. In the decade before World War I, for example, California Progressives matched their enthusiasm for "Americanizing" European immigrants with their determination to exclude Japanese as well as Chinese immigrants. Judges responded to cases challenging Chinese exclusion by allowing the Immigration and Naturalization Service to slip free from the oversight of judicial review.

In the decade after World War I, western politicians acquired national stature and western racial patterns were amplified into national immigration policy. In 1929, Herbert Hoover, the first American president born west of the Mississippi, took office. That same year, the U.S. immigration officials instituted a "national origins" policy (in the works since 1924) that would remain in place until 1965. As Mae Ngai points out in a brilliant article, the national origins system reconfigured an increasingly multicultural nation as a white republic and divided white "ethnicity" from nonwhite "race." It tipped the scales of European immigration toward northern Europe, legitimized Asian exclusion, and slaked agribusiness's continual thirst for cheap labor with immigrants from Mexico. Increasingly seen—and treated—as temporary migrant workers, Mexican immigrants escaped formal quota restrictions only to find themselves increasingly subject to the newly created border patrol.

The treatment of Asian Americans continued to provide a key symbolic link between citizenship and whiteness. In two cases originating in Hawaii and Oregon, the U.S. Supreme Court refused to allow Asian men to become naturalized American citizens. The first case was that of Takao Ozawa, a Japanese immigrant who had come to the United States as a teenager, learned English, and attended the University of California at Berkeley before making his home in Honolulu. The court denied his application for U.S. citizenship, declaring the term *white* synonymous with "Caucasian" and explaining that because Ozawa was "clearly of a race which is not Caucasian," he did not meet the federal requirement of being a "white person." The second case involved Bhagat Singh Thind, a Hindu man. Thind's lawyers argued that since ethnologists had determined that Hindus were "Aryan" and therefore "Caucasian," Thind could meet the whiteness standard. But the Supreme Court would have none of it. Eating some of its earlier words, the justices declared that "[T]he words 'free white person' are words of common speech, to be interpreted in accordance with the understanding of the common man, synonymous with the word 'Caucasian' only as that word is popularly understood."

This determination to draw the boundary of whiteness around American citizenship was so strong that it affected even American "nationals" like Filipinos, who were allowed to immigrate freely but refused the right to become naturalized U.S. citizens. In 1934, Congress finally agreed to grant the Philippines eventual independence, but Filipinos would henceforth be categorized as "aliens," and, although they were not technically subject to Asian exclusion laws, they were assigned the smallest immigration quota of any nation in the world, fifty people per year. In 1935 U.S. officials tried, largely unsuccessfully, to "repatriate" Filipino immigrants already in western states by paying their passage back to the Philippines.

WARTIME WEST

A third restructuring of democracy, citizenship, and race occurred during World War II. By the time the United States entered the war, a generation of western politicians and entrepreneurs stood ready, willing, and able to make the most of it. During the Great Depression, western politicians had funneled New Deal power and water projects to western entrepreneurs who translated them into personal and political success stories. During World War II, one of these entrepreneurs, Henry Kaiser, replaced Herbert Hoover as the iconic western business success story.

Hoover had urged voluntary cooperation between business and government, but Kaiser saw the two as virtually inseparable. During World War II, Kaiser relied on government capital to build an industrial empire that eventually ranged from cement, steel, and magnesium to aerospace, shipbuilding, and nuclear power. In a region starved for industrial employment, his enterprises drew workers like a magnet. Augmenting existing industrial labor pools by recruiting African Americans and women, Kaiser promised his workers high wages, company-built housing, unprecedented medical benefits, and even day-care centers. At the height of his power, Kaiser not only revitalized cities like Portland, Oregon, and Oakland, California, his headquarters, but he virtually created others, including the East Bay city of Richmond and southern California's Fontana.

From the point of view of a Progressive-era pacifist like Montana'a Jeannette Rankin, Henry Kaiser must have seemed like a classic example of her favorite argument that the only way to end war was to take the profit out of it. But if peace-leaning western politicians of the Progressive era and the 1930s, like Rankin, Hoover, and, before them, William Jennings Bryan, had assumed that the growth of democracy required peace, during World War II Americans linked democracy with war.

As a conveniently underdeveloped region rich in federal land and located on the coastline closest to the Pacific war, the West attracted more than its share of World War II defense contracts, military bases, and the nation's bomb development program. War contracts fueled the growth of Kaiser industries as well as Boeing in Seattle, Brown and Root in Houston, and Geneva Steel Works in Provo, Utah. Army, air, and naval bases covered the region so completely that during the war, four million soldiers were stationed in them. California and Texas attracted the lion's share, including the China Lake Naval Weapons Center, the Marine Corps Depot of Supplies, Goodfellow Field, and Camp Hood, but Utah boasted ten of its own, and Nevada acquired the Las Vegas Bombing and Gunnery Range, which stretched across 3.5 million acres of land. The isolated interior West provided especially attractive sites for the top-secret (and dangerous) atomic bomb project, including the atomic laboratories at Los Alamos, New Mexico, and the plutonium production plant at Hanford, Washington.

World War II military spending spurred western urban and economic growth, and western universities jumped on the bandwagon. The direction they would take was anticipated by Ernest Lawrence, a Nobel laureate, inventor of the cyclotron, and founder of the Radiation Laboratory at the University of California at Berkeley. During World War II, the Los Alamos atomic bomb program was administered through UC Berkeley. Immediately after the war, when many observers expected federal funding of weapons research to decline, Lawrence began to push for hydrogen bomb development. He eventually succeeded not only in keeping the Los Alamos facility open but also in establishing a second (and competing) UC weapons laboratory, later named Lawrence Livermore. These atomic development projects gave UC Berkeley a head start in attracting postwar weapons research contracts, but Stanford University soon closed the gap. Under the leadership of radio engineer Fred Terman, Stanford became, in the words of historian Rebecca Lowen, a leading "Cold War university" by blending support from private industry with government-sponsored Defense Department contracts. Stanford's Electronics Research Laboratory encouraged emerging electronics companies to locate in the university's newly formed industrial park, where they provided jobs for Stanford graduates while spurring the development of the Silicon Valley computer industry. From the 1950s clear through the 1980s, western higher education, western economic development, and the growth of western cities remained closely tied to the fortunes of the U.S. military.

In the meantime, World War II redrew the racial map of the West. One set of remappings drew racialized workers into the region. The lure of industrial jobs brought African Americans to western cities in numbers large enough to dwarf earlier black communities. Kaiser's Richmond shipyard alone brought 18,000 black workers to a town that before the war had only 270 African-American residents. Wartime farm labor shortages led the U.S. government to establish the "Bracero" program, a government-sponsored system of contract labor. The program brought 200,000 Mexican immigrants to the United States during the war, and was soon accompanied by an undocumented migration even larger than the official one. While industry and agriculture drew African Americans and Mexicans toward the West Coast, government officials pushed Japanese Americans away from it. Under the banner of "military necessity," government officials moved 110,000 Japanese Americans, 70,000 of whom were American born (and therefore American citizens) to internment camps.

During World War II, labor shortages combined with military rhetoric about American democracy to offer racialized westerners effective bargaining tools. African-American war workers demanded—and got—government support against discrimination in the Fair Employment Practices Committee. They used it to abolish racially segregated auxiliaries in the boilermakers' union at the Kaiser shipyards and racially segregated job assignments and water fountains at a major magnesium-processing plant in Las Vegas. In Southern California, Chicana cannery workers formed interracial unions that bargained successfully for maternity leaves, child care, and paid vacations. In Hawaii, the International Longshoremen's and Warehousemen's Union brought Filipinos, Japanese, and Hawaiian workers together. Chinese Americans played on their support for American war aims—and their opposition to Japan—to win a symbolic repeal of their exclusion from immigration quotas, and Filipino immigrants won the right to become naturalized citizens. Even Japanese Americans managed to wield their war records as a tool to fight racism, although not until after the U.S. Supreme Court had upheld internment. In 1945, when the Hood River, Oregon, chapter of the American Legion removed the names of sixteen Japanese-American veterans from its local war memorial, there was a national outcry.

Because women played a major role in wartime industrial work and workplace activism, historians of women often contrast World War II with the period of cold war domestic "containment" that followed. I would, however, emphasize a less-studied aspect of this development: the postwar use of sex, marriage, and the dream of the suburban good life to contain wartime racial remappings by crafting new forms of racial inclusion—and exclusion. In the years after the war, for example, veterans demanded and received exceptions to American immigration quotas so that they could bring their "war brides" home to live. After the California Supreme Court declared the state law against interracial marriage unconstitutional in 1948, western states began to repeal their miscegenation laws. In these same years, Hollywood built on the expansion of American military bases to showcase the exotic sexual appeal of Asian and Latin American women in films like *Something for the Boys* and *Sayonara*.

Yet the newest and most family-friendly government program of the period, the GI Bill of Rights, which provided subsidies for education and low-cost home loans, offered returning veterans a personal stake in what George Lipsitz has called "the possessive investment in whiteness." Under the terms of the GI bill, more than two million war veterans returned to college, getting a jumpstart up the occupational ladder and sparking a postwar expansion of colleges and universities. A million more purchased homes with government-insured loans. Between 1945 and 1960, California and Arizona, two states that attracted both wartime workers and returning veterans, had postwar real estate booms; both grew by more than 100 percent. But government officials refused to guarantee mortgages in neighborhoods that had been "red-lined" as racially mixed or economically risky. As a result, only 2 percent of the mortgage financing guaranteed by federal agencies between 1934 and 1962 was open to nonwhite buyers; much of that lay in segregated areas. In effect, then, home-loan policies and mortgage tax deductions helped whites move to the suburbs, bringing new schools and civil services along with them, while African Americans, Asian Americans, and Latinos remained fixed in crowded center cities where they had to compete with each other for space. In Los Angeles, where the African-American population had increased 168 percent during World War II, restrictive covenants and government loan policies excluded blacks from adjoining white neighborhoods, so African Americans moved into houses left by Japanese Americans placed in internment camps. As a result of internment, Japanese Americans lost much more than their civil rights; after the war, their property losses were estimated, probably conservatively, at $400 million.

Postwar government support for suburban home mortgages provided a sharp contrast to the collapse of support for the public housing projects that might have improved conditions for poor and minority westerners. In Portland, Oregon, when a 1948 flood wiped out the Vanport project that housed wartime workers, it left six thousand blacks homeless. Portland voters rejected a plan to replace it, and Portland businessmen asked the federal government to subsidize new private home construction instead. The spectacular growth of postwar western cities led to urban renewal and highway construction projects that also displaced existing minority residents. Los Angeles's famous freeway system, for example, was routed directly through East Los Angeles, the home of a wide variety of racial and ethnic groups, including the largest Mexican-American community in the United States. Ed Roybal, a Latino politician who had recently won a seat on the previously all-white Los Angeles City Council, criticized the plan, but was unable to stop either the freeway construction or the evictions that made it possible.

DEMOCRATIC WEST

Throughout the 1950s and into the 1960s, postwar prosperity and the possessive investment in whiteness fostered public complacency. Calling their country the leader of the "free world," American leaders exerted their economic muscle across the globe, patting themselves on the back for fostering democracy abroad and neglecting rumblings of discontent about democracy at home. But in the mid-1960s, these rumblings widened into a cultural earthquake that would once again restructure the western relationship between democracy, citizenship, and race. This restructuring—the fourth of my five—might be called "democratic" with a small "d" for the grass-roots movements that propelled it, and with a large "D" for Lyndon Johnson, the president who presided over it.

The model, directly or indirectly, for all these grass-roots democratic movements was the African-American campaign for civil rights. *Brown v. Board of Education*, the famous court case that declared racial segregation in schools unconstitutional, originated with African Americans in Kansas City, and in the late 1950s and early 1960s, civil rights demonstrations took place across the West as well as in the South. In 1958, Oklahoma blacks started a six-year campaign to challenge segregation in local restaurants; in Las Vegas, blacks protested segregation in hotels. In Denver, Colorado, where African Americans had protested against segregated movie theaters as early as 1943, demonstrators sat in at the governor's office in 1963. In schools, businesses, and public accommodations, civil rights protesters raised questions about American democracy that soon resonated well beyond the ranks of mid-century western African-American community leaders and their white liberal allies.

Mid-century western parents expected the rapidly expanding university system to pass all the features of postwar American democracy and world leadership—postwar prosperity, the suburban dream of domesticity, and the possessive investment in whiteness—on to their children, fitting them to be leaders of the next generation. But white college students who went to Mississippi for the "Freedom Summer" campaigns came back with their faith in American democracy shaken to the core. From Berkeley, California, where the first mass student protest erupted in 1964, to Austin, Texas, which would eventually boast one of the country's largest chapters of Students for a Democratic Society, civil rights campaigns set white as well as black students in motion. After students at the University of California at Berkeley accused the *Oakland Tribune* newspaper of racial discrimination, the university administration banned political activities on campus, and two hundred students held a sit-in at the administration building that spawned the campus Free Speech Movement. When university officials decided to prosecute the protest leaders, four hundred students returned for a second sit-in, which ended only after police dragged them out of the building.

In the West, both the nonviolent protests of the early civil rights movement and the rhetoric of black power that characterized the civil rights movement appealed to a wide variety of groups and causes. Farmworker organizer César Chávez built his pathbreaking United Farm Workers Union with sit-ins, marches, and boycotts that made effective use of support from liberal clergy, student radicals, and consumers. Mexican-American student activists dusted off an older, pejorative term, *Chicano,* and used it to claim a transnational identity that encouraged them to call for solidarity with Mexican immigrants. At San Francisco State College, the Black Student Union and the Third World Liberation Front, a coalition of Chicano and Asian-American students, shut down the university with a strike demanding the formation of Black and Ethnic Studies programs and the admission of all students of color rejected for admission by the university. The Oakland-based Black Panther party proclaimed itself "a nation within a nation" and established a range of community service programs, distinguishing itself from earlier civil rights groups by insisting on its right to armed defense. The Panthers' critique of police harassment provided the model for the American Indian Movement, AIM, which formed in Minneapolis in 1968, and spread rapidly across the urban West, revitalizing the movement for native sovereignty.

Protests against racism ignited—and were ignited by—protests against American participation in the Vietnam War. Asian-American antiwar activists linked the two causes, criticizing the war as the latest chapter in a century-long history of American imperialism in Asia. Claiming that it was the North Vietnamese, not the Americans, who stood for democracy, they demanded that the United States "stop killing our Asian brothers and sisters." They were joined by a wide range of students who, because they saw the war as the illogical outcome of a society so sick that its growth depended on weapons production, began to mount large-scale antiwar demonstrations. The issue of the war ran like a fault line through the society, setting students who protested against university involvement with the "war machine" on a collision course with post–World War II notions of patriotism, pitting Chicano war protesters against Mexican-American war veterans, and dividing Asian-American student radicals who admired Maoist China from their anti-Communist elders. And as the 1960s wore on, civil rights, black power, and antiwar protests spiraled from radical democratic politics and countercultural community formation to desperate antiestablishment violence.

The man who would both benefit from and try to keep a lid on this democratic ferment was Lyndon Baines Johnson, president of the United States from 1963 to 1969. Like William Jennings Bryan and Teddy Roosevelt before him, Johnson considered himself a product of western history. But fond as he was of posing on horseback on his Texas ranch (an image Ronald Reagan would later echo in California), the lessons Johnson drew from his particular western history reflected twentieth-century experiences rather than nineteenth-century cowboy symbolism.

One of these lessons was the habit of linking American democracy to military development. In Johnson's case, reliance on the military had little to do with frontier instinct; it was, rather, the necessary precondition for exerting political power in Texas. Like other mid-twentieth-century western politicians, Johnson's rise to power had begun during the New Deal and was cemented by securing the World War II military bases and defense contracts that ensured the postwar growth of Texas cities. By the time he became president, Johnson regarded supporting the military as the first axiom of economic and political survival. Unfortunately for antiwar protesters, he was unable to break the habit, even when his support for the Vietnam War doomed his presidency.

In another respect, too, Johnson was ill-equipped to deal with the social earthquakes erupting around him. A second lesson he had absorbed from twentieth-century western history was masculine privilege. Nurtured during his Texas boyhood, Johnson's arrogant masculinity was reinforced in the 1950s, when both scientists and social commentators contrasted male authority to female domesticity and grounded both in biology. These gender naturalisms were so prevalent that a succession of countercultures struggled long and hard to forge new patterns of sex and gender relations. One of these, the movement for homosexual rights, began in Los Angeles in 1951, when Henry Hay founded the Mattachine Society. Four years later, in San Francisco, Del Martyn and Phyllis Lyon founded the Daughters of Bilitis, the first organization for lesbians, but both organizations took care to keep the names of their members a secret. In North Beach, California, "beat" writers who renounced fatherhood, family life, and salaried work for art were caricatured more often than appreciated. During the 1960s, a much broader "sexual revolution" gathered enough steam to call traditional gender roles into general question; it was soon followed by increasingly political women's and gay liberation movements. All of these changes, though, were lost on Johnson.

Yet Johnson did draw another, much more unlikely, lesson from twentieth-century western history. During the 1950s, his quest for political power required defeating both the Republicans who governed his country and the conservative Democrats who governed his state. To do so, he would need the votes of two key Texas populations, African Americans and Latinos. As political historian Hugh Davis Graham explains, "[t]o Johnson the continued disfranchisement of . . . blacks was morally deplorable, and the prospect of so many nonvoting Democrats was politically intolerable." So Johnson turned his back on Texas tradition and tried to break the political circuit that wired American democracy to white supremacy.

In a country with such a long tradition of white political and economic entitlement, the results were historic. During Johnson's administration, the Civil Rights Act of 1964, the Voting Rights Act of 1965, and the Open Housing Act of 1968 set the pattern by countering white privilege in the political and economic arenas. Civil rights victories extended to education, with the passage of the first Bilingual Education Act, and marriage, when the U.S. Supreme Court built on a California court precedent to declare all the remaining state miscegenation laws unconstitutional. Perhaps the most significant achievement was the Immigration Act of 1965, passed in the wake of Johnson's landslide victory in the presidential elections of 1964. The act overhauled American immigration policy and discarded the racially based "national origins" system. When immigration officials put a new, race-neutral policy into practice, Latinos and Asians quickly became the principal immigrant groups. To take only a single example, 665,000 Filipinos came to the United States between 1965 and 1984. In the years after 1965, a wealth of these "new" immigrants would once again remake the racial map of the West, reconstituting the communities they entered and reshaping western politics.

At its best and broadest, Johnson's civil rights program promised racialized Americans full access to the benefits of American political, economic, and social citizenship. Like the Immigration Act of 1965, however, its rhetoric tapped into American ideas of democracy and equality by relying on the deliberate nonrecognition of race, or "color-blindness." Here, though, was the rub. In a society accustomed to taking white privilege for granted, refusing to recognize race was a strategy nearly as likely to reproduce white supremacy as to challenge it. To his credit, Johnson recognized that overturning America's deeply rooted racial hierarchies would require taking race into account—if not, as radical activists urged, in supporting black, Chicano, or Asian-American power movements—then at least in measuring progress toward equality. For a few short years, agreement on this point stretched across traditional party lines. Affirmative action programs designed to track progress toward racial and gender equality not only survived but grew under Johnson's Republican successor, Richard Nixon.

BORDER-PATROLLED WEST

Meanwhile, though, Nixon and the western Republicans who followed him were setting the stage for the century's fifth (and final) reformulation of democracy, citizenship, and race. For most of the twentieth century, western state governments had nurtured the liberal political conduits that had brought them the federal assistance needed to foster growth. The results could be seen in the post–World War II rise of California. By 1970, California had become the nation's most populous state, a shining example of regional economic growth and transnational capitalist potential. Not coincidentally, it was also a state in which the social movements of the 1960s had taken deep root and dramatic form. From the 1960s through the 1980s, race riots in Watts, the Indian occupation of Alcatraz Island, feminist campaigns for comparable pay for comparable work in Oregon, and Gay Pride marches in San Francisco highlighted some of the possibilities and the challenges of American diversity.

During the 1970s and 1980s, however, resurgent western conservatives began to describe social movements designed to diversify democracy as examples of unwarranted excess. Before long, they began to use them as a virtual road map for regaining national political power in a state with significant electoral clout. In 1966, Ronald Reagan won the California governorship in a campaign that criticized student radicals on the Berkeley campus, tapping into white voters' distress over a California open-housing law by changing the subject from civil rights to private property. In 1972, Richard Nixon expanded his narrow victory in the presidential election of 1968 into a substantial majority by labeling student radicals and antiwar and civil rights protesters as threats to law and order. Nixon's strategy was designed to attract disaffected white middle-class voters, a group he called the "silent majority" but pollsters called the "unyoung, unpoor, unblack."

Ronald Reagan's 1980 bid for the presidency perfected this strategy of drawing white voters into the "big tent" of late-twentieth-century conservatism. Campaigning against "big" government, Reagan drew white voters into his conservative camp by promising them tax cuts and a return to traditional sex and gender roles even as he cast contemporary symbols of white privilege by equating blacks and new immigrants with crime and criminals. Once in office, he expanded military funding, cut "social" programs, and turned attention away from civil rights issues for women as well as racial minorities by turning a critical eye on government "benefits." With Reagan's tacit approval and considerable help from grass-roots conservative women in Sunbelt states, Republican activists like Phyllis Schafly succeeded in halting ratification of the Equal Rights Amendment for women.

But in California as in much of the rest of the nation, electoral strategies built on appeals to conservative white voters rested on increasingly precarious calculations. By the time Reagan left office, opinion polls showed that a majority of Americans supported most feminist political causes, including that of the right to abortion. Post-1965 immigration from Asia and Latin America was turning so-called minority groups into the majority of California's population, and white Californians were beginning to reverse a century of westward movement by leaving the Pacific Coast for the states of the interior West. If California Republicans were going to remain in power, they would have to limit the rapidly increasing numbers of their opponents on the one hand and appeal to new constituencies on the other, and they would have to do so without offending an increasingly multicultural electorate by appearing to turn their backs on the principles of civil rights and equality.

Accordingly, conservatives began to enact a form of "border patrol" politics that translated white voting power into yet another version of white privilege. Choosing immigrants (a highly vulnerable population because so few of them could vote) rather than African Americans (whose political muscle was beginning to be felt in western cities) as their symbol of racial diversity, they used "illegal aliens" as lightning rods for attempts to roll back government programs and win the votes of white women voters who distrusted other Republican policies. In 1994, they offered voters Proposition 187, an initiative that denied illegal aliens access to health and education benefits; it passed with

58.9 percent of the vote. The majority reflected the continuing disparity between population figures and voting rolls. For a variety of reasons, including the relative youth of the immigrant population and the state's century-long tradition of white political privilege, Latinos, Asian Americans, and African Americans formed a near majority of California's population, but accounted for only 22 percent of the state's registered voters.

Republican leaders hoped to hold on to that edge. California governor Pete Wilson even suggested abandoning the traditional policy of granting automatic citizenship to every person born on American soil; by denying citizenship rights to the children of undocumented immigrants, his proposal would have prevented immigrant children from growing into adult voters. But two years after the passage of Proposition 187, California voters took an even bolder step, passing Proposition 209, an initiative designed to end state affirmative action policies. Entitled the "California Civil Rights Initiative," the antiaffirmative action proposal translated civil rights rhetoric into a tool to reinforce white privilege.

In the 1980s and 1990s, border patrol politics quickly spread beyond conservative groups. Liberals and radicals, too, drew fences around boundaries of various sorts. In the Clinton era, a number of prominent Democrats, including California senators Barbara Boxer and Dianne Feinstein, have supported anti-immigrant measures, though they have so far proved more supportive of programs like affirmative action. A growing number of western cities and towns have used environmentalist arguments to draw borders around urban economic growth, hoping to provide more "livable" space for current residents by keeping future residents out. Border patrol politics has even been used to challenge white privilege. To take the most striking example, American Indians have combined civil rights rhetoric with their own version of border patrol rhetoric, the argument for native sovereignty. This discourse has helped them win legal victories significant enough to reverse some of their nineteenth-century losses in fishing and water rights, and has helped sustain a rebirth of native power.

Border patrol politics and arguments for native sovereignty both reflect and reject late-twentieth-century western economic transformations. As the cold war receded, declining defense budgets and military base closures left western cities hard pressed to find alternative sources of economic growth. As geographer Ruth Gilmore shows in her Ph.D. dissertation, in California, prison building became the new government-sponsored growth industry. Although crime rates have been falling since the 1970s, popular fear of criminals sustained mandatory sentencing programs that spurred the state to spend more money on prisons than on higher education, while the most impoverished California towns competed with each other to attract the prisons they hoped would create local jobs. Prison jobs were appealing because, as American-based multinational corporations moved industrial processing overseas, the U.S. economy was increasingly divided into two major segments—a top tier of well-paid managerial workers and a bottom tier of badly paid service workers.

And these economic transformations, in turn, affect notions of democracy, citizenship, and race. Because higher education is the key to entering the top tier of the new economy, voter rejection of affirmative action programs at colleges and universities reconfigures white privilege. At the same time, though, the distinctions currently drawn between American citizens and "aliens" rely on national border lines that set the state and nation against multinational corporations, which increasingly rely on cheap labor outside as well as inside U.S. borders. Accordingly, the most recent attempts to restrict immigration pushed leading American corporations like Microsoft into the opposing camp. "To succeed in foreign markets," a Microsoft lawyer explained, "you need foreign personnel." By 1999, American racial formation was more closely connected to immigration than it had been at any time since the 1920s.

At the end of the twentieth century, both liberals and conservatives are accustomed to claiming that the civil rights movement of the 1960s was a turning point in American history. A survey of the historical past does, of course, reveal forms of early-twentieth-century racism that are so blatant that they seem to support this claim. But it also suggests that the same kind of values expressed in late-twentieth-century Americans' civil rights rhetoric—democracy, equality, anticolonialism—have often coexisted with, and even enabled the reproduction of—white privilege. In this sense, even in the early twentieth century, when the West could be characterized as an economically undeveloped province, its significance reached well beyond the region. To paraphrase one of my favorite western historians, Richard White, twentieth-century western politics has been—and continues to be—American politics, and American history.

SUGGESTIONS FOR FURTHER READING

A short essay cannot begin to do justice to the richness of historical work, old and new, on the history of the American West in the twentieth century. Readers in search of a general overview should begin with Patricia Nelson Limerick's pathbreaking *The Legacy of Conquest: The Unbroken Past of the American West* (New York: Norton, 1987) and the most comprehensive recent textbook, Richard White's *"It's Your Misfortune and None of My Own": A History of the American West* (Norman: University of Oklahoma Press, 1991). Recent articles on the development of the field include Richard White, "Western History," in Eric Foner, ed., *The New American History* (Philadelphia: Temple University Press, 1997); Paul Sabin, "Home and Abroad: The Two 'Wests' of Twentieth-Century United States History," *Pacific Historical Review* 66 (1997); and Sarah Deutsch, George J. Sánchez, and Gary Y. Okihiro, "Contemporary Peoples/Contested Places," in Clyde A. Milner II et al., eds., *The Oxford History of the American West* (New York: Oxford University Press, 1994). For a meticulous guide to specialized scholarship published through 1992, including many of the works used in this article, see Richard W. Etulain, ed., *The American West in the Twentieth Century: A Bibliography* (Norman: University of Oklahoma Press, 1994).

Readers interested in the complex history of "race" in the American West can now choose among several fine survey histories and collections of recent articles. Surveys of particular groups include: Quintard Taylor, *In Search of the Racial Frontier: African Americans in the American West, 1528–1990* (New York: Norton, 1998); Peter Iverson, *We Are Still Here: American Indians in the Twentieth Century* (Wheeling, Ill.: Harlan Davidson, 1998); Alexandra Harmon, *Indians in the Making: Ethnic Relations and Indian Identities around Puget Sound* (Berkeley: University of California Press, 1998); David G. Gutiérrez, ed., *Between Two Worlds: Mexican Immigrants in the United States* (Wilmington, Del.: Scholarly Resources, 1996); Vicki Ruíz, *From Out of the Shadows: Mexican Women in Twentieth Century America* (New York: Oxford University Press, 1998); Gary Y. Okihiro, *Margins and Mainstreams: Asians in American History and Culture* (Seattle: University of Washington Press, 1994); and Sucheng Chan, *Asian Americans: An Interpretive History* (Boston: Twayne, 1991). Collections that cover multiple groups include: Valerie J. Matsumoto and Blake Allmendinger, eds., *Over the Edge: Remapping the American West* (Berkeley: University of California Press, 1999); Elizabeth Jameson and Susan Armitage, eds., *Writing the Range: Race, Class, and Culture in the Women's West* (Norman: University of Oklahoma Press, 1997); Clyde A. Milner II, ed., *A New Significance: Re-Envisioning the History of the American West* (New York: Oxford University Press, 1996); and Sucheng Chan et al., eds., *Peoples of Color in the American West* (Lexington, Mass.: D.C. Heath, 1994).

Recent books, articles, and dissertations on the themes covered in this essay include Amy Kaplan and Donald E. Pease, eds., *Cultures of United States Imperialism* (Durham: Duke University Press, 1993); William G. Robbins, *Colony and Empire: The Capitalist Transformation of the American West* (Lawrence: University Press of Kansas, 1994); Tomás Almaguer, *Racial Fault Lines: The Historical Origins of White Supremacy in California* (Berkeley: University of California Press, 1994); Lisbeth Haas, *Conquests and Historical Identities in California, 1769–1936* (Berkeley: University of California Press, 1995); Philip J. Deloria, *Playing Indian* (New Haven, Conn.: Yale University Press, 1999); Sharon Delmendo, "The American Factor in José Rizal's Nationalism," *Amerasia* 24 (1998); Peggy Pascoe, "Miscegenation Law, Court Cases, and Ideologies of 'Race' in Twentieth-Century America," *Journal of American History* 83 (1996); William Deverell and Tom Sitton, eds., *California Progressivism Revisited* (Berkeley: University of California Press, 1994); Paul W. Hirt, *A Conspiracy of Optimism: Management of the National Forests since World War II* (Lincoln: University of Nebraska Press, 1994); Donald Worster, *Under Western Skies: Nature and History in the American West* (New York: Oxford University Press, 1992); Neil Foley, *The White Scourge: Mexicans, Blacks, and Poor Whites in Texas Cotton Culture* (Berkeley: University of California Press, 1997); A. Yvette Huginnie, "'Strikitos': Race, Class, and Work in the Arizona Copper Industry, 1870–1920," Ph.D. Dissertation, Yale University, 1991; George J. Sánchez, *Becoming Mexican American: Ethnicity, Culture, and Identity in Chicano Los Angeles, 1900–1945* (New York: Oxford University Press, 1993); Karen Anderson, *Changing Woman: A History of Racial Ethnic Women in Modern America* (New York: Oxford University Press, 1996); Mark David Spence, *Dispossessing the Wilderness: Indian Removal and the Making of the National Parks* (New York: Oxford University Press, 1999); Michael Rogin, "The Sword Became a Flashing Vision: D. W. Griffith's *The Birth of a Nation*," in Robert Lang, ed., *The Birth of a Nation* (New Brunswick, N.J.: Rutgers University Press, 1994); Albert S. Broussard, *Black San Francisco: The Struggle for Racial Equality in the West, 1900–1954* (Lawrence: University of Kansas Press, 1993); Lucy E. Salyer, *Laws Harsh as Tigers: Chinese Immigrants and the Shaping of Modern Immigration Law* (Chapel Hill: University of North Carolina Press, 1995); Mae Nagi, "The Architecture of Race in American Immigration Law," *Journal of American History* 86 (1999); Camille Guerin-Gonzales, *Mexican Workers and American*

Dreams: Immigration, Repatriation, and California Farm Labor, 1900–1939 (New Brunswick, N.J.: Rutgers University Press, 1994); Jordan A. Schwarz, *The New Dealers: Power Politics in the Age of Roosevelt* (New York: Knopf, 1993); Bruce Hevly and John M. Findlay, eds., *The Atomic West* (Seattle: University of Washington Press, 1998); Rebecca S. Lowen, *Creating the Cold War University: The Transformation of Stanford* (Berkeley: University of California Press, 1997); Gretchen Lemke-Santangelo, *Abiding Courage: African American Migrant Women and the East Bay Community* (Chapel Hill: University of North Carolina Press, 1996); Quintard Taylor, *The Forging of a Black Community: Seattle's Central District from 1870 through the Civil Rights Era* (Seattle: University of Washington Press, 1994); Judy Yung, *Unbound Feet: A Social History of Chinese Women in San Francisco* (Berkeley: University of California Press, 1995); Linda Tamura, *The Hood River Issei: An Oral History of Japanese Settlers in Oregon's Hood River Valley* (Urbana: University of Illinois Press, 1993); Valerie J. Matsumoto, *Farming the Homeplace: A Japanese American Community in California, 1919–1982* (Ithaca, N.Y.: Cornell University Press, 1993); Kevin J. Fernlund, *The Cold War American West, 1945–1989* (Albuquerque: University of New Mexico, 1998); George Lipsitz, *The Possessive Investment in Whiteness: How White People Profit from Identity Politics* (Philadelphia: Temple University Press, 1998); Stuart McElderry, "The Problem of the Color Line: Civil Rights and Racial Ideology in Portland, Oregon, 1944–1965," Ph.D. Dissertation, University of Oregon (1998); Eric Avila, "Reinventing Los Angeles: Popular Culture in the Age of White Flight," Ph.D. Dissertation, University of California, Berkeley (1997); Douglas C. Rossinow, *The Politics of Authenticity: Liberalism, Christianity, and the New Left in America* (New York: Columbia University Press, 1998); David G. Gutiérrez, *Walls and Mirrors: Mexican Americans, Mexican Immigrants, and the Politics of Ethnicity* (Berkeley: University of California Press, 1995); William Wei, *The Asian American Movement* (Philadelphia: Temple University Press, 1993); George Mariscal, ed., *Aztlán and Vietnam: Chicano and Chicana Experiences of the War* (Berkeley: University of California Press, 1999); Hugh Davis Graham, *Civil Rights and the Presidency: Race and Gender in American Politics, 1960–1972* (New York: Oxford University Press, 1992); Gerald Horne, *Fire This Time: The Watts Uprising and the 1960s* (Charlottesville: University Press of Virginia, 1995); Troy Johnson et al., eds., *American Indian Activism: Alcatraz to the Longest Walk* (Urbana: University of Illinois Press, 1997); William Riebsame, ed., *Atlas of the New West: Portrait of a Changing Region* (New York: Norton, 1997); Richard White, "The Current Weirdness of the West," *Western Historical Quarterly* 28 (1997); Lydia Chávez, *The Color Bind: California's Battle to End Affirmative Action* (Berkeley: University of California Press, 1998); Char Miller and Hal Rothman, eds., *Out of the Woods: Essays in Environmental History* (Pittsburgh: University of Pittsburgh Press, 1997); Ruth Gilmore, "From Military Keynesianism to Post Keynesian Militarism: Finance Capital, Land, Labor, and Opposition in the Rising California Prison State," Ph.D. Dissertation, Rutgers University (1998); Dana Takagi, *The Retreat from Race: Asian American Admissions and Racial Politics* (New Brunswick, N.J.: Rutgers University Press, 1992); Lisa Lowe, *Immigrant Acts: On Asian American Cultural Politics* (Durham: Duke University Press, 1996); and Juan F. Perea, *Immigrants Out! The New Nativism and the Anti-Immigrant Impulse in the United States* (New York: New York University Press, 1997).

12 | THE CHAMELEON WITH NINE LIVES
American Religion in the Twentieth Century

PAUL BOYER

The history of American religion in the twentieth century reminds one of the Broadway theater, that "fabulous invalid" whose death is constantly predicted but who miraculously revives and goes on to new heights. Influenced by nineteenth-century scientific positivists like Auguste Comte and Herbert Spencer, many observers early in the century foresaw a gradual process of secularization by which religion, once so powerful in American life, would give way before the forces of urbanization, modernization, and scientific advance. The bohemians and cultural rebels of Greenwich Village, self-conscious modernists, actively repudiated the piety and moralism that pervaded the late-Victorian genteel culture they found so stifling.

Religion hardly figures in the writings of such pre–World War I cultural critics as Herbert Croly, John Dewey, and Walter Lippmann. Croly, whose father embraced Comtean scientific positivism, was dedicated as an infant to Comte's "religion of humanity." Croly's influential work *The Promise of American Life* (1909) sees loyalty to the interests of society as a whole, as articulated by politically engaged journalists like himself, not religion or any religiously based moral code or reform activism, as the key to social progress. In *Drift and Mastery* (1914), Lippmann, a wholly secularized Jew, relegated religion to the fading "village" order being swept aside by the inexorable processes of modernity. Dewey, a secular academic with a Yankee Protestant heritage, offered a transformed public-school system as the institution that would gestate a new, more socially conscious citizenry, largely ignoring the role of other social institutions, including the church. One could read all the works of these and many other social thinkers from the 1900–1920 era and scarcely realize that such a thing as religion existed in America except as a residual, fast-fading cultural relic. To these shrewd and perceptive observers, the case for secularization seemed compelling.

Yet as the twentieth century ended, religion in America seemed if anything stronger than ever. Church membership remained at about 60 percent of all adults. The nation's 350,000 local congregations ranged from store-front black and Hispanic churches in the inner cities to suburban megachurches. Polls revealed levels of religious belief and practice far higher than in Europe. A 1995 cross-cultural survey of religious attitudes asked: "Is God very important in your life?" In Great Britain, 19 percent said yes; in France, 13 percent. In the United States, *58 percent*. According to a 1998 poll, 88 percent of Wisconsinites believe in heaven. (Only 73 percent believe in hell, however.)

Televangelists, religious periodicals, and mass-market religious paperbacks pervaded the media. Christian bookstores flourished. Periodic waves of religious questing, such as the Promise Keepers movement of the mid-1990s, which drew thousands of men to sports arenas across the land for emotional prayers, exhortations, and spiritual bonding, further underscored religion's importance. And the political power of conservative religious believers, channeled through such groups as the Christian Coalition, was acknowledged as a major electoral force. The secularization hypothesis, it appeared, if not utterly discredited, needed some fine-tuning.

But persistence is not the same as unchanging continuity. If the image of Broadway's fabled ability to confound the obituary writers is one useful way to think about twentieth-century American religion, the image of the chameleon is another. Just as striking as the vitality of American religion is its remarkable capacity to adapt to different social, cultural, and demographic realities. When St. Paul wrote, "I am made all things to all men, that I might by all means save some" (1 Cor. 9:22), he could have had American religion in mind. In antebellum America, slaves, slaveholders, and abolitionists all worshiped Jesus and found support for their ideas, or comfort for their lot, in the sacred texts, songs, and rituals of Christianity. Twentieth-century America presented equally diverse and even contradictory manifestations of Christian faith, from rock-ribbed conservatives to Christian Socialists in the Progressive era; from sophisticated "modernists" to cross-burning Klansmen fighting to preserve "white Christian civilization" in the 1920s; from soothing defenders of the status quo to civil rights protesters in the 1950s; from Reaganites to nuclear-freeze activists in the 1980s; from religiously inspired environmentalists, feminists, and advocates of gay marriage to cultural conservatives, racist survivalists, and shadowy militia groups preparing for Armageddon in the 1990s.

And all this diversity existed within only one part of the spectrum of U.S. religion: Protestant Christianity. Beyond that one band on the spectrum lay the full, rich array of American religious life in all its diversity. This diversity included not only Catholics and Jews—the remaining two-thirds of the reassuringly simple triad evoked in Will Herberg's 1955 work *Protestant/Catholic/Jew: An Essay in American Religious Sociology*. It encompassed groups from buggy-driving Amish to high-church Episcopalians; from messianic Jewish Lubavitchers to pentecostal African Americans. It included Muslims, Buddhists,

Eastern and Russian Orthodox, New Age self-actualizers, Gaia believers, Native American sweat-lodge visitors, and followers of America's many homegrown religions—Mormons, Unitarians, Christian Scientists, Seventh-Day Adventists, Jehovah's Witnesses, Scientologists, and new groups that have doubtless sprung up since you started reading this paragraph.

In short, any survey of twentieth-century American religion must guard against easy generalizations or sweeping assertions that obscure more than they reveal. Shape-shifting diversity within a framework of overall strength and continuity—a kind of spiritual Mall of America, or Cirque de Soleil—perhaps offers the best general model for framing the story. Bearing these preliminary reflections in mind, then, let us turn to examine how religion fared, what themes emerged, and what transforming changes occurred, in successive phases of American religious history between the presidencies of William McKinley and Bill Clinton.

1900–1917: SOCIAL GOSPEL OPTIMISM; FUNDAMENTALIST PESSIMISM; JAMESIAN THERAPEUTICS

The opening years of the century saw great ferment on the American religious scene. The nation's Jewish and Roman Catholic communities struggled to absorb a tide of immigrants, many desperately poor. As the Catholic population soared from six million in 1880 to nearly eighteen million by 1920, church leaders feverishly established new parishes, seminaries, parochial schools, and social agencies to serve the newcomers. Parishes like St. Sabina's on Chicago's South Side, founded in 1916, offered havens for Catholic immigrants in a hostile Protestant environment. Robert Orsi's *The Madonna of 115th Street* (1985) conveys the rich religious culture of an East Harlem Italian parish in these years. But the mere fact of a common religious faith proved no guarantee of amity. Ethnic tensions flared as an immigrant church dominated by Irish-Americans absorbed millions of Catholics from Italy, Germany, French Canada, and elsewhere. As parishes and parochial schools demanded priests and nuns of their own ethnic background, struggles broke out within the leadership and at the grass-roots level.

Tensions marked American Judaism as well. Down to the late nineteenth century, relatively few Jews had emigrated to America, primarily from Germany. Generally well educated and prosperous, they tended toward religious liberalism and assimilation. Rabbi Isaac Meyer Wise (1819–1900), a founder of Reform Judaism, was their greatest leader. But the immigrant waves of the late nineteenth and early twentieth centuries brought a tide of 2.5 million Jews from Poland, Russia, and elsewhere in Eastern Europe. Products of the *shtetl,* these newcomers were more orthodox in their beliefs and practices, more traditionalistic and exotic in their dress, diet, and language. Heavily concentrated in New York City, they became the object of anti-Semitic hostility. Some members of the more assimilated German Jewish community created philanthropies and social-service agencies to help their newly arrived co-religionists, despite the cultural gulf that separated them. Others reacted with scarcely concealed aversion, even advocating immigration restriction, creating resentments and divisions that would long persist.

Reflecting these patterns of immigration, American Judaism divided into three streams: Reform, favored by more acculturated German Jews; Orthodox, embraced by many of the Eastern European newcomers; and Conservative, a blend of tradition and accommodation. Migration to America proved a powerful solvent even among the Orthodox. A Lithuanian rabbi, visiting transplanted Orthodox Jews in New York in 1900, warned them that they were losing their *Yiddishkeit,* their entire Jewish mode of life.

But the United States remained overwhelmingly Protestant in these years. This was true not only numerically, but politically and culturally as well. While Irish bosses ran some big cities, power at the state and especially national level remained firmly in the hands of native-born Protestants. Book and magazine publishing, as well as the nation's museums, symphony orchestras, universities, and other high-culture institutions were controlled by the Protestant elite. Immigrants might be welcomed as museum visitors or concertgoers, as a gesture of noblesse oblige, but not as trustees or directors. Change was in the air, however. The accents of immigrant Catholics and Jews could be heard in the beer gardens, music halls, and vaudeville palaces of urban America, and soon in the movies, on radio, and in Tin Pan alley.

The immigrant tide aroused varied responses from the Protestant majority. Some favored exclusion. The Immigration Restriction League, led by Boston Brahmins who in many cases were Episcopalians, campaigned for a literacy test to cut the number of immigrants. In *The Passing of the Great Race* (1916), Madison Grant, a prominent New York civic leader and environmental activist, argued for the superiority of the "Nordic [mainly Protestant] 'race'" over the Catholics of Mediterranean Europe and the Jews of Eastern Europe, who aroused his special revulsion. Confronting the awkward fact that Jesus was a Jew, Grant observed: "[T]he Jews apparently regarded Christ as, in some indefinite way, un-Jewish. . . . [S]uch quasi-authentic traditions as we have of our Lord indicate his Nordic . . . physical and moral attributes."

But the influx of newcomers also stirred the reformist energies that had pulsed through American Protestantism since the antebellum era, when evangelicals had provided leadership to the abolitionist movement and many other reforms. Some older urban Protestant churches, now islands in a sea of Catholic and Jewish immigrants, turned themselves into social centers to serve their new neighbors. As early as the 1880s, rector William Rainsford converted St. George's Episcopal Church in New York City into a social-service oriented "institutional church" with the backing of its senior warden, banker J. P. Morgan.

The settlement-house movement, too, exuded a strong flavor of liberal, reformist Protestantism. Jane Addams, founder of Chicago's Hull House, reared a Quaker, had for a time considered becoming a foreign missionary. In "The Subjective Neccessity for Social Settlements" (1892), Addams praised settlement work as a means of expressing one's Christian faith. The settlement movement, she wrote, symbolized a rediscovery within Christianity of "its early humanitarian aspects . . . , [and] a bent to express in social service . . . the spirit of Christ." If less overt in Addams later writings, the religious theme was never far below the surface.

Indeed, Progressive-era reform in many respects represented a particularly intense manifestation of the social uplift (and social control) impulse of American Protestantism. When delegates to the Progressive party's 1912 nominating convention lustily sang "Onward Christian Soldiers," and when Theodore Roosevelt proclaimed, "We stand at Armageddon, and we battle for the Lord," it was a revealing symbolic moment. This reformist impulse moved in both coercive and positive directions. The Woman's Christian Temperance Union and the Anti-Saloon League, which spearheaded the drive for national prohibition, drew their leaders and their foot soldiers from Protestant—especially Methodist—churches. The campaigns against prostitution, obscenity, gambling, and dance halls had a similar Protestant cast.

But the campaigns against slums, child labor, tainted food, unsafe factories, and countless other Progressive-era issues also had a powerful religious component. As Upton Sinclair, the socialist author of *The Jungle* (1906), an exposé of the meatpacking industry, later observed: "[W]hat brought me to socialism more than anything else was Christianity; . . . the rebel carpenter, the friend of the poor and lowly."

The clearest evidence of the central role of liberal Protestantism in the reform movement was the Social Gospel. George Herron, Washington Gladden, W. D. B. Bliss, and Walter Rauschenbusch were only the best known of thousands of Protestant ministers who sought to channel the energies of the churches toward reform. In *Christianity and the Social Crisis* (1907) and *A Theology for the Social Gospel* (1917), Rauschenbusch offered a theological foundation, based on the doctrine of "the Kingdom of God," for calling on Christians to address the social consequences of rapid industrialization and explosive urban growth. The Federal Council of Churches (FCC), an ecumenical association of liberal Protestant denominations, gave institutional expression to the Social Gospel. The FCC's 1912 manifesto "The Social Creed of the Churches" offered a vast compendium of reform.

The Social Gospel impulse took many forms. The Salvation Army, a British import highly popular in America, represented an evangelical version. The reform impulse in American Catholicism found expression in such manifestos as the Rev. (later Monsignor) John A. Ryan's "The 'Living Wage' Philosophy" (1902) and James Cardinal Gibbons's "The Stake of the Catholic Church in the

Labor Movement" (1902). Meanwhile, Rabbi Stephen S. Wise, at his Free Synagogue in New York City (1907), preached a social justice message rooted in the ethical principles of Judaism.

Later "neo-orthodox" theologians such as Karl Barth, H. Richard Niebuhr, and Reinhold Niebuhr would harshly criticize the Social Gospel advocates; H. Richard Niebuhr, in a laborious Germanic witticism, claimed that they preached that "a God without wrath brought men without sin into a kingdom without judgment through the ministrations of a Christ without a cross." But in an era when the nation first awakened to the social consequences of unregulated industrial capitalism, the Social Gospel had powerfully reinforced the movement to revise the basic terms of the American social contract.

But other important currents in American Protestantism in these years have received less attention. Indeed, the history of early-twentieth-century American religion underscores its manifold and sometimes contradictory strands. While the liberal churches proclaimed the church's mission to transform society as a step toward achieving the Kingdom of God, other Protestants insisted with equal vigor on the futility of all efforts at human social betterment. In the nineteenth century, evangelicalism and reform had often gone hand in hand. In the early twentieth century, this relationship grew weaker, with important consequences for the future.

Evangelicalism, once the common profession of most Protestants, now became a distinct subcategory within the larger Protestant camp. Beliefs once held by nearly all American Protestants now became the defining creed of a Protestant subgroup who increasingly saw themselves under siege, as reform-minded liberal Protestantism seemed to sweep all before it. The intellectual challenges posed by Darwinism, critical study of the Bible, and the steady advance of science all added to the beleaguered mood. From this uneasy climate emerged *The Fundamentals* (1910–15), twelve short books financed by two wealthy California oilmen, Lyman and Milton Stewart. Widely distributed to Protestant clergy, *The Fundamentals* summed up what the authors believed to be the bedrock Christian beliefs, including biblical inerrancy ("a book dropped out of heaven," as one contributor put it), Christ's virgin birth and second coming, and the doctrine of sin and salvation. The series warned against skepticism and liberalism and called for a renewed commitment to personal piety and evangelism. Although less rigid than the later movement it helped galvanize, *The Fundamentals* represented a frontal challenge to the optimism and social reformism of liberal Protestantism. As one author warned, a preoccupation with "social service" was antithetical to creating "victorious soul-winners." Under the leadership of the World's Christian Fundamentals Association (1919); Bible schools such as Chicago's Moody Bible Institute and the Bible Institute of Los Angeles (funded by the Stewart brothers); and such stalwarts as the revivalist and writer Reuben A. Torrey; the Rev. A. C. Dixon of Massachusetts; and William Bell Riley, a Minneapolis minister and Bible-school founder, the fundamentalists stepped up their attacks on liberal Protestantism and the Social Gospel.

In terms of prophetic belief, the dispute between fundamentalists and their liberal (or "modernist") adversaries shaped up as a contention between "*pre*millennialism" and "*post*millennialism." Postmillennialists held that through Christian effort for human betterment, an infinitely better social order can be achieved in the present age, preparing the way for Christ's thousand-year earthly region foretold in the Book of Revelation. Premillennialists rejected this hopeful, activist vision. Human nature is congenitally evil because of Adam's sin, they insisted, and thus all human societies and social institutions must inevitably grow increasingly wicked and degenerate. When this downward spiral reaches its nadir, a demonic figure known as the Antichrist will rule the world. But then Christ will return as avenging warrior to destroy the Antichrist and his armies and establish his millennial kingdom. For premillennialists, all effort at social uplift was fundamentally fruitless, if not actually demonic. As evangelist Dwight L. Moody put it, reform effort was like polishing the brass fittings on a sinking ocean liner. The only hope lay in evangelism and missionary work to win individuals for Christ before it was too late. In short, this same early-twentieth-century era that saw an upsurge of reformist activity by liberal Christians also saw the emergence of a movement within Protestantism—by 1920 it came to be called "fundamentalism"—that held a much bleaker view of the human prospect. Seemingly at odds with American optimism and activism, this counter-strand exerted its own strong appeal to millions of Americans disturbed by unsettling social change.

A particular version of premillennialism, called dispensationalism, formulated in the mid-nineteenth century by the British churchman John Darby, soon spread to America. Citing an array of biblical texts, Darby foresaw a series of end-time events, beginning with the Rapture, when all true believers will join Christ in the air, followed by a seven-year Great Tribulation when the Antichrist will rule; the Battle of Armageddon, when Christ will return to defeat the Antichrist; Christ's thousand-year millennial reign in Jerusalem; and the Last Judgment. Dispensationalism was promulgated by books and periodicals; by summer prophecy conferences; by leading evangelical ministers who embraced Darby's scheme; and by educational centers such as Moody Bible Institute and Dallas Theological Seminary. Most influential of all was the Rev. Cyrus Scofield, a prophecy-conference lecturer and author of a popular reference Bible published by Oxford University Press in 1909, with footnotes elaborating the dispensationalist scenario. Selling millions of copies over predecades, the *Scofield Bible* reinforced the strand of evangelical thought that rejected social reform and deepened the fissure between liberal, reform-minded Protestants and those who saw no hope for human betterment in the present dispensation.

The Jehovah's Witnesses offered a variant of this pessimistic view of civil society. Founded by Charles Taze Russell, author of *Millennial Dawn* (1886), the movement grew steadily. Committed to door-to-door evangelism and streetcorner sales of *The Watchtower* and other church publications, the Witnesses taught that Christ's Second Coming has already begun, but that the Tribulation and Armageddon still lie ahead. Russell did introduce one hopeful note in his system: sinners will have a second opportunity to accept Christ during the millennium. Converts channeled their energies into proselytizing efforts, paying little attention to the larger society and dismissing all governments and other churches as part of a satanic world order that will be swept away when Christ's kingdom is established. Opposing military service; appealing especially to the poor; and presenting its message in simple, appealing terms, the Jehovah's Witnesses movement grew steadily despite persecution in many countries, including Russia and Nazi Germany. By 1960, worldwide membership stood at around one million.

Pentecostalism offered another variant on the premillennialist theme. Emerging from a 1906 Los Angeles revival, Pentecostalism featured emotional worship emphasizing the signs and wonders that followers believed heralded Christ's imminent return, including divine healing and glossolalia: the gift of speaking in strange tongues granted to Jesus' followers at Pentecost. Fired with missionary zeal, Pentecostalism won many converts at home and abroad, laying the groundwork for new denominations such as the fast-growing Assemblies of God Church (1914), which boasted more than half a million members by 1960, and the Church of God in Christ, an African-American denomination. Pentecostalism—also called "charismatic" religion—would remain a major force in American religion through the twentieth century.

These movements differed among themselves—fundamentalists were strongly patriarchal, whereas Pentecostalists welcomed women ministers, for example—but they shared a common skepticism toward the reform-minded ideology of the Social Gospel.

Another religious strand that would grow in importance as the century wore on, the therapeutic, was articulated in these years by the philosopher William James. In *The Will to Believe* (1896), James offered a "justification of faith," arguing that empirical science offers little help in life's most important choices, and that in many realms of experience, including the religious, one is justified in holding beliefs that can neither be proven nor disproven empirically, if they contribute to one's happiness and well-being. In *The Varieties of Religious Experience* (1902), James explored, and defended, religion's role in meeting the psychological needs of a wide variety of personality types.

Pragmatism, the philosophic position introduced by James in a 1907 work bearing that title, grew in part out of James's continuing concern with the therapeutic role of religious belief in promoting psychological health—a role it had played for him as a young man when he had struggled with depression and despair. James himself, reared on the mystical teachings of Immanual Swedenborg, embraced no specific creed himself, but played a crucial role for many Americans in defending the "right" to believe. As one observer noted, he was like a church bell, tolling others into church, while remaining outside himself.

A generation made uneasy by the spread of skepticism and by the ever-expanding domain of science welcomed James's message, glossing over its troubling subtext: if the test of the truth of a religious belief is how it makes one *feel*, what becomes of the exclusive truth claims of *specific* faith traditions? What possible basis for choosing among many different creeds did James's generalized defense of faith provide? Well before James's lectures and books, the religion-as-psychotherapy theme had been elaborated in Mary Baker Eddy's *Science and Health with Key to the Scripture* (1875) and embraced by Eddy's Christian Science Church. But thanks in part to James's imprimatur, it spread widely across the spectrum of American Protestantism.

In many ways, then, many key strands in the complex fabric of America's twentieth-century religious history were already clearly evident at the dawn of the twentieth century. In the decades that followed, these strands would lengthen, separate, and interconnect in fascinating ways.

WORLD WAR I AND THE INTERWAR YEARS

The outbreak of war in Europe in 1914, and America's entry into the conflict in 1917, profoundly affected the nation's religious climate. On one hand, in the initial burst of patriotism that followed President Wilson's war message, the reformist spirit of the Social Gospel seemed to reach its apotheosis. Wilson, son of a Presbyterian minister, spoke in exalted, quasi-millennialist terms of America's destiny to spread democracy and peace worldwide. Journalists and writers echoed Wilson's theme with prose and poetry sanctifying the war and the young men fighting in it. In this mood, the war seemed a global extension of the reformist cause that had burned so brightly in the nation for two decades. America's pulpits rang with religious defenses of the righteousness of the nation's cause and apocalyptic denunciations of the enemy. Turn Germany upside down, proclaimed the Presbyterian evangelist Billy Sunday, and you will find "Made in Hell" stamped on the bottom.

But the war also provided grist for the more pessimistic premillennialist view. As the struggle dragged on and the carnage of the trenches mounted, the hopeful vision of a world transformed through Christian effort rang increasingly hollow. Instead, the "wars and rumors of war" foretold by Jesus in Mark 13 as a sign of the Last Days seemed to be coming to pass. The war particularly excited Jehovah's Witnesses, since Charles Taze Russell in *Millennial Dawn* had seen 1914 as a key milestone on his road map of end-time events. The 1918 Balfour Declaration, which expressed Britain's support for a Jewish homeland in Palestine, stirred great excitement among dispensationalists, who had long predicted the Jews' return to the Holy Land as a key prophetic sign marking the imminence of Christ's return.

The Armistice of November 1918 ended America's brief—but culturally crucial—involvement in the European conflict. But the return of peace posed new challenges for the nation's churches. Indeed, the decades of the 1920s and 1930s, in different ways, brought severe strains to U.S. religious life, as they did to society as a whole.

The Twenties

Initially, the momentum of the Social Gospel and the prewar activist spirit continued. The young Reinhold Niebuhr, beginning his ministry in Detroit, angered Henry Ford by plunging into labor politics, which he saw as an expression of his Christian faith. Niebuhr's *Does Civilization Need Religion* (1929) restated the familiar themes of the Social Gospel.

The Rev. Harry Emerson Fosdick, a leading "modernist" (the fundamentalists' pejorative term for religious liberals), became pastor of New York's Park Avenue Baptist Church in 1925 and then, in 1931, of Riverside Church, built by John D. Rockefeller, Jr., a devout Baptist. Fosdick's *Adventurous Religion* (1926) and his radio program, "National Vespers," launched in 1922, brought his liberal Social Gospel message, including a pacifism rooted in his revulsion at the carnage of 1914–18, to a large audience.

But the larger cultural climate of the 1920s proved no more conducive to liberalism in the religious realm than in the political arena. The disillusionment with Wilsonian idealism that followed the vindictive Versailles peace treaty and the Senate's repudiation of U.S. membership in the League of Nations proved a bitter blow to liberal Protestants who in the high noon of the Progressive era had believed that the millennium could be achieved through committed Christian effort. The failure of national prohibition, painfully evident as the 1920s wore on, underscored the paradoxes of well-intentioned moral reform effort.

The hedonistic urban mass culture of the 1920s, with its emphasis on consumerism, leisure, and the idolization of movie stars and sports heroes, eroded traditional piety and undermined the minister's status as cultural leader. Church attendance remained high, but the cultural standing of religion subtly declined, particularly among college-age youth. Many 1920s' writers and journalists directed their satirical barbs against religion. Henry L. Mencken, editor of the *American Mercury* magazine, lampooned religious leaders of all stripes as mountebanks and charlatans. The leading minister in Zenith, the fictional midwestern city in Sinclair Lewis's *Babbitt* (1922), is an affable conformist who runs his church like an efficient business and confirms the prejudices of his comfortable middle-class parishioners. In *Elmer Gantry* (1927), Lewis offered the definitive fictional treatment of the minister as hypocrite. The revived Ku Klux Klan, which flourished in the early 1920s, wrapped its racist, nativist, anti-Semitic, and vengefully moralistic program in the language of fundamentalism, identifying this strand of Christianity with the decade's most bigoted and reactionary features.

The booming prosperity and new mass-culture technologies of the 1920s had important implications for religion. The explosive growth of radio, the movies, and phonograph records featuring jazz and other forms of secular music, not to mention the automobile beckoning to the open road, challenged the churches as competitors for parishioners' time and loyalty.

In *Middletown* (1929), a social study of Muncie, Indiana, Robert and Helen Lynd reported that religion seemed "a less spontaneous and pervasive part of the life of the city" than earlier. While religion remained important, the Lynds found declining concern with Sabbath observance and a generalized religiosity, particularly among the elite, rather than deep piety or concern with specific doctrines. H. Richard Niebuhr made a similar point in *The Social Sources of Denominationalism* (1929), arguing that considerations of social status, more than doctrinal issues, determined most Americans' denominational choices.

The 1925 Scopes trial in Dayton, Tennessee, stands as a defining moment in the religious and culture wars of the 1920s, with Charles Darwin's theory of evolution as the symbolic battleground. Religious liberals had long since made peace with evolutionary theory, but fundamentalists saw it as a radical threat to their literalist reading of the Bible. When the Tennessee legislature outlawed the teaching of evolution in the state's public schools, the American Civil Liberties Union offered free legal defense to any teacher willing to defy the law. John T. Scopes, a high-school biology teacher in Dayton, took up the challenge, encouraged by local boosters eager to promote their town. Famed Chicago lawyer Clarence Darrow led the defense team; William Jennings Bryan, three-time presidential candidate and former secretary of state, volunteered his services to the prosecution as an "expert witness" on the biblical account of Creation. H. L. Mencken led a horde of journalists who covered the event.

In the mythology of the trial, as popularized in the 1960 film *Inherit the Wind,* for example, Darrow exposed Bryan as an ignorant fool and heroically defended science and free speech against what he called "bigots and ignoramuses"; Mencken paraded the idiocies of Bible-thumping yokels before a jeering nation; and fundamentalism was demolished, never to rise again.

The reality was more complex. Darrow's view of "science" was nearly as simplistic as Bryan's, whose fundamentalism was not as rigid as legend had it. Bryan, in fact, had moments of eloquence at the trial as he articulated the anxieties of parents fearful that their children were being lost to the forces of modernity and an increasingly dominant urban mass culture.

While the Scopes trial may have given fundamentalism a black eye in the short run, it by no means killed it. Although less visible after the war than before, fundamentalism, and Protestant evangelicalism more broadly, continued to thrive at the local level. Evangelical and Pentecostal groups such as the Southern Baptist Convention, the Seventh-Day Adventists, and the Assemblies of God church experienced steady growth. (So did the Mormon church, the Jehovah's Witnesses, and other groups considered on the sectarian fringe.) Strong minorities within the generally liberal Methodist, Presbyterian, Lutheran, and Northern Baptist denominations resisted the Social Gospel orientation of their national leaders and espoused a stricter creed focused on evangelism; individual conversion; reverence for the Bible; and prohibitions on such behavior as smoking, drinking, dancing, and moviegoing. In some cases, the conservatives broke away to form separate denominations; in other cases, they remained as dissident elements within the larger body. But sustained by a vigorous publications program; Bible schools and missionary-training centers; and charismatic leaders like A. J. Gordon in Boston, Donald Gray Barnhouse in Philadelphia; James M. Gray of Moody Bible Institute, and William Bell Riley in Minneapolis, evangelicalism and fundamentalism remained potent forces in U.S. Protestantism. Sunday schools, a nineteenth-century innovation, sustained evangelicalism as well, as did gospel singing, which loomed large in evangelical worship services, both white and black, all across America.

In city missions and storefront churches, evangelicalism reached out to urban newcomers. The hundreds of churches of Harlem, for example, provided not only a familiar theology but also a crucial support network for thousands of African Americans pouring into New York City from the South. Black churches in other cities played a similar role. While some of the more affluent black churches echoed the worship patterns of the mainstream white congregations, the storefront churches, with their emotion-filled, often Pentecostal worship services, gospel singing, and fervent chant-and-response preaching bespoke the enormous vitality of this wing of American Protestantism. Also sustaining grass-roots religious life in this ostensibily secularist decade was an array of material-culture artifacts. Religious wall plaques, greeting cards, books and Bibles, children's stories, and everyday household objects bearing biblical verses all sustained the faith.

And the nation's religious leaders, keenly sensitive to trends in the secular culture, quickly saw not only the threat but also the potential of the new technologies. Religious radio programs proliferated. The automobile might lure parishioners from Sunday services, but it also enabled worshippers to come from greater distances, and helped touring evangelists move out of the cities into the small towns of rural America. And while the churches generally deplored the high life and loose morals on display in the movies, Cecil B. De Mille demonstrated the new medium's religious potential with his biblical epics *The Ten Commandments* (1923) and *The King of Kings* (1927), the latter portraying the Resurrection in two-color technicolor, a novelty at the time.

Demonstrating American religion's chameleon-like relationship to the secular culture, colorful evangelists such as Billy Sunday and Aimee Semple McPherson in Los Angeles adapted the techniques of modern advertising, ballyhoo, and celebrityhood to attract throngs to their services. "Sister Aimee," a product of Pentecostalism and the Salvation Army, turned the services at her 5,300-seat Angelus Temple into multimedia extravaganzas, and reached a still larger audience via radio.

American Judaism experienced its own tensions in the troubled 1920s. Hostility between acculturated German Jews and the newer Eastern European immigrants diminished as the latter entered the mainstream of U.S. life and moved from the immigrant ghettos. But divisions remained between the traditionalist and progressive branches of the faith. In *Religion in a Changing World* (1931), Rabbi Abba Hillel saw Judaism as beset by the same liberal-conservative struggles that divided American Protestantism.

Zionism, the movement to reestablish a Jewish state in Palestine, proved a further source of contention in American Judaism. Stephen S. Wise helped found the Federation of American Zionists in 1893, and lawyer Louis D. Brandeis became its head in 1914. But the movement remained divisive, with Conservative and Orthodox Jews generally supportive, and Reform Jews less so. (After World War II and the Nazi Holocaust, Zionism would win broad support across the entire spectrum of American Judaism.)

American Catholicism remained somewhat insulated from the culture wars of the 1920s. Still a parish-based immigrant church led by powerful prelates such as Boston's William Cardinal O'Connell and sustained by a network of parochial schools, U.S. Catholicism escaped the upheavals buffeting Protestant America in the 1920s. Ethnic tensions within Catholicism gradually diminished as well, as the immigrants became more assimilated.

But Catholicism's still precarious status in an overwhelmingly Protestant nation was underscored in 1928 when New York governor Alfred E. Smith, the Catholic son of Irish immigrants, won the Democratic presidential nomination. If this seemed a victory for tolerance, the election itself proved that the nation still had far to go. While Smith piled up large majorities in the immigrant cities, rural and small-town voters—even traditionally Democratic ones in the South and Midwest—rejected Smith in favor of the midwestern Protestant Herbert Hoover.

The contemporary media rarely treated seriously the vitality and diversity of grass-roots religion in the 1920s, and later historians generally followed suit. Frederick Lewis Allen's highly influential cultural history *Only Yesterday* (1930), treated religion only superficially. Yet this decade remains crucial for the later history of American religion. Both the fundamentalist and evangelical infrastructure established in the twenties, and the churches' quick appropriation of new technologies, helped shape much of what would follow on the religious scene.

Depression Decade

The 1929 stock market crash launched a depression that would hang on through the succeeding decade. President Franklin Roosevelt's New Deal, beginning as a depression-fighting program, was by the mid-1930s championing the underdog, supporting organized labor, and promoting major social-welfare legislation such as Social Security. With the depression and the New Deal dominating the nation's attention, religion seemed to be further marginalized. Roosevelt brought many Jews and Catholics into his administration, weakening the Protestant establishment's exclusive grip on national political power. But these newcomers were appointed for their political or bureaucratic expertise, and perhaps as representatives of important voting blocs, not for their religious faith, and their visibility in government had little bearing on the status of religion in the culture.

From the perspective of the historian of religion, the New Deal differed sharply from the Progressive movement, despite obvious continuities between the two. Progressivism exuded the spirit of liberal Christianity, as we have seen, and drew upon the moral energies of the churches. Progressive reformers fell easily into the language of Christian service and moral duty. The New Deal was much more secular, and its reforms more bureaucratic and structural, with little of progressivism's tone of moral uplift or aura of the Sunday morning sermon.

President Hoover, an ex-Progressive and a Quaker, while not rejecting governmental action, urged private philanthropic responses to the economic crisis, including charitable work by the churches. The New Deal, rejecting this approach as too little and too late, instead offered a panoply of federal programs to address the crisis and restore prosperity. The shift found symbolic expression in the Farm Security Administration photographs chosen for release by Roy Stryker, head of the FSA's documentary program. These visual images shaped contemporary impressions of 1930s' America, and continued to do so afterward. The rare church in these photographs is typically abandoned and boarded up. The New Deal, implicitly, offers the only hope. Religious life is largely missing from both the historical and visual record of the decade.

The mass media similarly paid scant notice to religion in the 1930s. A few religious movies were made, including *Green Pastures* (1936), with an all-black cast, in which Rex Ingram, as "De Lawd," translates familiar Bible stories into language and imagery accessible to southern black Sunday-school children. But in general, neither network radio, Hollywood, or the successful photo magazine *Life* (1936) devoted much attention to religion in the Depression decade.

This absence was not entirely a matter of governmental or media neglect. The Lynds, revisiting Muncie in 1935, found continued erosion in the relative status of religion. While religious faith remained for many "a personal source of strength and courage," they reported in *Middletown in Transition* (1937), its public manifestations were weakening, with empty pews, graying congregations, few revivals, and a further decline in Sabbath observance and the cultural standing of the clergy. As one minister lamented: "In the old days people went to preachers for consolation, information, and inspiration. They still come to us for consolation, but go to newspapers for their information and inspiration."

But despite the Lynds's evidence and the marginalization of religion by the New Deal and the mass culture, a closer look reveals a more nuanced picture. Depression-era religion not only remained important to millions of Americans, but it found public expression in some varied and highly visible ways. Indeed, American religion's capacity for adapting to shifting social realities was again very much on display in this decade. It was in these years of economic crisis, for example, that Norman Vincent Peale, embracing the religion-as-therapy theme, first honed his psychologically empowering message of happiness and fulfillment that would bring him fame in the 1950s and beyond. Peale launched his long ministry at New York's Marble Collegiate Church in 1932, and his first book, *Faith Is the Answer,* a collaboration with psychiatrist Smiley Blanton, appeared in 1940, as the nation moved from depression to war.

With the New Deal so dominant, the religious social-activist tradition found expression on the margins. In 1933 the Catholic convert (and ex-Marxist) Dorothy Day, with Peter Maurin, founded the Catholic Worker movement in New York City. Catholic Worker volunteers operated "hospitality houses" for the poor and homeless and peddled their *Catholic Worker* newspaper, a pioneer in advocacy journalism, on the city streets.

The 1930s also saw the heyday of the Universal Peace Mission in New York City, headed by an African American named George Baker who had proclaimed himself God and taken the name "Father Divine." In the depths of the depression, the Universal Peace Mission ran an employment office, purchased hotels (called "heavens") to house the homeless, and provided abundant free meals to the needy. Father Divine's ministry attracted such throngs that on one occasion he was arrested for disturbing the peace, fined five hundred dollars, and sentenced to a year in jail by a hostile white judge. When the apparently healthy 50-year-old judge dropped dead of a heart attack three days later, Father Divine commented: "I hated to do it."

In these same years, the radio broadcasts of the Canadian priest Father Charles E. Coughlin attracted a large midwestern following, especially among lower-middle-class Catholics. Initially sympathetic to the New Deal, Coughlin soon turned against FDR and laced his harangues with anti-Semitism, while preaching his own vaguely fascistic panacea called "social credit." Increasingly vitriotic, Coughlin was silenced by his superiors in 1939.

Meanwhile, the Rev. Charles E. Fuller of Long Beach, California, won a vast audience to his "Old-Fashioned Revival Hour," a nationally broadcast weekly radio program he had launched on a single station in 1925. With its lively gospel music and simple evangelical messages, Fuller's homey broadcast nostagically evoked an earlier, more bucolic era of American religious life for a vast audience of depression-era listeners.

Norman Vincent Peale, Dorothy Day, Father Divine, Father Coughlin, Charles E. Fuller: this quintet of religious figures, with little in common except their prominence on the 1930s' cultural horizon, remind us of the diversity of twentieth-century American religious life, and of the risks in offering sweeping generalizations about its nature and significance. And beyond the pulpit celebrities and media performers lay the thousands of local churches and synagogues where obscure ministers, priests, and rabbis ministered to congregations collectively numbering in the millions. This was the grass-roots reality of American religion in the 1930s, as in every other decade of the century: a reality frustratingly difficult to retrieve, yet crucial to the story.

WORLD WAR II AND THE COLD WAR ERA

Religion in Wartime

Religion played an important role in American life during World War II, at the front, at home, and in wartime propaganda. But its propaganda role differed in subtle ways from that of World War I. In 1917–18, images of a religious crusade lay at the heart of the propaganda justifying America's intervention. In World War II, the "religious crusade" theme was muted, and instead religion was simply folded into a bundle of evocative images defining the essence of the society the GI's were fighting to defend.

As in World War I, chaplains provided religious ministrations to servicemen. On the home front, the bereaved and families concerned about loved ones in combat turned to churches and synagogues for consolation. As in most wars, the nation's leaders invoked God's benediction on the U.S. cause. President Roosevelt's war message to Congress on December 8, 1941, called upon divine support in the coming conflict. A chaplain on Eniwetok Atoll in the South Pacific on August 6, 1945, prayed for God's blessing on the mission as the *Enola Gay* took off to drop an atomic bomb on Hiroshima.

But above all, wartime propaganda positioned religion at the heart of the cultural values the nation was determined to preserve. Artist Norman Rockwell, in a famous series of paintings illustrating the war aims proclaimed by President Roosevelt and British prime minister Winston Churchill in the Atlantic Charter, portrayed a congregation gathered in a simple New England church to illustrate freedom of religion. Warner Sallman's iconic "Head of

Christ" (1940) proved immediately popular in evangelical households. Irving Berlin's "I'm Dreaming of a White Christmas" (1942) evoked a religious holiday—albeit a largely secularized one—as a core image of a nostagically remembered America and a future nation again at peace.

Religion loomed large in wartime movies as well. Films set in England typically ended with a service in a bombed church. Even Hollywood's combat movies (far removed from *Platoon* and *Saving Private Ryan!*) had religious overtones, as in *A Wing and a Prayer* (1944) and *God Is My Co-Pilot* (1945). The wartime religious movies included several based on Catholic themes, such as *The Song of Bernadette* (1943), *The Keys of the Kingdom* (1944), Bing Crosby's Oscar-winning *Going My Way* (1944), and its sequel *The Bells of St. Mary's* (1945). (Catholic films had the added advantage of appeasing Joseph Breen, a devout Catholic who headed the powerful Production Code that rated the movies for moral content.)

Wartime propaganda featuring a generic commitment to "religion" for its own sake strengthened a growing ecumenical movement in America that downplayed differences among the various faiths and celebrated a shared commitment to the idea of religion itself. This ecumenical spirit was epitomized by a much publicized incident on January 29, 1943, when four chaplains—two Protestants, a Catholic priest, and a rabbi—gave up their lifejackets to others and went down together when the *U.S.S. Dorchester,* a navy transport, was torpedoed by a German U-boat off Newfoundland. Commemorated by a U.S. postage stamp and in an interfaith chapel, the "Four Chaplains" came to personify the spirit of ecumenical amity and brotherhood that would figure prominently in American religious life of the 1950s and beyond.

The Cold War Years

As the postwar era dawned, many observers noted a revival of interest in religion in America. Church membership soared from 64 million in 1940 to 114 million in 1960. Biblical epics such as *Quo Vadis* of 1951 (with Peter Ustinov as a particularly odious Nero); *The Robe* (1953); and *Ben-Hur* (1959) filled the movie theaters. A wave of church construction (often involving the same prefabrication techniques used in suburban housing developments) struggled to keep up with the demand. The evangelistic crusades of Billy Graham, Oral Roberts, and others attracted hundreds of thousands.

The boom in religion had multiple sources, including demographic patterns. As the birthrate soared and Americans flocked to the suburbs, the media and the popular culture celebrated domesticity and family life. Church attendance figured prominently in this apotheosis of the suburban nuclear family as the American ideal. The Advertising Council summed up the theme in a ubiquitous public service slogan: "The family that prays together stays together."

As families left farms and older ethnic neighborhoods for the suburbs, church affiliation provided both a social network in unfamiliar surroundings and evidence of one's social aspirations. As William H. Whyte wrote in *The Organization Man* (1956): "[W]hen young people [new to the suburbs] see how many other people are going to church regularly, they feel they ought to." Whyte further observed: "Acclimation to suburbia . . . stimulates switches in religious affiliations, and the couple from, say, a small Ozark town is likely to discard their former fundamentalist allegiance to become Methodists or Presbyterians."

As Whyte's comments suggest, these sociological analyses often implied a criticism of postwar American religion as superficial, driven mainly by social anxieties and opportunism. Echoing H. Richard Niebuhr' earlier critique, Will Herberg in *Protestant, Catholic, Jew* harshly criticized a religious culture in which support for "religion" as simply one component of the "American way of life" threatened to displace genuine piety and commitment to a specific faith tradition.

One may take such judgments seriously without embracing them uncritically. They often reflected an outsider's impressions rather than an in-depth probing of individuals' actual reasons for church attendance. In any event, William James would have understood: if religion provided emotional rewards, and helped people get on with their lives, this was evidence for its truth. And was it perhaps precisely this "shallowness" and adaptability to different social realities that gave American religion such tenacity and strength?

The cold war ideological climate also helped fuel the postwar upsurge of religion. As Washington mobilized the nation for a protracted struggle with the Soviet Union, politicians and the media insisted that the contest was not only military and strategic, but ideological and cultural as well. And a vital distinction between the United States and the Soviet Union was America's religious freedom and encouragement of religion, as contrasted with the Communists' atheism and materialist ideology. When Congress in 1954 added "under God" to the Pledge of Allegiance, and "In God We Trust" to U.S. currency and coinage, the gesture underscored religion's importance in the nation's cold war self-image. In 1967, sociologist Robert Bellah would identify this melding of piety and patriotism as America's "civil religion."

John Foster Dulles, secretary of state from 1953 to 1959 and a prominent Presbyterian layman, embodied this religious dimension of the cold war. So did ex-Communist Whittaker Chambers, who in *Witness* (1952) portrayed the cold war in apocalyptic, quasi-religious terms, and numerous contributors to William F. Buckley's conservative *National Review* (founded in 1955). Reinhold Niebuhr, having evolved from Social Gospel advocate in the 1920s to Marxist in the early 1930s to avid cold warrior in the 1950s, strengthened the quasi-theological strand of America's anti-Communist ideology in his early postwar polemical writings.

Further reinforcing the postwar turn to religion was the new menace of thermonuclear war. Post-Hiroshima prophecy interpreters quickly reminded their readers of biblical prophecies of Earth's destruction by fire ("[T]he heavens shall pass away with a great noise, and the elements shall melt with fervent heat, the earth also and the works that are therein shall be burned up," 2 Pet. 3:10). Nuclear war, they warned, could well fulfill this frightening vision. "This Atomic Age and the Word of God," a November 1945 essay by prophecy writer Wilbur M. Smith of Moody Bible Institute, sold fifty thousand copies and was condensed in *Reader's Digest.*

Young Billy Graham was preaching in a tent revival in Los Angeles in the fall of 1949 when Russia successfully tested an atomic bomb. In his staccato, doom-laden voice, Graham immediately cited the prospect of atomic war as another reason for sinners to repent. Los Angeles ranked third on Moscow's target list, after New York and Chicago, proclaimed Graham, adding: "Time is desperately short. . . . I say to you, the message of the Lord has not changed! . . . [P]repare to meet thy God!" Jonathan Edwards had once terrified his audiences by comparing them to spiders dangling above a fire by a thin thread; Graham in 1949—and for years thereafter—invoked not just metaphorical but real images of fiery destruction to win converts.

The atomic bomb was only one of a combination of developments that heightened postwar interest in Bible prophecy. In *The Late Great Planet Earth* (1970), a popularization and updating of the dispensationalism of Darby and Scofield, Hal Lindsey wove together the nuclear threat, the creation of Israel in 1948, the Israelis' recapture of the Old City of Jerusalem in 1967, the rise of the European Common Market, the menace of communism, and growing wickedness worldwide to argue that the Rapture might occur at any moment. An eager public snapped up Lindsey's book, making it the nonfiction bestseller of the 1970s. In this era of cold war anxieties and nuclear alarm, scores of prophecy popularizers, on TV, in paperback books, and in local pulpits, capitalized on the growing preoccupation with biblical visions of the End.

Other religious writers exploited the stresses of the early cold war era to offer a soothing message of religion as therapy. Rabbi Joshua Liebman's popular *Peace of Mind* appeared in 1946, as awareness of atomic danger eddied through the culture. Norman Vincent Peale's many best-selling books included *A Guide to Confident Living* (1948), *Faith Is the Answer* (1950), and *The Power of Positive Thinking* (1952). Peale's national radio program and successful magazine *Guideposts* added to his audience. He was perfectly attuned to his historical moment: the early cold war years of atomic fear and rapid geographic mobility. Americans were "afraid of the future," Peale noted in 1948, going on to offer his "cure for fear": "Say confidently to yourself: 'Through God's help and the application of simple techniques, I will be free from fear.' Believe that—practice it, and it will be so." Religion not only helps you overcome fear, Peale taught; it also will make you popular and successful. "Christianity . . . teaches that one basic trait will go far toward getting people to like you," he wrote in *The Power of Positive Thinking;* " . . . a sincere and forthright interest in and love for people." Half a century after William James, Peale demonstrated the market potential of James's psychotherapeutic justification of religious faith.

As American popularizers of religion have always done, the religious figures of the 1950s used the latest technologies—in this case, television, jet travel, and cheap paperbacks—to spread their message. Graham soon moved from tents to football stadiums to television with his popular "Hour of Decision" program. His sign-off comment: "Just write to me, Billy Graham, Minneapolis, Minnesota; that's all the address you need. And God bless you real good," was heard around the world. (An African listener, misunderstanding the instructions, addressed his letter: "Billy Graham, Many Applause, Many Sorrows." It was promptly delivered.)

Bishop Fulton J. Sheen became a 1950s celebrity with his program "Life Is Worth Living." The media-savvy Sheen insisted on lighting that brought out his sharply etched features and piercing eyes. Accepting an award for his show, he began: "First, I would like to thank my writers, Matthew, Mark, Luke, and John." These and other postwar religious superstars wrote paperbacks that broke out of the religious-publishing ghetto into the mass-market outlets of airports, supermarkets, and chain stores.

As the simultaneous popularity of Graham, Lindsey, and Peale makes clear, both the evangelical/fundamentalist and the liberal/therapeutic strands of American Protestantism flourished in postwar America. The evangelical Southern Baptist Convention added 2.7 million members in the 1950s. Billy Graham got his start with Youth for Christ, a postwar evangelical movement aimed at the younger generation. Saturday-night Youth for Christ rallies featuring musical performers, religious films, and youth-oriented sermons attracted thousands, laying the groundwork for an evangelical resurgence. The National Association of Evangelicals, created in 1941 by denominations defining themselves by this label, helped coordinate the postwar evangelical revival through its publications and annual conventions.

Despite all these postwar trends—the allegedly superficial and self-satisfied religion of the suburbs, the popularity of feel-good books by Peale and others, the resurgence of evangelicalism's traditional emphasis on personal salvation—the reformist energies associated with liberal Christianity and the Social Gospel found a powerful new outlet in the later 1950s and beyond: the civil rights movement. African-American ministers played a crucial role as the movement took shape in the South. Martin Luther King, Jr., founder of the Southern Christian Leadership Conference, was only the best known of many black ministers who rallied to the cause, bringing national visibility, strategic guidance, and moral authority to a grass-roots, often church-based movement. King's April 1963 "Letter from the Birmingham Jail," and his "I Have a Dream" oration at the Lincoln Memorial that August, seminal movement documents that stand as classics of American religious literature, are saturated in biblical language and the Judeo-Christian moral world. Drawing upon the language of Isaiah, the Christian gospels, and the hymnody of the black church, King at the Lincoln Memorial offered a postmillennial vision of a future age of justice and equality for all, when Americans white and black, "Jews and Gentiles, Protestants and Catholics, will be able to join hands and sing in the words of that old Negro spiritual, 'Free at last! Free at last! Thank God almighty, we are free at last.'"

As the southern freedom struggle captured the nation's attention, religious leaders of all faiths, particularly the more liberal groups historically drawn to social action, supported the cause with sermons and resolutions, and joined in civil rights demonstrations. A Unitarian minister, James Reeb, was murdered by white racists in Selma, Alabama, in 1965. The National Council of Churches (successor to the Federal Council of Churches) worked strenuously for the Civil Rights Act of 1965, supplying lobbyists, organizing marches and letter-writing campaigns, and holding daily prayer services in a church near the Capitol while the bill was being debated.

Some white evangelicals were drawn into the cause as well. Billy Graham made a significant symbolic gesture in adding African Americans to his evangelistic team and insisting that his southern crusades be racially integrated. The civil rights crusade represented perhaps the moment of maximum peacetime unity and social engagement for American religion in the twentieth century.

With the coming of the Vietnam War, however, America's historic religious fault lines reemerged. Many liberal ministers, priests, and rabbis followed William Sloan Coffin, the Yale University chaplain, in opposing the war, preaching and marching against it, and supporting draft resisters. The Berrigan brothers, Daniel and Philip, both Jesuit priests, went further, engaging in acts of civil disobedience, such as pouring blood on draft records, that periodically landed them in jail. (The Berrigans also opposed the nuclear arms race, and their direct-action protests on this front, such as trespassing on missile sites, got them into further hot water.)

On the other hand, prominent Catholic prelates like Francis Cardinal Spellman of New York, aware of Vietnam's large and firmly anti-Communist Catholic population, vigorously supported the war. And some conservative Jewish leaders, mindful of the crucial importance of the United States in shielding Israel from aggression by hostile neighbors, supported the U.S. effort to keep South Vietnam from being swallowed by Communist North Vietnam.

American evangelicals, including such well-known figures as Billy Graham, generally backed the war as well. When Graham introduced Clebe McClary, who lost an arm and an eye in Vietnam, at a Southern California rally in 1969, McClary received a standing ovation. The Rev. Jerry Falwell hailed McClary (who went on to become an evangelist in his own right) as "a champion for Christ." Declared the Rev. Stephen Olford, an evangelical Baptist minister, after a 1969 visit to Vietnam: "America may be confused; other nations may have little idea of why we are in Vietnam, but . . . I did not find one soldier, from the ranks to the generals . . . , who was not solidly convinced of our enemy and our cause."

This unwavering support won evangelicals the gratitude of the military, and strengthened the campaign for the appointment of more evangelical, fundamentalist, and pentecostal chaplains. Evangelical religious activities in the military increased dramatically in the 1970s. For a time, so many prayer breakfasts, prayer luncheons, and Bible-study groups were convening in the Pentagon that one wonders how any military planning got done.

Both the deep divisions in American religion and the dramatic resurgence of evangelicalism, so vividly on display during the Vietnam War and its aftermath, would continue as the twentieth century drew to a close.

TO THE END OF THE CENTURY: EVANGELICALISM REDIVIVUS; A CHANGING RELIGIOUS LANDSCAPE

The end of the twentieth century saw some stirrings of the activism by liberal churches that had emerged so strongly in the Progressive era and again in the later 1950s and 1960s. The anti-nuclear weapons campaign of the early 1980s won the support of liberal Protestant and Jewish leaders and many Catholic activists. The U.S. Catholic bishops' 1983 pastoral letter *The Challenge of Peace,* while stopping just short of condemning the building and possession of nuclear weapons as immoral, sharply criticized America's massive nuclear arsenal and the deterrence theory (if you attack us, we'll annihilate you) that underlay it. Even Billy Graham displayed a new interest in nuclear disarmament and social justice issues in his 1983 book *Approaching Hoofbeats.*

The liberal churches were active on other fronts as well in the 1980s and 1990s, from gay rights, feminist theology, the ordination of women, and AIDS support groups to anticolonialist liberation theology and environmental activism. Robert Booth Fowler's *The Greening of Protestantism* (1995) documented the latter movement.

But the activism of religious progressives paled in comparison with the energies on display at the other end of the spectrum. In fact, the center of growth and activism in American religion shifted sharply rightward after the mid-1960s, reflecting a broader conservative turn that led to strong presidential challenges by Alabama governor George Wallace, the election of Richard Nixon, and Ronald Reagan's eight years in the White House. Evangelical, fundamentalist, and charismatic churches were the fastest growing sector of American Protestantism in these years. Established bodies such at the fifteen-million-strong Southern Baptist Convention—America's largest Protestant denomination—and the Assemblies of God Church (2.5 million) expanded rapidly. Newly founded independent "Christian fellowships," "gospel taberna-cles," and "Bible churches" enjoyed phenomenal growth. In a religious paral-lel to the Wal-Mart superstores, suburban megachurches, some with many thousands of members, proliferated. A team of sociologists, returning to much-studied Muncie, Indiana, in the late 1970s, found the churches thriv-ing—but little interest in social action.

Television ministries reached across the nation and the world via commu-nications satellites. Pat Robertson's Christian Broadcasting Network and the Trinity Broadcasting Network provided full-time evangelical programming via cable, often utilizing the popular talk-show format. The spectacular fall of tel-evangelists Jimmy Swaggart, arrested not once but twice for consorting with prostitutes, and Jim Bakker, imprisoned for fraud, proved temporary embar-rassments, but not serious setbacks. Evangelical and charismatic magazines, videotapes, and even Internet discussion groups flourished

The nation's Christian bookstores—most of them evangelical—repre-sented a three billion dollar business by the 1990s, with six thousand outlets nationwide, many in suburban shopping malls. Evangelical Christian schools gained popularity, and enrollment at evangelical colleges grew from 97,000 in 1990 to 129,000 in 1999. A student at Illinois Wesleyan University explained her motivation: "[I want to] stick with people who think the same way I do." In short, all the hallmarks of twentieth-century American religion—its capac-ity for renewal, its chameleonlike ability to adapt to shifts in the cultural and political winds, and its skillful use of the latest technologies—were vividly on display in the decade's final years.

Interest in Bible prophecy remained intense despite the cold war's end and the diminished threat of nuclear holocaust. Post–cold war prophecy pop-ularizers focused on new menaces as signs of the Last Days: environmental hazards, Islamic fundamentalism, and the "new world order" of electronic data, communications satellites, international organizations, and multina-tional conglomerates. The "Left Behind" prophecy novels, a projected twelve-volume series that became multimillion bestsellers in the 1990s, offered a fic-tional version of the dispensationalist scenario. Coauthored by Tim LaHaye, a far-right religious activist, and Jerry B. Jenkins of Moody Bible Institute, the se-ries featured the U.N. secretary general as the Antichrist and the U.S. president as his willing dupe. The message of the series reinforced the distrust of gov-ernment already pervasive in late-twentieth-century America: society is de-generate; international organizations and even your own government are sus-pect; the only hope is to withdrew and form survivalist enclaves for the dark days ahead.

The mainstream liberal denominations, meanwhile, hemorrhaged mem-bers in these years. Methodist church membership fell from 9.8 million in 1961 to 8.5 million in 1997. Those who remained were often elderly, while the younger generation turned to dynamic evangelical and charismatic churches that offered extensive programs for children, youth, and families. In their passion for social activism, critics charged, the liberal churches had failed to provide emotional support and spiritual sustenance for their own members, and had paid a high price in consequence. With their ranks thinning, the liberal denominations seemed to lose direction, and their voice on social issues weakened.

In this climate, post-1970 political and cultural activism flourished mostly on the conservative side of American religion. A series of Supreme Court decisions, notably *Engel v. Vitale* (1962), forbidding prayer in the public schools, and *Roe v. Wade* (1973), legalizing abortion, coupled with an increasingly secular and sexualized mass media, convinced many conservative Catholics, evangelical Protestants, and Orthodox Jews that the government and the culture were turning against them. To mobilize these feelings politically, Jerry Falwell of Lynchburg, Virginia, a fundamentalist Baptist and popular TV preacher, founded the Moral Majority in 1979. Energizing evangelical voters for Ronald Reagan in 1980, Falwell was a frequent guest in the Reagan White House. Reagan, in turn, addressed such evangelical groups as the National Association of Evangelicals and the National Association of Religious Broadcasters. It was at the NAE's 1983 meeting in Orlando that Reagan famously characterized the Soviet Union as an "evil empire" and "the focus of evil in the modern world."

Falwell disbanded his Moral Majority in 1989, but it was succeeded by the Christian Coalition, founded by another superstar of religious broadcasting, Pat Robertson. Son of a U.S. senator and a Yale Law School graduate, Robertson experienced a charismatic religious conversion as a youth and went on to a career as a TV evangelist and founder of his own religious network. Under the savvy leadership of young Ralph Reed, the Christian Coalition focused on grass-roots organizing and electing "stealth candidates" to school boards, town councils, and local Republican committees. Through the 1990s, the Christian Coalition—and evangelicals generally—played a major role in Republican party politics and in focusing attention on a wide range of cultural issues, including abortion, pornography, gay rights, "radical feminism," school prayer, home schooling, the teaching of "Creation Science," federal support for religious schools, and sexually suggestive TV shows and pop music. As sociologist Robert Wuthnow noted in *The Restructuring of American Religion* (1988), the formation of pan-denominational "special purpose groups," by both liberals and conservatives was a key trend in postwar American Protestantism.

In another manifestation of this newly aggressive conservative religious activism, the Rev. Paige Patterson of Texas, a prominent Southern Baptist minister and fundamentalist, with his millionaire backer Paul Pressler, organized a systematic and ultimately successful campaign to purge all "liberals" who held leadership roles in the Southern Baptist Convention, served on SBC committees, or taught at Southern Baptist colleges and universities.

In *The Culture of Disbelief* (1993), Yale Law School professor Stephen L. Carter an evangelical, blasted the alleged denigration of religious faith in the public sphere. "The message of contemporary culture," Carter complained, "seems to be that it's perfectly all right to *believe* that stuff, . . . but you really ought to keep it to yourself." Evangelical activism at century's end seemed clearly designed to challenge this alleged cultural conspiracy to relegate conservative religious faith to the private sphere.

These newly mobilized religious energies on behalf of conservative causes mirrored the activism of the Social Gospel leaders early in the century, as they addressed the appalling conditions in urban-industrial America. Although at opposite ends of the political and cultural spectrum, the two groups shared a zeal for translating faith into practice.

Beneath the activism, however, lurked the deep premillennial pessimism about transforming the present social order. By the end of the 1990s, increasing numbers of evangelicals were withdrawing from social engagement and returning to their traditional emphasis on saving souls. Throughout this period, in fact, evangelicals and pentecostalists had never abandoned conversion efforts, planting churches, carrying on their vast media ministries, and dispatching foreign missionaries to Africa, Latin America, and elsewhere.

The American Catholic and Jewish communities faced dilemmas and divisions in these years as well. Conservative Catholics expressed growing dissatisfaction with the liberalizing trends introduced by Pope John XXIII after the historic Second Vatican Council (1962–65). Liberal Catholics, by contrast, viewed Pope John Paul II, the "Polish pope" who took office in 1978, as a bastion of conservatism on a range of issues from abortion and contraception to the celibate priesthood, the ordination of women, and the authority of the papacy. American Catholicism at the end of the century also faced an institutional crisis: as recruitment into the priesthood declined, the church had difficulty staffing its parishes, schools, and social institutions. Exacerbating the problem was a heavy influx of Hispanic immigrants, most of them Catholic. By 2050, demographers predicted, Hispanics would comprise 25 percent of the U.S. population, surpassing African Americans as the nation's largest minority. As the Hispanic population burgeoned, the implications for the Catholic church specifically, and for American religious life more generally, were difficult to calculate.

The tripartite division of American Judaism continued as the century ended: Reform Judaism represented about 30 percent of Jews; Conservative, some 40 percent; and Orthodox, about 10 percent. The remaining 20 percent were nonpracticing or expressed no denominational preference. As in other religious groups, Jews, too, divided on liberal/conservative lines on a range of domestic cultural issues.

The high rate of Jews who married outside the faith raised serious concerns, as leaders feared the gradual erosion of Judaism through assimilation, and debated what to do about it. Before World War I, only 3 percent of Jews married non-Jews. By the 1980s, about one-third of Jews were marrying non-Jews. In Los Angeles and other western cities, the figure approached 40 percent. What Hitler had failed to achieve by violence, the seemingly inexorable processes of assimilation threatened to accomplish peacefully.

American Jews also divided on issues related to Israel, some supporting the hard-line expansionist policy of the Likud party, others backing the Israelis who sought accommodation with their Arab and Palestinian neighbors. Meanwhile, the effort of Israel's powerful Orthodox rabbinate to define who was a Jew stirred dismay and anger in liberal American Jewish circles.

While the traditional "Big Three" of American religion—Protestant, Catholic, Jew—grappled with new social issues and internal conflicts, the overall profile of American religion was shifting as the twentieth century ended. U.S. membership in the Jehovah's Witnesses neared one million by the 1990s, with three and one-half million worldwide. The most successful of America's homegrown religions, the Church of Jesus Christ of Latter Day Saints (Mormons), boasted some five million U.S. members in 1999, and ten million globally.

As the number of Muslims in America grew, Islam was poised by the end of the century to replace Judaism as America's second largest religion, after Christianity. And in the fin-de-siecle religious marketplace, increasing numbers of Americans opted for Buddhism (nearly 800,000 by the later 1990s), other Eastern religions, New Age mysticism, or no religion at all.

Despite religion's continuing strength, the process of secularization (or what historian David Hollinger provocatively calls "cognitive demystification"), especially among intellectuals and academics, was taking its toll as the century ended. Evangelicalism and other forms of conservative religion might show great numerical strength, but among the nation's intellectual elite, cultural leaders, and media masters, it was drastically underrepresented. Stephen Carter's complaints in *The Culture of Disbelief* were not without foundation. In this respect, the change wrought by the passage of a century was profound.

CONCLUSION

Amid all these changes, critics and cultural observers continued to assess and evaluate American religious life. Some, echoing a familiar criticism, faulted its blandness and superficiality, and its easy accommodation to shifts in the secular culture. Others, like Stephen L. Carter, criticized the prevalent social expectation that believers should confine their specific and distinctive religious principles and practices to the private realm, with the public sphere reserved for a benignly affirmative attitude toward "religion" in general.

Yet, as this chapter has suggested, what these critics deplored might also be seen as great strengths. Twentieth-century American religion, ever adaptable, did indeed accommodate itself to shifting social, economic, and cultural realities, all the while maintaining sufficient variety that nearly everyone could find a niche that fit his or her particular world view. In this very process, religion again demonstrated its remarkable hold on the nation, and its striking powers of endurance. Similarly, the public-sphere/private-sphere distinction, while perhaps diminishing religion's voice in public discourse, may also at the same time have diluted religion's divisive potential—so painfully evident elsewhere in the world—while maximizing its role as a force for social cohesion.

The criticism of religion's superficiality and lack of public impact also perhaps gave insufficient attention to those moments in the twentieth century when religious belief did in fact play a highly influential role in the public arena. Whether from the liberal or the conservative side, these upsurges of activism constitute an important if episodic part of the story.

For all the criticism, cautionary notes, and premature obituaries, American religious life remained vital and pervasive as the twentieth century ended, its capacity for adaptation and self-renewal seemingly undiminished. In 2000, as in 1900, religion in the United States continued to exhibit the kaleidoscopic diversity, quicksilver adaptability, and complex symbiotic relationship with the larger culture that both helped to ensure its survival and to make it so maddeningly elusive for scholars attempting to pin it down and analyze it.

BIBLIOGRAPHY

Useful surveys include Sydney E. Ahlstrom, *A Religious History of the American People* (New Haven, Conn.: Yale University Press, 1972), pts. VII–IX; Winthrop S. Hudson and John Corrigan, *Religion in America,* 6th ed. (Upper Saddle River, N.J.: Prentice-Hall, 1999), pts. III–IV; Charles H. Lippy and Peter W. Williams, eds., *Encyclopedia of the American Religious Experience* (New York: Scribner, 1988); Charles H. Lippy, ed., *Twentieth-Century Shapers of American Popular Religion* (New York: Greenwood Press, 1989); Michael J. Lacey, ed., *Religion & Twentieth Century American Intellectual Life* (New York: Cambridge University Press, 1989); Richard W. Fox, "Experience and Explanation in Twentieth-Century American Religious History," in Harry S. Stout and D. G. Hart, eds., *New Directions in American Religious History* (New York: Oxford University Press, 1997); R. Laurence Moore, *Religious Outsiders and the Making of Americans* (New York: Oxford University Press, 1986) and *Selling God: American Religion in the Marketplace of Culture* (New York: Oxford University Press, 1994).

On Roman Catholic, Jewish, Mormon, Christian Science, and Jehovah's Witness history, see James J. Hennesey, *American Catholics* (New York: Oxford University Press, 1981); Jay P. Dolan, *The American Catholic Experience: A History from Colonial Times to the Present* (Garden City, N.Y.: Doubleday, 1985); Jacob Neusner, *American Judaism* (Englewood Cliffs, N.J.: Prentice-Hall, 1972); Jan Shipps, *Mormonism: The Story of a New Religious Tradition* (Urbana: University of Illinois Press, 1985); Stephen Gottschalk, *The Emergence of Christian Science in American Religious Life* (Berkeley: University of California Press, 1973); and J. J. Penton, *Apocalypse Delayed: The Story of Jehovah's Witnesses* (Toronto: University of Toronto Press, 1985). On Islam, see Yvonne Yazbek Haddad and Adair T. Lummis, *Islamic Values in the United States: A Comparative Study* (New York: Oxford University Press, 1987).

On new religious movements, Jacob Needleman and George Baker, eds., *Understanding the New Religions* (New York: Seabury Press, 1978); R. S. Ellwood, *Alternative Altars: Unconventional and Eastern Spirituality in America* (Chicago: University of Chicago Press, 1979); and Catherine L. Albanese, *Nature Religion in America* (Chicago: University of Chicago Press, 1990).

Useful collections of primary documents include William R. Miller, ed., *Contemporary American Protestant Thought, 1900–1970* (Indianapolis: Bobbs-Merrill, 1973) and Aaron I. Abell, ed., *American Catholic Thought on Social Questions* (Indianapolis: Bobbs-Merrill, 1968).

Biographical studies include Robert Moats Miller, *Harry Emerson Fosdick: Preacher, Pastor, Prophet* (New York: Oxford University Press, 1985); Richard Fox, *Reinhold Niebuhr* (New York: Pantheon, 1985); Edith Blumhofer, *Aimee Semple McPherson: Everybody's Sister* (Grand Rapids, Mich.: Eerdman's, 1993); Carol George, *God's Salesman: Norman Vincent Peale and the Power of Positive Thinking* (New York: Oxford University Press, 1993); William Martin, *A Prophet with Honor: The Billy Graham Story* (New York: William Morrow, 1992); and James H. Cone, *Martin and Malcolm and America* (Maryknoll, N.Y.: Orbis Books, 1991), on Martin Luther King, Jr.

Studies of specific time periods and movements include George Marsden, *Fundamentalism and American Culture: The Shaping of Twentieth Century Evangelicalism, 1870–1925* (New York: Oxford University Press, 1980); William R. Hutchison, *The Modernist Impulse in American Protestantism* (Cambridge, Mass.: Harvard University Press, 1976); Robert D. Cross, *The Emergence of Liberal Catholicism in America* (Cambridge, Mass.: Harvard University Press, 1958); Edward J. Larson, *Summer for the Gods: The Scopes Trial and America's Continuing Debate over Science and Religion* (New York: Basic Books, 1997); Paul A. Carter, "In God Some of Us Trusted," chap. 3 in *Another Part of the Twenties* (New York: Columbia University Press, 1977); Horace C. Boyer, *How Sweet the Sound: The Golden Age of Gospel* (Washington, D.C.: Elliot & Clark, 1995); Robert Weisbrot, *Father Divine and the Struggle for Racial Equality* (Urbana: University of Illinois Press, 1983); Martin E. Marty, *Under God, Indivisible, 1941–1960*, vol. 3 of *Modern American Religion* (Chicago: University of Chicago Press, 1996); Robert Wuthnow, *The Restructuring of American Religion: Society and Faith since World War II* (Princeton, N.J.: Princeton University Press, 1988); James Hudnut-Beumler, *Looking for God in the Suburbs: The Religion of the American Dream and Its Critics, 1945–1965* (New Brunswick, N.J.: Rutgers University Press, 1994); Patrick Allitt, *Catholic Intellectuals and Conservative Politics in America, 1950–1985* (Ithaca, N.Y.: Cornell University Press, 1993); Robert C. Liebman and Robert Wuthnow, eds., *The New Christian Right* (Hawthorne, N.Y.: Aldine, 1983); Paul Boyer, *When Time Shall Be No More: Prophecy Belief in Modern American Culture* (Cambridge, Mass.: Belknap Press of Harvard University Press, 1992); Robert Booth Fowler, *The Greening of Protestant Thought* (Chapel Hill: University of North Carolina Press, 1995); and Rosemary Radford Reuther and Eleanor McLoughlin, eds., *Women and Religion in America: A Documentary History* (San Francisco: Harper & Row, 1985).

Interpretive studies include Mark A. Noll, *The Scandal of the Evangelical Mind* (Grand Rapids, Mich.: Eerdmans, 1994); Mark A. Noll, ed., "The Modern Period," pt. 3 of *Religion and American Politics* (New York: Oxford University Press, 1990); William R. Hutchison, ed., *Between the Times: The Travail of the Protestant Establishment in America, 1900–1960* (New York: Cambridge University Press, 1989); and James D. Hunter, *American Evangelicalism: Conservative Religion and the Quandry of Modernity* (New Brunswick, N.J.: Rutgers University Press, 1983).

13 | IMMIGRATION AND ETHNICITY IN THE AMERICAN CENTURY

GARY GERSTLE

Any reckoning with the role of immigration and ethnicity in the American century ought to begin with some statistical measures. America in 1900 had a population of approximately 76 million. Into this society, in the years between 1880 and 1920, came about 24 million immigrants, a majority of whom arrived between 1900 and 1914. By 1914, a full third of Americans were either immigrants themselves or living in households with at least one immigrant parent. This calculation implies that immigrants were evenly distributed throughout the country, which of course they were not. Relatively few immigrants went to the South or the interior West. They concentrated themselves in urban and industrial areas in the northeast quadrant of the country (from the Mississippi River east and the Ohio River north) and on the West Coast. A true measure of their demographic weight in those areas can be gleaned from census reports on the ethnic composition of specific cities. The following figures are from the 1920 census, and they combine the first and second generations—the immigrants themselves and their children who were born in America: In Boston, New York, Chicago, and Milwaukee, they accounted for more than 70 percent of the total population; in Buffalo, Cleveland, Detroit, Minneapolis, and San Francisco, more than 60 percent; and in Philadelphia, Pittsburgh, and Seattle, more than 50 percent. A large majority of these immigrants, approximately 75 percent, were from Europe and increasingly from southern and eastern Europe. On the eve of World War I, Germans were still the single largest immigrant group, but their numbers along with those from Ireland and other countries from northwest Europe were being eclipsed by the cumulative weight of three to four million Italians, two million Russian and Polish Jews, two million Hungarians, approximately four million Slavs, and one million Lithuanians, Greeks, and Portuguese. Some states received significant numbers of non-European immigrants—Chinese, Japanese, and Filipinos in California; Mexicans in California and the Southwest; and French

Canadians in New England—whose presence profoundly affected regional economies, politics, and culture.

A social phenomenon of this magnitude is bound to generate a mythology about the role of immigrants in the making of the American nation, and in this case it did. By mythology I do not mean views that are necessarily false, but rather views so powerful and so embedded in the national imagination that they come to have a life independent of actual experience; or, to put it another way, the myths themselves become a constitutive part of experience. The mythology that enveloped these immigrants from Europe is one familiar to us all. It portrays America as a land of freedom—religious, political, and economic. Here an immigrant could either practice his or her faith in ways denied in intolerant Europe or abandon religious faith altogether in favor of a "modern," secular existence; here, an immigrant obeying the laws could quickly gain full citizenship rights and enjoy the political and social benefits that such rights conferred; here, economic opportunities abounded for anyone willing to work hard and show some pluck and adventuresomeness. Here a person could take charge of his or her own destiny. In some versions of this mythology, control over one's destiny was thought to endow an individual with extraordinary freedom, either to cultivate a religious, ethnic, or regional culture that authorities in Europe had repressed or to construct a radically new way of living. But in the dominant versions of the mythology, it was expected that immigrants, once they breathed the intoxicating air of freedom in America, would choose to build new lives and become new men and new women. This mythology took shape long before the immigrants of the late nineteenth and early twentieth centuries arrived. The French-American farmer, Hector St. John de Crevecoeur, expressed it powerfully in his eighteenth-century musings on the American as a "new man" who had left "behind him all ancient prejudices and manners." And it received a powerful boost in the late nineteenth century with the placement of the Statue of Liberty in New York harbor. Surely, there were few more resonant symbols of freedom anywhere in the world. Boatloads of weary and anxious Europeans, the "huddled masses" of Emma Lazarus's imagination, raised their eyes—their first act in this new land of freedom—to gaze upon this monument to liberty.

And there was a great deal of freedom to be gained and enjoyed in America. For much of the nineteenth century, the United States was remarkably open to immigrants, accepting virtually anyone from any part of the globe as long as they were able to reach our shores. A steady procession of groups found in America refuge from political or religious oppression: the Puritans and Quakers in the seventeenth century, the Mennonites in the eighteenth, the German '48ers in the nineteenth, and Russian Jewry in the early twentieth. The mythology of American freedom had often penetrated the imaginations of these and other groups before they had left homelands, becoming a factor in their decision to emigrate. Eastern European Jews spoke of America in the years before Zionism became strong as the Promised Land, or as the *Goldene Medina*, the "golden land"; prospective Chinese immigrants talked excitedly among themselves about America as the *Gam Saan*, or "Gold Mountain." "To these hopeful migrants," Ronald Takaki writes, "America possessed an alluring boundlessness." And many of those who were here (though few Chinese, as we shall soon see) enjoyed an exceptional freedom, which they used to practice their faith as they wished, or to make money and rise in the social order, or to reinvent themselves with new names, new occupations. One poor group of German-Jewish immigrants who arrived in the mid-nineteenth century built a glamorous (and lucrative) New York City empire of department stores by century's end; Amadeo P. Giannini, the son of Italian immigrants, parlayed his savings from a San Francisco fruit and vegetable stand into the Bank of America, at one point the nation's largest financial institution. Japanese immigrant farmers, specializing in fresh vegetables and fruits, generated one-tenth of California's agricultural revenue by 1919. President John F. Kennedy's grandfathers, meanwhile, themselves the children of penniless Irish immigrants, gained wealth and fame as powerful politicians in early-twentieth-century Boston. We could fill many pages with similar stories of poor immigrants who "made it"—and remade themselves—in America.

But, of course, this mythology, as do all mythologies, clouds as much as it reveals. Thanks to an extraordinary body of work produced by scholars of immigration and ethnicity since the 1960s, we now have a keen sense, in ways we did not before that time, of the many ways in which the actual experience of immigrants differed from the mythology that surrounds them. In virtually all periods of American history, we now know, a majority of immigrants were looking for work, not for a political or religious refuge. When the American economy was booming, they came; when it plunged into one of its many recessions, they stayed away. Many treated America as a place of sojourn, not as a place to make one's home. These sojourners were not primarily interested in making themselves over into new men or women; rather they wanted to save enough money to return home and buy land in their native villages and gain stature in their local societies. Among some groups, rates of repatriation were remarkably high: 50 percent among Chinese in the mid-nineteenth century and 50 percent among Italians in the early twentieth century; as high as 80 percent among early-twentieth-century Balkan immigrants. Not everyone went home, of course; and among those who did, many would fail to achieve their dreams and would return a second or third time to the United States.

Most, after all, had not made fortunes in this country. The vast majorities had been unskilled or semiskilled workers laboring long hours for low wages. In the first decade of the twentieth century, immigrant men and their male children constituted 70 percent of the work force in fifteen of the nineteen leading U.S. industries. Their concentration was highest in industries where work was the most backbreaking. Immigrants built the nation's railroads and tunnels; mined its coal, iron ore, and other minerals; stoked its hot and some-times deadly steel furnaces; and slaughtered and packed its meat in Chicago's putrid packinghouses. In 1909, first- and second-generation immigrants—es-pecially Greeks, Italians, Japanese, and Mexicans—comprised 96 percent of the force that built and maintained the country's railroads. Of the 750,000 Slo-vaks who arrived in America before 1913, at least 600,000 headed for the coal mines and steel mills of western Pennsylvania.

Immigrants also performed "lighter" but no less arduous work. Jewish and Italian men and women predominated in the garment manufacturing shops of New York City, Chicago, Philadelphia, Baltimore, and Boston. In 1900, French-Canadian immigrants and their children held one of every two jobs in New Eng-land's cotton textile industry. By 1920, the prosperity of California's rapidly growing agricultural industry depended primarily on Mexican and Filipino labor. In these industries, immigrant women and children, who worked for lower wages than men, formed a large part of the labor force. Few states re-stricted child labor. More than 25 percent of boys and 10 percent of girls aged 10 to 15 were "gainfully employed."

A fortunate minority within this vast immigrant labor force rose into the ranks of skilled laborers, where they were able to earn wages greater than what they would have earned in Europe. But skilled work was beyond the reach of most immigrants, who remained mired in poverty. Most working families re-quired two or three wage earners to survive. Strained economic circumstances confined immigrant families to cramped and dilapidated living quarters. Many of them lived in two- or three-room apartments, with several sleeping in each room. The lack of windows allowed little light or air into these apartments, and few had their own toilets or running water. The population density of New York City's Lower East Side—the principal area of settlement for Jewish im-migrants there—reached seven hundred per acre in 1900, a density greater than that of the poorest sections of Bombay, India. Overcrowding and poor sanitation resulted in high rates of deadly infectious diseases, especially diph-theria, typhoid fever, and pneumonia.

The American dream did not grip many of the immigrants who lived in these districts, either because they still clung to their hope of returning home or because their own living circumstances belied the myth that America re-warded those willing to work hard. Many immigrants, as a result, were disin-clined to take up American ways, and some openly defied Americanization processes. This defiance took many forms—refusing to learn English or to send children to public, Americanizing schools; resisting an "American" work ethic imposed by hard-driving employers; obstructing the efforts of American-born social workers who, in the name of an "American" standard of hygiene, placed immigrant households under moral surveillance; celebrating one's Old World religion and culture, even when they conflicted with American religious and cultural practices; and embracing a socialist or anarchist ideology that depicted

America as Mammon, so given over to the worship of money and the exploitation of labor that nothing short of a revolution could achieve a just society.

To visit America during the years of peak immigration, then, was to enter a multicultural land, its cities in particular home to a dizzying array of peoples, cultures, and ideologies. This brazen "foreignness," in turn, provoked anger among the native born, leading to recurrent outbursts of nativism—an ideology that called on America to rid itself of aliens and restore power and authority to long-settled natives: not Indians, of course, but those who variously called themselves Protestant, British, Yankee, Know-Nothing, Anglo-Saxon, Nordic, the White Knights of the Ku Klux Klan, or just plain American or white. Many of these outbursts turned ugly, culminating in riots through foreign-born districts; the torching of immigrant churches and schools; the elaboration of frankly, and sometimes vicious, racist ideologies; and the implementation of punitive anti-immigrant legislation. The targets of the nativists varied across time and place. In the nineteenth century, they were Irish-Catholic immigrants, depicted both as a subhuman species unfit for habitation in America and as clever servants of the pope who had been sent to deny Americans their Protestant destiny. By the early twentieth century, nativist attention had shifted to the immigrants from eastern and southern Europe; the animus against Catholicism remained strong, now augmented by a vigorous anti-Semitism deployed against Russian Jews. The racial stigmatization of immigrant groups, meanwhile, had intensified, and the Italians and Jews, in particular, were seen to be carriers of anarchism, socialism, and other dangerous European ideologies.

Non-European immigrants were subject to some of the worst abuse. In 1790, the first Congress had passed a law restricting naturalization to immigrants who were free and white; this law meant that Asian and black immigrants could not become American citizens. While this law was amended in 1870 to exempt black immigrants from its provisions, the prohibition against Asian naturalization remained on the books and was enforced (with only a few exceptions here and there) until 1952. The Supreme Court resoundingly affirmed its constitutionality in 1922 and 1923. Here was powerful testimony to how much America wanted to be a European or white nation—a wish that rarely appears in the mythology described earlier.

We cannot dismiss these antiforeign impulses as a residue from an earlier time, when a young America was still trying to shake off its Old World origins, including, perhaps, a lingering desire for religious, racial, or national uniformity. Antiforeign impulses, ideologies, and legislation intensified as America approached and then crossed the threshold into its twentieth-century modernity. The first big blow came in 1882 in the form of Chinese exclusion. A total of 300,000 Chinese immigrants had come to America between 1850 and 1880, and this number would probably have grown to several million by the second decade of the twentieth century had the stream not been dammed. Imagine how different America would have been in the twentieth century had the Chinese been allowed to take their place alongside the Germans, the Irish, the Italians, and the Jews as one of the nation's largest immigrant groups. But it was precisely this prospect of "Orientals" overrunning America that prompted Congress to pass a Chinese exclusion law and to keep it in place until 1943.

This law marked the beginning of a period of immigration restriction that gathered steam in the early years of the twentieth century, climaxed in the 1924 Immigration Restriction Act, and profoundly shaped American society—immigrants and nonimmigrants alike—through the 1960s. The 1924 act was stunningly successful, reducing annual immigration from outside the Western Hemisphere from approximately 1 million a year to 150,000, an 85-percent drop. The law affected southern and eastern European immigrants even more dramatically, as their annual arrivals fell from 750,000 (the annual prewar average) to a mere 18,500, a 97-percent decrease. The legislation effectively stopped the immigration of Italians and Jews, seen as two of the most racially objectionable and politically dangerous immigrant streams. While the barriers against Asian immigration hardly needed reinforcing, they were, as the law declared that any immigrant ineligible for naturalization was heretofore barred from entering the United States. Japan, in particular, regarded this provision as a humiliation; in domestic politics there, this American law weakened the influence of Western-oriented liberals and strengthened the hand of anti-Western and imperial-minded militarists. In such ways did the 1924 act push America and Japan down the road to war.

Increased Mexican immigration partially offset the loss of Europeans; bowing to pressure from agribusiness interests in the Southwest, Congress had refused to place a ceiling on immigration from Mexico or anywhere else in the Western Hemisphere. But the Mexican stream proved susceptible to administrative control, as government officials demonstrated in the 1930s when they forced 500,000 Mexican immigrants to return home, and again in the 1940s through a tightly controlled system of contract labor known as the "Bracero" program. The 1924 law, in combination with other measures, then, dramatically reduced the ability of foreigners to enter and to remain in America.

The movement for immigration restriction drew on several impulses. One was a Progressive desire to inject more rationality and order into the processes of receiving and Americanizing immigrants, processes that had reached such volume and unpredictability that they seemed to threaten the very integrity of the American nation. This desire manifested itself in the establishment of a federal Bureau of Immigration and related governmental institutions endowed with the power to supervise the arrival of immigrants, to identify certain groups of diseased, pauperized, and morally or politically questionable immigrants as unacceptable imports (and to deport them), and to set up passport and visa systems in foreign lands to control the immigrant flow at its point of origin. A second impulse driving immigration restriction was the belief that immigrants had made the labor force too large and that wages and social mobility for American workers had suffered accordingly. Initially, this argument emerged most forcefully from the labor movement itself but, by the 1920s, corporations agreed that it was time for the massive influx of foreign labor to end.

A third impulse was racial: a concern that immigration was undermining the high quality of American "stock" by filling up the United States with races of lower intelligence, little capacity for self-government, and no discernible moral restraint. These immigrants were, in the eyes of the restrictionists, drinking too much, mixing promiscuously with other races (thus threatening America with mongrelization), and reproducing at unacceptably high rates. Racial concerns emerged first in connection with the Chinese and then the Japanese. But, in a move that many of us might regard as surprising, they had spread by the 1920s to immigrants from southern and eastern Europe. This is how one restrictionist congressman, Fred S. Purnell of Indiana, described the threat of eastern European Jews, Italians, Poles, and Greeks in the 1920s. "There is little or no similarity," Purnell declared, "between the clear-thinking, self-governing stocks that sired the American people and this stream of irresponsible and broken wreckage that is pouring into the lifeblood of America the social and political diseases of the Old World." On the floor of the House, Purnell quoted approvingly the words of a Dr. Ward, who claimed that Americans deceived themselves into believing that "we could change inferior beings into superior ones." Americans could not escape the laws of heredity, Ward argued. "We can not make a heavy horse into a trotter by keeping him in a racing stable. We can not make a well-bred dog out of a mongrel by teaching him tricks." The acts that Ward dismissed as "tricks" included the learning by immigrants of the Gettysburg Address and the Declaration of Independence.

Congressman J. Will Taylor of Tennessee, meanwhile, approvingly read to his colleagues a 1924 *Boston Herald* editorial warning that America was entering the same period of eugenic decline that had doomed Rome:

> Rome had [mistaken] faith in the melting pot, as we have. It scorned the iron certainties of heredity, as we do. It lost its instinct for race preservation, as we have lost ours. It flooded itself with whatever people offered themselves from everywhere, as we have done. It forgot that men must be selected and bred as sacredly as cows and pigs and sheep, as we have not learned.

"Rome rapidly senilized and died," the editorial concluded, and so would the United States unless Congress took note of hereditarian principles and passed the 1924 restriction legislation.

Overwhelming numbers of congressmen and senators voted for this legislation. Many of them were not eugenicists, at least not in the extreme way of a Purnell or Taylor. Nonracial impulses motivated a significant number, who wanted to inject more order into immigrant processes, or who hoped to curtail the labor supply in the interests of raising the wages of American workers, or who desired to control the immigrant population at a time when a vast state-sponsored Americanization program seemed too dangerous an undertaking. But very few were free of racialist thinking altogether. This was true even of a small, hardy band of liberal congressmen from midwestern and northeastern cities—Chicago, Detroit, New York, Providence—with heavily immigrant constituencies. Bravely they opposed the 1924 act and the racialist ideology it embodied. Led by Adoph Sabath of Chicago and Samuel Dickstein of New York, these congressmen mounted an eloquent defense of America's civic nationalist tradition, holding forth even after the act's passage had become a fait accompli. Thus, one of their band denounced the 1924 bill as "the worst kind of discrimination against a large class of individuals and absolutely opposed to our American ideas of equality and justice." Another declared that the stigmatization of certain European races as inferior would render his America unrecognizable: "This is not the America I belong to. That is not the America that I was brought up to love and worship. That is not the America that I want to be a part of."

But when discussion in the House shifted from European to Japanese immigrants, who were also to be excluded by the 1924 act, these liberals changed their tune. Sabath declared that he, Dickstein, and others were "all in favor of exclusion of the Japanese." Dickstein, himself, made the same point in dramatic fashion, interrupting an anti-Japanese tirade by a California congressman to "make it clear" that he shared the Californian's point of view. Only Fiorello LaGuardia showed some sympathy for Japanese plight, but Sabath was quick to cut him off and shut him up. Young and inexperienced, LaGuardia did not challenge Sabath's gag order.

Why did they do it? Sabath, Dickstein, and others evidently grasped how much a campaign against the Japanese might benefit immigrants from southern and eastern Europe. Whenever talk focused on the Japanese, the racial standing of the southern and eastern Europeans seemed to rise. The latter were no longer racially despised peoples, but simply Europeans, racially and culturally indistinguishable from the Germans, English, and Scandinavians. The designation of the Japanese and, by extension, all "yellow" people as the racial other had magically fused all Europeans into members of a single superior race. The eastern and southern Europeans no longer had to listen to charges that they were racially degenerate, mongrelized, and unassimilable. Denigrating the Japanese elevated the new immigrants and allowed them to claim identities that at least some of their leaders desperately wanted—as Americans, white Americans, Caucasians. When they saw how America's fondness for racial distinctions might benefit their people, Sabath, Dickstein, and their supporters made the fateful decision to play America's racial game.

The immigration act and the racial ideologies it embodied profoundly influenced immigrants, ethnics, and American society for forty years. Most obviously, the act dramatically reduced the number of immigrants; within twenty years, America had ceased to be an immigrant society. The act shrank to insignificance the number of unwanted immigrants from eastern and southern Europe and from Japan. The annual quotas for eastern and southern Europeans degreed by the 1924 legislation were ridiculously small: 5,982 for Poles, 3,845 for Italians, 2,248 for Russians, 473 for Hungarians, and so on.

For immigrants already in America, the 1924 act, over the long term, exercised at least three kinds of influence. First, it intensified pressures to Americanize. Some of this pressure arose from demographic change. As the number of immigrants declined, so did knowledge of and access to Old World cultures. Meanwhile, within ethnic communities, a second generation more at home in the United States began emerging into leadership positions. But this pressure was more than demographic; it arose, too, from the stigma that had become attached to foreignness and the desire of immigrants and their children to hide markers of their ethnic identity, at least from public view. Numerous such markers lost their visibility in the two decades following immigration restriction. The number of foreign-language publications and Catholic national parishes plummeted; so, too, did the volume of conversations being conducted in some language other than English. If a group's Old World language survived into the second generation, by the third it was mostly gone. Cultural movements that today we would call multicultural—movements that insist on maintaining the integrity of particularist ethnic cultures even at the cost of keeping one's American identity or loyalty weak—went into eclipse.

During this time, many immigrants, from Hollywood stars seeking nationwide celebrity to Communists intent on revolution, Americanized their names. In Hollywood, Mladen Seklovich transformed himself into Karl Malden and Margarita Carmen Cansino reinvented herself as Rita Hayworth; Muni Weisenfreund became Paul Muni; Lucille Le Sueur became Joan Crawford and Julius Garfinkle became John Garfield; Bernie Schwartz metamorphosed into Tony Curtis while the jazz band leader Arthur Arshawsky converted himself to Artie Shaw. The Communist revolutionaries Stephanos Mesaros and Avro Halberg recreated themselves as Steve Nelson and Gus Hall, respectively, while their comrades Itzhak Granich and Saul Regenstreif became Mike Gold and Johnny Gates.

Hollywood filmmakers, meanwhile, many of them of eastern and southern European origin, were reluctant to reveal anything about their own ethnic identity in their movies. Thus, the Italian-born Frank Capra, arguably the most successful of the 1930s film directors, always cast Anglo-Saxon types—most notably Gary Cooper and Jimmy Stewart—as the virtuous men who, in his populist parables, stood up for the people against the vested interests and the cynics. Even for a scene in *Mr. Deeds Goes to Town*, a 1936 movie set in New York City, Capra chose to fill an unemployment line with farmers from the Midwest rather than the Italian and Jewish workers who, in real life, would have been the ones on New York City relief rolls. Exactly why Capra's midwest farmers went to New York City for unemployment relief and how they got there were details that didn't seem to trouble Capra or any of the reviewers who loved this film. But they are details that should, if not trouble us, then at least catch our attention, for they signify a deep impulse on Capra's part to keep his own people, and thus his own identity, off the silver screen.

The second broad influence exercised by immigration restriction was indirect but no less significant: it made eastern and southern Europeans determined to increase their political influence in American society. As powerful as immigration restriction was as a tool in the hands of conservatives and eugenicists, it suffered from a crucial weakness. It could do nothing to stop the European immigrants who were already here from asserting their rights as Americans and pursuing political power. And this they began to do, often with a fury and dedication that took their opponents by surprise. Eastern and southern European immigrants started naturalizing and then voting in large numbers, making their voices count in politics, first in local elections and then in state and national ones. The 1928 Democratic nominee for the presidency, the Irish-Catholic governor of New York Alfred Smith, was their candidate, and Franklin D. Roosevelt was their president. These same ethnic Americans also played a crucial role in the labor movement and especially in the Congress of Industrial Organizations, the upstart labor federation founded in 1935 (for more on the CIO, see chapter 5 in this volume). The political mobilization that gathered in immigrant districts in the late 1920s and then allied itself with labor's resurgence in the 1930s was an extraordinary development, and it helped to secure the ascendancy of a liberal Democratic party for almost forty years. A liberal and egalitarian nationalism held this mobilization together, celebrating an America in which the rich did not live at the expense of the poor and in which religious or racial prejudice was not tolerated. World War II further strengthened this liberal nationalism and bolstered the claim of European immigrants and ethnics that America belonged to them as much as to anyone else. The Americanizing ethnics who participated in these movements came to believe that they not only had altered themselves but had also changed the America that the restrictionists had bequeathed to them. In some very important ways they had. Through their support for the New Deal, they had impressed on America the need for the government to mitigate the effects of untrammeled market capitalism, to contain disparities between the rich and the poor, and to care for those unable to help themselves. And through their enthusiastic support for the war against Hitler they forced a serious reexamination of racist ideologies abroad and at home. By 1945, a revulsion against religious and racial discrimination had spread to large sectors of the American population, as did a desire to identify and eradicate all prejudice.

For all these reasons, many ethnic Americans came to regard this New Deal era of the 1930s and 1940s, of depression and war, not only as a time of suffering and sacrifice but also as an era of advance. The prosperity of the postwar years strengthened this conviction, as it put economic security, if not affluence, within their reach. This was the America that millions of European ethnic Americans eagerly embraced; this was the America that made Frank Capra a wealthy and famous man and engendered in him a lifelong love for his adopted land. These years, in other words, gave the mythology of America as a land of freedom and opportunity a great boost.

But, once again, to focus only on the mythology is to miss an important part of the story: of European ethnics not only becoming American but also becoming white and increasing their social distance from nonwhites. These Europeans ethnics were settling into a society still encoding its racialized notions into law and culture. We have already seen how the 1920s' Supreme Court upheld the 1790 law barring the naturalization of nonwhite immigrants and how the 1924 Congress passed into law a racialized program of immigration restriction. The 1920s were also a time when many state governments strengthened their laws against miscenegation. Virginia, for example, passed a law in 1924 prohibiting a white from marrying a black, Asian, American Indian, or "Malay." At the same time, it changed the definition of who counted as a black person from anyone who was at least one-sixteenth black to any individual possessing at least one black ancestor, no matter how remote. This statute stayed on the books until 1967. The liberal and labor movements of the 1930s and 1940s attacked aspects of the American racial order, protesting discrimination against racial minorities and insisting that they be given their full rights as Americans. But it is also true that numerous labor organizations and New Deal agencies reinscribed racism into their practices, if not their ideals. Many labor unions deferred to the wishes of their white majority, which did not want to see blacks—even those who were union members—gain access to "their" jobs. New Deal housing agencies, meanwhile, endorsed racialized real estate practices in northern cities; that meant giving racially mixed neighborhoods (as well as homogeneous black ones) low "grades," thereby denying people in those neighborhoods access to treasured federal loans, lowering the value of their property, and encouraging the white homeowners among them to flee to racially pure and high-value neighborhoods. And in World War II, as America was fighting a war to rid the world of racial prejudice, the government placed the West Coast Japanese-American population (110,000 people) into prison camps and constructed an army that not only segregated blacks from whites but, by and large, refused to let the "inferior" black servicemen fight. Virtually no black soldiers participated in the initial D-Day assaults on the Normandy beaches on June 6, 1944, a fact accurately reproduced by Steven Spielberg in his celebrated 1998 film, *Saving Private Ryan*. But there were hundreds of thousands of black servicemen stationed in Great Britain, many of them restive because the army had confined them to the "domestic" chores of building roads, ferrying supplies, and preparing meals for the white soldiers on the frontlines.

When we tell this story, we like to frame it in terms of racism's last stand; by the early 1950s, this tale goes, racism had been thoroughly delegitimized, its supporters outside the South, if they survived at all, driven underground. And, indeed, much evidence supports this view. The barriers against Asian immigration and naturalization began to fall in the 1940s and early 1950s, Truman desegregated the armed forces in 1948, and the Supreme Court rendered Jim Crow unconstitutional in 1954. But to tell the story in this way is to misrepresent the experience of the 1930s and 1940s, or, at least, to read too much of the future into the past. For if we recognize that the period from the mid-1920s to the mid-1940s were the critical years of European ethnic Americanization, then we can plausibly argue that the pressures working for racialization were as powerful as those working against it. In other words, as the civil rights movement was gathering steam in these years, America's commitment to a racialized society was being reinvigorated. Both processes unfolded simultaneously, and both shaped the Americanization experience. In this context, the European ethnics learned to value not only America's commitment to freedom but also America's commitment to whiteness. And this double education helps to explain what happened in numerous ethnic districts in northern cities in the postwar years, as residents there greeted African-American efforts to move into their neighborhoods with furious and often violent resistance. These European ethnics, as Tom Sugrue, Arnold Hirsch, and others have shown, had acquired whiteness and were determined to enjoy its privileges.

The persistence of this racialized sense of America is what makes the peak years of the civil rights movement, 1963 to 1968, a revolutionary moment in American society. While the movement could not eradicate entrenched racist attitudes overnight, it did tear down the legal edifice on which those attitudes had long depended. The Civil Rights Act of 1964 outlawed racial discrimination in all public and many private institutions. The Voting Rights Act of 1965 undermined the byzantine web of laws and practices that southern states had used for sixty years to keep blacks in those states from getting to the polls. The antiracist energy and idealism of the movement made itself felt, too, in immigration. The Immigration Act of 1965 finally overturned the odious 1924 law, erasing the remaining barriers against Asian immigrants and eliminating altogether the system of quotas based on national origins. No longer did American immigration law presume that certain races or nationalities were more desireable than others.

Although the 1965 Immigration Act did not reestablish the open immigration system that had prevailed through much of the nineteenth century, it did double the annual ceiling on total immigrants (from 150,000 to 300,000). Moreover, the law's generous provision for family reunification would eventually allow several hundred thousand more immigrants to enter a year. The law did introduce one significantly new method of restriction by imposing a ceiling—120,000 a year—on the number of immigrants from the

Western Hemisphere. This ceiling would intensify the problem of illegal immigration in the 1970s and 1980s, and increase suspicions of those groups, especially Mexicans and other Latinos, identified as the main sources of the illegal stream.

At least two other important changes affecting immigrants occurred in the 1960s. First, the civil rights revolution swept away the large body of state laws prohibiting individuals classified as white from marrying those classified as Negro or colored. The Supreme Court delivered the critical blow in 1967, declaring Virginia's 1924 law to be "so directly subversive of the principle of equality" that it was unconstitutional. States could no longer prevent Americans from crossing the color line for purposes of marriage. It took some time for this legal change to work its way through the culture, but by the 1980s and 1990s, the number of racial intermarriages had risen dramatically.

The other change occurred as much in culture as it did in law. Until 1965, the civil rights movement had strengthened the mythology of America, its adherents believing that the racist realities of American society could yet be overturned through mobilization around American ideals of freedom, equality, and opportunity. No figure more fully articulated and embraced these ideals than Martin Luther King, Jr., who, in an address to several hundred thousand protesters who had marched on Washington for "jobs and freedom" in August 1963, described how the Declaration of Independence still allowed him to dream that his "four little children will one day live in a nation where they will not be judged by the color of their skin but the content of their character." But the vicious racism that civil rights workers encountered in the South had worn down their belief in King's dream; their trust in the federal government had also weakened as the FBI and other federal institutions seemed reluctant to ferret out and punish the South's Negro-haters. Then the violent protests of the black poor in northern cities, beginning with the Watts riot in 1965 and culminating in the devastating crescendo of violent protest that ripped across urban America in 1967 and 1968, focused attention on patterns of institutional racism that had long shaped housing, employment, and school practices in the urban North and West. An increasingly unpopular war in Vietnam further challenged the notion that the United States stood for freedom and equality.

As a result of these developments, growing numbers of Americans began depicting their society as one compromised by racism, inequality, and empire. The resurgence of black nationalism, first under the leadership of Malcolm X and then of secular black militants such as Stokely Carmichael, H. Rap Brown, and the Black Panther Bobby Seale, signified this anti-American turn. A wide variety of groups, from white and Latino radicals who celebrated the Black Panthers to white ethnics who loathed them, emulated the cultural style of black power. Encapsulated in the magnetic phrase, "Black is beautiful," this style demonstrated how any group that had been marked as different and as marginal could shake off nagging feelings of inferiority and celebrate its particular identity or inheritance. Groups transfixed by the cultural assertiveness of black nationalists began to question the desirability of assimilation, preferring to tally up its costs. By the 1970s and 1980s a new ideology, multiculturalism, had arisen as an alternative to assimilation. It called on groups to invest their hopes and dreams in some identity—racial, ethnic, sexual—other than the now discredited nation.

While this ideology was strongest among the groups that had suffered most from discrimination, it also gained influence among those, such as the descendants of eastern and southern Europeans, who had enjoyed some success in America but who now rallied to the banner of the "unmeltable ethnics." It also gained adherents among portions of the governing elite, especially among those located in federal agencies concerned with civil rights and social welfare and in philanthropic institutions, such as the Ford Foundation, that had responded to the racial crises of the 1960s by embracing the cause of racial equality. These elites did not revile the nation, but they believed that the treatment of minorities had severely compromised it; the state, as the representative of the nation, was thus obligated to compensate the aggrieved groups. These elites thus welcomed and helped to legitimate affirmative action policies, which required the government to identify those groups that had suffered the most from racial discrimination. By the 1970s, all federal agencies classified their employees as white, black, American Indian, Asian or Pacific Islander, and Hispanic; many private institutions soon followed suit. The last four groups in this pentagon of ethnoracial classification (plus women of all races) were the groups deemed worthy of affirmative action. By the 1980s, the government demanded that virtually all institutions, public and private, demonstrate their openness to these minorities. Lawsuits and loss of government contracts and subsidies loomed for any that failed to do so. Through such policies did the government hope to overcome the country's long history of racial discrimination and to restore legitimacy to the nation's egalitarian ideals.

Affirmative action's creators saw their program as a way to address past wrongs and thus to strengthen the nation's hold on its people; affirmative action, they believed, would spur assimilation. But the very process of identifying certain groups as deserving of assistance and of tying substantial benefits to membership in those groups strengthened the corporate identity of those groups. And within those groups arose leaders, influenced by the anti-American sentiments of the 1960s, who insisted that their followers cultivate their ethnic or racial identity at the expense of a national one. Thus one unintentional effect of affirmative action programs may well have been to weaken the government's role in promoting assimilation and to fray further the American sense of "nation-ness." The decline of nationalist feeling was not a development generated by domestic politics alone, however, as global economic forces everywhere challenged the authority of governments and the integrity of nation-states.

The profound changes in 1960s law and culture together with convulsions in the international economy made possible the reemergence of America as an immigrant society and opened up the country to a variety of groups to whom it had long been closed. Whereas in the late nineteenth and early twentieth centuries most immigrants had come from Europe, now most arrived either from Latin America or East and South Asia. Mexicans formed the largest group by far, as 2.7 million of them came to the United States between the early 1960s and 1990s. In these same years (1961–90), the country attracted almost a million Filipinos, 700,000 Cubans, 700,000 Chinese, 650,000 Koreans, 600,000 Vietnamese, 500,000 Dominicans, and 500,000 Indians. The sizes of these groups, with the exception of the Mexicans, are not as large in absolute terms as the sizes of the leading groups of the early-twentieth-century immigrants, nor do the immigrants as a whole represent as great a proportion of the American population as they once did. Indeed, it is difficult to imagine that immigrants will once again become as large a presence as they were early in this century; for that to happen, the number currently coming a year, about one million, would have to quadruple to four million and maintain that level for a decade or more. On the other hand, this immigrant era is still under way, and millions of Latin Americans and Asians are still keen on coming to the United States. And while a restrictionist movement has coalesced in the last few years, the forces behind it have yet to demonstrate the broad base of support that would be required to force deep cuts in the immigrant stream. We can expect another ten to fifteen million immigrants before this era ends.

As in previous waves, the motives of many in this one are economic. Medical and agricultural advances in poor and developing countries the last fifty years have triggered large increases in population, increases not matched by their native economies' ability to absorb the new people into well-paying jobs. Many of these immigrants, especially those arriving from Latin American countries, are from poor backgrounds, though generally not from the lowest strata in their societies. In the United States, they fill many of the poorest paying jobs. They make computer chips in Silicon Valley and garments in New York City sweatshops; pick the fruits and vegetables in California's agricultural valleys; serve as stockers and cashiers in supermarkets, as busboys and waiters in fast food restaurants, and as housekeepers, kitchen help, laundry workers, and aides in hotels and hospitals. Finally, they provide the new urban rich in New York, Miami, Los Angeles, and elsewhere with a variety of personal services ranging from domestic service to landscaping to child care. While comparatively few of these jobs are in manufacturing, these immigrant workers suffer from many of the same problems as their early-twentieth-century predecessors who labored in steel mills, automobile plants, and textile mills. For the majority, wages are poor and vulnerability to the boss's or supervisor's authority great; many have no protection from being laid off or fired, no recourse should they feel that they have been unfairly treated.

A significant portion of the immigrants, however, especially those coming from Asian countries, are not poor at all; they are highly trained professionals and managers who have decided that their skills will be more fully used and rewarded in the United States than at home. Thus the proportions of professionals and managers in the immigrant streams arriving from the Philippines, India, Taiwan, and Korea have regularly reached or exceeded 50 percent. This tendency represents a new departure in American immigrant history, for a professional immigrant stream of this magnitude appeared in none of the groups that came in the nineteenth or early twentieth century. It grows directly out of the 1965 law, which categorized professionals and managers as preferred immigrants. It reflects, too, the political and career frustration experienced by many of these professionals in their own societies. In the 1950s and early 1960s, professionals in countries like India were, on the whole, too committed to building their own nation to contemplate emigration, even if that commitment entailed accepting fewer career opportunities and a lower standard of living. These professionals partook of the nationalist euphoria engulfing their newly formed nations, and they fervently believed that their abilities and skills would enhance their nation's prosperity and prestige. As those expected results failed to materialize and as the task of building nations proved to be more arduous and corrupting than most had anticipated it would be, these elites lost their nationalist ardor. If they had become too settled to contemplate emigration themselves, their children felt differently and were more eager than their parents to fulfill personal dreams, even if that meant living permanently abroad. This reorientation made emigration to the United States a far more attractive proposition than it had been.

If the current immigrant stream contains a larger proportion of professionals than the last one, it may also contain a larger proportion of refugees. Russian Jews, we have noted, were the most notable example of refugees of the early twentieth century; their religious beliefs had put them in peril with czarist authorities. Among these Jews, moreover, and present in most other groups of southern and eastern European immigrants at the time, were radical émigres—Socialists, anarchists, and later Communists—who had fled their countries because their *political* beliefs had cost them their jobs and their personal safety. Jail and even death awaited those who lingered too long at home. Today's refugees are also fleeing political, rather than religious, oppression, but they are not Socialists or Communists. To the contrary, they are in flight from Communist regimes, especially those in Cuba, Vietnam, China, and the former Soviet Union. Their loathing of Communist forms of rule has turned many into political conservatives and inflected ethnic politics with a strong right-wing presence—in sharp contrast to the left-wing influence that was so prominent a force in immigrant politics of the early twentieth century. Thus, the most vivid political figure among the immigrants today is not some young Jewish woman or man in New York City stumping for socialism, but the equally fervent Cuban exile in Miami using powerful radio transmitters to saturate the Caribbean with anti-Castro broadsides.

Initially, the political refugees from Communist societies such as Cuba and Vietnam were drawn from the more advantaged sectors of their home societies, where their wealth and their connections with American business and government circles made them targets of the new Communist rulers; for these same reasons, American political authorities were eager to hustle these individuals to American safety. Possessing considerable human capital in the form of education or experience in running their own businesses, these refugees were well positioned to take advantage of opportunities in American society. Thus, many Cubans in south Florida and Vietnamese in Southern California and the Washington, D.C., metropolitan area, have prospered from their time in America. But, in the case of both these groups, many of the immigrants who followed the pioneers—including the Cubans who participated in the so-called Mariel exodus in the early 1980s and the Hmong villagers who fled Communist Laos—did not bring the same skills or contacts with them and have had to endure a harsh poverty. Refugees fleeing right-wing regimes in Guatemala, El Salvador, and Haiti in the 1980s have also had a difficult immigrant experience, first because they faced an American government reluctant to grant them official status as refugees (in the government's eyes, the perils of life under right-wing regimes were not as great as those under Communist ones), and second because they too tended to be without economic resources. For all these reasons, the immigrants of today may well be a more diverse lot than they were early in the twentieth century, more varied in their countries of origin, in their economic background, and in their motives for coming.

Another important difference between the immigrants of today and those earlier in the century is that the former are much more likely to live in family units. This tendency, too, is encouraged by immigration law, which allows any immigrant to sponsor immediate family members—parents, siblings, and children—still living outside the United States. In this way, today's immigrants differ from the millions of Italians, Greeks, Slavs, and other southern and eastern Europeans who, in the early twentieth century, "sojourned" in the United States alone. In some respects, a family orientation spurs assimilation: the children in these families quickly become English speakers and are likely to be immersed in sports, music, clothing, and other aspects of American mass culture. On the other hand, political pressures to assimilate—those generated by American political authorities—are significantly less than they were earlier in the century, as multiculturalism, itself a virtual government policy in many areas where immigrants concentrate, encourages the newcomers to retain their native traditions. Despite a flurry of anti-immigrant agitation in the mid-1990s, the pressures on immigrants to Americanize and to shed stigmatized

Old World cultures are still not nearly as strong as they were in the second and third decades of the twentieth century. The comparative weakness of these political pressures allows immigrants to maintain a strong identity with their homelands without having to fear economic or political reprisals. Meanwhile, governments and political parties in the immigrants' homelands do more than their counterparts in the early twentieth century did to keep emigrants informed of and involved in political and social developments at home. Some foreign governments allow their emigrants to exercise citizenship rights; thus, Colombians in New York regularly participate in elections in Colombia, while New York Hasidim make two-day trips to Israel to vote when their participation is deemed to be critical to the outcome of parliamentary contests there. Among Colombians, it is even possible to run for office in a Colombian election and to serve as an elected Colombian official while living in New York City! These immigrants, like most others, participate in far-flung diasporas whose effective functioning is made possible by various foreign governments' diligent policies, the low cost and speed of international travel, and the instantaneous character of modern communication.

The non-European origins of many immigrants, the large number of professionals and political refugees among them, their family orientation, the ease of maintaining diasporic connections, and the American state's commitment to multicultural rather than assimilative policies are all features of this wave of immigration that distinguish it from the last. But how different the current immigrants' experience ultimately becomes may well depend on two other factors: their orientation to whiteness and their ability if not to prosper, at least to achieve economic security in America. The civil rights revolution of the 1960s mounted a stunning assault on the privileges of whiteness: in one area after another—the use of public accommodations, employment, housing, voting rights, immigration, marriage—the revolution undercut the legislative edifice that had long encoded white superiority, north and south, into law. This revolution transformed the field of immigration as much as any other, making possible, for the first time in the history of the American nation, an immigrant stream that was overwhelmingly nonwhite. At the same time, the revolution generated hopes that race would lose its salience as a source of division and friction in American society. Some signs, from the emergence of a dynamic black middle class and the racial integration of American celebrity culture to accelerating rates of intermarriage across various color lines, suggest that race is indeed declining in significance. The intermarriage data are particularly interesting in this regard. The 1990 census revealed that approximately half of Asian immigrants and about one-third of Latino immigrants aged 25 to 34 had married outside their immigrant group. In light of these statistics, it seems reasonable to suppose that rates of intermarriage among the children of Asian and Latino immigrants are even higher. We do know that the intermarriage rates among some groups, such as Japanese-American women, exceed 70 percent.

Rates of black-white intermarriage are far lower, but, by some measures, have risen dramatically since the 1960s; thus, the number of African Americans marrying whites has increased from less than 3 percent in 1970 to more than 12 percent in 1993. If we project these statistical trends fifty to one hundred years into the future, it is possible to imagine that America will become a "brown nation," one thoroughly hybridized and in which racial distinctions have lost most of their force. This would be a great achievement, should it come to pass, and the new immigrants will have played a pivotal role in bringing it about.

But there is a less sanguine way of reading these intermarriage statistics, and that is to stress that gap that has emerged between immigrant and African-American intermarriage rates. Thus Latino immigrants are almost three times and Asian immigrants more than four times as likely as African Americans to marry whites. Moreover, rates of intermarriage among Asians and African Americans and among Latinos and African Americans are so low that they are barely discernible. In this sense, the golf *wunderkind*, Tiger Woods, who is of mixed African-American and Asian ancestry, should be viewed not as the representative of a large group of similarly mixed people but rather as a striking exception. Blacks may simply have more catching up to do, and the 2000 census may show their rate of outmarriage converging with those of other non-European groups. But a familiar historical pattern may be reestablishing itself: blacks may find their opportunities for integration limited even as white Americans open their arms (literally, in the case of marriage) to nonblack immigrants. In this way, Asian and Latino immigrants may, at some point, come to define their Americanness in terms of being white or, at least, of not being black. Meanwhile, Afro-Carribean immigrant parents from Jamaica, the Dominican Republic, Haiti, and other West Indian nations who have settled in New York and other eastern cities observe their children assimilating into an angry African-American youth culture, a tendency that many of these parents regard as injurious to their kids but which they feel powerless to resist. These patterns suggest that "whiteness" and "blackness" are still charged with meaning in 2000 America and may continue to structure patterns of immigrant assimilation well into the twenty-first century. If that happens, the civil rights revolution will come to be judged a failure, and the future will indeed come to resemble the past.

The large number of professionals in this immigrant stream and the success they have enjoyed should not be allowed to obscure the majority that labors in poorly paid manufacturing, agricultural, and service jobs. Many of these immigrants are determined to improve their lot, going to university at night, picking up second jobs as taxidrivers and doormen, saving money to start their own small garment shop or landscape service. Some will make it, just as did poor immigrants in the early twentieth century. America has always given opportunities to those with talent willing to work hard and lucky enough to be blessed with good fortune. But the majority of immigrants will not succeed in this way; their hope of rising in the social order will depend more on collective than on individual struggle. Historically, immigrant groups have often developed their own institutions of collective self-help, and in associations of Korean grocers and Mexican contractors we see these patterns, so vital to economic success, being reproduced. But these have not been sufficient in the past to assist the ordinary wage earner, which is why labor unions have played an important role in enabling immigrants or their children to improve their economic condition.

The great labor breakthrough for the southern and eastern European ethnic workers came in the 1930s through the allied efforts of the CIO and the New Deal. It will take an effort of similar breadth and energy today to lift up today's immigrant poor, especially in areas, such as southern California, and among groups, such as Mexican Americans, in which patterns of impoverished immigrant wage-earning are most entrenched. The circumstances of these immigrant workers are made all the more vulnerable because of the nature of the global economy in which corporations have become adept at shifting investments and jobs from one country to another at lightning-like speed. In this economic setting, the power of any one state, the American one included, to influence economic trends is correspondingly reduced. So, too, is the ability of nationalism to function as an ideology of rights around which Americans might mobilize and sway public opinion to their side. It is thus hard to see how a labor movement the size and influence of the 1930s one might reappear. In an age in which socialism has been discredited and in which nationalism no longer exerts the same hold on the imagination of Americans, what ideology is capable of generating transethnic solidarity among immigrant workers? In this age of declining state power, to what authority will immigrants turn as they seek to reign in the power of global capital? How successfully the immigrant poor answer these questions will shape their fate as Americans. In the process they will determine whether the vaunted mythology of America as a land of freedom and opportunity survives into the twenty-first century or whether it comes to be seen as a quaint artifact of an earlier time, no longer relevant to our own.

SUGGESTIONS FOR FURTHER READING

For overviews of American immigration, consult Roger Daniels, *Coming to America: A History of Immigration and Ethnicity in American Life* (New York: Harper Collins, 1990); Leonard Dinnerstein, Roger L. Nichols, and David Reimers, *Natives and Strangers: A Multicultural History of America* (New York: Oxford University Press, 1996); and Ronald Takaki, *A Different Mirror: A History of Multicultural America* (Boston: Little, Brown, & Co., 1993). The best synthesis of the European immigration experience in the first half of this century is John Bodnar, *The Transplanted: A History of Immigrants in Urban America* (Bloomington:

Indiana University Press, 1985); for Latino and Asian immigration in the century's second half, consult Alejandro Portes and Rubén G. Rumbaut, *Immigrant America: A Portrait*, 2nd ed. (Berkeley: University of California Press, 1996); Reed Ueda, *Postwar Immigrant America: A Social History* (Boston: Bedford, 1994); and David R. Reimers, *Still the Golden Door: The Third World Comes to America* (New York: Columbia University Press, 1985). For a synthesis that places women and gender at the center of the immigrant experience, see Donna R. Gabaccia, *From the Other Side: Women, Gender, and Immigrant Life in the U.S., 1820–1990* (Bloomington: Indiana University Press, 1994).

The literature on individual immigrant groups is so vast that it cannot be included in a short bibliography. Those who seek such information should begin with Stephan Thernstrom, ed., *Harvard Encyclopedia of American Ethnic Groups* (Cambridge, Mass.: Belknap Press of Harvard University Press, 1980); in addition to containing individual entries (with bibliographies) on every imaginable immigrant group, the encyclopedia contains invaluable thematic essays on many issues of concern to immigration scholars. This volume is less useful for contemporary immigration, so it should be supplemented with Charles Hirschman, Philip Kasinitz, and Josh DeWind, eds., *The Handbook of International Migration: The American Experience* (New York: The Russell Sage Foundation, 1999). See also Rudolph J. Vecoli, "Ethnicity and Immigration," in Stanley I. Kutler, ed., *Encyclopedia of the United States in the Twentieth Century*, Vol. 1 (New York: Scribner's, 1996), pp. 161–193. As for so many other topics, *The Historical Statistics of the United States, Colonial Times to 1970* (Washington, D.C.: Government Printing Office, 1975), is an indispensable source of statistical information on the numbers, origins, naturalization rates, and residential patterns of immigrants.

Gary Gerstle, "Liberty, Coercion, and the Making of Americans," *Journal of American History* 84 (September 1997): 524–558, traces the influence of American mythology on the work of American immigration historians. The classic work on nativism and immigration restriction is John Higham, *Strangers in the Land: Patterns of American Nativism, 1860–1925* (New Brunswick, N.J.: Rutgers University Press, 1992), though it should be supplemented with Ian Haney López, *White by Law: The Legal Construction of Race* (New York: New York University Press, 1996). On European ethnics, labor, and the New Deal, consult Lizabeth Cohen, *Making a New Deal: Industrial Workers in Chicago, 1919–1939* (New York: Cambridge University Press, 1990) and Gary Gerstle, *Working-Class Americanism: The Politics of Labor in a Textile City, 1914–1960* (New York: Cambridge University Press, 1989). On these groups' pursuit of whiteness, see Matthew Frye Jacobson, *Whiteness of a Different Color: European Immigrants and the Alchemy of Race* (Cambridge, Mass.: Harvard University Press, 1998); Thomas J. Sugrue, *The Origins of the Urban Crisis: Race and Inequality in Postwar Detroit* (Princeton, N.J.: Princeton University Press, 1996); and Arnold R. Hirsch, *Making the Second Ghetto: Race and Housing in Chicago, 1940–1960* (New York: Cambridge University Press, 1983). Consult Hugh Davis Graham, *The Civil Rights Era: Origins and Development of National Policy* (New York: Oxford University Press, 1990) for a history of the legislative changes that accompanied the civil rights revolution. For thoughtful reflections on immigrants, citizenship, and nationalism in fin-de-siecle America, see the essays in Noah M. J. Pickus, ed., *Immigration and Citizenship in the 21st Century* (Lanham, Md.: Rowan & Littlefield, 1998). On immigrant workers in the postindustrial economy, consult Roger Waldinger, *Still the Promised City? African Americans and Immigrants in Postindustrial New York* (Cambridge, Mass.: Harvard University Press, 1996). For an example of late-twentieth-century nativism, see Peter Brimelow, *Alien Nation: Common Sense about America's Immigration Disaster* (New York: Random House, 1995).

14 | THE IRON CAGE AND ITS ALTERNATIVES IN TWENTIETH-CENTURY AMERICAN THOUGHT

JACKSON LEARS

Twentieth-century life has been haunted by images of imprisonment. One of the most enduring is the "iron cage" introduced by Max Weber at the conclusion of *The Protestant Ethic and the Spirit of Capitalism* (1904). The Puritans had believed that the care for material goods should be worn like a cloak, lightly; but, as Weber wrote, "fate decreed that the cloak would become an iron cage." Iron cages connote death camps and *gulags*, but Weber was not alluding to totalitarian states; he was referring to the broader process of rationalization embodied in modern (and mostly American) corporate capitalism. Weber understood that what he called the disenchantment of the world raised large and perhaps unanswerable questions about the corrosive impact of capitalist rationality on human meaning and purpose.

In our contemporary cultural climate, when the "free market" is equated with liberty and democracy, Weber's image jars. How could a thinker of Weber's subtlety have mistaken a liberating force for an iron cage? Maybe he was simply mistaken—misled by his romantic nostalgia, blinkered by the blinders of privilege into overlooking the long-term beneficence of corporate capitalism for ordinary folk—liberation from want, expansion of leisure, all the developments celebrated by our official thought leaders as evidence of progress. One way to accept the iron cage is to declare that it's really not a cage at all.

This was the strategy adopted by Weber's contemporary, the economist Simon Nelson Patten. In *The New Basis of Civilization* (1907), Patten presented a bold departure in American social thought—a rearticulation of the relation between production and consumption. Moralists had long distrusted consumption as a temptation to idleness, frivolity, and extravagant display. Patten declared that, on the contrary, good consumers would make good producers. The desire to buy things would not undermine labor discipline but would reinforce it. Patten looked forward to a society where production and consumption were in dynamic equilibrium, where workers strove constantly for betterment and employers benefited from their striving. Many twentieth-century Americans would embrace this vision; indeed by mid-century it had become virtually synonymous with the American Way of Life.

But many Americans remained skeptical. The growing dominance of corporate capitalism provoked widespread discontent, both inchoate and articulate. Some dissenters simply thought the cage was too small, too exclusively the property of a white male elite; their solution was to use government pressure to enlarge the cage, let in the outsiders, and put them on the escalator to the top floor. But others shared Weber's deeper dis-ease: the fear that the iron cage cut its inmates off from first-hand experience—physical, emotional, even spiritual.

Weber's iron cage was not simply a set of material structures, but a managerial cast of mind. The Weberian capitalist was obsessed with efficiency, productivity, the peak performance of both his employees and his investments. Disenchantment not only reduced work to a repetitive routine for the vast majority of workers; it impoverished the available store of symbolic meanings. No wonder the rise of Weberian rationality coincided with an unprecedented proliferation of longings for intense reality, for authentic, unmediated experience. A rationalist version of modernism provoked an irrationalist one.

Tensions between calculating rationality and spontaneous reality ranged widely, shaping debates in social thought, arts and letters, religion and philosophy. It is possible to see Weber's iron cage as a useful scaffolding for twentieth-century American thought. The process of rationalization promoted apologetics and ambivalence, defense and dissent. If we recognize that the iron cage is not merely an economic framework but a frame of mind, we can see the spread of managerial rationality as a way of linking American thought with broader social developments, and of provisionally periodizing a chaotic century.

The history of twentieth-century American thought can be seen (at least in part) as a three-stage pattern: the formation, consolidation, and fragmentation of a managerial ethos—which could also be considered a rationalist version of modernism. The managerial ethos played a central role in debates over public policy: it sanctioned a Keynesian partnership between big business and big government, a strategy for deploying the iron cage in the service of economic growth. John Kenneth Galbraith captured this vision by stressing the centrality of "the technostructure" in *The New Industrial State* (1968). Yet the iron cage or the flight from it also energized educational thought, success mythology, psychotherapy, philosophy, and religion: it promoted departures from individualism, including an emerging emphasis on assimilation to the new world of large organizations. The managerial outlook fostered a new attention to the importance of "system"—its ultimate intellectual expression may have been the sociologist Talcott Parsons's functionalist theory of society, *The Social System* (1951). The underlying assumptions behind this mode of thought were a faith in statistical expertise as a means of predicting and controlling the contingencies of fate and a pragmatic stress on mid-range means rather than ultimate ends, techniques rather than values. As the poet Allen Tate observed in 1953: "We do not ask 'is this right?' we ask: 'will it work?'"

The managerial ethos emerged gradually, through the sometimes conflicting efforts of social reformers and corporate apologists. The years from the turn of the century to the late 1930s marked its formation; from the late 1930s to the late 1960s, its consolidation; and from the late 1960s to the present, its fragmentation. During the last third of the century, the iron cage survived and spread in fluid, multinational forms, but it lost the coherent rationale of the mid-century decades. Despite unprecedented prosperity, the fin de siecle was pervaded by feelings of disintegration and drift. Americans (many of them, anyway) were doing better, but feeling worse. Disenchantment had corroded larger frameworks of belief, provoking fundamentalist reactions in a variety of religious idioms. But in public discourse, the only sense of the sacred lay in the sanctity of the bottom line.

Throughout the century, celebrants and critics of the iron cage have alike appealed to reality as the ultimate standard of judgment. Reverence for reality could feed an anti-intellectual fascination for the pseudoconcrete, creating a cult of numbers and a timidly majoritarian, poll-driven politics, allowing business apologists to define themselves against the effete unreality of the intelligentsia. But the pursuit of the real could also promote more venturesome forms of thought. The recoil from rationalization occurred at a visceral level, challenging Cartesian categories, melding body and mind. The fear that one was living life at second hand, the desire to grapple directly with raw experience—these impulses could lead thinkers toward more complex definitions of the real, toward longings for transcendance as well as a taste for slumming.

The quest for intense experience—physical, emotional, spiritual—was intertwined with the rise and fall of the managerial ethos. As this chapter traces the formation, consolidation, and fragmentation of a managerial consensus, it will also try to illuminate the ways that consensus shaped and reshaped the search for an ever-elusive reality.

FORMATION

Across the political spectrum in 1900, Americans were preoccupied with taming the operations of chance in economic life. Seeds of a managerial outlook were sprouting all over the place. The turn-of-the-century merger wave was the most dramatic and successful example of this new mentality at work. Figures like John D. Rockefeller epitomized the triumph of Weber's rational capitalist ethic. Ruthlessly self-controlled, he sought predictable profits through systematic power over markets and elimination of rivals. Determined to contain entrepreneurial chaos, Rockefeller and his contemporaries created a new world of corporate behemoths in control of entire industries.

Humanitarian progressives were as preoccupied as robber barons with the taming of chance, but for different purposes. They wanted to salve the abrasions of accident in workers' lives through social insurance schemes, to transform what Brand Whitlock called "the hideous anarchy and accident" of American cities into coherent public space—and in general, to underwrite social democracy with statistical expertise. As Daniel Rodgers has recently shown, progressives on both sides of the Atlantic became convinced that protecting the public interest from potential corporate predators required granting countervailing power to government institutions. That conviction marked the birth of modern liberalism.

Universities played a critical role in the parturition process, easing the transition from Protestant to managerial modes of thought. In 1900, even at research universities remaking themselves on the Prussian model, curricula contained a heavy residue of Protestantism. Economics had only recently separated from moral philosophy; sociology was often a secular surrogate for the Social Gospel, and many sociologists were former ministers or ministers' sons.

Yet there was a significant shift under way in the prevailing cognitive style of the American academy. For decades Darwinian analogies had seeped into social thought. Many sanctioned wealth and power, but others aimed to undermine any form of static hierarchy—"laying hold of the sacred ark of the Permanant," as John Dewey put it, posing an evolutionary challenge to all fast-frozen principles, demanding that ideas demonstrate what William James called their "cash value" through their actual consequences in everyday life.

This pragmatic "revolt against formalism," as the philosopher Morton White characterized it, cut across disciplinary lines. It was articulated by James and Dewey in philosophy, Thorstein Veblen in economics, Oliver Wendell Holmes in law, Charles Beard in history, and a host of lesser makers of modern liberal thought. The antiformalist turn led to a powerful critique of existing pieties, many of which served the interests of the economic status quo.

The problem with pragmatism was that even its most sophisticated practitioners never figured out how to fuse the pragmatic method with an enduring set of values or social goals. It seemed to lead instead to a more immediate focus on processes rather than purposes, means rather than ends. Its resistance to fixed ideals, its opennness to multiple interpretations meant that pragmatism could be transformed into an apologia for power as well as a weapon against privilege—especially if the power justified itself with reference to superior technique. For all these reasons, a debased version of pragmatism became embedded in the discourse of managerial rationality.

One can sense its presence in the preoccupation with efficiency that spread from factory to school and household in the first two decades of the century. Women as well as men were swept up in unprecedented efforts to banish unpredictability from everyday life and bring systematic control to the home, the work place and, ultimately, the gene pool. The home economists Christine Frederick and Ellen Richards created the neologism *euthenics* to characterize their ultimate aim: founding "the science of the perfectly controlled home environment." The feminist Charlotte Perkins Gilman was so traumatized by the suffocating privacy of Victorian domestic life that she promoted various schemes for a more efficient division of household labor though cooperative apartments; she also became involved in the eugenics movement. The dreams of a managerial utopia led from sanitizing the household to perfecting the race.

The masculine, corporate version of the efficiency cult was far more pervasive and influential. Frederick Winslow Taylor's *Principles of Scientific Management* (1911) encapsulated the methods he had been using for years on the shop floor: most involved dividing each task into discrete measurable units, timing the swiftest performance of each, and recombining the fragments into a more efficient whole. Taylor's system replaced direct craft knowledge with disembodied managerial knowledge; the manager's brains, which had proverbially been under the worker's cap, were removed to the planning department. Henry Ford and other pioneers of the assembly line accomplished results similar to Taylor's. They achieved increased productivity at the cost of degrading artisanal traditions; they rewarded workers willing to accept labor discipline with increased buying power off the job. They laid the foundation, in short, for the fulfillment of Patten's vision.

During the 1920s, despite the eclipse of progressive reform, managerial ideas were still afloat amid a sea of resurgent laissez faire ideology. The Great War had demonstrated how a government-business partnership could mobilize production and propaganda. Enlightened capitalists like Edward Filene (the Boston department store magnate) and Owen D. Young (the head of General Electric) developed corporate versions of social insurance and other social democratic programs—an embryonic welfare capitalism. To old-stock elites, the passage of immigration-restriction legislation in 1924 created the prospect of an increasingly stable working class. Dreams of a new era of well-managed prosperity spread among corporate prophets of progress.

The crash dashed their hopes. The persistence of catastrophe retilted the balance in favor of government's role in managing economic chance. Progressives pulled plans from file drawers where they had been mouldering for twenty years; Social Security was their most conspicuous achievement. By the end of the 1930s, steel and auto manufacturers had grudgingly accepted the power of industrial unions; labor and capital struck an implicit bargain: steady work and decent pay in exchange for labor discipline—numbing dullness on the job in exchange for some extra cash, a little time to enjoy it, and an unprecedented sense of economic security. A dynamic equilibrium between production and consumption was in sight. The stage was being set for the fulfillment of Patten's vision.

Yet the further one moves from the arena of public policy, the more likely one is to see evidence of doubts and longings that could not be satisfied in the realm of managerial rationality. When Jane Addams wrote of "the subjective necessity of social settlements" in 1910 she referred to the cravings of privileged young women like herself for a direct connection with palpitating unpredictable actuality. For her and many of her contemporaries, that meant the reality of the streets. Similar impulses linked numerous sociological pilgrimages with the novels of Theodore Dreiser, the photographs of Lewis Hine, the paintings of John Sloan and his Ash Can school. The discovery of urban poverty involved more than the objective needs of the poor; it drew strength, as well, from the subjective necessities of the discoverers.

Pragmatism displayed comparable psychological origins—at least in the life of William James. Like so many other late Victorian intellectuals, James was haunted by fears of a vague and looming unreality, a state of near nonbeing, embodied for him when he was a young medical student by a hopeless epileptic patient he saw in an insane asylum; "that shape am I," James thought. He spent much of his career trying to exorcise that vision, to reaffirm his faith in "pure experience" as the ultimate ground of meaning and truth. That project energized the development of pragmatism.

If behind James's pragmatism was a religion of experience, behind Henry Adams's pessimism there was an experience of religion—or at least a vicarious one, the ecstatic faith he attributed to thirteenth-century French Catholics in *Mont-St.-Michel and Chartres* (1907). But readers of Adams's posthumously published *Education* (1918) were less likely to respond to his medievalist reverence for the Virgin than to his modernist disdain for Victorian gentility and managerial rationality—both, in his view, destroyers of instinctual vitality. Adams's vitalism struck a persistently resonant response.

Even among liberal Protestants, whose bland affirmations and compromises had done so much to promote the spread of spiritual banality, desires for revitalization spread. The Rev. Harry Emerson Fosdick called for an *Adventurous Religion* in a book of 1923, though the ultimate point of that adventure remained frustratingly obscure. And Bruce Barton revealed *The Man Nobody Knows* (1925) to be Jesus himself, who in Barton's telling was in need of rescue from Sunday-school sentimentality. He was no weak-kneed lamb of God, Barton insisted, but a virile, magnetic fellow, "the most popular dinner guest in Jerusalem" and the founder of modern advertising. His parables, Barton wrote, were "the hottest ad copy in all history." These risible assertions, often taken as evidence of business complacency in the 1920s, actually can be seen as signs of self-doubt, of a sense that something was missing from mainstream Protestant tradition.

Among literati, the search for creative vitality often depended on continued hostility to the "genteel tradition." Even before George Santayana had named it in 1913, identifying it with everything tepid and anemic in American culture, American artists and writers were obsessed with gentility as the source of all falsity, insincerity, and unreality. In the first two decades of the century the main alternatives to gentility had been found among the virtuous poor but also among the buccaneer businessman—the chief actors in the modern urban drama; by the 1920s, though, at least for some rebellious bohemians, the revolt against gentility led to a celebration of advertising—the glittering iconography of managerial capitalism. Writing in *Broom* in 1922, Matthew Josephson rejected "the piffle of the teacup type" of poet in favor of the "terse vivid slang" produced by advertising copywriters. This would not be the last time a self-conscious cultural radical confused corporate-sponsored spontaneity with the real thing.

The assault on Victorian gentility often stemmed from familiar masculine anxieties about the effeteness of the literary life, but sometimes led in more interesting directions. F. Scott Fitzgerald's *The Great Gatsby* (1925) explored the hollowness at the heart of self-made manhood, and the desperate longing for the past behind the impulse to deny its power. Ernest Hemingway's Jake Barnes, in *The Sun Also Rises* (1926), gave palpable form to modern feelings of impotence and embodied a stoic alternative to self-pity. Lanston Hughes and other poets of the Harlem Renaissance brooded on the difficulty of deriving authentic experience from Africa, "so far away." Georgia O'Keefe filled canvases with enormous female flowers in haunting desert landscapes, ensuring that notions of "virgin nature" would never be the same.

The Great Depression profoundly reshaped the discourse of authenticity. For intellectuals who had bristled at corporate fatuities about a New Era, "there was something exhilerating about the collapse of that stupid gigantic fraud," the capitalist system. So Edmund Wilson recalled. But most Americans did not share his enthusiasm. As Franklin Roosevelt brilliantly realized, the dominant response to economic disaster was not radicalism or even resentment, but fear—"stark unreasoning terror." When the bottom dropped out, as Warren Susman has perceptively shown, middle-class Americans groped for feelings of connectedness; they yearned for economic, social, and emotional security; they wanted to belong to a larger whole, to immerse themselves in a transcendant collective identity.

The longing to belong shaped a host of cultural tendencies, from an emerging psychology of adjustment to a success mythology of team play, from Dale Carnegie's *How to Win Friends and Influence People* (1936) to the Popular Front slogan: "Communism is twentieth century Americanism." Under the impact of unprecedented economic strain, the notion of intense experience became collectivized; the favored embodiment of the real became the people, the virtuous folk—epitomized in the American scene paintings of Thomas Hart Benton and Grant Wood, the photographs of the Farm Security Administration, and John Ford's bowdlerized film version of John Steinbeck's *The Grapes of Wrath* (1940).

The collectivization of the real fostered rapprochement between the iron cage and its critics. A vague civil religion, keyed to the worship of an even vaguer American Way of Life, fostered cultural nationalism and distrust of idiosyncratic intelligence. The very vagueness of the American Way of Life allowed it to be redefined by corporate apologists during World War II, from a soupy haze of populist slogans to an equally murky rhetoric of free enterprise. There was a fundamental continuity, surpassing political fashion, between the "radical" thirties and the "conservative" fifties. Depression-bred yearnings for security found fulfillment in the conformist suburban culture of the postwar era. Patten's vision came to rest at last.

Yet idiosyncratic intelligence did survive. More than a few writers and artists, influenced by European modernism, realized that human experience was too complex and various to be represented in literalist or nationalist formulas. In *Call It Sleep* (1934), Henry Roth set out to write a proletarian novel and ended by producing an astonishingly powerful account of a Jewish immigrant boy's coming of age in a strange new land; in *Let Us Now Praise Famous Men* (1941), James Agee set out to present a documentary report on Alabama sharecroppers and ended by producing a revealing meditation on his own obsession with subordinating art to reality. Like Agee and Roth, the editors of *Partisan Review* refused to use politics as a refuge from the terrors of the inner life. They pioneered an inward, psychological turn that redefined reality with unprecedented subtlety even as it ended in accommodation to the managerial consensus.

CONSOLIDATION

World War II and its aftermath marked the noontide of the managerial consensus. The war brought prosperity, the rise of a well-paid working population. This was key: for the first time in more than a decade, people had some loose change in their pockets. The war itself was a crusade for comfort, an effort to restore the American Way of Life on a firmer economic foundation: this at least was the message increasingly being sent to the population by national advertisements and the corporate-dominated Office of War Information. No more inflated Wilsonian rhetoric about making the world safe for democracy; ensuring domestic tranquillity was a wide enough war aim.

Meanwhile, major changes had been brewing in managerial economic thought. In *The General Theory of Employment, Interest, and Money* (1936), John Maynard Keynes provided a sophisticated rationale for government intervention in the economy: public investment could boost aggregate demand, the key to sustaining prosperity. Private investment could boost it too, but was too chaotic and indifferent to social goals to serve as a sensible basis for policy. Or so Keynes thought. His alternative to the "casino" of stock market speculation was the judicious use of fiscal and monetary policy to stimulate investment during slack times and dampen it during booms. Keynes was an aristocrat and social democrat who wanted to flatten the curves in the business cycle for humanitarian as well as financial reasons. His assumptions characterized managerial thought at its most humane.

Keynesian ideas penetrated the New Deal in the late thirties, went underground during the war, and emerged during the postwar period in considerably more businesslike garb. To be sure, the Full Employment Act of 1946 seemed an official affirmation of Keynesian ideas in their broadest sense: the government was symbolically underwriting Patten's vision of a society in dynamic equilibrium between production and consumption. But the specific provisions of the act were so minimal in effect as to be virtually meaningless. What actually occurred was the emergence of a right-wing Keynesian consensus based largely on military spending and private investment. Not the sort of strategies Keynes had in mind, but nicely attuned to the developing cold war economy.

The managerial consensus shaped the built environment as well as the economic climate—particularly the process of suburbanization, as Lizabeth Cohen shows in Chapter 7 of this volume. Returning veterans and their brides were eager to start families, in places with light and air and a little plot of green; the government provided cheap loans and built highways to town. IBM and other corporations resurrected welfare capitalism, providing middle managers with security and social mobility at the price of geographic mobility; they wanted pleasant predictable places with decent schools and people like themselves; suburbs filled the bill. A huge swath of the working class were union members, with steadier jobs and higher wages than ever before; they liked the idea of more space, too. No wonder the suburbs spread like crabgrass. With standardized houses and well-clipped yards, they approximated the managerial dream of a safe, controlled environment.

Of course there were structural problems with this apparent idyll. The cold war economy depended on a constant stream of expensive weaponry and a constant public mood of near-hysterical alarm. The construction of a unified mass culture depended on the systematic exclusion of black people—except as comic or pathetic characters. Outside the suburbs (and the managerial consensus) were rich vernacular traditions that explored the darker dimensions of life—one need only recall Hank Williams singing about cheatin' hearts and Billie Holiday about lynching and suicide, during this epoch of bland, sunny optimism. And it would not be too long before Elvis Presley appeared to embody Sam Phillips's deepest wish. (The producer of Sun records had said: "if only we could find a white man who sings like a black man, we could make a million bucks.") Soon youthful pulses would be quickening to the rhythms of rock n' roll, a music calculated to cross the carefully drawn boundaries of the managerial consensus.

But the triumphalist mood of the postwar era made it easy for many Americans to ignore those "pictures from life's other side," as Hank Williams called his songs. Even when African Americans created a mass movement for civil rights, the sense of guilt and wrongdoing could be projected onto the hapless, backward South. The rest of the country could feel self-satisfied. Black people, after all, were not challenging the managerial consensus; they were demanding admission to it. And the cold war? However alarming, it seemed a permananent state of affairs; it reassured Americans of their own magnanimity and moral superiority; it provided a convenient allegorical figure on which to project fears and hostilities.

By the late 1950s, even intellectuals felt that history had somehow ended, with the United States atop the heap. When Daniel Bell described *The End of Ideology* in 1960, he was explicitly articulating what many of his contemporaries had been suggesting for years: that the entire free world had reached some common conclusions regarding the inevitability and comparative beneficence of big organizations, the necessity of pragmatic interest-group politics and a "mixed economy"involving government-business cooperation, and the irrelevance of old labels like left and right, as well as old concepts like class domination.

The idea of American culture as a classless, monolithic "way of life," which was rooted in the cultural nationalism of the thirties and forties, became the conventional wisdom of the fifties. It required a systematic inattention to power relations, a view of American politics as a roistering egalitarian melee— this characterized the pluralist political theory popularized by Bell and David Riesman. The refusal to engage questions of power led to the reification of abstract concepts into things that acted autonomously on people. Parsons's "social system" was the most egregious example, but many more could be culled from the literature of "modernization" or culture-and-personality anthropology. Historians followed social scientists into awkward reification, as David Potter chose the abstraction "abundance" as the deus ex machina hovering over two centuries of American history. Most of mainstream social thought depended on an attribution of omnipotence to abstract collective entities—society, abundance, the economy, the organization.

The tendency toward reification reflected the *embourgeoisement* of left-wing social thought, the assimilation of ex-radicals to institutional roles in publishing, the universities and foundations, and government policy positions. This was a crucial part of the consolidation of the managerial consensus. As early as 1950, the critic Lionel Trilling was able to observe (uncritically) that "intellect has associated itself with power, perhaps as never before in history, and is now conceded to be itself a kind of power." In such an atmosphere, it should come as no surprise that pragmatism lost virtually all its critical edge, becoming a handmaiden of positivism in university curricula, and a justification for "tough minded realism" in the foreign policy arena.

But the story of mid-century intellectual life was more interesting—and more tragic—than the dreary saga of accommodation with power. Indeed that saga started with wholly understandable motives. It began with the late 1930s' "imagination of disaster" (in Henry James's phrase)—the growing recognition, fed by the spread of totalitarianism, that the liberal imagination was unable to encompass reality in all its dark complexity. Trilling's classic essay, "Reality in America" (1940), brought the indictment against liberal literalism by satirizing the views of the progressive historian Vernon Parrington: "there exists . . . a thing called reality; it is one and immutable, it is wholly external, it is irreducible. Men's minds may waver, but reality is always reliable, always the same, always easily to be known."

Parrington's simpleminded epistemology was wholly incompatible with the modernist sensibility Trilling and his friends were cultivating at the *partisan Review*. They were reading Dostoevsky and Kafka, Conrad and Proust—these were authors for whom human motives were ambiguous and often self-defeating, depths were more revealing than surfaces, and reality was disturbing and elusive. The effort to locate dark truth by plumbing hidden depths became a characteristic move of high modernism. It linked Trilling and other devotees of psychoanalysis with neoorthodox theologians like Reinhold Niebuhr. The Freudian unconscious could become a secular equivalent of original sin. And original sin acquired new currency in the age of the dictators. Niebuhr assaulted religious liberals for their pacifism in the thirties, dismissing them as "foolish children of light" who failed to recognize a monster when they saw one. A more realistic religion, Niebuhr believed, would be one that recognized the tragic necessity of confronting evil in an imperfect, fallen world.

Occasionally secular radicals bristled at intellectuals' newfound interest in religion. In a *Partisan Review* symposium called "Religion and the Intellectuals," the philosopher Sidney Hook castigated the newly religious for their "new failure of nerve"—their apparent inability to live without the crutch of creed, myth, and ritual. But despite such complaints, the discourse of authenticity turned decisively toward spiritual matters during and after the war. Even Catholicism acquired an appeal, in the wake of T. S. Eliot's famous conversion to the Anglican version. Literary figures like Allen Tate and Robert Lowell found the Church of Rome to be (at least temporarily) a satisfying alternative to the pieties of progressive liberalism—and a basis for their developing critique of technocratic authority. Existentialists, Christian and humanist, flourished in the pages of *Partisan Review*, where everyone from Sartre to Silone and Kierkegaard found a hearing.

The quest for dark truth animated a broad shift in cultural taste, away from the unproblematic social realism of the 1930s and toward the literary modernist exploration of depth and complexity. Ambiguity was always "rich" in the 1940s and 1950s. American scene painting was out; abstract expressionism was in. Emerson's stock was falling; Melville's was rising. This was not simply a matter of shifting fashion; it was an understandable response to the flatness of liberal reality.

What gradually happened, though, is that modernist high seriousness became assimilated to the culture of the cold war. Niebuhr's "tough-minded realism" sanctioned acceptance of existing foreign policy; "life's tragic complexity" became a justification for the curtailment of intellectual freedom in the national security state.

On the domestic scene, as intellectuals shifted their attention from Wall Street to Madison Avenue, questions of power were redefined as matters of taste. Mass culture became identified as a menacing, standardizing force. Endless chatter about conformity became a kind of in-house critique of the managerial consensus. This occurred as the war receded and the imagination of disaster gave way to more overtly aesthetic concerns. Literary intellectuals like Trilling and Irving Howe had long fought for an art independent of political criteria. But an autonomous art ran the risk of becoming a trivial art—isolated, disembodied, cut off from the vicissitudes of history and biography. This was what happened to the study of literature as the New Criticism spread throughout the academy. And it was what happened to cultural criticism that focused exclusively on the standardization of taste.

To be sure, the critique of conformity could transcend mere aestheticism, especially when it came from less mandarin sources. In *Mad* magazine (1952–), a mostly New York Jewish subculture produced brilliant satires of mass market entertainment and managerial culture, exposing (in the modernist mode) the depths of aggression, rage, and madness beneath the surface of bonhomie. Amid a managerial obsession with control, abstract expressionists and "beat" poets (again mostly regional or ethnic outsiders) explored the frontiers of artistic spontaneity. An aesthetics of accident—a willingness to embrace and even play with the vagaries of chance—these tendencies linked Jackson Pollock's painting with the writing of Jack Kerouac and Charles Olson and the music (if that's the right word) of John Cage. Though Pollock denied accident and Cage encased it in Zen significance, there is no doubt that these artists, among others, were seeking a backdoor exit from the iron cage—an experience of pulsating spontaneity in an over-organized society. Sheer play, they realized, could still be a very serious thing.

The oppressiveness of managerial consensus led many intellectuals to believe that the stakes in mass culture criticism were high indeed: "there is slowly emerging a tepid, flaccid middlebrow culture that threatens to engulf everything in its spreading ooze," Dwight MacDonald wrote in 1953. This ludicrously apocalyptic imagery revealed some of the deepest fears behind the critique of conformity. It was rooted in the feeling articulated by MacDonald: the sense that the enveloping force of mass culture threatened the thoughtful individual with a kind of asphyxiation.

Fears of asphyxiation were not really subject to political remedy. They required a dose of authentic experience; even a vicarious dose would do. For many intellectuals, from Arthur Schlesinger, Jr. to Norman Mailer, the rise of John F. Kennedy provided it: he and his entourage provided the "breath of fresh air" that many intellectuals craved after a decade of suffocating conformity. For a time, the managerial consensus received an injection of legitimacy from the youthful style and bravado of the Kennedy administration—the resuscitation of pragmatism as risk taking and realpolitique, the romance of counterinsurgency, the pop existentialist rhetoric that composed the Kennedy legend after his death (and that was brilliantly satirized in Donald Barthelme's "Robert Kennedy Saved from Drowning.")

At the same time, though—the early 1960s—longings for regeneration began to lead in more interesting political directions. Sylvia Plath captured the plight of the educated woman whose talent had nowhere to go in *The Bell Jar* (1963). She dissected the role of therapy as social control, explicitly associating her frustration with feelings of asphyxiation. That same year, Betty Friedan exposed "the problem that has no name" in *The Feminine Mystique:* suburban housewives were cut off from participation in the realities of the masculine world; they were drowning in weightless unreality. The second wave of feminism was beginning to stir.

So was the youthful rebellion that became known as the New Left. The authors of "The Port Huron Statement" (1962) used an existentialist idiom of authenticity to indict the managerial consensus for its dehumanizing effects. Here as elsewhere in the 1960s, an avowedly political movement was demanding changes in the quality of subjective experience. The "old politics" had been reduced to terminal boredom by the managerial preoccupation with technique and disdain for ideology; by now all "responsible debate" took place inside the iron cage, in a denatured language of efficiency, productivity, and kill ratios. So it should come as no surprise that a "new politics" would attempt to put passion back into public debate by placing ideology in the service of personal identity. For many young men, facing a war no one could convincingly justify, it was a matter of life and death. No wonder the personal became political, and vice versa.

By the late 1960s, the turn toward identity politics was well under way in a variety of venues. For feminists, New Leftists, and advocates of black power, agendas broadened to include selfhood as well as social justice. Rancorous demands multiplied. An emergent identity politics stemmed from the implicit realization that managerial consensus could not solve the crisis of meaning in the modern world. The "social system" fed the body but starved the soul.

By the late 1960s, though, bodies as well as souls were threatened by managerial policy. Counterinsurgency tactics in Vietnam proved less romantic than Kennedy's minions had thought. Robert McNamara's "systems analysis" approach to strategy was mired in the rice paddies of the demilitarized zone. The war shattered the bipartisan foreign policy and exposed the complicity of "value-free" social science with power. And it provoked a wholesale rejection of managerial rationality in the name of personal authenticity.

The antiwar counterculture has often been caricatured as merely an orgy of hip consumerism. There is no denying the fatuities of countercultural excess, as therapies of adjustment gave way to therapies of self-realization, and advertisers courted the "youth market" with an array of "alternative lifestyles." But behind the day-glo and paisley there was a serious critique of technocratic society, summarized in Theodore Roszak's *The Making of a Counterculture* (1970). The intellectual lineage of the counterculture stretched from William Blake and Henry David Thoreau to the communitarian anarchist Paul Goodman and the Beat poet Allen Ginsberg. Their critique stressed the disenchanting impact of the iron cage, its corrosion of natural and supernatural meanings, and its destruction of opportunities for serious play. From this perspective, the consumerist vision of a "leisure society" involved no genuine leisure at all. It merely substituted a frenetic alternation between working and spending for the linear, plodding work ethic—a hamster cage for an iron one. Countercultural critics rejected the ponderous tone of High Modernism, but preserved much of the modernist critique of managerial rationality.

Foreign policy failure combined with emergent identity politics to begin the splintering of managerial consensus. An economic downturn finished the job. By the early 1970s, the social as well as ideological foundations of the consensus had begun to crumble. Kevin Phillips, a Republican party consultant, cooked up a "southern strategy" to capitalize on conservative resentment against the alleged excesses of hippies and black militants. White middle-class resentment became an emotion to be mobilized. The OPEC oil boycott of 1973 demonstrated that American corporations could no longer remain indifferent to overseas rivals. Major employers looked to lower labor costs by closing unionized factories at home and exporting jobs abroad. The bargain of the late thirties no longer held. The foundation of Keynesian policy—an economically secure working population—was becoming a thing of the past.

FRAGMENTATION

The structures of corporate capitalism did not come apart during the last third of the twentieth century: corporations became more powerful than ever, more global in their reach, less subject to government regulation. What came apart was the coherent culture that had legitimated powerful institutions, private and public, during the mid-century decades. The idea of the American Way of Life, oppressively conformist to some, was sustaining and reassuring to many. It offered an optimistic, energetic vision of national purpose—an agenda for progress that, if flawed, could always be expanded or modified, at least in its more flexible and humane versions.

The breakup of that unifying vision left an unsatisfying void. Complaints of decline and drift became staples of public discourse. Countercultural dreams of social transformation soured amid a million therapies that promised self-fulfillment but often delivered adjustment. To be sure, there was still some serious countercultural thinking going on. Even amid the plethora of New Age cults and gurus, religious thinkers like James Wallace (of *Sojourners* magazine) and Michael Lerner (of *Tikkun*) made sustained efforts to connect social commitments with Christian and Jewish traditions. But generally, the cultural left became a hotbed of hyperindividualism, and a constant provocation to the resurgent fundamentalist right.

Countercultural hopes for a rebirth of hedonism disappeared amid a resurgent (usually corporate-sponsored) performance ethic stressing the maintenance of peak efficiency in all areas of life, from the boardroom to the bedroom. What the economist Juliet Schor has called "the unexpected decline of leisure" has resulted in part from employers' tendency to use job insecurity as a means of enforcing labor discipline. With business having reneged on its side of the late 1930s' bargain, and unions in decline, many Americans saw little alternative to the hamster cage model of life.

As multinational corporations entered a new era of hegemony without responsibility, many artists and writers took a postmodern turn. They extended the countercultural agenda, rejecting the modernist preoccupation with depths as well as its ponderous tone. Postmodern art and culture were characterized by a celebration of glittering meaningless surfaces, a delight in the unending play of floating signifiers, a pervasive mood of ironic detachment. The avant garde baton passed from Jackson Pollock to Andy Warhol, whose disdain for emotional intensity was legendary. "I want to be a machine" he said, and "frigid people really make it" This was a far cry from the familiar reverence for palpitating actuality.

The accession of Ronald Reagan to the presidency in 1980 marked the triumph of postmodern politics. His convincing simulation of commitment to "traditional values" concealed their irrelevance to the resurgent free market of the 1980s and 1990s. It was a special cultural moment, when postmodern speculators and free-market fundamentalists could cohabit the same virtual terrain, surf the same net, thumb down the same information highway. The astonishing success of the computer industry helped solidify the notion that corporate capitalism was the cutting edge of hip. As in the New Era of the 1920s, CEOs became culture heroes and entrepreneurial mythology made a comeback. In the bull market atmosphere, it became hard to see public policy as anything more than an instrument for promoting economic growth, which mostly meant getting out of the entrepreneurs' way. Even environmental consciousness, the one lasting contribution of the counterculture to mainstream social thought, began to be eclipsed by a resurgent and heavily debt-financed consumerism.

Among intellectuals, the last third of the century saw fundamental definitions of reality challenged, refashioned, and transformed. In the humanities and social sciences, the positivistic synthesis of the mid-century decades met fundamental challenges from hermeneutics, the sociology of knowledge, and (by the 1980s) a postmodern emphasis on the cultural construction of allegedly "natural" categories—particularly gender, race, and sexual preference. Hayden White, Judith Butler, and diverse other critics participated in this latest revolt against positivism.

The deconstruction of positivist certainties accomplished a great deal. It posed a bracing challenge to the literalist or narrowly quantitative definitions of reality embedded in most mid-century formulations. It sensitized cultural analysis to the many ways reality could be constituted through language. It called reification into question, by reasserting an active human agency in the creation of cultural meaning. And it revealed the flimsy basis of many social categories—including the categories that lay at the heart of identity politics. This last accomplishment created confusion among many left academics, who celebrated authentic ethnic or sexual identities even as their epistemology dismissed any notion of the authentic as a form of "essentialism."

Ultimately, the deconstruction project succeeded almost too well. By the 1990s it was almost impossible to find a professor in the humanities who would use the word "reality" without inverted commas (except for some stubborn historians). The postmodern turn in the academy led to a blithe disregard for intractable social realities—especially the realities of concentrated economic power—as well as for the realities of the natural world. As Frederic Jameson wrote in 1991, "Postmodernism is what you have when the modernization process is over and nature is gone for good." Such statements make it clear that postmodernism was a provincial urban and academic phenomenon. The idea that "nature is gone for good" proved a tough sell west of the Hudson, east of the Quinnipiac, or outside the humanities building.

In fact, precisely at the time when academic postmodernists were deconstructing everything "natural" in sight, a number of influential scientists and science popularizers were resurrecting the hereditarian thought of the earlier twentieth century. Sometimes the resurgent biologism carried overtly racial connotations, as in the notorious claims of Richard Herrnstein and Charles Murray in *The Bell Curve* (1994) that poor academic performance by African Americans could be traced to their genetic impoverishment. More often, as in the work of the sociobiologist E. O. Wilson, the argument for the genetic origins of culture muted any racist claims and (at least rhetorically) rejected reductionism.

The problem with sociobiology was not simply that it could be used to shore up existing social hierarchies on spuriously scientific grounds (though that danger was surely present). There was, after all, nothing inherently wrong with reasserting the claims of nature against culturalists' casual disregard of it.

The fundamental difficulty was that sociobiologists participated with their postmodern opponents in sustaining the demented dualism that has reinforced so many simpleminded oppositions in American thought—in this case, the opposition between nature and nurture. Nature may be culturally constructed, but culture is also naturally constructed. To say this is not to start a slide down the slippery slope to soil worship. It is simply to acknowledge what so many postmodern theorists seem to forget: there are some kinds of reality that cannot be contained in quotation marks.

It may be that the confusions of late twentieth-century American thought are the signs of a new synthesis waiting to be born. Even if they are not, there is no reason to suppose that intellectual drift and fragmentation are undesirable developments. The managerial consensus was oppressive and limited; the new directions in social thought are filled with humane possibilities, many so far unrealized. But how can they be fruitfully connected with everyday life in an era when the market is god?

As our experience of reality becomes increasingly virtual, the iron cage becomes increasingly protean—a shape-shifting structure with hundreds of formal variants but one overriding imperative: the primacy of the bottom line. As Weber said, "no one knows who will live in this cage in the future." But we can be pretty sure it will be a lot of us.

BIBLIOGRAPHY

Belgrad, Daniel. *The Culture of Spontaneity: Improvisation and the Arts in Postwar America.* Chicago: University of Chicago Press, 1998. Good on the mid-century avant garde and its revolt against managerial values.

Blake, Casey. *Beloved Community: The Cultural Criticism of Randolph Bourne, Van Wyck Brooks, Waldo Frank, and Lewis Mumford.* Chapel Hill: University of North Carolina Press, 1990. Compelling account of Dewey's early disciples and critics.

Cott, Nancy. *The Grounding of Modern Feminism.* New Haven, Conn.: Yale University Press, 1987. The best book we have on the subject.

Degler, Carl. *In Search of Human Nature: The Decline and Revival of Darwinism in American Thought.* New York: Oxford University Press, 1992. Comprehensive but unconvincingly polemical in its assault on sociobiology.

Fox, Richard Wightman. *Reinhold Niebuhr: A Biography.* Ithaca, N.Y.: Cornell University Press, 1986. Masterful biography of a key critic of liberalism.

Gitlin, Todd. *Twilight of Common Dreams.* New York: Metropolitan Books, 1995. Sensitive history and critique of identity politics.

Graff, Gerald. *Professing Literature: An Institutional History.* Chicago: University of Chicago Press, 1989. Lively and insightful account of the professionalization of one discipline.

Gurstein, Rochelle. *The Repeal of Reticence.* New York: Hill and Wang, 1998. A challenging, historically informed brief for privacy and against therapeutic "openness."

Herman, Ellen. *The Romance of American Psychology.* Berkeley: University of California Press, 1995. Great on role of therapy in mid-century consensus.

Hollinger, David. *In the American Province.* Baltimore: Johns Hopkins University Press, 1989. Penetrating essays on pragmatism and other matters.

Kevles, Daniel. *In the Name of Eugenics: Genetics and the Uses of Human Heredity*. New York: Knopf, 1985. Comprehensive and learned.

Kuklick, Bruce. *The Rise of American Philosophy*. New Haven, Conn.: Yale University Press, 1977. On the importance of the Harvard philosophy department, 1870–1930.

Lasch, Christopher. *The New Radicalism in America: The Intellectual as a Social Type, 1889–1963*. New York: Knopf, 1965. Brilliant on "the anti-intellectualism of the intellectuals."

Lears, T. J. Jackson. *No Place of Grace: Antimodernism and the Transformation of Amrican Culture, 1880–1920*. New York: Pantheon, 1981. Discusses the complex origins of the twentieth-century quest for "real life."

Leja, Michael. *Reframing Abstract Expressionism: Subjectivity and Painting in the 1940s*. New Haven, Conn.: Yale University Press, 1993. Deftly integrates art and mid-century cultural ferment.

Lekachman, Robert. *The Age of Keynes*. New York: Random House, 1965. The best introduction to Keynesian economic thought and its policy consequences.

Lewis, David Levering. *When Harlem Was in Vogue*. New York: Knopf, 1981. Elegant appraisal of an important cultural moment.

Marcus, Greil. *Mystery Train: Images of America in Rock 'n Roll Music*. New York: Dutton, 1978. Ragged, self-indulgent, but still rewarding.

Marsden, George M., and Bradley Longfield, eds. *The Secularization of the Academy*. New York: Oxford University Press, 1992. An important and neglected story.

Miller, Mark Crispin. *Boxed In: The Culture of TV*. Evanston, Ill.: Northwestern University Press, 1988. Wittiest and most perceptive media critic in the business.

Nasaw, David. *Going Out: The Rise and Fall of Public Amusement in America*. New York: Basic Books, 1993. Demonstrates the centrality of race in the creation of mass culture.

Noble, David F. *America by Design: Science, Technology, and the Rise of Corporate Capitalism*. New York: Knopf, 1977. Spells out the key institutional connections.

Oliver, Paul. *Blues Fell This Morning*. 2nd ed. New York: Cambridge University Press, 1994. Illuminating interpretation of lyrics.

Pfister, Joel, and Nancy Schnog, eds. *Inventing the Psychological: Toward a Cultural History of Emotional Life in America*. New Haven, Conn.: Yale University Press, 1997. Pathbreaking essays.

Posnock, Ross. *Color and Culture: Black Writers and the Making of the Modern Intellectual*. Cambridge, Mass.: Harvard University Press, 1998. Good on the complex interplay of universal and particular.

Rodgers, Daniel. *Atlantic Crossings: Social Politics in a Progressive Age*. Cambridge, Mass.: Harvard University Press, 1998. Superb study of intellectual sources of public policy.

Ross, Dorothy. *Origins of American Social Science*. New York: Cambridge University Press, 1991. Comprehensive, balanced, thoughtful.

Singal, Daniel, ed. *Modernist Culture in America*. Belmont, Calif.: Wadsworth, 1991. Useful essays.

Susman, Warren. *Culture as History*. New York: Pantheon, 1984. Important essays on 1930s culture.

Trachtenberg, Alan. *Reading American Photographs*. New York: Hill and Wang, 1988. Subtle and historically informed.

Westbrook, Robert. *John Dewey and American Democracy*. Ithaca, N.Y.: Cornell University Press, 1991. Challenging interpretation of the pragmatist as democrat.

index

Abortion, 52, 69, 76, 169, 172, 242, 270. *See also Roe v. Wade*
Adams, Henry, 1, 10, 12, 301
Addams, Jane, 251, 301
Affirmative action, 199, 241, 288
  and African Americans, 195
  and education, 197
  enforcement of, 143
  rejection of, 244
  support for, 243
African Americans, 3, 6, 311
  Afrocentricity, 196
  citizenship, 153, 178
  and communism, 68–69
  consumerism, 150–51, 152–53
  culture, 182–83, 195
  discrimination against, *see* Jim Crow
  and economics, 179
  the family, 130, 135, 184–85, 222
  and the Great Society, 136
  housing discrimination, 137, 183–84
  liberalism, 56
  "manhood," struggles with, 177–78, 180–81, 185, 195, 200, 222
  militancy, 36
  poverty, 126, 129–30, 132, 134, 137, 222
  and progressivism, 58
  and religion, 182
  and the vote, 58, 61, 70, 178–79, 203
  white primaries, 232
  women, 166, 178–79, 184
Agricultural Adjustment Act (AAA), 114, 148
Aid to Families with Dependent Children (AFDC), 132, 135, 136, 142
Albright, Madeline, 84, 99
American Civil Liberties Union (ACLU), 42, 257
American Exceptionalism, 3, 83

American Federation of Labor (AFL), 105, 108, 112, 117, 138
Anarchism, 9
Anti-Communism, 44–45, 47, 67–68, 72, 155, 267
Anti-Semitism, 38, 40, 41, 46, 60
Antitrust legislation, 63, 147. *See also* Clayton Antitrust Act
Apocalypse, 1, 37, 248. *See also* Millennium
Arthur, Chester A., 11
Assemblies of God, 258, 268
Atomic bomb, 22, 23, 262, 265
  arms race, 94
  Enola Gay, 262
  Los Alamos Project, 235
  nuclear energy, 47
  and religious ideology, 265
Atomic Energy Commission, 24
Automobile, 107
  and consumerism, 145, 147

Baker, Ella, 69, 151, 187–89, 190, 193
Baker, George ("Father Divine"), 261, 262
Baker v. Carr, 72
Balfour Declaration, 255
Barenblatt v. United States, 72
"Beat" writers, 240, 307, 309
Bell, Daniel, 33, 43
Bilingual Education Act, 240
Billy Sunday, 255, 259
Birth control, 61, 76, 172
Blacks. *See* African Americans
Black nationalism, 191, 287–88, 308. *See also* Malcolm X
Black Panther party, 190–91, 239, 287–88. *See also* Black nationalism
Bolshevism, 38–39
Boxer Rebellion, 11